WILLIAM BARCLAY

The Gospels and Acts

VOLUME ONE

The First Three Gospels

SCM PRESS LTD
BLOOMSBURY STREET LONDON

Volume One first published separately 1966
First published in this two-volume edition 1976

© SCM Press Ltd 1966, 1976

Filmset by Specialised Offset Services Ltd, Liverpool
Printed in Great Britain by
Redwood Burn Limited, Trowbridge & Esher

CONTENTS

Christianity is Christ, and nearness to him and to his image is the end of all your efforts. Thus, the Gospels, which continually present to us one pattern, have a kind of precedence among the books of Holy Scripture.

W. E. Gladstone

If the footprints of Christ be anywhere shown to us, we kneel and adore. Why do we not rather venerate the living and breathing picture of him in these books? If the vesture of Christ be exhibited, where will we not go to kiss it? Yet were his whole wardrobe exhibited, nothing could represent Christ more vividly and truly than these evangelical writings. Statues of wood and stone we decorate with gold and gems for the sake of Christ. They only profess to give us the form of his body; these books present us with a living image of his most holy mind. Were we to have seen him with our eyes, we should not have so intimate a knowledge as they give of Christ speaking, healing, dying, rising again, as it were in our actual presence.

Erasmus

Among the four Gospels that of St Mark became my favourite from the sudden and direct manner in which it at once brings Christ into contact with a suffering world, and shows him surrounded from morning until latest eve with the direct aspects of human distress and woe.

Dora Greenwell

The Gospel which the publican wrote for us, with its perfect Sermon on the Mount, and mostly more harmonious and gentle fulness in places where St Luke is formal, St John mysterious, and St Mark brief – this Gospel according to St Matthew, I should think, if we had to choose out of all the books in the Bible for a prison or a desert friend, would be the one we should keep.

John Ruskin

I find great pleasure in lecturing, and a large portion of my studies are conducted with a view to it. I have got to the end of the first ten chapters of Luke, and continue to like it more and more. Nothing has disabused my mind more of the first impressions made by Strauss than the regular and close examination of the Gospel history. The difficulties grow ever less and less the more one works into the substance of the history and applies to it the ordinary laws of historical evidence.

John Cairns

PREFACE

This book is a revision and a reissue of a previous volume entitled *The First Three Gospels*. The science of New Testament introduction never stands still and certain additions have been made.

In the first volume there are two new chapters, one on developments in general and one on redaction criticism in particular. The second volume is entirely new. When I had occasion to revise the material on the gospels it seemed a good idea to add an introduction to John and an introduction to the Acts of the Apostles and both of these introductions ran to a length which I did not contemplate when I began to write them.

My debts are too many to mention. I hope I have acknowledged most of them in the notes and in the text, but much of the material in these two volumes was used continuously throughout the years as lectures and I may have debts of which I am not even aware. If so, I ask pardon from the people I have quoted without acknowledgment and express my gratitude to them.

I am particularly indebted to John Bowden, the Editor of the SCM Press, who had such patience with my long delays and who finally shook me into activity. His help, his patience and his encouragement have been of great value.

I would be sadly lacking in courtesy if, in particular, I did not express a very great debt of gratitude to Miss Jean Cunningham, who not only prepared this manuscript for the press but who continually improved it in the preparation. I am very grateful for her scholarly and courteous help.

The study of the gospels will never come to an end, and any book which is written on the gospels cannot be more than an interim report, but it is my hope and my prayer that these two volumes will help the reader better to understand how these gospels came into being.

Glasgow 1975   WILLIAM BARCLAY

1

THE NATURE OF THE GOSPELS

There can be few Christians who will dispute the claim that for the Christian the gospels are the most important books in the world; and their supreme importance lies in the fact that they are our only sources for the life and the teaching of Jesus. Without them we would know very little that Jesus said, and almost nothing that Jesus did.

Until comparatively recently an opening paragraph such as I have just written would have commanded almost universal consent. Today there are many who would accept it only with the most serious reservations, and there are those who would hold it to be not only untrue but also precisely the wrong way to begin a book on the gospels. When F.C. Burkitt wrote his famous book *The Gospel History and its Transmission* in 1906, he was able without hesitation to use the word 'history' in the title, and he was able to say in his opening paragraphs that he believed that there was such common consent that the gospel history was of such vast importance that no one would grudge the 'discussion of dry and tiresome details' to study it closely. That is to say, some sixty years ago the juxtaposition of the words 'history' and 'gospels' was something which could be assumed.

Today the reverse is true. Let us set side by side two quotations. The first is from Burkitt's book:

> It is not to get new ideas of religion or of philosophy that we need a minute and searching historical criticsm; rather do we need to test the ideas we already have by the historical facts, and we cannot get the facts without criticism . . . And the attempt to return to the historic Christ is the only way by which we can escape from the tyranny of the last generation's theories about Christ (pp. 30f.).

For Burkitt the historical study of the gospels was of primary importance, and its aim was to delineate the portrait of the historic Christ. On the other hand Ernst Käsemann, in his *Essays on New Testament Themes*, speaks of 'the impoverishment and distortion of the Gospel which takes place wherever the question of the Jesus of history is treated as decisive for theology and preaching' (p. 15).

So then there is today what can only be described as a flight from history. In *Jesus and the Word* (p. 11) Bultmann speaks of history, in the sense of that which may be learned from historical research, as no more than 'a walk through a museum of antiquities'. In the same book (pp. 14f.) he writes:

Interest in the personality of Jesus is excluded – and not merely because in the absence of information I am making a virtue of a necessity. I do indeed think that we can now know almost nothing concerning the life and personality of Jesus, since the early Christian sources show no interest in either, are moreover fragmentary and often legendary; and other sources about Jesus do not exist ... We can strictly speaking know nothing about the personality of Jesus.

As J.M. Robinson says in his *New Quest of the Historical Jesus* (p. 12), for Bultmann search for the historical Jesus is 'historically impossible and theologically illegitimate'. And on the latter point Martin Dibelius says: 'What is asserted by faith cannot be proved by history. Indeed, faith would not be faith if it could be demonstrated to every comer' (*Jesus*, p. 8).

Lest it be thought that this point of view is to be found only in what may be regarded as the more radical theologians, it must be noted that Barth and Brunner think on almost exactly the same lines. Barth can write:

Jesus Christ is also the Rabbi of Nazareth, historically so difficult to get information about, and when it is obtained the one who is apt to impress us as a little commonplace alongside more than one other founder of a religion, and even alongside many later representations of his own religion.[1]

The Jesus of history and the Christ of faith have no necessary connection. As Donald Baillie said in *God was in Christ* (p. 36): 'The attempt to write the life of Jesus and to reconstruct his personality is in Barth's view quite irrelevant to Christian faith.' 'Faith presupposes, as a matter of course,' says Brunner in *The Mediator* (p. 184), '*a priori*, that the Jesus of history is not the same as the Christ of faith.' 'In faith,' he says again (p. 159), 'we are not concerned with the Jesus of history, as historical science sees him, but with the Jesus Christ of personal testimony, who is the real Christ.'

Here is this flight from history which denies that we go to the gospels for history at all.

It is quite obvious that a revolution has taken place. It is not a revolution which everyone has accepted, but nonetheless it is one which has been of very great effect in modern theology and in the modern study of the gospels. Let us see if we can trace how it came about. Of the latter part of it, the part which more directly leads up to the present situation, there is an excellent summary in Stephen Neill's *The Interpretation of the New Testament 1861-1961* (pp. 4-12).

It is quite clear that this modern view of the gospels involves a view of scripture which in a sense brings scripture under the judgment of the minds of men rather than bringing the minds of men under the judgment of scripture.

The earliest doctrine of the inspiration of scripture, a doctrine which was widespread, if not universal, was almost mechanical. It conceived of the Spirit of God so using men that men were no more than passive instruments in the hand of God. Their minds did not enter into the matter at all; they were simply used by God. Justin Martyr spoke of the divine plectrum descending from heaven and using righteous men as instruments like a harp or lyre.[2] Athenagoras said the Spirit breathed through the writers of scripture as a musician breathes through a flute.[3] Chrysostom said that John and Paul were musical instruments played upon by the Spirit.[4] Before this Philo had held that the prophets, when they were speaking or writing, lost their own consciousness, and did not even know what they were saying. It was not they but God who spoke.[5] According to Tertullian[6] the inspired writers were *inundati*, inundated, submerged, by the Spirit. Since this is so, on this view there can be no contradiction in scripture;[7] there can be no such thing as a lapse of memory;[8] there can be no possibility of a mistake.[9] As Novatian said of the writers of inspired scripture, '*numquam fallunt*', which to all intents and purposes means, 'They are infallible'.[10]

If all this is so, there is a duty to dovetail and to harmonize, but never to question or to doubt. It is, of course, true that there are some who still hold this. There are some who have departed from it, but who still hold that in a very real sense scripture is the word of God and inspired by God; but there are also those who have departed from it, as it were, *simpliciter*, and who see in scripture a human record, which has to submit to the judgment of the mind of man and the criticism of scholarship. It is the rise of this last view that we must look at.

The roots of a revolution may lie very deep. Or a revolution may be likened to a stream which begins with only a trickle of water, and which travels a long, long way before it becomes a flood, wide and deep and fast enough to sweep everything before it. Stephen Neill begins his tracing of the roots of this revolution with J.D. Michaelis (1717-1791) who was Professor of Oriental Languages at Göttingen, and a very great scholar. Up to his time the theory of inspiration, as we have seen, was founded on a mechanical basis; this mechanical basis presupposed inerrancy; and therefore the main task of scholarship was to exercise all its skill and ingenuity in harmonizing the apparent contradictions with which the gospels presented it. But Michaelis shifted the basis of inspiration. He held that what guarantees inspiration is not inerrancy, but apostolic authorship. This for the study of the gospels obviously had immediate repercussions, for it meant that Matthew and John were inspired scripture in a way that Mark and Luke were not, for no one had ever claimed that Mark and Luke were apostles. Michaelis did not in the least wish to jettison Mark and Luke. For him they were generally reliable and valuable and of the greatest use. But theoretically at least they were non-canonical, for they were not apostolic.

Michaelis might never have been heard of in England but for the fact that Herbert Marsh, one of the very few Englishmen at that time to study in Germany, had studied under Michaelis in 1785. He became Professor of Divinity at Cambridge in 1807, and later successively Bishop of Llandaff and Peterborough. Between 1793 and 1801 he translated into English Michaelis' *Introduction to the New Testament*. Of course it aroused violent opposition. John Randolph, Bishop of Oxford, accused Marsh of 'derogating from the character of the sacred books', and said that the book was 'injurious to Christianity as fostering a spirit of scepticism'. So far the thing was no bigger than a cloud the size of a man's hand on the horizon, but a process had been started, a process which nothing could now stop, and whose end at that time none could have foreseen.

The next factor in the situation was the emergence of a book which was in itself a great book and which had an incalculable influence on all subsequent work in its own field. This was G.B. Niebuhr's *History of Rome* (1810-1812). With this book the modern writing of history was born. Niebuhr had one aim – 'to approach history without presuppositions'. He had two basic questions to ask – What is the evidence? What is the value of the evidence? The old traditions have to be submitted to the acid test, and the fact that they are venerable and constantly repeated is simply irrelevant. Niebuhr had, of course, no difficulty in showing that the so-called early history of Rome was myth and legend and fiction. It was in fact he who introduced the conception of 'myth'.

Once again Niebuhr was fortunate in finding his translator in Connop Thirlwall (1797-1875). The *Quarterly Review* declared the whole approach to be 'pregnant with crude and dangerous speculation', but the fact remains that the approach to history could never be the same again, and also that inevitably the astringent approach of Niebuhr was bound to find its way into the realm of biblical history, not only in the sphere of the Old Testament, but also of the gospels and Acts.

But Connop Thirlwall was not finished translating. For some reason he chose to translate Schleiermacher's *Essays on the Gospel of St Luke* (1821). The gist of this essay was that 'Gospel material had circulated in the form of brief memorabilia, on which the evangelists had later worked, each with a particular understanding of the life of the Lord in his mind'. This comes very near to stating the principles of form criticism in embryo, and it certainly does away completely with anything like verbal inspiration.

Thirlwall was but ill rewarded for his courage and enterprise as a translator, for from the point of view of ecclesiastical preferment his work as a translator was the equivalent of suicide. Ultimately he was given the impoverished diocese of St David's but in the eyes of 'the establishment' of his day his translating work was a millstone round his neck.

Next in the chain of events there followed an odd, and in some ways a tragic, interlude. A certain Hugh James Rose (1795-1858), who travelled and studied in Germany, found German scholarship repugnant and dangerous and said so in four Cambridge sermons on *The State of the Protestant Religion in Germany*, in which he talked of the German Church's 'abdication of Christianity'. E.B. Pusey, later to become the focus of the Tractarian Movement and a pillar of orthodoxy, was then in Germany learning oriental languages. At that time he was much more sympathetic to German scholarship than Rose had been and in 1821 he wrote *An Historical Enquiry into the Probable Causes of the Rationalistic Character of the Theology of Germany*. In it he took the point of view that faith has nothing to fear from scientific enquiry and from scholarly research. He stated that in his opinion 'the historical parts of the Bible in which no religious truth is contained should never be regarded as equally inspired with other passages of Scripture'. It looked as if Pusey had opened his mind to the new scholarship, and, if he had done so, his later position in Oxford would have made his opinions extremely influential. But Pusey was to make the great recantation; he was to become the champion of the ancient orthodoxy, and in his will of 19 November 1875 he was to give strict orders that this early book of his was never to be republished.

The storm broke in Oxford with the publication in 1860 of *Essays and Reviews*.[11] Jowett had already written to Dean Elliot: 'There will be no religion in Oxford among intellectual young men, unless religion is shown to be consistent with criticism.' The aim of the book is written in its own preface:

> This volume, it is hoped, will be received as an attempt to illustrate the advantage desirable to the cause of religious and moral truth from a free handling, in a becoming spirit, of subjects peculiarly liable to suffer by the repetition of conventional language, and from traditional methods of treatment.

It pleads that the Bible must be submitted to the tests to which any other book is liable, that that which as physical fact is now scientifically untenable should be recognized without abandoning its spiritual truth and value, that the differing authority of the differing books of the Bible must be frankly and freely investigated and admitted. It is all now part of the stock-in-trade of biblical scholarship. But it raised an astonishing storm. There was an attempt to prosecute for heresy H. B. Wilson, the editor of the book, and Rowland Williams, one of its contributors. The attempt was dismissed by the sceptical Lord Chancellor Westbury, who, as it was said, 'dismissed Hell with costs and took away from orthodox members of the Church of England their last hope of everlasting damnation'. The orthodox, as J.S. Mill said, were lost 'in the dead slumber of a decided opinion', and bitterly resented being forcibly awakened. And now Pusey was leading the opposition. To acquiesce in these evils was to be like a man sleeping in the snow – which is death. The struggle, as he saw it, was for the life and death of the University as a place of religious learning. He wrote to Wilberforce:

> One can hardly think of anything for the hidden blasphemy of that judgment which declares that to be uncertain which our Lord taught, and for the loss of the countless souls which it will involve, if not repudiated by the Church.

The Church of England, Pusey insisted, 'in common with the whole Catholic Church maintains without reserve or qualification the inspiration and divine authority of the whole canonical Scriptures, as not only containing but being the word of God'. It was a fight to the bitter end, and leading the fight was that same Pusey who had once seemed to be about to lead the van of progress against the obscurantists.

We must now return to the main stream of New Testament critical development, and, when we do, we come to two men whose influence on all subsequent study has been immense.

The first of them is not connected so much with the gospels in particular as with the whole New Testament field. His name is Ferdinand Christian Baur (1792-1860). He went to Tübingen in 1826 and he remained there for the rest of his life. He was one of the very few men who had a vision of the field as a whole. He saw that you could not interpret the New Testament by itself, that you needed what went before, that you needed its whole environment, that you needed the study of church history and of Christian theology, before a true picture would emerge. He was a man of incredible industry. He was at his desk every morning at 4 a.m. Stephen Neill says that he produced 10,000 pages of manuscript during his lifetime, that a further 6,000 pages were produced from his notes after his death, which amounts to a book of 400 pages every year for forty years. He believed that the New Testament scholar must be a trained philologist in order to be an exegete, a trained historian in order to be a church historian, and a trained philosopher in order to be a systematic theologian.

Baur's point of view was due to the fact that in 1833 he came under the influence of Hegel, who saw all progress in terms of a thesis, and then an opposing antithesis, with a final unification into a synthesis. Baur was rightly convinced that study must start from the Pauline letters, which are the earliest Christian documents. Of these letters he regarded only four as unquestionably genuine – Romans, I and II

Corinthians and Galatians. Now I Corinthians already shows us a conflict within the church (I Cor. 1.12); and so Baur saw the whole Christian church, in its early stages, as a conflict between Judaistic Christianity centring on Peter, and Pauline Christianity, centring on Paul; and the conflict finally emerged into the unity of the Catholic Church under the pressure of attack and heresy. Judaistic Christianity is the thesis; Pauline Christianity, the antithesis; the Catholic Church, the synthesis. Acts is the book which tries to show a harmony between the two, so that in Acts whatever Peter does Paul must do too and *vice versa*. Baur then went on to assign every book in the New Testament to one side or the other, an arrangement which led him to some fantastic conclusions. For our purpose we may note only one of these conclusions. Luke is the Pauline gospel; Matthew is the Judaistic gospel; and since in Mark there is no trace of the conflict, Mark must come from a time when the conflict was over, and therefore must be dated sometime in the first half of the second century! Mark becomes the latest instead of the earliest of the gospels.

So Baur sees the New Testament rather as the production of a church conflict than as the production of a mechanical inspiration.

We come finally to the last of what may be called the pre-modern leaders of this revolution, David Friedrich Strauss (1808-1874), and his famous, or notorious, *Life of Christ*, first published in 1835. Strauss introduced a new conception into the whole position. He was quite unable to accept the supernatural view of the gospels, and he did not believe that a process of rationalization could really provide any true solution. He therefore introduced the conception of the *mythical*. Myths were for him of three kinds. There were the myths of the ancient Greek gods, which are only crude and pictorial attempts to understand nature and the world. There were myths which are majestic stories, quite unhistorical, but nonetheless having within them a deep understanding of the human situation, like the myths of the early chapters of Genesis. There are the myths, like the Oedipus myths, which are really dramatizations and projections of man's own struggle to understand a bewildering destiny. A myth, unlike a legend, has no historical foundation. Stephen Neill illustrates this thus. Gideon in history is a self-taught military genius. Gideon in legend is an instrument in the hand of God. But the legend arises directly out of Gideon as he historically was. Myth, on the other hand, comes not from history but from the mind of man.

Now, as Strauss sees it, the gospel stories are for the most part myths which arise from two desires, the desire to show Jesus as surpassing the highest supernatural events and experiences of the Old Testament, and the desire to show Jesus as the Messiah. For instance, the transfiguration story is due to a desire to repeat the transfiguration story of Moses on a still higher level (Ex. 24.15-18; 34.29). It is due

Lions

also to the desire to show Jesus in contact with his forerunners, Moses and Elijah. And it is due to the desire to confirm his dignity by the heavenly voice of approval (Matt. 17.5; Mark 9.7; Luke 9.35). There is no history here. There is a deliberately constructed myth to show Jesus as superior to anything in the Old Testament and to show him as Messiah.

In the end Strauss reduced everything to myth. Stephen Neill speaks of Strauss's 'volatilization' of the story of Christ.

Strauss held that since Jesus defies human categories the story cannot in any event be told in any other way. To try to write a life story of Jesus in historical fact, to try to iron out the contradictions and the disharmonies, is impossible, for these are questions which never even occurred to the first writers of the gospels, who are rather constructors of myths designed to prove their faith in Christ.

Of course, there is a substratum of truth here, for Strauss never for a moment denied that Jesus existed, but that substratum of truth is quite beyond reconstruction. Even the order of the incidents is quite without historical foundation. What we have is 'a necklace of pearls of which the string is broken'. Even the sayings of Jesus cannot be placed. Neill (pp. 15f.) quotes Strauss's vivid metaphor:

> The hard grit of the sayings of Jesus has not indeed been dissolved by the flood of oral tradition, but they have been worked away from their original position and like rolling pebbles have been deposited in places to which they properly do not belong.

In Strauss history is dissolved in myth. The gospels tell us not what Jesus was but what the writers believed him to be. The revolution is complete. It is easy to see how far this has moved from the idea of the factual inerrancy of the gospels.

We have now reached the development in work on the New Testament which had more influence than any other on the question of history and the gospels – the development of form criticism. The principles of form criticism were stated almost simultaneously by K.L. Schmidt and Martin Dibelius in 1919 and Rudolf Bultmann in 1921. We shall postpone a detailed examination of the methods and results of form criticism until the next chapter of this book. At the present we will simply state its broad outlines and its claims.

There is a certain difficulty, which must be frankly stated and faced, in the evaluation of the work of the form critics. There is no doubt that the student of the New Testament who began his study on what may be called orthodox and traditional lines is at first sight repelled by the seeming destructiveness of form criticism. Ernst Käsemann writes in *Essays on New Testament Themes* (p. 15):

> The work of the Form Critics was designed to show that the message of

Jesus as given to us by the Synoptists is, for the most part, not authentic but was minted by the faith of the primitive Christian community in its various stages.

It seems at first as if form criticism deals a death blow to the value of the gospels and destroys and undermines the very foundations on which Christianity is built. But if, in spite of his shock, the student will persevere, he will find that it is true to say that the main aim of form criticism, and nowhere more so than in the case of Bultmann, can only be called evangelical, that its whole idea is to make relevant and challenging and contemporary the demand of the Christian faith. Its theology is a theology of encounter with the living Christ, and its demand is the demand for decision. When a student has reached this point, he then may take the very opposite point of view from that with which he began, and he may find himself in a position in which he holds that there is no other possible approach to the understanding of the New Testament. The form-critical approach is apt to generate either horror or adoration; it is indeed apt to begin with the one and issue in the other. We must try to exercise a sane and balanced judgment on it.

The literary aim of form criticism was to penetrate to the form of the Christian tradition before that tradition was set down in the written gospels; it was with the *form* of that tradition that it was concerned. Its discovery was that, before it was set down in writing, the gospel tradition consisted of units of tradition, circulating in stereotyped patterns and forms, which are easily identifiable. The fact that the gospel tradition circulated in these detached, stereotyped units means, according to the form critics, that we never can have anything like a chronology of the life of Jesus. As Martin Dibelius says (*Jesus*, p. 25):

> Any reader, even of the English translation, can see that the narratives in Mark 1-12 are completely self-contained units, whose positions can be interchanged without affecting the picture of Jesus' activity. . . . We are obliged, therefore, to forgo chronological order from the outset as well as the reconstruction of any development in Jesus, in his success, in his conflict with his enemies. A biography of Jesus in this sense cannot be written. All we know is individual incidents, not interconnected events.

The original is always the single unit of narrative, the single saying, not the connected text. It is the gospel writers who supply the transitions and the junctions in a quite artificial way, for they knew no more of the connected order than we do.

So then on this basis all that we have is what Strauss already called a necklace of pearls of which the string is broken. With one exception, the passion narrative, what we have is a miscellaneous collection of single units whose background and place in the tradition is unknown. Any reconstruction of growth and development is therefore precluded.

The very idea of biography is wiped out. The gospels are not literary works; they are not independent portrayals of the life of Jesus; they are not based on personal experience and enquiry. They are simply in Dibelius' phrase 'compilations of tradition'. They simply take the already existing units and arrange them in their own way. 'They are not to be compared with biographies, either modern or ancient' (*Jesus*, p. 8). As long as 1896 Martin Kähler, in his book *The So-called Historical Jesus and the Historic, Biblical Christ*, only recently translated into English, had said just exactly that and had said it forcibly:

> We do not possess any sources for a 'Life of Jesus' which a historian can accept as reliable and adequate. I repeat: we have no sources for a biography of Jesus of Nazareth which measure up to the standards of contemporary historical science (p. 48).

In view of these very strong and very definite words we may well ask – indeed we are bound to ask – what do we possess? The answer of the form critic is clear and unmistakable – and unquestionably true. Why were these units of tradition ever constructed? Why were they preserved? How did they become stereotyped? What produced them so that they were ready to hand when the gospel writers began to compile their gospels? The answer is obvious – *they were used for preaching*. They are the preaching material of the early church. This clearly gives them a special characteristic. They were not written simply to preserve the facts; that is to say, they are not primarily history. They were written to awaken faith; that is, they are primarily apologetic. They are the product of faith and they are written to awaken faith. That is to say, they are *kērygma*, they are proclamation. *Kērygma* means 'a herald's announcement', and it has become a technical term which scholars use to describe the basic proclamation of the Christian faith by the early preachers.

This apparently simple fact has become the very basis of the form critics' approach to the gospels, and the very centre of the whole discussion of the connection of the gospels with history.

Paul Althaus sums it up in *The So-called Kerygma and the Historical Jesus* (p. 21): 'The gospels are not in the least like historical sources, as the historian understands the term; the evangelists are "preachers".' This is reiterated again and again. Donald Baillie in *God was in Christ* (p. 25) says that what R.H. Grützmacher claimed to get from the gospels was 'the faith portrait which was the basis of the Christianity of the early Church, and must be the basis of our Christianity too.' The story, says Käsemann, as we have already quoted him, was 'minted by the faith of the early community'. 'We can learn nothing at all about the historical Jesus except through the medium of primitive Christian preaching.' We may quote still another fairly lengthy passage from Käsemann's *Essays*, because it shows not only this point of view, but the deduction which the form critics make from it:

> The historical Jesus meets us in the New Testament, our only real and original documentation of him, *not* as he was in himself, *not* as an isolated individual, but as the Lord of the community which believes in him. Only in so far as, from the very outset, he was potentially and actually this Lord, does the story of his earthly life play any part in our Gospels. Anything else there was to him is completely overshadowed, so that we are no longer in a position to delineate with even approximate accuracy and completeness his portrait, his development, the actual course of his life: we are for the most part groping in absolute darkness so far as these are concerned. The significance of this Jesus was so profound for faith, that even in the very earliest days it almost entirely swallowed up his earthly history. The living experience of him which later generations enjoyed made the facts of his earthly life simply irrelevant, except in so far as they might serve to reflect the permanent experience (p. 23).

The position here is that because the gospel portrait is the product of faith and is designed to awake faith, it is not in any normal sense of the term history at all.

Ernst Fuchs writes in his *Studies of the Historical Jesus* (p. 19):

> New Testament scholarship today is generally agreed that these gospels owe their form to kerygmatic considerations, and that their matter subserves this form. The evangelists were not mere compilers of their material, but had what may be described as a theological plan.

Dibelius says that the gospels are the work of people who marvel at God's doings rather than ponder over questions of detail.

> It is foreign to this sort of narrative to raise critical questions, or to examine whether or why this thing could have happened or that thing could have been said. Our positive knowledge of Jesus' history rests therefore on what the primitive communities handed down from the life of their master, and it is limited by the special nature of the transmitted material (*Jesus*, pp. 13f.).

It can now be seen that this approach uses the fact that the early records are the records of the faith of the community to divorce the story from history.

So then this point of view holds that it is not possible to penetrate behind and beyond the preached message of the early church. What we have is not the earthly facts about the life of Jesus, but the church's interpretation of these facts. What we have is not the record of Jesus as he was in the days of his flesh, but of Jesus as the church experienced him to be in the light of the resurrection.

But it is possible to go further than this. As a first step, we can say that we regard it as a great loss that we cannot penetrate behind the witness of the Christian community to the historic facts which lie behind it. But it is then possible to take another, and a much more far-reaching, step, and to say that it is wrong and misguided and mistaken even to want the historical facts, using that term in the normal sense. This is not so much a flight from history; it is a release from history.

It will be necessary first of all to understand a distinction which this school of thought draws, and which is quite essential to its thinking. In German there are two words for 'history' – *Historie* and *Geschichte*. A clear distinction – justifiably or unjustifiably – is drawn between their meanings. *Historie* is that which is past; it is what someone has called 'a piece of happenedness'. It may have no relevance at all to the present, other than that it is a built-in part of the past which has led to the present. It demands no reaction from us at all; it is something which is outside us. *Geschichte* is that which, although it is past, still demands a verdict, a judgment, a response, a decision from us. Carl E. Braaten in his introduction to Kähler's *The So-called Historical Jesus and the Historic, Biblical Christ* (p. 21) suggests that the two words represent the difference between objective history and existential history, between outer history and inner history, or even between writing history and making history. It is the difference between coming to the past with no other interest than the annalist or the chronicler, who is simply setting down past events, and going to the past, as Bultmann put it in *Jesus and the Word* (p. 12), 'seeking an answer to the questions which agitate him'. In English the difference is usually expressed by using the adjective *historical* to express that which is merely past, and *historic* to express that which is past but which still demands decision from me. An historical event is simply an event which happened; an historic event is an event which is still operative in its effect to this present day, and which demands a response from me. The fact that the Battle of Hastings was fought in AD 1066 and that in it William the Conqueror defeated Harold demands no decision from me; I do not have to do anything about it. The fact that Jesus Christ came into the world is an event which to this day, and at this present moment, demands a decision from me. As Bultmann very rightly says, the object of this kind of history is 'encounter'. Our object is not to find out what Jesus Christ *was* and *did*, but what Jesus Christ *is* and *does*.

That is exactly and precisely why the gospels are witnesses to a community's experience of the living Christ, and not records of one who belongs to the past. This is why Bultmann can say:

> Christ, the crucified and risen, meets us in the word of preaching and nowhere else. . . . The word of preaching meets us as God's word, and when we confront it we cannot ask any questions as to its legitimacy. Rather does it ask us whether we are willing to believe or not. . . . The Christian Easter faith is not interested in the historical question. To ask retrospectively whether the claim of the historic preaching is historically

justified is tantamount to rejecting it. This question has to be exchanged for the question which the questioner puts to himself, Will he acknowledge the lordship of Christ?[12]

It is not in the dead record of the past that we encounter Christ but in the living witness of faith.

Here then is the point of view that we do not find Jesus Christ in past events, however well or ill attested these events may be. It is actually in the faith of the community that we do find him.

This line of thought presents us with another dilemma, which Bultmann in the passage just quoted puts to us. To ask for historical legitimization of the act of faith which is demanded from us is, so it is claimed, the reverse of faith. Dibelius asserts the same point: 'What is asserted by faith cannot be proved by history. Indeed, faith would not be faith if it could be demonstrated to every comer' (p. 8). It is claimed that this interest in history is in fact the denial of faith, for it is demanding an attested and guaranteed series of facts upon which faith may be based. 'For Kähler,' writes Carl E. Braaten in his introduction (p. 18), 'modern historicism represented a particularly faithless form of objectivism.'

The insistence on factual history has two further results, it is claimed. If we insist that we must believe in an actual historical record of the deeds and acts of Jesus, then we run the risk of forming a Jesus-cult, and of worshipping, or even hero-worshipping, Jesus instead of God. Barth[13] protested that the insistence on history leads to a kind of Jesus-cult, which is the apotheosis of a religious hero, and is nothing more than a substitute for the Christian faith. Braaten points out (p. 25) that, as Kähler saw, this tends to replace Christology with Jesuanism. And, as Harnack said long ago,[14] 'The Gospel as Jesus proclaimed it has to do with the Father only, and not with the Son.' It is the action of God that we see in Jesus Christ, and a hero-cult of Jesus is not Christianity.

There remains one objection to the stressing of historicity which, at least at first sight, seems peculiarly impressive. Long ago Lessing said that accidental historical truths can never serve as proofs for eternal rational truths. The accidental and the eternal belong to different spheres.

Now it is obvious that historical research does not provide us with what we might call an agreed picture of Jesus. Different scholars come up with widely differing pictures of Jesus, each of them claiming that they have arrived at their picture through historical research. Further, historical research can never issue in static results. Additional material, better techniques, new understandings will produce differing pictures. Historical research provides us with a picture of Jesus which fluctuates and varies from person to person and from age to age.

This has been noted. Bornkamm in *Jesus of Nazareth* (p. 9) says succinctly: 'Certainly faith cannot and should not be dependent on the change and uncertainty of historical research.' Tillich in his foreword to *The So-called Historical Jesus and the Historic, Biblical Christ* (p. xii) says: 'I do believe that one emphasis in Kähler's answer is decisive for our present situation, namely, the necessity to make the certainty of faith independent of the unavoidable incertitudes of historical research.'

Kähler himself looked at this from another – and a pastoral – angle. If faith is to be dependent on the production of a reliable portrait of Jesus by methods of historical research, then what is to happen to the· simple person who has no scholarship, and who, since he can neither carry out nor evaluate research, would need to be dependent on an authoritarian acceptance of what the experts tell him?

> Faith must not be dependent on the uncertain conclusions about a reputedly reliable picture of Jesus which is tortured out of the sources by the methods of recently developed historical investigation. ... For in relation to the Christ in whom we have the duty and the privilege of believing, the most learned theologian must be no better off and no worse off than the simplest Christian.... How can Jesus Christ be the proper object of the faith of all Christians, if what and who he was can only really be established by a complicated investigation, and if it is only the science of our time which has shown itself equal to the task? How can this uncertain deposit left by the corrosive acids of criticism (i.e. the historical Jesus), how can this figure whom now for the first time scholarship can discern through the mists of antiquity, be the object of the faith of all Christians? ... Historical facts which can be established only by science cannot *as such* be experiences of faith.[15]

If it is so difficult, and even so impossible, to establish a picture of the historical Jesus, then such a picture cannot be essential for faith.

This then is the position of those who feel that it is no longer either possible or desirable to regard the gospels as historical documents. The older and the traditional view quite simply regarded the gospels as telling the story of Jesus; the new view does not regard that as the primary aim of the gospels at all. Let us once again very briefly summarize what we have called the new position. The gospels consist of separate and independent units, the connection of which the gospel writers did not know. With the exception of the passion and the resurrection narratives the connections are editorial and artificial, and we therefore cannot construct a chronology from the gospels at all. This precludes all talk of growth and development. The gospels are the product of the faith of the early community. In them we see Jesus, not as he actually was, but as the community believed him to be, in light of the resurrection faith. The gospels are not history but preaching; they are written out of faith, and their aim is to beget faith. But it is carefully to be noted, and it is always to be remembered, that the aim of all this is not destructive but evangelical. The aim is to make Jesus

Christ real, living, and freely available to all. The aim is to present Jesus, not as a figure in a book belonging to the dead past, a figure whose history we study and whom we know through research, a figure about whom we know, but rather as a living presence, whom we know and encounter, and who demands here and now our decision. Any evaluation of this whole approach must never forget the personal faith and devotion of its exponents, and must remember that the whole aim is to enable the simplest person to encounter the living Christ.

Our problem is whether or not we must accept all this. Are we to share in this flight from history? Must we abandon the gospels as history? Or can we still hold in some sense or other to their historical character and value? Are we to regard this new approach as a release and as a powerful evangelical instrument. Or are we to agree with H.E.W. Turner when he says in *Historicity and the Gospels* (p. 72): 'It needs to be plainly stated today that if statements of a historical order about the life and teaching of Jesus can no longer be made, Christianity as it has been classically understood would be wounded in a vital place'? These are the questions which we must try to answer and they are obviously of the first importance.

Our problem is not an easy one. As R.W. Hepburn has said,[16] our problem would be much easier, if we could regard the gospels either as completely infallible documents or as completely mythical documents; but these are exactly the two alternatives which are excluded. It is precisely the peculiar character of the gospels which makes the whole question so difficult.

(i) We may begin by agreeing that the gospels are not biographies in any recognizable sense of the term. They give us no personal description of Jesus. For the first thirty years of his life they supply almost no material at all. It is only in the last weeks of Jesus' life that there is any possibility of following Jesus day by day in the events in which he was involved.

F.C. Burkitt, in his book *The Gospel History and its Transmission*, from whose introductory chapter we shall have occasion to quote more than once in this section, points out (p. 20) that at a minimum Jesus' mission lasted four hundred days and we have information about perhaps forty of them, and that Jesus' teaching, as we have it in the gospels, could all have been delivered in about six hours. Whatever this is, it is not biography.

Modern biography, as Burkitt remarks (pp. 19 f.), tends to think in terms of a two-volume 'Life and Letters', followed by newspaper articles full of intimate and gossipy and often spicy reminiscence by people who knew the subject well in some capacity or other. The gospels are not in the least like this.

It will be well to remember as a basic fact that the gospels were bound to be selective. Nowadays there is no reason why a book should not run to vast length; seven or eight hundred pages and a quarter of a million words are perfectly practicable. But the material with which the gospel writers were working was the papyrus roll, and the maximum practical length of the papyrus roll was thirty feet – beyond that it became too difficult to handle – and that is almost exactly the length of Matthew, Luke and John. Within these limits a writer was bound to select; he had no other course.

It is further to be pointed out that sheer length does not necessarily provide a characterization of the person written about. Burkitt points out that Lady Macbeth's part in Shakespeare's play has only some two hundred and fifty lines in it, and yet the portrait of Lady Macbeth is living and vivid and unforgettably memorable. 'The chronicling of events,' says Burkitt (p. 23), 'is one thing, and the characterization of personality is another.'

Burkitt uses an illustration. Suppose you wished to describe St Paul's Cathedral to someone who had never seen it and who would never see it. You could get a photograph; you could get a set of architect's drawings; you could get an impressionist painting; and it is perfectly possible and even likely that the painting would best of all give the character of the cathedral. Of course, it would not have the detail, but it would have the 'personality' of the building.

Assuming for the moment that the facts as narrated in the gospels are reliable, the question, as Burkitt sees it, is not, Have we all that we might want? but, Have we as much as we need? That is to say, have we as much as we need to give us a living, recognizable portrait of Jesus Christ? We certainly have. This not even the radical critics deny. Martin Kähler writes:

> All the biblical portrayals evoke the undeniable impression of the fullest reality, so that one might venture to predict how [Jesus] might have acted in this or that situation, indeed, even what he might have said. This is why to commune with Jesus one needs nothing more than the biblical presentation.... The biblical picture of Christ, so lifelike and unique beyond imagination, is not a poetic idealization originating in the human mind. The reality of Christ himself has left its ineffaceable impress upon this picture (pp 78f.).

And Dibelius writes (*Jesus*, pp. 9f.):

> It is not a case of our having to forgo a picture of Jesus or of having to doubt even the historicity of his figure.... A unified basic tradition was at hand.

Jesus, Bultmann would not for one moment doubt, was the friend of outcasts and sinners, and, as it were, opened the messianic banquet to them.

Biography we do not have; characterization we most certainly have. Photograph we do not have; portrait we certainly possess. It is perfectly true that there may be more than one portrait. F.C. Burkitt says (p 23): 'One man may be the subject of many adequate portraits.' If a man was going to write a portrait study of Teilhard de Chardin he might show him as scientist, for he was a most distinguished scientist; he might show him as mystic and theologian, for these things he most certainly was; or he might write a study of the church's unsympathetic treatment of him, for that too was certainly part of his life. We may think, for instance, of the widely differing characterizations of T.E. Lawrence. But there are limits to this. As H.E.W. Turner says (p. 19): 'You may doubt that Caligula was as mad as he was supposed to be – but you can't make him into a balanced and far-sighted statesman.' The basic picture remains.

The fact is that from the gospels a recognizable person emerges, and it is equally true that the personality there depicted is in accordance with the facts.

We may here take in the claim that there is no possibility of constructing a chronology of the life of Jesus, because the material came to the writers of the gospels in completely independent and disconnected units. This has always seemed to me a completely rash and illegitimate statement. Leaving aside altogether for the moment for future discussion the possible apostolic connection with the gospels – and it cannot be blandly disregarded – it is surely an incredible implication that by the time Mark's gospel was written in the middle of the sixties of the first century there was no one left alive who knew the general pattern of Jesus' life. That such was the case is frankly beyond belief. Further, the Marcan pattern, which became the generally accepted pattern, makes sense. We have already quoted Dibelius's statement that any reader of the English translation can see that 'the narratives in Mark 1-12 are completely self-contained units whose position can be interchanged without affecting the picture of Jesus' activity'. This statement is frankly simply untrue. The Marcan pattern makes sense – preparation, conflict, tragedy, triumph. And it is surely preposterous to say that you can take the narratives, say, of the temptations and the baptism and put them at the end rather than at the beginning. No one would claim that the exact and precise place of every incident and bit of teaching was known; but surely equally no one can claim that thirty years after Jesus was crucified no one knew the general pattern of his life, and no one remembered when an incident took place.

No one is going to claim the chronological accuracy of a railway timetable or a conference programme for the gospels, but we believe it impossible reasonably to deny that their general chronology makes dramatic sense, and is on the whole correct, for the simple reason that there were many people who still remembered it.

(ii)　We shall readily agree and always remember that before we

can use the gospels as history we must remember that they move in
the thought-world of the first century, and that not only the words but
the ideas and the categories of thought have to be translated into the
idiom of the twentieth century.

It is perfectly true that the ancient world was accustomed to think
in terms of myth in the sense in which Bultmann used that word. He
himself, in *Jesus Christ and Mythology* (pp. 141-8), defines myth as
that which gives 'worldly objectivity to that which is unworldly'. Or
again, myth renders objective and pictorial that which is an inward
experience. Myth is no phenomenon which is confined to the ancient
world; it can frequently be found, for instance, in dreams to this day.
To take an example far from the field of theology, Simenon in one of
his Maigret books, *Maigret in Society*, confronts Maigret with a
problem which is in a world of birth and aristocracy to which he is a
stranger and in which he feels himself inadequate and helpless. During
the investigation Maigret has a dream in which he is in a room with all
the people who are involved in the case. They are smiling at him
amusedly; one of them in explanation points at his legs; and in the
dream he sees that he is wearing a boy's short trousers. In other
words, the dream is a mythological way of saying that these people,
who are out of his sphere altogether, are in fact treating him as a child.
The inner experience is objectified in the concrete picture.

To take the most obvious examples, the attribution of disease to the
influence of demons and the occupation of a man's body by evil spirits
is myth; the descent of the Holy Spirit in the form of a dove is myth;
the temptation story with the apparently visible devil and the
mountain from which the whole world can be seen is myth. But, as
Burkitt said (p. 4), we have not only to listen to our witnesses, we have
also to cross-examine them; and it is not difficult to find the truth in
the myth. The fact that we can no longer speak of the creating activity
of God as of a child who makes things out of plasticine does not mean
that we have to abandon the idea of God as the power behind and
within the world. That fact that we can no longer regard disease as the
work of demons does not mean that we can no longer say that Jesus
healed those who were ill. The fact that we can no longer speak of a
personal devil called Satan does not mean that there is not a power of
evil in the world, and that Jesus met and conquered that power, as we
must do. The fact that we can no longer speak of Jesus' coming down
and going up does not mean that we need to abandon the idea that
God in a special way entered the world in Jesus Christ and triumphed
over sin and death.

The fact that the New Testament story is often told in mythical
terms does not mean that the history of the story is dissolved; it only
means that we have to translate the myth into terms which are relevant
to the twentieth century.

(iii) But we are as yet only on the fringe of the real problem involved in the flight from history. There are two interconnected lines of thought.

(a) There is the insistence that what we have in the gospels is in fact the deposit of the faith of the early community, that this is *kērygma*, that this is preaching and proclamation, that this is the belief of the church. Leave the matter there and no one will have the slightest objection to that statement. The fourth gospel is unequivocally definite that these things are written that those who read may come to believe that Jesus is the Messiah and that in that belief they may find life (John 20.31). No one is going to deny this. No one is going to plead that the primary interest of the gospel writers is literary or historical; they were not writing biography or history; they were writing out of faith and in order to produce faith. They themselves had encountered God in Jesus Christ, and they wished others to experience the same encounter.

But it is the conclusion which is drawn from that which is by no means so convincing, for, to put it bluntly, the conclusion is that because they were writing in faith they were not interested in fact, and because they were preachers they had no interest in history. The second conclusion is far from being a necessary deduction from the first.

Let us put this in another way. *We are seeing Jesus through the eyes of the early Christian community.* This is unanswerably true – and what is unusual about it? There is no other kind of history. History is always the past seen through someone else's eyes. H.E.W. Turner in *Historicity and the Gospels* (pp. 3f.) quotes Marc Bloch on this very point – that the knowledge of the historian is always indirect. 'No Egyptologist has ever seen Rameses. No expert in the Napoleonic Wars has ever heard the sound of the cannon of Austerlitz.' You cannot have first-hand knowledge of the distant past; that knowledge is necessarily mediated through other sources. Turner goes on to quote the saying of another historian, François Simiand: 'The historian's knowledge of all human activities in the past is *a knowledge of their tracks.*'

To say that the gospels represent the faith of the early community in Jesus is simply to say that our knowledge of the earthly life of Jesus is mediated to us through the writings of the early church – which is the only possible way in which it could come to us. There is no possible way in which anyone can see any event in the past other than through the eyes of someone else.

But it may be argued that even admitting this there are still two things to be said about the gospels which make them different from other documents.

First, in the case of the gospels it is claimed there is no 'control'.

That is to say, there is no other account by which their statements may be checked and evaluated; there are no parallel sources which can act as controls on the gospel stories. This is true, for any information we have outside the gospels about Jesus is negligible in its value. But it cannot be claimed that the gospels are the only historical sources which stand alone. There are many accounts of the past which go back to the witness and the evidence of one person or one book, and the weight given to them must be assessed by an evaluation of the source. An account cannot simply be ruled out as unhistorical because there is no parallel account.

Second – and at first sight this seems a serious charge – the community which produced the gospels is so committed that it is both impossible and unreasonable to look for a fair and impartial account. It is indeed not possible to look for an impartial account in documents which are admittedly pleading a case. The aim of the gospels is not to describe Jesus but to commend Jesus.

Of the committedness of the gospel writers there is no question, and of their object there is no question, but is it really true that such an attitude disqualifies them from all claims to being historians? It cannot be said, without doing violence to his own statement, that Luke was an uncritical and slavish follower of his sources (Luke 1.1-4). His claim is to investigation and to research.

It is in any event true to say that an attitude of complete and total detachment could succeed in compiling a chronicle, but could never succeed in writing a history. Burkitt said (p. 22): 'A true impression is on the whole and for most people better conveyed by a friend than by an observer wholly dispassionate.' It has been said that a good biography could be written by a man who loves his subject and a good biography could be written by a man who hates his subject, but a good biography could never be written by a man who is totally indifferent to and detached from his subject.

This is so for the simple reason that history presupposes a standpoint. An historian cannot simply relate the facts; he must pass some kind of judgment upon them. The history of a man must not only tell us what the man did; it must tell us something of the kind of man he was; it must evaluate his effect on current and consequent events. And this necessarily involves a standpoint from which such a judgment can be made. A biography of Adolf Hitler would be an odd book without some kind of judgment of his effect upon Germany and Europe and the world; a relation of the events of Belsen or Auschwitz would be an odd thing without some judgment of the governing body which regarded these places as legitimate governmental enterprises.

To demand history in detachment is both an impossibility and a contradiction in terms.

It is further true that even the most prejudiced historians have not been dismissed as totally valueless. Tacitus is highly selective and tendentious, yet he is not abandoned as an historian. Suetonius was a court gossip and scandalmonger, yet his Lives of the Caesars are not without value. Macaulay wrote history as a Whig, yet his history is not valueless. It is quite certainly true that even if the general character of an historical work is prejudiced and partial, this does not in the least detract from the value of individual incidents which it may give. To say that the gospels are pleading a case or witnessing to a belief is simply to say something which could be said about at least half the histories that have ever been written.

And, finally, it may not be completely naïve to suggest that even if the gospel writers are pleading a case, they might well have served their case best of all by telling about Jesus as he was and relating what he did say.

(b) But there is another problem in relation to history which we must face. We have already seen the distinction which is commonly made between *Historie* and *Geschichte*. *Historie* is that which is merely historical, that which is simply past, that which may be interesting enough, but has no particular relevance to my life, that which makes no special demand on me. *Geschichte* is that with which I am still faced, that which still demands a response and decision from me, that which I do not merely know, but on which I must base my actions.

No one will question this decision. It is a fact that the two thieves were crucified on Calvary, but this does not demand any decision from me; it is a fact that Jesus Christ was crucified on Calvary, and this does demand a decision from me. I encounter the cross of Christ in a way that I do not encounter the other two crosses. This is true. But this does not in the least affect the truth that that which is *Geschichte* is also what H.E.W. Turner (p. 15) called 'a piece of happenedness'. *Geschichte* has the quality of 'presentness', but it has the quality of 'passedness' also.

What we may call the non-historical line of thought would say that it does not really matter whether it happened or not; what matters is the faith of which it is the expression.

But this issues in the very curious position that my encounter is not really with an always contemporary event, but with what is really no more than a projection of my own mind. I am encountering what my faith produced rather than what God has done – and where in the first instance did my faith come from?

Let us take a very simple and even crude analogy. If a total stranger comes up to me on the street and asks me to trust him with my wallet and all my money, it will not be faith but folly to give it to him. But if someone whom I know and love and whom I have again and again proved to be absolutely reliable and devoted to my best interests asks me to trust him with the administration of my affairs, then I will trust him. *I trust him because I know what he is like.* And that is not making faith dependent on knowledge; it is making faith dependent on the certainty of character and personality. It is not a series of facts and arguments I trust; it is a person.

Now here is the point. The desire is encounter with Jesus Christ, so that I may entrust my life to him. But I cannot possibly make that act of encounter and follow it with the act of trust if the name of Jesus means no more to me than the letter X. I must be able to put some content into the name Jesus. The flight from history has completely forgotten the one inevitable fact that no one can even mention this name without a picture rising in the mind; no one of the scholars who insist that history is irrelevant can speak the name Jesus without a mental picture embedded in their minds. When I speak the name Nero a picture arises; when I speak the name Hitler a picture arises. When I speak the name Jesus a picture arises. If I can know nothing about this Jesus, if his personality and character remain a closed book to me, I cannot encounter him, because I cannot encounter that which is simply a name; I can only encounter a person. It is completely necessary for me to have a picture of Jesus before I can encounter him, and I cannot have a picture unless I believe that the gospels give me a reliable picture of him, at least in broad outline.

There is a distinction here. It is claimed that we cannot believe in the resurrection unless we bring faith to the alleged facts. It is claimed that no amount of 'proof' that the grave was empty and that Jesus appeared to his disciples can make *me* believe unless I already have the faith to believe. This is true. But reverse the argument and see what happens. If it could be proved to me that the whole resurrection story if pure fiction, that it is nothing more than the objectivizing of an idea that arose in the minds of the first disciples, then this is going to make a disastrous difference to me, for the simple reason that there is nothing left to have faith in.

The facts will not in themselves beget faith, but unless the facts are there faith cannot even arise, for I am not surely called upon to have faith in the faith of the early church, but to have faith in the action of God expressed in events.

(iv)   And this brings us to the matter in which this whole question reaches its climax. We were impressed by the argument that you cannot make faith dependent on the chances and the changes of historical research, as Bornkamm said. We were impressed by Kähler's plea that faith must be as open to the non-scholar and the simple person as it is to the theologian and the qualified historian. But there is another side to this.

If we believe in anything that may be called an incarnation or, as Nels Ferré calls it, an 'enmanning of God', then we are committed to history. The incarnation, as H.E.W. Turner puts it (pp. 33f.), is 'a unique involvement in history'. And therefore, 'The Christian cannot enjoy the advantages of an historical revelation without the possible disadvantages of historical analysis and explanation.'

This is the hard and simple fact. Belief in the incarnation means that the Christian message is anchored in history. This does not mean that we are back to a Jesus-cult. We believe in the self-revelation of God in Jesus Christ. As Paul Althaus says in *The So-called Kerygma* (p. 45): 'In the picture of the man Jesus we lay hold of the character of God, in the spiritual countenance of Jesus we behold the countenance of God.' What the gospel demands of me is that I should cast myself upon God. That I can never do unless I can know what God is like. I must be sure that he wants me to do this, and I must be sure that I will be enfolded in his love and not blasted by his wrath. My only proof that when I submit to God I submit to love, lies in the life of Jesus. Unless I can be quite sure that Jesus was the friend of outcasts and sinners, I can never be sure that God is just that. Unless I can be quite sure that God is like Jesus I cannot make the act of faith. I must therefore be able to believe that when the gospels tell of Jesus' attitude to men they are telling the truth, or I cannot know the character of God.

This does not mean that I must literally and exactly and mechanically accept everything; but it does beyond all doubt mean that I must be able to regard the picture of the gospels as historically and factually reliable in general.

As we see it, this can be summed up in a double statement. The gospels are certainly the product of the faith of the early church; but the gospels are equally certainly the reliable record of the events on which that faith is founded. The gospels are certainly *kērygma*, but they are also the record of that self-revelation of God in Jesus Christ which the *kērygma* preaches. I respond to God because I know that God is like Jesus, and the only way in which I can know Jesus, and therefore the only way I can know God, is through the record of the life of Jesus in the gospels, and, no matter what historical research and analysis can do to that record, they cannot alter the historical rightness of its total impression on the mind and heart.

2

THE INITIAL STAGE

The general consensus of opinion is that Mark is the earliest of the gospels, and that the date of Mark is about AD 65. This at once presents us with an initial problem which forces itself upon our attention. This is to say that the earliest written gospel did not emerge until almost forty years after the life of Jesus in the flesh. Obviously we are bound to ask what was happening to the story of Jesus in these years between.

Before we try to answer that question, we must ask a prior question. What was it that caused this delay? Why did so long pass before the story was committed to writing? There is more than one answer to that question. There was indeed a whole series of contributory factors.

(i) Apart from the main centres of culture like Athens and Rome, the first half of the first Christian century was still a non-literary age. It is hard to think oneself out of a situation in which, if a man has something to say, he naturally writes a book. The days of printing and of mass circulation lay still many centuries ahead. The writing of books was not then the natural and inevitable procedure that it is now.

Further, in the initial stages of Christianity the Christians were not the kind of people who either would or could write books. Not many wise, or powerful, or noble were among them as the world evaluates these things (I Cor. 1.26f.). They were simple people to whom the pen would have been an unfamiliar tool, and the book something that was strange to their way of life.

This was particularly true of Jewish society. The great mass of Jewish law and tradition was passed down by word of mouth. The teaching of the rabbis was oral. The *Mishnah* is the codified summary of the Jewish law, and it was not put into writing until the third century AD. According to Jewish standards, a good student was not a great reader, because there were no books to read, but a good listener, and a good rememberer who was like 'a well plastered cistern which never loses a drop of water'. The reverence which a Jewish scholar accorded to the scriptures of the Old Testament made him utterly unwilling himself to put anything into writing, lest he might appear to be putting his productions on a level with the sacred and the holy writings. 'Commit nothing to writing,' was the rabbinic maxim.

Nor was this attitude to the written word absolutely confined to Judaism. When Papias, the bishop of Hierapolis, towards the end of the second century, was collecting every possible scrap of information about Jesus and the early days, he said: 'I did not think that I would get so much profit from the contents of books as from the utterances of a living and abiding voice.'[1] Even Quintilian, the Roman master of oratory, and one of the world's great educationalists, held the same point of view. He said of the education of children that the children certainly must have their books, but the living voice gives richer nourishment, especially if it be the voice of a teacher whom the pupils love and trust.[2] In such circumstances the memory was highly developed. Xenophon relates how Niceratus told how his father wished him to grow up a good man, and therefore made him learn by heart all the forty-eight books of Homer's *Iliad* and *Odyssey*. He could still recite them by heart and so could many of his contemporaries.

The fact that the gospel events were so long in being committed to writing was far less surprising in the ancient world than it would be now.

(ii)   A not inconsiderable factor in the situation was the cost of committing anything to writing, if it was properly and expertly written by a scribe. By this time something like mass production had arrived, for books were produced in quantity by dictating them to large numbers of scribes. But that was only true of popular poets and the like, and the New Testament in the early days would have to be copied one copy at a time.

We have the information to deduce the cost of a properly and expertly scribed book. The unit of measurement of a book was the *stichos*. The *stichos* is not a line, for of course the number of lines in a book would vary according to the size of the parchment sheet and the writing of the scribe, and the line could not be the standard of measurement. A *stichos* was the average length of an Homeric hexameter line of poetry, which was about sixteen syllables. This then was the unit of measurement. There is one New Testament codex which gives the number of *stichoi* in the various books, the Codex Claromontanus. In Matthew there are 2600 *stichoi*; in Mark, 1600; in Luke, 2900; in John, 2000. That is to say there are 9,100 *stichoi* in the whole four gospels, and there are rather more than 18,000 in the whole New Testament. In AD 310, in a time of severe inflation, Diocletian issued a wide-ranging price-fixing edict.[3] By that edict the pay of a good scribe was 20-25 *denarii* per 100 *stichoi*. This compares with 25 *denarii* per day as a labourer's or mule-driver's wage, or 50 *denarii* per day for a skilled craftsman, a mason or a carpenter or smith. So a properly scribed copy of the four gospels would cost the equivalent of a craftsman's wages for about six weeks. There is little wonder that there was no haste to commit things to writing.

(iii)   There remains one further reason why the gospel story was not committed to writing and it may well have been the dominating reason. In the early days the Christian expected the *parousia*, the second coming, the return of Jesus in glory, at any moment; the world was hastening to its end. In a situation as temporary as that books were simply irrelevant. With the last day liable – even, as they believed, certain – to come at any moment, no one was going to spend time committing things to writing for a future which was not going to exist.

Such, then, were the main factors which delayed the production of a written gospel. What were the factors which in the end brought about the production of such gospels?

(i)   The form of the Christian service encouraged the production of a Christian literature. Very naturally the services of the early church were modelled on the services of the synagogue, and central in the synagogue service was the reading of the law and of the prophets. At first the Old Testament was the only book which the Christians possessed, and it was it that they used, but quite inevitably a literature of their own was bound to grow up beside it. The first description of a Christian service is in Justin Martyr's *First Apology* (67) which dates to AD 155. Justin's account begins:

> On the day called Sunday all who live in cities or in the country gather together to one place, and the memoirs of the apostles or the writings of the prophets are read as long as time permits; then, when the reader has ceased, the president verbally instructs and exhorts to the imitation of these good things.

So from the first we find the reading of scripture embedded in the Christian service as it had been in the Jewish. The very existence of Christian worship would tend to encourage and even necessitate the production of Christian literature.

(ii)   The missionary propaganda of the church would necessitate the production of the gospels. One of the outstanding features of the work of Paul is the speed with which he passed from place to place. Since he himself could not stay long in any place, it was necessary that he must have some account of Jesus to leave behind.

That such an account was given is not really open to doubt. 'I appeal to you,' he writes to the Corinthians, 'by the gentleness and the magnanimity of Christ' (II Cor. 10.1, NEB). These qualities must have been illustrated from the life of Christ. When Peter writes to his friends, he says:

> It is for you to follow in his steps. He committed no sin, he was convicted of no falsehood; when he was abused he did not retort with abuse; when he suffered he uttered no threats, but committed his cause to One who judges justly. In his own person he carried our sins to the gibbet, so that we might cease to live for sin and begin to live for righteousness (I Peter 2.21-24, NEB).

A passage like that could only have been written to people who already knew the facts of Jesus' life and death. It has to be read in the context of an already existing knowledge of Jesus. The New Testament letters are quite clearly written to those who know the story, either in the beginning through the spoken word, or later through the written word.

(iii)   Closely related to this, in fact another aspect of this, is that it may well be that the first formulated accounts of the deeds and of the teaching of Jesus were constructed for catechetical purposes. We read of the teachers in the early church (Acts 13.1f.; I Cor. 12.28f.; Eph. 4.11). The early converts must have been handed over to the teachers for catechetical instruction, and thus the account of the life and teaching of Jesus must have assumed a standardized form.

(iv)   There were two interconnected reasons why a written and authoritative 'official' gospel was likely to come into being.

(a)   In matters of life and in matters of discipline both the church and the individual needed the example and the command of Jesus. When a man or a church was faced with a decision, it was of the greatest value to have some deed of Jesus to cite as an example, or some word of Jesus to quote as an instruction and command. A compendium of the life and teaching of Jesus was a practical necessity.

(b)   When the church was threatened with heresies and with mistaken ideas, it was again essential to have some agreed version of the teaching of Jesus. The true gospel had to be available to quote against the false gospel, and the 'real' teaching of Jesus had to be available to quote against the alleged private revelations of the heretics.

(v)   There were two reasons connected with persecution which must have had their influence on the production of a written gospel.

(a)   It was necessary to have an official account of the life and teaching of Jesus in order at least to attempt to prove the innocence of Christianity to the government. It is certain that Acts had an apologetic aim, and it may well be that the gospels, too, were accounts which sought to show that such a faith as this should not offend.

(b)   When persecution did break out, it was necessary to have that which would keep high the hearts of the Christians in their trials, and what better source of courage could there be than the demands and the promises of Jesus, and his own personal example in the face of the cross?

The gospels could be used as Christianity's defence against the persecutor, and as the Christian's inspiration in persecution.

(vi)   When we turn to the tradition of the early church, one reason is again and again advanced for the writing of the gospels.

Traditionally, the supreme figures in the church were the apostles.

They were the repositories and the guardians of the tradition about Jesus. They were the men who had been with Jesus throughout his ministry and who had been witnesses of the resurrection (Acts 1.21f.). As Clement of Rome says in his *First Epistle* (42):

> The apostles were made evangelists to us by Jesus Christ; Jesus Christ was sent by God. Thus Christ is from God, and the apostles from Christ. He and they came into being in harmony from the will of God.

By the beginning of the fourth century Serapion could say: 'We receive Peter and the other apostles as Christ.'[4] In the Revelation the foundation stones of the holy city bear the names of the twelve (Rev. 21.14).

But the apostles were human, and death came to them. With the exception of John, the disciples were all dead by AD 70, and it is possible, though not indeed probable, that even John was martyred early. *Tradition saw the written gospel as the necessary substitute for the living voice of the apostles.* Irenaeus says that it was after the death of Peter and Paul that Mark and Luke wrote their gospels, thus enshrining the preaching and teaching of their masters. Mark, says Clement of Alexandria, at the express request of the church wrote out what he remembered of the preaching of Peter.[5] Mark, said Tertullian, edited what Peter said.[6] Jerome in the preface to his *Commentary on Matthew*, said that Mark narrated those things which he had heard Peter his master preach. Elsewhere he says: 'Mark, the disciple and interpreter of Peter, when asked by the brothers at Rome, wrote a short gospel according to what he had heard Peter reporting.'[7] Eusebius in his *History* (3.24.15) tells us that what Luke gives us in his gospel is 'the reliable account of the things whose truth he had well learned with the help of his association and sojourn with Paul and his conversation with the other apostles'. Of the writing of Matthew's gospel he says (3.24.5f.) that Matthew originally preached to the Hebrews. When he was about to leave them for other spheres, he committed his gospel to writing, and thereby 'compensated by his writing for the loss of his presence'.

Tradition is unanimous that the written gospel was the substitute for the living voice – and in principle it may well be right, as we shall see when we now turn our attention to what was happening to the gospel tradition before it was written down.

Before we begin to study this in detail, there are certain general principles at which it will be well to look.

We may begin with one certainty. Whatever was happening to the gospel material in its unwritten period, it was quite certainly always being used as preaching material. From the beginning the church was a missionary church, and therefore from the beginning the church was a preaching church. For Irenaeus what the gospels brought to men was *the plan of salvation*. In his book *Against Heresies* (3.1.1) he describes the work of the gospel writers as he saw it:

> After our Lord rose from the dead, and when they were endued from on high with the power of the Spirit who came upon them, they were filled with that power in respect to all things, and had perfect knowledge, and went out to the ends of the earth proclaiming those good things which are ours from God, and announcing heavenly peace to men.

The sole object of the early preachers, and therefore the sole object of the early tradition, was to confront men with the saving action of God in Jesus Christ.

So then quite certainly the early tradition is preaching. There must first of all have been a process of translation. Jesus himself spoke and taught in Aramaic, and the early communities in Jerusalem and in Palestine must have used that language. As Dibelius points out (*Jesus*, p. 21), the process of translation into Greek was not like the modern translation of a book. A translator nowadays has a book to work on and sits down to translate it as a whole in a single process. Dibelius describes early translation as a 'multiple' process. This simply means that in a bilingual community like Antioch the sayings of Jesus and the stories about Jesus were translated in the telling. No one ever sat down and translated the material as a whole; the preacher and the teacher and the missionary put it into Greek piecemeal as they needed it.

But along with this process of multiple translation another process was going on, as it were, parallel with it. There was a process of stereotyping. The same story began to be told in exactly the same form, and the same saying began to be quoted in exactly the same way.

A process like this is much easier and much quicker and much more definite in a community where boooks are neither known nor used. For instance, anyone who tells favourite stories to children knows that the form of the story must not vary. The child wants it — and sees that he gets it! — in exactly the same form. He does not want variation; he protests against variation; he wants it in the form in which he knows it. Similarly, sagas of stories arise round even many modern personalities, around preachers and teachers and scholars, especially if they are 'characters' with a certain eccentricity in them. And in that case, too, the story tends to stereotype, so that, no matter who is telling it, it remains the same. In the circumstances it is only to be expected that the stereotyping of the stories about Jesus would be a process both quick and firm.

When we get this length, one extremely important conclusion emerges. This unwritten tradition has not got an author as a book has an author. It is in a sense anonymous. Its creator is the community; its custodian is the community; and its guarantor is the community. This is not to say that some individual man did not tell the story for the first time or make the translation for the first time; but this was being done at the same time in all sorts of communities; and the men who did it never thought of themselves as authors or translators but simply as preachers and teachers transmitting what they knew about Jesus.

Up to this point there will be substantial agreement from almost all schools of thought; but it is here that we encounter two opposite points of view.

There are those who would regard this whole situation as the best guarantee of the basic reliability of the Christian tradition. F.C. Grant on the opening page of *The Gospels* writes:

> The tradition was a 'social' possession, the common property of the early Christian churches, and was not limited to the 'recollections' of a few individuals. . . . The significance of this view is obvious. The memories of a few individuals might be mistaken − since human recollection is notoriously fallible − but the testimony of a group, even if anonymous, is more likely to have been verified, criticized, supported, culled, and selected during the course of the first generation of early church evangelism. The possibility of fabrication by one or two individuals is completely ruled out. . . . Although the tradition was no doubt modified in the course of transmission, its basic trustworthiness is beyond doubt; for it rests, not upon one man's recollections − say Peter's − or those of two or three persons, but upon the whole group of the earliest disciples.

From this point of view the way in which the tradition grew up and was stereotyped is the best guarantee of its substantial accuracy.

But, as we have already seen, there are those who take precisely the opposite point of view, and who hold that what we have in the tradition represents not the facts of the life of Christ, but the faith in him of the early church, in the light of the resurrection; that we have theology rather than history, that in fact there was no interest in history.

We have already dealt with the two points of view, but it is well to see just from where they take their rise.

It would obviously be of the greatest interest and importance, if it were possible to discover the form in which the gospel tradition circulated before it was written down. We can assume that it did circulate in detached units which were used in preaching and in teaching. In recent years there has widely developed a branch of New Testament study called form criticism, whose aim it has been to identify the *forms* in which the tradition came to be stereotyped and in which it did circulate. It is to be noted that form criticism began by being interested in the forms. That is to say, it began by being literary-critical. But it has gone further than that. It has made it its business to pass judgment on the historical value of these units of tradition, and to say which of them may go back to Jesus, and which, in its opinion, are the production of the community of the early church. It has tended to be on the whole radical in its approach, and to assign much to the activity of the Christian community and comparatively little directly to Jesus himself.

Let us then see what 'forms' the form critics have identified; let us see the kinds of unit in which they believe that the gospel tradition circulated before it was reduced to writing.

(i) There are what are variously called *paradigms, apophthegms,* or *pronouncement stories*. These are units whose sole purpose is to enshrine some saying of Jesus. Their interest is neither in events nor in persons; it is solely in the saying of Jesus. The scene is usually quite vague; the people are often not even identified, but are simply 'they'. Such narrative as there is simply provides the irreducible minimum to give the saying some kind of setting. A very good example of this kind of unit is the story about Jesus and the children (Mark 10.13-15; Matt. 19.13-15; Luke 18.15-17):

> And they were bringing children to him that he might touch them; and the disciples rebuked them. But when Jesus saw it he was indignant, and said to them: 'Let the children come to me and do not hinder them; for to such belongs the kingdom of God. Truly, I say to you, whoever does not receive the kingdom of God like a child shall not enter it.'

There is no indication of where this happened; there is no indication of who it was who brought the children; there is no indication of why the disciples stopped them. The unit exists simply to tell the saying of Jesus. The unit in Mark 6.1-4 which tells of Jesus' visit to Nazareth exists only for the saying of Jesus: 'A prophet is not without honour except in his own country, and among his own kin, and in his own house.' The unit in Matthew 22.15-22 is designed to preserve the saying of Jesus: 'Render to Caeser the things which are Caesar's, and to God the things that are God's.' In Luke 9.57-62 the three would-be followers of Jesus are brought upon the scene simply that Jesus' answers to them should be recorded.

With this no one is likely to differ. It is indeed obvious that these units are in fact designed to preserve the saying of Jesus in which they culminate, and that everything else is subordinate to that.

But the form critic does not stop there. He may go on to say two things.

(a) Let us remember that all these units are preaching material, and let us remember that they arose in the community in the very natural and proper desire for guidance from the example and the words of Jesus. Now, it can be seen that these stories often end with a kind of double-barrelled saying of Jesus. Certain of the form critics — for instance, Dibelius — hold that these stories led up to a saying of Jesus, and then to that actual saying the Christian community added a further sentence which makes the original saying of Jesus into a

general principle for the church. This second and attached saying is therefore not a saying of Jesus, but rather the interpretation by the church of what Jesus said. Let us take two examples, and what the form critics mean will become clear. Let us take first Mark 2.15-17:

> And as he sat at table in his house, many tax-collectors and sinners were sitting with Jesus and his disciples; for there were many who followed him. And the scribes of the Pharisees, when they saw that he was eating with sinners and tax-collectors, said to the disciples, 'Why does he eat with tax-collectors and sinners?' And when Jesus heard it, he said to them, 'Those who are well have no need of a physician, but those who are sick; I came not to call the righteous, but sinners.'

This line of thought holds that the actual saying of Jesus ends with the words: 'Those who are well have no need of a physician, but those who are sick.' And that then the community added the interpretation: 'I came not to call the righteous, but sinners', for this was the very principle on which the missionary work of the Christian church was based. In other words the community has, as it were, put into the mouth of Jesus a general principle which is the expansion and the interpretation of a particular saying.

Let us take, second, Mark 3.31-35:

> And his mother and his brothers came; and standing outside they sent to him and called him. And a crowd was sitting about him; and they said to him, 'Your mother and your brothers are outside, asking for you.' And he replied, 'Who are my mother and my brothers?' And looking around on those who sat about him, he said, 'Here are my mother and my brothers! Whoever does the will of God is my brother, and sister, and mother.'

This line of thought holds that Jesus' actual words end with, 'Here are my mother and my brothers!' and that then from this the community extracted a quite general principle: 'Whoever does the will of God is my brother, and sister, and mother.' The community has extracted from a particular word of Jesus on a particular occasion a word for all time.

It is the point of view of Dibelius that this is perfectly natural. In *A Fresh Approach to the New Testament* (p.34) he wrote:

> These Christians believed themselves to be more faithful to their Master when they explained his sayings by expanding them, and then followed them with understanding, than if they had abhorred any addition and passed on the original form of his words.

It might indeed well be held that this is precisely the fulfilment of the promise of Jesus when he said that the Holy Spirit would take what he had said and declare it to his disciples. This point of view – and we may well in principle accept it – simply says that in the units which are designed to preserve a saying of Jesus we may sometimes get not only the saying, but the interpretation of it by the early church.

(b) But the form critic may go a step further than that. The unit in Mark 2.23-27 has to do with sabbath observance, and finishes with the saying: 'The sabbath was made for man and not man for the sabbath; so the Son of man is Lord even of the sabbath.' Our former point of view would say that the actual words of Jesus end with the saying: 'The sabbath was made for man and not man for the sabbath', and that the final saying: 'The Son of man is Lord even of the sabbath' is the general and interpretative principle added by the community. But Bultmann in his *History of the Synoptic Tradition* (p. 16) goes much further than this. He notes that Jesus is questioned not about his own behaviour but about his *disciples'* behaviour. He therefore holds that this unit is not authentic history but a production of the church, formulated to justify through the words of Jesus its own use of the sabbath. This point of view would thus make this whole unit a production of the community.

With this there will be much less general agreement, for indeed the fact that it is the conduct of the disciples that is called in question is a somewhat slender foundation on which to erect the edifice of such a conjecture.

We may or may not accept the further developments, but must accept the principle that there were certain units of the tradition whose sole aim was to preserve a saying of Jesus.

(ii)   The second kind of form that has been identified consists of units which Dibelius called *Novellen* or 'tales' and which Bultmann called simply *Wundergeschichten* or 'miracle stories'. (For this whole section see Dibelius, *From Tradition to Gospel*, ch. IV, pp. 70-102, and Bultmann, *The History of the Synoptic Tradition*, IIA, pp. 209-44.) These are stories of wonderful things that Jesus did. The interest is not as in the first group of units in something Jesus said; the interest is not in his words but in his action.

By no means all the miracle stories fall into this group, for there are certain miracle stories which are more important for the sayings of Jesus which they contain than for the action of Jesus. Such stories are at least to some extent paradigms, or apophthegms, or pronouncement stories rather than specifically miracle stories. In the real miracle stories, using the term as the form critics use it, Jesus hardly speaks at all, apart from the words which contain or command the cure.

The story of the healing of the man with the withered hand (Mark 3.1-6) is really a pronouncement story, for the real point of it is the use of the sabbath — 'Is it lawful on the sabbath day to do good or to do harm, to save life or to kill?' The story of the healing of the centurion's servant belongs to the same class (Matt. 8.5-14), for the salient thing in it is Jesus' recognition of the unique faith of a Gentile, and his

statement that the believing Gentiles will be guests at the messianic
banquet while the unbelieving Jews will be shut out. The story of the
Syro-Phoenician woman (Mark 7.24-30) falls into the same group, for
the interest is as much in Jesus' conversation with the woman as it is in
his action. The story of the healing of the man sick with the palsy
(Mark 2.1-12) really falls into both groups. The action of Jesus is
important and the story follows the pattern of the miracle stories, as
we shall see, but at least equally important is the claim of Jesus to
convey to men the forgiveness of sins.

The genuine miracle stories all consist of what we might call a
scenario in three acts. First, there is a statement of the circumstances
and of the illness. Second, there is a statement of the cure. Third, there
is a statement of the result.

The simplest of them all, yet, short as it is, with the pattern
complete, is the story of the healing of Peter's wife's mother (Mark
1.29-31):

> And immediately Jesus left the synagogue and entered the house of Simon
> and Andrew, with James and John. Now Simon's mother-in-law lay sick
> with a fever, and immediately they told him of her. And he came and took
> her by the hand, and lifted her up, and the fever left her, and she served
> them.

In this story Jesus does not speak at all. But the three-strand pattern is
clearly there.

   i.   The circumstances: Simon's mother-in-law was sick with a
       fever.
   ii. The cure: Jesus took her by the hand and lifted her up.
   iii. The result: The fever left her and she served them.

No matter how the story is elaborated the pattern remains the same.

Many of the 'tales' are much more elaborate. Dibelius lists what he
reckons as the real tales in Mark.

The healing of the leper (1.40-45)
The stilling of the storm (4.35-41)
The Gerasene demoniac (5.1-20)
The raising of the daughter of Jairus and the healing of the woman
    with the issue of blood (5.21-43)
The feeding of the five thousand (6.35-44)
The walking on the sea (6.45-52)
The deaf and dumb man (7.32-37)
The blind man at Bethsaida (8.22-26)
The epileptic boy (9.14-29)

In the fourth gospel also these tales are represented:

The turning of the water into wine at Cana (2.1-11)

The healing of the official's son (4.46-54)
The healing of the helpless man at Bethzatha (5.1-18)
The healing of the man born blind (ch.9)
The raising of Lazarus (ch. 11)

In the longer of these tales anyone can see that there is an interest in detail. We do not have here the austere economy in words and in facts that we have in the paradigms and the pronouncement stories proper. There is, for instance, an interest in numbers, as Dibelius points out (p. 77). In the feeding of the five thousand alone (Mark 6.35-44), it is suggested that 200 *denarii* would not buy the bread needed; there are 5 loaves and 2 fishes; the people sit in ranks of 100s and 50s; 12 baskets of fragments are taken up; there are 5,000 people. Jairus' daughter is 12 years of age (Mark 5.42). Jesus came walking on the water at the 4th watch. The helpless man had been paralysed for 38 years. The 6 water jars held 20 to 30 gallons apiece (John 2.6). There are 2,000 swine in the Gerasene story (Mark 5.13). There are 153 fishes in the miraculous catch (John 21.11).

Dibelius sees here what might be called a 'secular' interest. There is more than just an interest in the 'salvation' value of the story. There is 'pleasure in the narrative itself' (p. 70). 'The description does not arise from a religious tendency or theory but from joy in lively graphic description' (p. 78).

This may be seen in the vivid relation of the reaction of the disciples. In the story they cry out: 'Teacher, do you not care if we perish?' (Mark 4.38). They regard Jesus' question about who touched him as a ridiculous question to ask in the middle of a jostling crowd (Mark 5.31). They have their own ideas about how the crowd should be fed (Mark 6.37).

Almost always the method of healing that Jesus used is related. Sometimes Jesus acts with a word (Mark 1.25). Sometimes the Aramaic word is kept (Mark 5.41; 7.34). Sometimes he heals with a touch (Mark 1.41; 7.33; 9.27). Sometimes he uses spittle (Mark 7.33; 8.23).

Bultmann (p. 241) notes that this kind of desire for detail developed in the church. In the gospels themselves only two cured people have names – Bartimaeus (Mark 10.46) and Lazarus (John 11). But in the *Gospel of Nicodemus* (7) the woman with the issue of blood is called Veronica, and in Macarius Magnes (1.6) she has become a princess of Edessa. In the *Pseudo-Clementine Homilies* (2.19; 3.73) the Syro-Phoenician woman and her daughter have become Justa and Bernice.

The form critics, in particular Dibelius and Bultmann, use this very detail to suggest that here we are not in the realm of history at all, but in the realm of non-authentic development of tradition. This indeed is why Dibelius calls these stories *Novellen*, by which he means to suggest that they are secular tales. On the whole miracle is rejected, unless in the case of the miracle stories which are also paradigms and pronouncement stories. The pure miracle stories are regarded as traditional developments. How then did they arise?

(a)	A saying of Jesus could become the basis of a miracle. For instance, the saying of Jesus that he is the light of the world could be worked up into the story of the man born blind and given his sight (John 9).

(b)	A parable could be 'dramatized' into an event. For instance the parable of the barren fig-tree (Luke 13.6-9) may have been dramatized into the alleged miracle of the blasting of the fig-tree (Mark 11.12-14, 20f.).

(c)	Old Testament miracles could be transferred to Jesus that he might surpass them. For instance, Elisha's feeding of a hundred men with twenty loaves with something left over (II Kings 4.42-44) could be the origin of the feeding of the five thousand. Or that miracle could go back to the rabbinic tradition (*Yoma* 39a) that in the days of Simon the Just there was a blessing on the shewbread as a result of which every priest who ate a piece even the size of an olive was satisfied, and the bread never grew less.

(d)	Miracles performed by others could be transferred to Jesus. It is here that the form critics go a long way. Bultmann (pp. 234f.) tells a story of a Jewish child on board a ship. There was a storm; all prayed to their gods; the storm did not abate. The child prayed; the storm ceased; all glorified the God of the Jews. This, says Bultmann, must have been a widespread story, for it reappears in Jonah 1, and this, or something like it, is the origin of the story about Jesus stilling the sorm. 'I cannot myself doubt,' he says, 'that in this instance an alien miracle story has been transferred to Jesus.'

Dibelius (pp. 87-9) holds that the story of the Gerasene demoniac loses all its difficulties if it is regarded as a bazaar story of a famous exorcism by some Jewish exorcist which was transferred to Jesus. Bultmann (p. 238) connects the story of the turning of the water into wine with the alleged miracle at the Greek festival of Dionysus, at which three jars of water left overnight were regularly found to be filled with wine in the morning.

The whole non-historical approach to the miracle stories may best be seen in the parallels which are cited to them. Let us look at some of these alleged parallels.

Take first of all a very simple thing. In the healing in the Decapolis of the dumb and stammering man, it is said of Jesus that he looked up to heaven 'and sighed' (Mark 7.34). Dibelius (p. 85) cites a series of passages to prove that this was part and parcel of the healing paraphernalia of the heathen wonder-workers. So in a Leyden Papyrus there is the instruction: 'Enter, act with your eyes shut, bellow as much as you can, then take in your breath with a sigh, and let it out again with a whistle.'[8] In the *Mithrasliturgie* we find: 'Breathe the radiance in, three times, as strongly as you can.' And again: 'Draw in the spirit-breath to yourself while looking away from the deity.'[9] So Dibelius concludes that the sigh 'belongs to the technique of mystical magic'. It is part of the popular 'healing media'.

Take another simple example. In Mark 2.11 the paralysed man is told to take up his stretcher and to go. Both Dibelius (p. 89) and Bultmann (p. 225) mention a story from Lucian's collection of marvels, *The Lover of Lies* (11), in which it is said of a man who was healed that he picked up his stretcher and went off with it.

It might not be altogether unfair to call these parallels little better than trivial. Take still another comparatively small matter. Sometimes Jesus is depicted as speaking in Aramaic, as when he says *Talitha cumi* to Jairus' daughter (Mark 5.41), or *Ephphatha* to the deaf and dumb man (Mark 7.34). Bultmann (p. 222) has pointed out that in the heathen wonder stories the healing word is frequently spoken in an unintelligible or a foreign language. It might well be answered that the whole point of the gospel stories is that the word was not unintelligible, since it was in Aramaic which was the native language of the person to whom it was addressed.

Let us come to something far more important. In Matthew we have the combined story of Jesus walking on the water, and Peter's attempt to walk on the water (Matt. 14.22-33). Bultmann (p. 237) quotes a Buddhist story.

> It tells of a disciple who wanted to visit Buddha one evening and on his way found that the ferry boat was missing from the bank of the river Aciravati. In faithful trust in Buddha he stepped on the water and went as if on dry land to the very middle of the stream. Then he came out of his contented meditation on Buddha in which he had lost himself, and saw the waves and was frightened and his feet began to sink. But he forced himself to become wrapt in the meditation again and by its power he reached the far bank safely and reached his master.

It is actually suggested by Garbe, from whom Bultmann draws the parallel, that the gospel story was borrowed from the Buddhist tradition. In this case not only a parallel but a dependence is claimed.

Let us take another important incident, the raising of Jairus' daughter (Mark 5.21-24, 35-43). Both Dibelius (pp. 89f.) and Bultmann (pp. 233f.) instance the following parallel from the *Life of Apollonius of Tyana (4.45)*:

> A girl had just died in the hour of her marriage, and the bridegroom was following her bier lamenting, as was natural since his marriage was left unfulfilled, and the whole of Rome was mourning with him, for the maiden belonged to a consular family. Apollonius saw their grief and said, 'Put

down the bier for I will stay the tears that you are shedding for the maiden.' So he asked what her name was ... Merely touching her and whispering in secret some spell over her, he at once woke up the maiden from her seeming death; and the girl spoke out loud, and returned to her father's house.

Here, it is claimed, we have a parallel to the raising done by Jesus, and the story about Jesus may well be no more than the transference to him of the same kind of wonders that other wonder-workers were supposed to perform.

Let us again take some of the smaller matters in which these parallels are found. It was a common belief in the ancient world that to know the name of a demon was to have power over the demon (Mark 5.9). The heathen accounts of the exorcism of demons have close parallels to the gospel accounts. Bultmann (pp. 231f.) quotes such a description from Lucian (*The Lover of Lies*, 16):

I would greatly like to ask you what you think of all those who free demoniacs from the spirits that trouble them, and so manifestly exorcize spectres. ... Whoever he [the exorcist] came to, the moonstruck, those who rolled their eyes or foamed at the mouth, he really put right and dismissed them cured for a high fee, after he had freed them from their affliction. For when he came up to some prostrated person and asked when the affliction had come into the body, the sick person himself kept silent, but the demon answered in Greek or some foreign tongue or in that of its own country, and told how and whence it had come into the man. But the Syrian then used his exorcisms, and, if the demon failed to respond, he would cast him out with threats. I have myself seen one come out, black and dark in colour.

The rolling around and the foaming at the mouth is the picture of the epileptic boy in Mark 9.26.

One extraordinary parallel has been found to Mark 2.4. Mark tells how because of the crowd the paralysed man had to be let down through the roof. It is claimed that the removal of the roof was not because of the crowd, but because an exorcist had to conceal from a demon the proper way into the house where the sick person was, and it was for this reason that the roof and not the door was used. So Bultmann suggests that Christian tradition either forgot or altered this into the picture of the crowd. It is difficult to regard that as convincing.

As we have already seen, the feeding of the five thousand has been traced back to the legend of the shewbread that never diminished. It has also been said to be founded on the story of the manna (Ex. 16). What Moses did, Jesus must be made to do still better. And Bultmann (p. 236) cites in parallel a Finnish fairy story of a maid who prepared food for a whole army out of three barley corns, and another story of a miraculous loaf which fed a whole army.

We have already seen that the Dionysus legend from classical mythology has been quoted as a parallel to the changing of the water into wine. Dibelius produces an extraordinary parallel to the story of the pigs in the healing of the Gerasene demoniac (Mark 5.1-20). One of the best known of all classical legends is the snatching away of Persephone by Pluto the god of the underworld, and the resultant grief of Demeter. Now part of that legend was that, when Persephone was snatched into the underworld by Pluto, there was close by a swineherd Eubouleus, who was also swallowed up in the earth with his pigs. This is quoted as a parallel to the death of the pigs in the sea.[10]

Finally, we return to the exorcisms of the demons. It is true that the ancient world knew many such stories, Josephus in his *Antiquities* (8.46-8) tells how Solomon had the secret of exorcism. This secret was passed down. A Jewish exorcist called Eleazar gave a demonstration of it. By the aid of a ring with a certain root in it he drew the demon out of the sufferer's nose, and the proof of the demon's coming out was the upsetting of a basin of water. When Apollonius of Tyana exorcized a demon it overturned a statue when it came out (*Life*, 4.20). In the apocryphal Acts of Peter (2) a demon exorcized by Peter damaged a statue of the emperor. Lucian (*Lover of Lies* 11), has a story in which a piece of stone from a virgin's tombstone cured an injured foot.

We have quoted these so-called parallels up to this point without comment. But the fact is the more so-called parallels that are quoted, the more it becomes quite clear that they are not parallels. The characteristic of all these stories is what we can only call magic and spells; they are like witchcraft and conjuring tricks. There is nothing like this in the gospel miracles at all, with the possible exception of the story of the Gerasene demoniac. There is a simplicity and restraint in the gospel narratives which is quite different. Both Dibelius and Bultmann in fact note this. Dibelius writes: 'In the gospel Tales we must recognize a certain shyness towards such practices.' Bultmann says that the New Testament authors 'are extremely reserved in this respect, since they hesitate to attribute to the person of Jesus the magical traits which were often characteristic of the Hellenistic miracle worker'.[11] It is the plain fact that the alleged parallels read like fiction; the gospel narratives do not. What really stands out is not the likeness of Jesus to contemporary miracle workers, but his difference from them.

It is true that the form critics do not cite these parallels as the actual and direct sources of the gospel miracle stories. What they do say is that the gospel tradition grew up and developed in an age which was full of such stories, and that the gospel tradition was therefore bound to be affected by, if not modelled upon, them. Dibelius quotes Aelius Aristides: 'Sacred cupboards full of sacred books contain numberless examples. Market-places, harbours, and the big squares of the town are full of such stories.'[12] Bultmann writes (pp. 238f.):

> It is clear that the material cited cannot be reckoned as the source for the miracle stories in the Synoptics, or only in the rarest cases. But it illustrates the atmosphere, shows motifs and forms, and so helps us to understand how miracle stories came into the Synoptic tradition.

So then we may sum up. According to Dibelius (p. 95) the miracle stories are in the synoptic tradition to show the life of Jesus as a series of 'divine epiphanies'; they are there to prove his messianic status and his superiority to all Old Testament prophets and to all heathen gods. It is not claimed that all are completely unhistorical. But they come from a variety of sources. Some are based on the Old Testament. Some are sayings turned into dramatic actions. Bultmann, for instance, would suggest (pp. 230f.) that the story of the miraculous catch of fishes really goes back to the saying about fishers of men (Mark 1.16-20; Luke 5.1-11). Some of them are folk stories transferred to Jesus, and Bultmann (p. 210) would definitely class the story of the Gerasene demoniac in this category. Some are the transference of stories to Jesus. Dibelius writes (p. 100):

> Such a transference may at times have taken place as an unconscious process. Jewish-Christian narrators would make Jesus the hero of well-known legends of prophets or rabbis. Gentile-Christian narrators would hand on stories of gods, saviours, and miracle-workers, re-cast as applying to the Christian Saviour.

Bultmann would even cite the alleged parallel of the *Arabian Nights*: 'In the Thousand and One Nights Harun al Raschid has been made the hero or participant in countless fairy stories' (p. 229).

What do we say about this? We may say three things.

i.   It tends to forget that Jesus was in fact a unique person, and that he therefore did unique things. Of course, what he did is seen through first-century eyes; but it is possible so to strip Jesus of unique action that there is no explanation of his impact on men left.

ii.   There is no attempt in all this to allow for the connection of the gospel tradition with eyewitness account. It is not, for instance, possible, and it is certainly not good scholarship or criticism, to wave away the possible connection of Mark with Peter, as we shall later see.

iii. And it seems to us that one thing is completely forgotten. Surely this process of the transference to Jesus of all kinds of material would take time. Now Mark can hardly be later than the middle of the sixties of the first century. On the claim of the form critics themselves, when Mark got the material it was already stereotyped. There is little more than thirty years between Mark and the death of Jesus. Stereotyping takes time, and if that stereotyping is to be done within thirty years, it is done within a period when there were many still alive who well knew the facts. It seems to us frankly incredible that first the transference, and then the stereotyping will all go into thirty years, and all into a period in which eyewitnesses existed in large numbers. It is very hard to see how the process involved will fit into the time available. There must be far more fact and history in the tales than the form critics will allow, for the degeneration of the tradition which the form critics postulate cannot be fitted into the time available.

(iii)   The third class of passages which has been identified is the class which contains what are known as 'legends'. The word 'legend' is here correctly and technically used. In popular language that which is legendary is unhistorical, but this is not so when the word is technically used. The word 'legend' comes from the Latin verb which means 'to read', and literally means 'that which ought to be read'. Legends were technically stories of the life and death of holy men, particularly if these men were saints and martyrs; and these stories were designed to be read – hence their name – on the saint's day on which the man about whom they were composed was commemorated. The legend is therefore by no means necessarily unhistorical, although it is always liable to growth and development, and to elaboration and embellishment. None the less, this kind of story will always have value, because even in its growth and its elaboration it will still tell us what kind of a man its subject must have been. The legends – in the popular sense of the term – which gather round any great man, even if they have been invented, have been invented to fit, and will be a witness to, the man's character and personality. Dibelius in his chapter on 'Legends' (*From Tradition to Gospel*, ch. IV) defines the material of legend:

> The deeds and experience of a man, who for his piety and sanctity is honoured by God with a special fate, stand as the middle point of a typical personal legend. He works miracles, reconciles enemies, tames animals; distress and danger lead him to salvation, and even as a martyr he is surrounded by signs of divine grace.... The trait of the precocity of the hero, a wise man, or a saint, who even in youth shows the promise of his later calling, and thereby shames or at least astonishes his elders, is naturally widespread.

Dibelius has pointed out (pp. 108f.) that there is what he calls *a law of biographical analogy*, through which the same kind of things are said of all great figures around whom legend has gathered. Portents surround the birth and the death of such a person; even in his youth his future calling is forecast; his death throws its shadows in advance on the pathway of his life. Divine power is always ready to help him and often bears wonderful and supernatural testimony to his merits.

Sometimes, before the appointed end comes, there are wonderful escapes from danger and from trouble.

About Jesus himself there are very few legends in the gospel tradition. The two clearest are the story of him as a boy in the temple (Luke 2.41-51), and the story of the preaching and of the miraculous escape from the anger of the crowd in Nazareth (Luke 4.16-30).

But there are in the gospel tradition a fair number of legends about other people. Naturally the desire to know more about those who came near to Jesus arose, and in the gospel tradition a legend is typically a story which involves Jesus, but of which he himself is not, so to speak, the centre; it is a story designed to tell us more about someone in the story other than Jesus. Of course, even a story like that tells us much about Jesus in his attitude and his words to the other person, but it is the other person about whom the story is being told. In fact, in Dibelius' treatment of the material the legend is characteristically a story which tells of characters in the gospel tradition other than Jesus. So there are legends of Peter in his recognition of Jesus (Mark 8.27-33), and his attempt to walk on the water (Matt. 14.28-33). There is the legend of the death of John the Baptist (Mark 6.17-29); of Judas Iscariot (Matt. 27.3-8); of Nathanael (John 1.45-51); of Zacchaeus (Luke 19.1-10); of Nicodemus (John 3.1-21); of the Samaritan woman (John 4.1-42); of the ass for the triumphal entry and the room for the last supper (Mark 11.1-7; 14.12-16); of the woman who was a sinner (Luke 7.36-50); of Martha and Mary (Luke 10.38-42). In all these stories the central figure is not Jesus himself, but someone brought into contact with Jesus.

In what may be called the Gospel of the Childhood of Jesus there are several legends. There is the legend of the birth of John the Baptist (Luke 1.5-25) and of the Magi (Matt. 2.1-13). In the first two chapters of Luke there is a group of three legends – the legend of the Virgin (1.26-38), the legend of the shepherds (2.1-9), the legend of Simeon and Anna (2.22-38).

The attitude of the critics to these legends varies. The more radical see almost all of them as productions of the community, composed to show what Jesus was like by putting him in contact with other people. There are others who would allow a good deal of historical value to these stories; and the vividness of their characterization does seem to make it likely that they are telling real and not manufactured stories.

(iv)   The fourth area of material in the gospel tradition consists of the *sayings of Jesus*. This is clearly an area of immense importance, for here we are in direct contact with the teaching of Jesus, and it is obviously a matter of supreme importance to decide what parts of this material go back to Jesus himself, and what parts of it are later productions of the church.

Bultmann in *The History of the Synoptic Tradition* has a section entitled 'Dominical Sayings' (pp. 69-205), in which he treats this part of the material very fully. He divides the material into four sections: wisdom sayings, prophetic and apocalyptic sayings, legal sayings and church rules, and 'I' sayings. We shall go on to examine them under these headings. But before we look at the material itself, we must look at the forms in which it is expressed. It is always to be remembered that we are moving in a time when the printed book did not exist. In such conditions the teacher would be bound to fail in his objective, unless he could make his material memorable. It had to be easy to carry in the memory, for it could be possessed in no other way.

(a) Much of the material is poetic in form. Hebrew poetry does not have rhyme, but it does have rhythm. Take a passage like Matthew 6.25-32. We give it in the Moffatt version, for Moffatt prints it as poetry.

> Therefore I tell you,
>> never trouble about what you are to eat or drink in life,
>> nor about what you are to put on your body;
> surely life means more than food,
>> surely the body means more than clothes!
> Look at the wild birds;
>> they sow not, they reap not, they gather nothing in granaries,
>> and yet your heavenly Father feeds them.
> Are you not worth more than birds?
> Which of you can add an ell to his height by troubling about it?
>> And why should you trouble over clothing?
> Look how the lilies of the field grow;
>> they neither toil nor spin,
> and yet, I tell you, even Solomon in his grandeur was never robed like
>> one of them

That is poetry designed to lodge in the memory.

(b) Jesus used patterns, made all the more memorable by repetition and reiteration. If we take a passage like Matthew 5.17-37 (NEB), and strip it of all the additional and incidental material, we get a pattern like this:

> Do not suppose that I have come to abolish the Law and the prophets;
> I did not come to abolish, but to complete . . .
>
> You have learned that our forefathers were told,
>> Do not commit murder;
> Anyone who commits murder
>> must be brought to judgment.
> But what I tell you is this:
>> Anyone who nurses anger against his brother
>> must be brought to judgment.

You have learned that they were told,
    Do not commit adultery;
But what I tell you is this,
    If a man looks at a woman with a lustful eye,
    he has already committed adultery with her in his heart.

You have learned that they were told,
    Do not break your oath,
    and, Oaths to the Lord must be kept;
But what I tell you is this,
    You are not to swear at all. . . .
Plain 'Yes' or 'No' is all you need to say;
    anything beyond that comes from the devil.

The pattern and the reiteration are clear.

In a passage like Luke 6.32-35 (NEB) the rhythmic pattern is even clearer:

If you love only those who love you,
    what credit is that to you?
    Even sinners love those who love them.

If you do good to those who do good to you,
    what credit is that to you?
    Even sinners do as much.

If you lend only where you expect to be repaid,
    what credit is that to you?
Even sinners lend to each other
    if they are to be repaid in full.

But you must love your enemies,
    and do good, and lend, never despairing,
And you will have a rich reward.
    You will be the sons of the Most High.

The rhythmic verse pattern is clear and memorable.

(c) Parallelism is characteristic of Hebrew style. The Hebrew writers tended to say everything twice, restating, developing, amplifying the statement first made. There are three types of this parallelism in Hebrew style and all are exemplified in the gospel account of the teaching of Jesus.

There is *synonymous parallelism,* in which the second line reiterates the first.

Is it permitted on the sabbath
    To do good or to do evil,
    To save life or to destroy it? (Luke 6.9)

There is *antithetical parallelism,* in which the second line contrasts with the first.

The sabbath was made for man,
Not man for the sabbath (Mark 2.27).

There is *synthetic parallelism*, in which the thought continues in a series of parallel lines.

They go about with broad phylacteries,
And wear deep fringes on their robes.
They like to have places of honour at feasts,
And chief seats in synagogues,
To be greeted respectfully in the street,
And to be addressed as Rabbi (Matt. 23.5-7, NEB).

Rhythm is accentuated by making not only the whole lines, but also the phrases within the lines correspond.

Give not
     the holy thing
          to the dogs,
And cast not
     your pearls
          before swine. (Matt. 7.6)

He that is faithful
     in little
          is faithful
               in much;
He that is dishonest
     in little
          is dishonest
               in much (Luke 16.10f.).

It would only be natural that the teaching of Jesus would be cast in Old Testament moulds. However new the subject matter of his teaching, its form would be the form with which his listeners were familiar. In the wisdom literature of the Old Testament Bultmann identifies certain basic forms (pp. 70-81).

i.   There are what might be called *impersonal principles*.
      Where no oxen are,
      the crib is clean (Prov. 14.4)

ii.   There are *personal formulae*.
      Like a gold ring in a swine's snout,
      so is a beautiful woman without discretion (Prov. 11.22).

iii. There are *blessings*.
      Happy is the man who finds wisdom (Prov. 3.13).

iv.   There is the argument *a maiore ad minus*, the argument which runs, *how much more . . .*
      Sheol and Abaddon lie open before the Lord,
      how much more the hearts of men? (Prov. 15.11).

v.   There are *exhortations*.

> Hear, my son, your father's instruction,
> and reject not your mother's teaching (Prov. 1.8).

vi.   There are *questions*.

> Can a man carry fire in his bosom
> and not be burned?
> Or can a man walk upon hot coals
> and not be scorched? (Prov. 6.27-28)

These are the forms in which the wisdom teaching of the Jews was expressed and all these forms meet us in the recorded *wisdom sayings* of Jesus.

'Let the day's trouble be sufficient for the day' (Matt. 6.34), 'A city set on a hill cannot be hid' (Matt. 5.14), 'No good tree bears bad fruit, nor again does a bad tree bear good fruit, for each tree is known by its own fruit' (Luke 6.43f.), are all *impersonal principles*. 'The labourer is worthy of his hire' (Luke 10.7), 'No one can serve two masters' (Matt. 6.24), 'Those who are well do not need a physician but those who are ill' (Mark 2.17), are all *personal formulae*. 'Blessed are those who hear the word of God and keep it' (Luke 11.28), as are all the Beatitudes (Matt. 5.1-11), is a *blessing*. 'If God so clothes the grass of the field, which today is alive and tomorrow is thrown into the oven, will he not much more clothe you, O men of little faith?' (Matt. 6.30) is an argument *a maiore ad minus*. 'As you wish others to do to you, so do you to them' (Matt. 7.12), 'Enter in by the narrow gate' (Matt. 7.13) are *exhortations*. 'What good will it do a man to gain the whole world and to forfeit his own soul?' (Mark 8.36), 'Who by worrying about it can add a cubit to his height?' (Matt. 6.27) are *questions*.

The forms of the wisdom teaching all appear in Jesus' teaching too.

The form of the wisdom teaching is most commonly the short, pithy, memorable saying, which in Hebrew is known as the *mashal*. The *mashal* in this connection may be a riddle, or an epigram; but perhaps the word 'proverb' comes nearest to covering it.

The *mashal* may have one strand, or one arm.

> He that is not against us is for us (Mark 9.40).
>
> Many that were first shall be last, and the last first (Mark 10.31).
>
> A city set on a hill cannot be hid (Matt. 5.14).

Often the *mashal* can be double-stranded with two balanced arms.

> There is nothing hid except to be made manifest,
>   Nor is anything secret except to come to light (Mark 4.22).
>
> Can a blind man lead a blind man?
>   Will they not both fall into a pit? (Luke 6.39)

These forms are the basic forms and the raw material of the wisdom teaching, and in them the teaching of Jesus is expressed.

Within these simple forms development takes place. The simple, short saying is expanded with illustration, sometimes including direct speech. So the command to love enemies is expanded with illustrations from human and divine conduct (Matt. 5.43-48). The command not to worry is illustrated from nature and from the futility of human anxiety (Matt. 6.25-33). This is like the development and elaboration of a simple theme.

There is a tendency to group together similar sayings, for we find sayings grouped in one gospel, which are separated in another. Take the case of the group of sayings in Mark 8.34-38 with the parallels in Matthew 16.24-26 and Luke 9.23-26.

8 ³⁴If any man would come after me, let him deny himself and take up his cross and follow me.

³⁵For whoever would save his life will lose it; and whoever loses his life for my sake and the gospel's will save it.

³⁶For what does it profit a man to gain the whole world and forfeit his life?

³⁷For what can a man give in return for his life?

³⁸For whoever is ashamed of me and of my words in this adulterous and sinful generation, of him will the Son of man also be ashamed when he comes in the glory of his Father with the holy angels.

Luke has the whole passage as it stands with slight variations; but Mark 8.34 is also in Luke 14.27, and Mark 8.35 is also in Luke 17.33, and Mark 8.38 is also in Luke 12.9. Matthew has the whole passage except that he has a different version of Mark 8.38; but Mark 8.34f. are also in Matthew 10.38f. and Mark 8.38 is also in Matthew 10.33. If we tabulate this, the variations will become clear.

Mark 8.34   = Matt. 16.24 = Matt. 10.38 = Luke 9.23
                        = Luke 14.27
        8.35   = Matt. 16.25 = Matt. 10.39 = Luke 9.24
                        = Luke 17.33
        8.36 ⎫
        8.37 ⎭ = Matt. 16.26 = Luke 9.25
        8.38   = Matt. 10.33 = Luke 9.26 = Luke 12.9

It is plain to see that these sayings exist in two forms: they exist in one piece; and they exist in detached units. The entire probability is that the unified passage came into being by the association of similar sayings into one composite unit. From the point of view of memory and of teaching it would be very convenient to have them united into one piece.

An even more natural way of grouping sayings is to associate sayings which have in them a common key-word. So, for instance, in

Mark 9.49f. we have a series of sayings based on the word *salt*.

> 9 ⁴⁹So everyone will be *salted* with fire.
> ⁵⁰*Salt* is good; but if the *salt* has lost its saltness, how will you season it?
> Have *salt* in yourselves and be at peace with one another.

There are three *salt* sayings there in Mark. Matthew (5.13) and Luke (14.34f.) both have an amplified version of the second one, but they have it in different contexts. By far the most probable conclusion is that here Mark has made a little easily memorable collection of *salt* sayings.

Another development is that often, when a saying is already in circulation, a further saying is added to it, because this additional saying is either occasioned by the first saying, or is analogous to it in form. We can see this happening very plainly in Christian literature outside the New Testament.

In the longer version of Ignatius' *Letter to the Magnesians* (9) we read:

> Let him who does not work not eat,
> for in the sweat of your brow you shall eat your bread.

The first line of that passage is II Thessalonians 3.10; the second line is Genesis 3.19. They are very closely analogous sayings, and they have been run together to form one new composite saying. Clement of Rome has a whole series of sayings formed on the analogy of the Beatitude, 'Blessed are the merciful, for they shall obtain mercy' (Matt. 5.7). Clement's passage runs (13.2):

> Have mercy that you may receive mercy;
> Forgive that you may be forgiven;
> As you do, so it will be done to you;
> As you give, so it will be given to you;
> As you judge, so you will be judged;
> As you are kind, so you will receive kindness.
> With what measure you measure, it will be measured to you.

So Clement of Alexandria in his *Stromateis* or *Miscellanies* (4.6.41) quotes as a saying of Jesus:

> Happy are those who are persecuted for righteousness' sake,
>   for they will be perfect;
> And happy are those who are persecuted for my sake,
>   for they will have a place where they will not be persecuted.

Oxyrhynchus Papyrus 654.5 has the following addition to Matthew 10.26:

> Everything that you cannot see, and everything that is hidden from

you will be revealed to you.
For there is nothing hidden which will not be made manifest,
And there is nothing buried which will not be raised up.

The last line is an additional analogous formation.

It is even possible to see the development process of this kind of thing in action. Here are three stages in the development of one saying.

i. Mark 2.17: I came not to call the righteousness, but sinners.

ii. Luke 5.32: I came not to call the righteousness, but sinners *to repentance*.

iii. Justin Martyr, *Apology*, 1.15: I came not to call the righteous, but sinners to *repentance, for the heavenly Father desires the repentance of the sinner rather than his punishment.*

Here is an example of the growth of a saying as the years went on.

Bultmann suggests that it is possible to see this process of development within the New Testament itself. Take the case of the parallel passages Matthew 5.27-30; Matthew 18.8f.; Mark 9.43-48. In the first of these passages the instruction is that, if the right eye or the right hand are a cause of sin, they must be removed and cast away. But in the second and the third passages *the foot* has been added to the eye and the hand. In the context it is true that the foot comes in much less naturally, and Bultmann would think it possible that *the foot* has been added to the eye and the hand by analogous formation.

So Bultmann suggests that in the following passages, amongst others, there may be development by this analogous formation. The new wine may be added as an additional illustration of the new patch (Mark 2.21f.). In the master and servant passage Matthew 10.25 may be a later formation added to Matthew 10.24. In Matthew 6.24 the original may have been quite simply: 'No man can serve two masters', and the rest of the verse may be additional expansion.

It is again possible to show this expansion in action. We take four parallel passages.

Mark 11.22f.: Truly I say to you, whoever says to this mountain, 'Be taken up and cast into the sea,' and does not doubt in his heart, but believes that what he says will come to pass, it will be done for him.

Luke 17.6: If you had faith as a grain of mustard seed, you could say to this sycamine tree, 'Be rooted up and be planted in the sea,' and it would obey you.

Matthew 21.21: Truly I say to you, if you have faith and never doubt, you will not only do what has been done to the fig-tree, but even if you say to this mountain, 'Be taken up and cast into the sea,' it will be done.

> Matthew 17.20: Truly, I say to you, if you have faith as a grain of mustard seed, you will say to this mountain, 'Move hence to yonder place,' and it will move; *and nothing will be impossible to you.*

Out of the four parallel sayings the last generalized truth only appears in one; and all the probability is that it is a later addition added to turn a particular saying into a general truth.

Frequently there are what we might call by the general name of *underlining additions*. There are additions which emphasize the thought of a passage, or which make still clearer the implication of the passage. We may compare the following parallel passages in which the italicized words form this kind of addition.

> Luke 6.31: And as you wish that men would do to you, do so to them.

> Matthew 7.12: So whatever you wish that men would do to you, do so to them; *for this is the law and the prophets.*

> Matthew 8.22: Follow me, and leave the dead to bury their own dead.

> Luke 9.60: Leave the dead to bury their own dead, but as for you, *go and proclaim the kingdom of God.*

There is a whole series of passages, especially in Luke, in which *the kingdom of God* is introduced in this way.

> Mark 1.38: Let us go on to the next towns, that I may preach there also; for that is why I came out.

> Luke 4.43: I must preach *the good news of the kingdom* to the other cities also; for I was sent for this purpose.

> Matthew 10.1: And he called to him his twelve disciples and gave them authority over unclean spirits to cast them out, and to heal every disease and every infirmity.

> Mark 6.7: And he called to him the twelve, and began to send them out two by two, and gave them authority over the unclean spirits.

> Luke 9.1f.: And he called the twelve together and gave them power and authority over all demons and to cure diseases, *and sent them out to preach the kingdom of God* and to heal.

> Mark 6.34: As he landed he saw a great throng, and he had compassion on them, because they were like sheep without a shepherd; and he began to teach them many things.

> Luke 9.11: When the crowds learned it, they followed him; and he welcomed them, and *spoke to them of the kingdom of God*, and cured those who had need of healing.

> Matthew 19.29: And everyone who has left houses or brothers or sisters or father or mother or children or lands for my name's sake will receive a hundredfold.

> Mark 10.29f.: There is no one who has left house or brothers or sisters or

mother or father or children or lands for my sake *and for the gospel* who will not receive a hundredfold.

Luke 18.29f.: There is no man who has left house or wife or brothers or parents or children *for the sake of the kingdom of God* who will not receive manifold more.

It is further to be noted that in the last series of passages Mark alone (10.30) adds to the list of things to be received in reward *with persecutions*. We take one more example from the chapter which tells of the signs and the happenings of the last times.

Matthew 24.33: So also, when you see all these things, you know that he is near, at the very gates.

Mark 13.29: So also, when you see these things taking place, you know that he is near, at the very gates.

Luke 21.31: So also, when you see these things taking place, you know that *the kingdom of God* is near.

It is quite clear that defining, explaining, underlining additions have been made to shorter and simpler statements.

In point of fact this kind of addition can be made almost unconsciously. Bultmann quotes a modern lecturer's citation of John 15.5:

Without me you can do nothing;
With me you can do everything.

The second line is the lecturer's own — perhaps quite unconscious — addition to the actual words in John.

Sometimes in the development of the sayings-tradition we get *the transformation of sayings*. Sometimes this transformation is no more than a change of the words and form in which the saying is expressed. For instance, in the following two versions Luke shortens and simplifies Matthew.

Matthew 10.24f.: A disciple is not above his teacher, nor a servant above his master; it is enough for the disciple to be like his teacher, and the servant like his master. If they have called the master of the house Beelzebul, how much more will they malign those of his household.

Luke 6.40: A disciple is not above his teacher, but every one when he is fully taught will be like his teacher.

Sometimes a statement becomes a question, or *vice versa*.

Mark 4.21: Is a lamp brought in to be put under a bushel, or under a bed, and not on a stand?

Matthew 5.15: Nor do men light a lamp and put it under a bushel, but on a stand, and it gives light to all in the house.

> Luke 11.33 (cf. Luke 8.16): No one after lighting a lamp puts it in a cellar or under a bushel, but on a stand, that those who enter may see the light.

Mark's question becomes a negative statement in Matthew and Luke. We see the same process at work in the following examples.

> Matthew 7.16: Are grapes gathered from thorns or figs from thistles?

> Luke 6.44: Figs are not gathered from thorns, nor are grapes picked from a bramble bush.

> Matthew 15.14: If a blind man leads a blind man, both will fall into a pit.

> Luke 6.39: Can a blind man lead a blind man? Will they not both fall into a pit?

If we remember that the original sayings were in Aramaic, and that what we have is a translation, this will not surprise us.

But there is another kind of transformation, which completely transforms a saying without altering a syllable of it. This happens when a saying is read against a new background and in a quite different context of thought. Here Bultmann is very interesting, for he sees in many sayings attributed to Jesus quite secular proverbial sayings which are completely transformed in meaning by being read in a Christian context. Let us take some examples. Take the saying in Matthew 5.25f. = Luke 12.58f.:

> Make friends quickly with your accuser, while you are going with him to court, lest your accuser hand you over to the judge, and the judge to the guard, and you be put in prison; truly I say to you, you will never get out till you have paid the last penny.

Read in a human context, that is a piece of practical, worldly-wise common sense; read in the context of the second coming and the day of judgment it is very different.

Take the case of Mark 8.36:

> For what does it profit a man to gain the whole world and forfeit his life? For what can a man given in return for his life?

Read in a human context, this simply says that life is the most precious thing a man possesses and is quite irreplaceable. It can be paralleled from any literature. In the *Thousand and One Nights* we have:

> You can easily exchange your estate for another,
> But you can find no substitute for your life.
> Bondservants indeed you can find in plenty,
> But for your life you can find no substitute.

In its secular sense this is simply a proverb and a truism which occurs in every literature in the world. But read in the light of eternal life and in the consequence of rejecting Jesus Christ for worldly things, it has a very different meaning. 'If salt has lost its taste, how can its saltness be restored?' (Matt. 5.13), or, 'A city set on a hill cannot be hid' (Matt. 5.14) are very ordinary proverbial sayings, but they change their meaning when they are read in the context of the obligation of Christian conduct. 'He who is not with me is against me' (Matt. 12.30) is the kind of thing a man might say at any committee meeting, but it has a very different meaning when read in the light of allegiance to Jesus Christ. 'The harvest is plentiful but the labourers are few' (Matt. 9.38) could be said by any farmer, but it changes its meaning when it is read in the light of Christian mission.

It is unquestionably true that the gospel tradition contains many, many secular sayings which in their context are transformed.

We must now ask what conclusions in view of all this are to be drawn in regard to that part of the gospel tradition which may be called the wisdom sayings of Jesus. A minor conclusion is obvious. Even assuming that all the gospel material went back directly to Jesus, it would still obviously be very difficult to be certain as to the *exact form* in which it was first spoken. As we have seen, the same saying exists in different forms, and sometimes in different contexts. But this difference in form would be of little consequence, and, as we have already noted, would be no more than might be reasonably expected in material which has been translated from Aramaic into Greek, and which certainly began by being orally transmitted. A much bigger question and a much more important question is whether the wisdom material can be assigned to Jesus himself, or whether parts of it at least must not be regarded as having been later worked into the gospel tradition. Bultmann and the form critics would regard very little of it as going back all the way to Jesus.

There are, says Bultmann, three possibilities. First, Jesus could have taken secular proverbs and sayings, and used them, and altered them to his needs. Second, Jesus could, and no doubt on occasion did, himself coin wisdom sayings. Third, secular wisdom sayings could have been used by the church in its teaching, not at first as sayings of Jesus at all, and later could have become attributed to him, especially when they had undergone a transformation of meaning in the context of the Christian message.

That the third possibility could have happened is not open to doubt. There are, for instance, two New Testament sayings, which are repeatedly attributed to Jesus in all ages of the church down to the present day. The one is, 'Love covers a multitude of sins' (I Peter 4.8; James 5.20), and the other is, 'Do not let the sun go down on your anger' (Eph. 4.26). These two sayings continuously get themselves attributed to Jesus.

Further, there is no doubt at all that there are rabbinic parallels to many of the gospel sayings. Bultmann (pp. 106-8) quotes many of them, of which some of the closest are as follows:

> Fret not over tomorrow's trouble, for thou knowest not what a day may bring forth, and peradventure tomorrow [a man] is no more: thus he shall be found grieving over a world that is not his (Sanh. 100b).

(This also has parallels in Egyptian and Arabian literature:

> Do not prepare for the morrow before it comes; for no one knows what evil it brings.
> The god of the morrow will care for the morrow.
> Every day brings its own sufficiency with it.)

These are several parallels to sayings about judgment.

> He who calls down (Divine) judgment on his neighbour is himself punished first (Rosh ha-Shanah 16b).
> Judge every man by his good side (Pirke Aboth 1.6).
> Judge not thy friend until thou comest into his place (Pirke Aboth 2.4).
> He who judges his neighbour in the scale of merit is himself judged favourably (Shabbath 127b).

On the student studying the law:

> When he knocks, the door is opened for him (Pesikta 176a).

> God says of the Israelites: To me they are upright as doves, but to the nations they are wise as serpents (Midrash on S. of Sol. 2.14, 101a).
> Not a bird falls to the ground without heaven (=God), so how much less does a man?
> Physician, rise and heal thine own lameness (Gen. Rabba 23, 15c).
> The sabbath is given over to you, not you to the sabbath.

There are other parallels, also very close.
Bultmann holds that there are a large number of sayings in the gospels which have nothing original in them. They are 'observations on life, rules of prudence and popular morality, sometimes a product of humour or scepticism, full now of sober popular morality, and now of naïf egoism' (p. 104). Such sayings, Bultmann suggests, were secular popular wisdom sayings, which were used in preaching and teaching for their practical value, and which were in time attributed to Jesus. Among such sayings, according to Bultmann, are the following:

> Mark 8.36: What does it profit a man to gain the whole world and forfeit his life?

> Mark 8.37: What can a man given in return for his life?

> Matthew 8.20; Luke 9.58: Foxes have holes, and birds of the air have nests, but the son of man has nowhere to lay his head. (Here *son of man* means *a man*, and the point is man's homelessness in the universe.)

Mark 6.4: A prophet is not without honour, except in his own country . . .and in his own house.

Mark 9.50: Salt is good; but if the salt has lost its saltness, how will you season it?

Mark 4.21: Is a lamp brought in to be put under a bushel, or under a bed, and not on a stand?

Mark 2.21-22: No one sews a piece of unshrunk cloth on an old garment . . . No one puts new wine into old wineskins.

Matthew 12.30: He who is not with me is against me.

Matthew 10.24: A disciple is not above his teacher, nor a servant above his master.

Matthew 6.27: Which of you by being anxious can add one cubit to his span of life?

Matthew 5.14: A city set on a hill cannot be hid.

Matthew 5.42: Give to him who begs from you, and do not refuse him who would borrow from you.

Matthew 7.6: Do not throw your pearls before swine.

Luke 10.7; Matthew 10.10: The labourer deserves his wages.

Luke 14.11; Matthew 23.12: Everyone who exalts himself will be humbled, and he who humbles himself will be exalted.

Luke 16.10: He who is faithful in a very little is also faithful in much; and he who is dishonest in a very little is dishonest also in much.

Matthew 7.12; Luke 6.31: Whatever you wish that men would do to you, do so to them.

Bultmann's comment on this last saying (p. 103) is:

> It is a piece of self-deception to suppose that the positive form of the rule is characteristic for Jesus, in distinction from the attested negative form among the Rabbis. The positive form is purely accidental, for whether it be given positive or negative formulation, the saying, as an individual utterance, gives moral expression to a naïf egoism.

All these sayings, and many others, are held by Bultmann to have nothing distinctively Christian in them, nothing characteristic of Jesus, and are to be regarded as secular wisdom sayings which were originally used in the church and later attributed to him. Before we make any comment on this, we will go on to look at the sayings which, as Bultmann considers, may be with some probability assigned directly to Jesus.

What then are the characteristics of the sayings which Bultmann regards as being probably assignable to Jesus?

(a) Sayings which have in them 'the exaltation of the eschatological

mood' are likely to go back to Jesus. That is to say, sayings which have a strong consciousness that the end-time has been reached, that God has broken into history, that the power of the demons and the prince of demons is shattered, reflect the thought of Jesus. Thus such a passage as Mark 3.24-27 with its picture of the defeat and the binding of the strong man may go back to him.

(b) Sayings which are the product of 'an energetic summons to repentance' may go back to him.

> No man who puts his hand to the plough and looks back is fit for the kingdom of God (Luke 9.62).

> How hard it will be for those who have riches to enter the kingdom of God! . . . It is easier for a camel to go through the eye of a needle than for a rich man to enter the kingdom of God (Mark 10.23, 25)..

> Leave the dead to bury their own dead (Luke 9.60).

> Enter by the narrow gate; for the gate is wide and the way is easy, that leads to destruction, and those who enter it are many. For the gate is narrow and the way is hard, that leads to life, and those who find it are few (Matt. 7.13f.).

These sayings have the mark of going back to Jesus.

(c) What may be called reversal sayings may go back to him.

> Many that are first shall be last and the last first (Mark 10.31).

> Many are called, but few are chosen (Matt. 22.14).

Such sayings as these have his accent.

(d) Sayings 'which demand a new disposition of mind' sound as if they belonged to Jesus.

> There is nothing outside a man which by going into him can defile him; but the things which come out of a man are what defile him (Mark 7.15).

> Whoever does not receive the kingdom of God like a child shall not enter it (Mark 10.15).

> What is exalted among men is an abomination in the sight of God (Luke 16.15).

In this group we may include the whole passage on love and forgiveness (Matt. 5.38-48).

Of these passages Bultmann says (p. 105), 'Here if anywhere we can find what is characteristic of the teaching of Jesus.'

There are certain things to be said about this whole approach. In the last analysis, that which is accepted and that which is rejected are rejected and accepted on largely subjective grounds; and the proof of this is that no two critics accept and reject the same passages. It is, for example, true to say that Bultmann has every right to put forward his opinion regarding the Golden Rule (Matt. 7.12) as an opinion; he has no right at all to state it as a fact, and a fact which is self-evident. The trouble about this is that the critic really retains what is in accord with his own view of Jesus and rejects that which is not.

Further, nothing could be more likely than that Jesus would use and adapt the material which lay ready to his hand, and because a proverb is a secular proverb there is no reason to suppose that he would not have used it and reminted it for his own purposes. The good teacher will frequently make evident new meanings in that which his hearers already know.

And still further, if the sayings of Jesus began to be written down and systematized a good deal before AD 60 there does not seem to be time for such copious additions as this point of view visualizes.

We need not doubt that teaching material did get into the gospels, but we may well doubt that the process was so wholesale as the more radical critics suggest.

The second section into which Bultmann divided the sayings of Jesus consists of the *prophetic and the apocalyptic sayings*. We would expect to find both these kinds of sayings in the gospel tradition. Jesus both regarded himself (Luke 4.24) and was regarded by others as a prophet (Matt. 21.11; Luke 24.19). We will therefore expect to find prophetic announcements among his sayings, always remembering that a prophet was the *forthteller* of the will of God in any human situation rather than a *foreteller* of the future. Apocalyptic is the technical term for that kind of literature which aimed to lift the veil from the things which will happen in the last times and at the end of things as they are, and, since Jesus announced the coming of the kingdom, we shall also expect to find that kind of material in his teaching.

In both these areas Bultmann and his school discern a very great amount of material which in their opinion does not go back to Jesus himself, but which is partly Jewish material which has been adapted to and woven into the Christian tradition, and partly the production of the Christian community.

(a) It is held that there is much that is attributed to Jesus which is *post eventum* or *ex eventu* prophecy. That is to say, it was read back into the words of Jesus *after* the events had happened. Foremost amongst this kind of material are the sayings of Jesus which tell of the persecutions which were to fall upon the church. Such a passage is Matthew 5.10f. (cf. Luke 6.22f.):

Blessed are those who are persecuted for righteousness' sake, for theirs is the kingdom of heaven. Blessed are you when men revile you and persecute you and utter all kinds of evil against you falsely on my account. Rejoice and be glad, for your reward is great in heaven, for so men persecuted the prophets who were before you.

It is fair to say that this passage is in fact different from the rest of the
Beatitudes. This Beatitude is much longer than any of the others, and
its form is different, although the English translation does not show
this. In all the other Beatitudes there is no *are*. They are exclamations
rather than statements, and should really begin, 'O the blessedness of
...'. By contrast, in the Beatitude of the persecuted the *are* is
expressed, and it is a statement and not an exclamation. It is different in
character and form.

A similar and even more definitely detailed passage is Matthew
10.17-22 (cf. Mark 13.9-11, 13):

> They will deliver you up to councils, and flog you in their synagogues, and
> you will be dragged before governors and kings for my sake, to bear
> testimony before them and the Gentiles ... You will be hated by all for
> my name's sake.

Another kind of passage is that which describes the fall and
destruction of Jerusalem. For instance, Luke 19.43 has a reference to
the fall of Jerusalem in which not only is the attack on the city forecast
but the great bank or mound which the Romans built to overlook the
fortifications of the city is mentioned. This is regarded as at least a
prophecy transmitted by someone who had seen the events described.

It is difficult to go the whole way with the more radical critics in this
matter, although it is easy to go some of the way with them. There is
no case for simply eliminating all prophecy as *post eventum*, for there
always have been men who could read history. Further, it would be
astonishing if Jesus did not foresee trouble for his people in the days to
come. If he violently collided with orthodox religion, so would they, if
they followed his way. No one can surely hold that Jesus did not warn
his followers of trouble to come. But it is easy to believe that, when
that trouble did come, and when men desperately needed all the
encouragement they could find, these warnings were filled out with
detail taken from what actually happened. It would be wrong to hold
that Jesus did not foretell persecution at all, but it would probably be
right to hold that his words were amplified in the light of experience.

(b) It is argued that certain things which are put into the mouth of
Jesus are only intelligible *in the light of his completed earthly ministry*.
The claim is that these sayings do not belong to a time when his
ministry was running its course, but must come from a time when it
was, so to speak, possible to stand back and to see it as a whole. The
most significant of these passages are the woes on the Galilaean cities
(Matt. 11.21-24; Luke 10.13-15).

> Woe to you, Chorazin? Woe to you, Bethsaida! for if the mighty works
> done in you had been done in Tyre and Sidon, they would have repented
> long ago in sackcloth and ashes. But I tell you it shall be more tolerable
> on the day of judgment for Tyre and Sidon than for you. And you,

Capernaum, will you be exalted to heaven? You shall be brought down to Hades. For if the mighty works done in you had been done in Sodom, it would have remained until this day. But I tell you that it shall be more tolerable on the day of judgment for the land of Sodom than for you.

It is said that a passage like this looks back on Jesus' ministry as something which has been completed. The same is true of a passage like Matthew 7.22f. and its parallel Luke 13.26f. The people will say to Jesus, as Luke has it: 'We ate and drank in your presence, and you taught in our streets.' The claim is that things like this can only be said when the ministry of Jesus had already been completed and when it is possible to look back upon it.

This may be so, but it is by no means absolutely necessary, for in the midst of present rejection, it would surely be possible to look forward to the consequences of that rejection, when the day of reckoning comes. Again, the sayings of Jesus may well have been heightened and detailed, but it is not necessary totally to reject them.

(c) It is claimed that Jewish material has been taken into the gospel tradition, and has been ascribed to Jesus. The woes to the rich, the full, the happy and the popular (Luke 6.24-26) could have come from any of the earlier prophets. The picture of the last days with wars and rumours of wars, with nation rising against nation, with the spread of a hatred which wrecks the closest human relationships, and its earthquakes and its famines, and its doom of Jerusalem (Mark 13.7f., 12, 14-22) can be almost verbatim paralleled from Jewish apocalyptic works. Parabolic material may have been taken over from Jewish sources. Bultmann would, for instance, trace the parable of the sheep and the goats (Matt. 25. 31-46) to a Jewish source. He quotes a parallel from the Talmud (Sotah 14a):

In reference to Deuteronomy 13.5 it is asked: How can a man walk after God? . . . The meaning is that you acquire his properties. Just as God clothes the naked (Gen. 3.21), so must you clothe the naked. Just as God visits the sick (Gen. 18.1), so must you. Just as God comforts the mourner (Gen. 25.11), so must you. Just as God buries the dead (Deut. 34.6), so must you.

There are two very well known passages in which this takeover is claimed and in which it is very subtly explained. The first is the saying in Matthew 24.36 = Mark 13.32:

But of that day and hour no one knows, not even the angels of heaven, nor the Son, but the Father only.

Bultmann would suggest that that sentence most probably originated as the last sentence of a Jewish apocalyptic writing; that it was taken over with the reference to the Son inserted; and then that finally it was omitted by Luke – it is not in Luke – for the theological reason that

Luke was unwilling to attribute ignorance to Jesus. So then we would have a saying which was in turn taken over, adjusted and discarded.

The second passage is one of the best known passages in the New Testament – Jesus' lament over Jerusalem (Matt. 23.37-39):

> O Jerusalem, Jerusalem, killing the prophets and stoning those who are sent to you! How often would I have gathered your children together as a hen gathers her brood under her wings, and you would not! Behold, your house is forsaken and desolate. For I tell you, you will not see me again, until you say, Blessed be he who comes in the name of the Lord.

The passage is also in Luke 13.34f.

In Matthew this is immediately preceded by another passage about the messengers of God, which is also repeated in Luke, although in Luke the two passages do not come together and are in different contexts. In this other passage there is a significant difference between the versions of Matthew and Luke. Let us set them both down:

> Matthew 23.34f.: Therefore I send you *prophets* and *wise men* and *scribes*, some of whom you will kill and crucify, and some you will scourge in your synagogues and persecute from town to town, that upon you may come all the righteous blood shed on earth.

> Luke 11.49f.: I will send them *prophets* and *apostles*, some of whom they will kill and persecute, that the blood of all the prophets, shed from the foundation of the world, may be required of this generation.

Now the significant thing is that in Matthew the people in question are *prophets, wise men*, and *scribes*; that is to say, this moves in purely *Jewish* terms; but in Luke they are *prophets* and *apostles*, which brings the thing into *Christian* terms. The argument then is that this was originally a Jewish prophecy, in which terms Matthew has kept it, but that it has become a Christian prophecy, in which altered form Luke has it.

But that is not the end of this argument. As we have said, the two passages in question come one after another in Matthew 23.34-39, but in Luke they are separated (11.49-51 and 13.34f.). Bultmann brings forward the regular argument that Jesus could not have said that he would often have gathered the people of Jerusalem together, and they refused, for the very simple reason that according to the synoptic gospels *this was his first visit to Jerusalem*. The normal answer to this would be that the fourth gospel in its early chapters describes a Jerusalem ministry, and therefore Jesus had been in Jerusalem before. This argument Bultmann does not notice here. But what he does suggest is this. He holds that Matthew is correct in bringing the passages together. Now suppose that they should be together, how does Luke introduce the first passage about the prophets and apostles? In Matthew it is simply an unintroduced word of Jesus; but

Luke begins (11.49): *Therefore also the Wisdom of God said.* Bultmann would apply this beginning to both the saying about the prophets and the apostles *and* the lament over Jerusalem, and so reaches the conclusion that the lament over Jerusalem was not originally a word of Jesus at all, but comes from a Jewish work in which Wisdom laments that men will not receive her. Thus a Jewish saying, on this view, has been put into the mouth of Jesus.

This is an ingenious argument which can neither be proved nor disproved. In the end one has to make a subjective judgment, and our own judgment would be that the lament over Jerusalem has the accent of Jesus.

(d) There are passages which are claimed to be *community formulations*. That is to say, they are passages produced by the Christian community, as it were, in the name of Jesus, in order to meet some contemporary need.

Matthew and Mark give us the initial message of Jesus slightly differently:

> Matthew 4.17: Repent, for the kingdom of heaven is at hand.

> Mark 1.15: The time is fulfilled, and the kingdom of heaven is at hand; repent, and believe in the gospel.

Mark's 'and believe in the gospel' is the way in which *the church* put Jesus' demand, and Matthew's simpler version is the more original. Luke 12.47f., with its insistence on the responsibility which special privilege brings, is the church's warning to its office-bearers and leaders. Mark 13.5f. and Matthew 7.15, with their warning against false teachers, come from the days when heresies had already arisen. Mark 13.31 is on this view the church's affirmation of its faith in Jesus rather than a statement of Jesus himself. Luke 12.32, with its promise of the kingdom to the little flock, is the encouraging word of a Christian prophet rather than of Jesus himself. Mark 9.1 with its parallels, with its promise that some who are still alive will see the consummation of things, is a word of encouragement produced when the second coming was unexpectedly delayed. Matthew 8.11f. = Luke 13.28f., with its picture of the Gentiles admitted to the messianic banquet and the Jews shut out, is part of the church's polemic against a rigid and a narrow and exclusive Judaism. Luke 23.28-31, with its prophecy of tragedy to come, is the word of a Christian prophet rather than of Jesus. On one passage in particular Bultmann has an interesting comment to make.

> Luke 21.34-36: But take heed to yourselves lest your hearts be weighed down with dissipation and drunkenness and cares of this life, and that day come upon you suddenly like a snare; for it will come upon all who dwell upon the face of the whole earth. But watch at all times,

praying that you may have strength to escape all these things that will take place, and to stand before the Son of man.

Bultmann's comment on this passage (p. 119) is:

> This is a quite late Hellenistic formulation with a terminology so characteristic of and so akin to Paul's that one could hazard a guess that Luke.was here using a fragment from some lost epistle written by Paul, or one of his disciples.

It may seem strange even to assume that men would put sayings which he did not say into the mouth of Jesus. But it must be remembered that they had no idea at all that they were doing that. They conceived of Jesus as still speaking. Bultmann writes (pp. 127f.):

> The Church drew no distinction between such utterances by Christian prophets and the sayings of Jesus in the tradition, for the reason that even the dominical sayings in the tradition were not the pronouncements of a past authority, but sayings of the risen Lord, who is always a contemporary for the Church.

In other words, the church believed that Jesus meant it when he said, as he is made to say in the fourth gospel: 'I have yet many things to say to you, but you cannot bear them now. When the Spirit of truth comes, he will guide you into all the truth' (John 16.12, 13).

We would do well to remember that it is true that the risen Lord still speaks. We need not go the whole way with the more radical critics, but we have no reason to deny that the church believed that Jesus Christ still speaks, and that they meant it when they attributed to him the truth they discovered and the warnings they needed.

Bultmann's third class of the sayings of Jesus consists of the sayings which he calls *legal sayings* and *church rules*. As soon as the church became an institution and developed an organization, it had to have rules and regulations to guide and to control the conduct, worship and belief of its members. In these rules were laid down the beliefs and duties which distinguished the Christian from the Jew and from the pagan, and which directed his conduct within the fellowship of the church. Of such sayings there are various kinds.

(a) There is the saying in which Jesus in effect abrogates all Jewish food laws, the saying in which he lays it down that nothing which goes into a man from outside can defile him, the saying by which, as Mark comments, he made all foods clean (Mark 7.15, 19). There is the saying in which he lays down the Christian attitude to the sabbath, the saying in which it is laid down that the sabbath is made for man and not man for the sabbath, so that the Son of man is lord also of the sabbath (Mark 2.27f.), and the question which demands whether it is right to do good or to do evil on the sabbath (Mark 3.4).

Here too comes the saying which speaks about it being quite right to rescue a sheep which has fallen into a pit on the sabbath day (Matt. 12.11f.). There are the sayings which abolish fasting for the Christian, because he lives in the joy of the bridegroom's presence and company (Mark 2.19). There are the sayings which point out the inadequacy of the Pharisaic law (Matt. 23.23-26).

It is suggested that these are not, at least as they stand, really sayings of Jesus, but that they are sayings in which the church summed up the teaching of Jesus for the guidance of its members.

(b) There are sayings which begin with phrases like, 'If any man . . .', or 'Whoever', or 'Whenever'. These are to be regarded as general rules in which Christian principles are laid down. Such a saying is: 'Whoever divorces his wife and marries another, commits adultery against her' (Mark 10.11f.; cf. Matt. 19.9). The form of these sayings makes them general rules and principles, and it is suggested that the formulation of them is the work of the early church.

(c) There are sayings which lay down principles which govern the religious activities of the Christian. For instance, the right way of almsgiving, of prayer, and of fasting is laid down (Matt. 6.1-18). It is laid down that reconciliation with our fellow men is the precondition of answered prayer (Matt. 5.24). There are the sayings which govern the taking of oaths (Matt. 5.33-37; 23.16-22). There is the group of sayings which in a series of antitheses draw out the difference between the Christian attitude and the ancient law (Matt. 5.21-48).

Once again it is suggested that, if the principles are the principles of Jesus, the voice is the voice of the church.

(d) There is a group of sayings, which have all to do with some point of conduct or belief, and which give a decision, and then support it by the citation of a passage from the Old Testament. It is suggested that such sayings are community sayings, in which the church stated what it believed to be the mind of Jesus and then supported its decision with a quotation from scripture. There is the passage in which, according to the story as it stands, Jesus justified his disciples for plucking and eating the ears of the corn on the sabbath day. Their action is justified by the conduct of David in taking the tabernacle loaves for himself and his men when they were hungry (Mark 2.25f.; I Samuel 21.1-6); it is further justified by Matthew (12.5f.) by the fact that the priests in the temple can do all the necessary work for the sacrifices on the sabbath and be guilty of no infringement of the law; and in Matthew 12.7 it is further and finally justified by the quotation of Hosea 6.6, which declares that God will have mercy and not sacrifice. Here three citations are made to justify Christian freedom on the sabbath.

In Mark 7.6-8 Jesus accuses the scribes and Pharisees of breaking the essence of the law by their manipulation of it to make it fit their own traditional and oral law, and the Christian point of view is justified by a quotation from Isaiah 29.13 which condemns lip service, when the attitude of the heart is wrong. In Mark 12.23-25 an argument for the resurrection of the dead is supported by the quotation of Deuteronomy 25.5f. and Exodus 3.6. In Mark 12.29-33 the question about the greatest commandment is answered with Deuteronomy 6.4f.; Leviticus 19.18; I Samuel 15.22. In Mark 12.35-37 an argument about Jesus as Son of David and Lord is answered in terms of Psalm 110.1. Bultmann's view is that a theological problem like the last, the problem of the connection between the titles Son of David and Lord, is something which would never have crossed Jesus' horizon, and that here we have the reflection of the church on the person of Jesus, with the faith of the church expressed and confirmed with the argument from scripture.

It is true that this method of argument is typically and characteristically rabbinic; a rabbi would never make a statement, unless he could buttress it with a quotation from scripture and with the opinion of other rabbis, while the thing about the teaching of Jesus which struck his contemporaries was that he needed no authority but his own.

(e) There are certain passages which, it is suggested, are the product of the arguments and the controversies and the activities of the early church. There are five passages or sets of passages which are good examples of this.

i. There is the very difficult passage about the Christian attitude to the law in Matthew 5.17-20:

> Think not that I have come to abolish the law and the prophets. I have not come to abolish them but to fulfil them. For truly I say to you, till heaven and earth pass away, not an iota, not a dot will pass from the law, until all is accomplished. Whoever then relaxes one of the least of these commandments and teaches men so, shall be called least in the kingdom of heaven; but he who does them and teaches them shall be called great in the kingdom of heaven. For I tell you, unless your righteousness exceed that of the scribes and Pharisees, you will never enter the kingdom of heaven.

This is normally printed as one paragraph, but it is likely, and it makes better sense, that the last sentence about the greater righteousness should be printed as the first sentence of the next section which is about the great antitheses between the old and the new law.

The rest of the paragraph is so far from the normal New Testament teaching that it demands explanation. The probable explanation is that this forms part of the debate between the narrower and more conservative attitude of Jewish Palestinian Christianity and the more liberal attitude of Gentile Hellenistic Christianity; and the condemnation of the liberal teachers and the praise of the rigid teachers is part of the polemic against the teachers of the Hellenistic church, who would break away from Judaism.

By far the most likely explanation of this passage is that it is the deposit left in the tradition from the struggle and debate between the Palestinian and the Hellenistic church.

ii.   There is the passage which gives to Peter the authority of discipline and doctrine (loosing and binding) within the church (Matt. 16.18f.). It has indeed been suggested that this represents the polemic of the Petrine Palestinian party against the Pauline Hellenistic party. There is no reason to doubt that Jesus gave to Peter a leading place, but this is the leading place expressed in terms of the church as an institution.

iii.   The clearest of all the 'church' passages is in Matthew 18.15-17:

If your brother sins against you, go and tell him his fault, between you and him alone. If he listens to you, you have gained your brother. But, if he does not listen, take one or two others along with you, that every word may be confirmed by the evidence of two or three witnesses. If he refuses to listen to them, tell it to the church; and if he refuses to listen even to the church, let him be to you as a Gentile and a tax-collector.

This with its reference to the ostracized Gentile and tax-collector obviously comes from a Jewish background, and from the Palestinian church. We have no reason to doubt that Jesus gave the initial advice in the passage about the necessity of the restoration of personal relationships; but it is quite clear that in the end the passage goes on to think and to advise in terms of a situation in which the church has become an institution and an organization.

iv.   There is the famous passage on prayer:

Again I say to you, if two of you agree on earth about anything they ask, it will be done for them by my Father in heaven. For where two or three are gathered in my name, there am I in the midst of them (Matt. 18.19f.).

The latter half of this saying can hardly be anything else than what we might call a saying of the risen Christ; it is the expression of the church's faith in and experience of its risen Lord.

v.   There are certain passages which are the expression of the church's realization of its missionary task and of its confidence in the help of the risen Christ for it. Such passages are Mark 6.8-11; Matthew 10.5-16; Luke 10.2-16. These are at least as much the instructions of the risen Christ to his missionaries through the church as they are charges to the original twelve. And this is particularly true of Matthew 28.19f., with its vision of a worldwide task carried out in the continual presence of the risen Lord, and with the instruction to baptize in the name of the Father, the Son and the Holy Spirit. Here the church formulates its task and affirms its confidence.

Throughout this section we have been stating certain deductions as if they were assured. It may be, it almost certainly is, the case that the point of view stated here has been taken too far, but there can be no real doubt that there are at least some passages in the gospels which must be taken as the faith and confidence of the Christian community in their risen Lord.

The fourth and the last group of the sayings of Jesus identified by Bultmann consists of what he calls the *'I' sayings* of Jesus. These are the sayings in which Jesus is depicted as making some special claim or demand for himself. It will be better if in this case we state at the beginning the general way in which Bultmann and the form critics regard these sayings. From the form-critical point of view these sayings are regarded, not so much as sayings of Jesus, but as affirmations in which the church expresses its faith in, and its experience of, its Lord. To take an example from the fourth gospel, the idea is that, 'I am the way, and the truth, and the life; no one comes to the Father but by me' (John 14.6), is not an actual saying of Jesus, but is the affirmation of that which the church had found to be true of him. To put it in a kind of paradoxical way, as the form critics see it, in these sayings Jesus is made to claim to be that which the church knew him from experience to be. Let us see how Bultmann works this out.

(a)   There are certain prophetic sayings of Jesus with which there is no difficulty. 'The blind receive their sight and the lame walk, the lepers are cleansed and the deaf hear, and the dead are raised up and the poor have the good news preached to them. And blessed is he who takes no offence at me' (Matt. 11.5) is a prophetic claim. 'Why do you call me "Lord, Lord", and not do what I tell you?' (Luke 6.46) is a similar prophetic saying. But there are sayings which do not so much demand obedience to the words of Jesus as they demand a theological acceptance of his person. They demand not that his words be accepted as true but that he be accepted as the Son of God. We can in fact see this process developing. There are four forms of the one saying:

> Mark 8.38. Whoever is ashamed of me and of my words in this adulterous and sinful generation, of him will the Son of man be also ashamed, when he comes in the glory of his Father.

> Luke 9.26 is almost exactly the same.

> Matthew 10.32f. Everyone who acknowledges me before men, I will also acknowledge before my Father who is in heaven; but whoever denies me before men, I will also deny before my Father who is in heaven.

> Luke 12.8f. is almost the same.

The point is this – in Mark and in the first version of the saying in Luke, what is demanded is the acceptance of Jesus' words and

teaching and personal loyalty to him, whereas in Matthew and in the
second version of Luke what is demanded is the theological confession
of the sonship of Jesus. The first demand can easily be the demand of
Jesus; the second demand, so it is claimed, is the theologizing demand
of the church.

So the Bultmann principle is that sayings which demand a
theological view of the person of Jesus are church formulations.

(b)   There are sayings which tell definitely about the death and the
resurrection of Jesus. 'As Jonah was three days and three nights in the
belly of the whale, so will the Son of man be three days and three
nights in the heart of the earth' (Matt. 12.40). 'I tell you that Elijah has
already come, and they did not know him, but did to him whatever
they pleased. So also the Son of man will suffer at their hands' (Matt.
17.12). 'First he must suffer many things and be rejected by this
generation' (Luke 17.25). The suggestion is that these sayings are to
be regarded rather as the church's description of what did happen
than as Jesus' prediction of what was to happen.

(c)   There are sayings about 'the name' of Jesus. The suggestion is
that these sayings come from a time when Christians had come to
worship in the name of Jesus, and when Jesus was not, as it were, a
localized human figure, but the universal Lord and Master of the
church. Such sayings are:

> Whoever receives one such child in my name, receives me (Mark 9.37).

> Whoever gives you a cup of water to drink because you bear the name of
> Christ, will by no means lose his reward (Mark 9.41).

> Lord, Lord, did we not prophesy in your name, and cast out demons in
> your name, and do many mighty works in your name? (Matt. 7.22).

> Where two or three are gathered in my name, there am I in the midst of
> them (Matt. 18.20).

The suggestion is that these sayings come from the time when Jesus is
worshipped rather than from the days of his flesh.

(d)   It would be an equally valid way of expressing this to say that
there are certain sayings which are sayings of the risen Lord
transferred back to the days of his flesh. The promise to be with his
people whenever they meet is clearly a promise possible only for the
risen and ever-present Christ (Matt. 18.20). The commission to go out
to all nations and the promise of the perpetual presence is given as a
word of the risen Lord (Matt. 28. 19f.). The promise of the Spirit to
equip them for their task is also given as a saying of the resurrection
(Luke 24.49).

There are two sayings on which Bultmann's verdict (p. 157) is: 'The
legendary character of both passages, in which the sayings occur, is
beyond question.' They are Jesus' statement that he has prayed for

Peter (Luke 22.32), and his promise to the dying and penitent thief
that he would be with him in paradise (Luke 23.43). It is not so much
that these sayings are so obviously legendary as that they imply a
power in Jesus which is the power of the risen Christ rather than the
power of Jesus of Nazareth. Such, for instance, is the promise to Peter
(Matt. 16.28), and the promises of future glory made to the disciples
(Luke 22.28-30; Matt. 19.28).

The argument is that such passages fit the risen Christ rather than
the human Jesus and that therefore they are formulations of the
church under the influence of its risen Lord.

(e) On this view it is suggested that the persecution sayings and
the sayings about the disruption of family relationships are church
formulations. 'Do not think that I have come to bring peace on earth;
I have not come to bring peace, but a sword. For I have come to set a
man against his father, and a daughter against her mother, and a
daughter-in-law against her mother-in-law; and a man's foes will be
those of his own household' (Luke 12.51-53; Matt. 10.34-36). This,
for instance, almost exactly reproduces Micah 7.6, and, further, the
picture of the disrupted family relationships becomes a standard part
of the Jewish picture of the events of the last days. 'In that age, when
the Son of David comes, the daughter will rise against her mother, and
the daughter-in-law against her mother-in-law' (Sanhedrin 97a). So it
is suggested that in the experience of persecution the church took and
put its own experience and its own faith into the mouth of Jesus.

On this it need only be said that it would be a very strange thing, if
Jesus did not foresee that loyalty to himself would lead to trouble.

(f) There is another and wider aspect of this. It is suggested that
all the sayings about the cross are formulations of the church rather
than words of Jesus, and in particular the most famous perhaps of all
sayings: 'If any man would come after me, let him deny himself and
take up his cross and follow me' (Mark 8.34; Matt. 16.24; 10.38;
Luke 9.23; 14.27). It is argued that such sayings only become
meaningful in the light of the cross of Jesus, and that they must have
been formulated *after* Jesus himself had carried his cross. This is
undoubtedly partly true. But there is something more to be said. In
Psalm 22.17 there is a reference to crucifixion: 'They have pierced my
hands and feet'. The Jews themselves used the picture: 'Abraham took
the wood for the burnt-offering and laid it on his son Isaac (Gen.
22.6), just as one does who carries his cross on his shoulder' (Gen. R.
56). Plato in the *Republic* (326A) speaks of the crucifixion of the
righteous. And, more significant than any of these references, the
Romans used crucifixion to punish revolutionaries, and there were
times when the roads of Galilee had been lined with men on crosses. It
may well be best, in regard to this saying, to hold not that it could not
be said until after the crucifixion of Jesus, but that the cross of Jesus

gave to the cross of the Christian a meaning and a significance that it could not have had until the death of Jesus.

(g) On this view all the sayings which represent Jesus as saying that he came to do something or was sent for some purpose are church formulations. The argument is that such sayings 'look back to the historical appearance of Jesus as a whole'. They are, so to speak, verdicts which are passed in the light of the whole life of Jesus. They are therefore, so it is claimed, not sayings of Jesus, but affirmations of the faith of the church, in which the church expressed its own experience of all that Jesus was and did. Sayings of this type include the following:

Mark 2.17: I came not to call the righteous, but sinners.

Luke 19.10: The Son of man came to seek and to save that which was lost.

Matthew 10.34: I have not come to bring peace, but a sword.

Mark 10.45: The Son of man came . . . to give his life a ransom for many.

Matthew 11.19: The Son of man came eating and drinking, and they say, Behold a glutton and a drunkard, a friend of tax-collectors and sinners!

Luke 10.16; Mark 9.37; Matthew 10.40: He who receives me receives him who sent me.

It is not without significance that this kind of saying is found among the apocryphal sayings of Jesus. For instance, Jerome gives a saying of Jesus: 'I came to destroy sacrifices.'

The argument is that such sayings 'gather up the significance of Jesus as a whole', and that therefore they are not so much his sayings as they are the expression of the experience and the faith of the church.

It may well be that there are sayings in which the early church expressed its faith in Jesus, but it is not necessary to assume that Jesus had no idea of what he came to do, and that he never expressed the object of his coming in words.

The general view is that when Jesus says 'I' and goes on to describe either himself or his work, it is the voice of the church that we are hearing.

(h) We may finally in this section gather up a series of sayings of Jesus which on the form-critical view arise from certain situations in the early church.

'Think not that I have come to abolish the law and the prophets: I have not come to abolish them, but to fulfil them' (Matt. 5.17) comes from the controversies about the relationship of the Christian to the law. 'I was sent only to the lost sheep of the house of Israel' (Matt. 15.24) is one of the sayings from the controversies about the Gentile mission. 'If I cast out demons by Beelzebul, by whom do your sons cast them out?' (Matt. 12.27) comes from the controversies about the exorcisms carried out by the church. Matthew 11.25-30, with its statement of teh Son's unique relationship to the Father and its promise of a light yoke and of rest, comes from the contrast between the legalistic piety of the scribes and the difference of the new faith. 'Whoever does the will of God is my brother and sister and mother' (Mark 3.35), and the demand to set loyalty to Christ far above loyalty to any earthly tie (Luke 14.26), come from the time when to be a Christian was to cut oneself loose from one's family. Luke 22.28-30 and Matthew 19.28, with its promise that the apostles will be the future judges, comes from the controversies about the place of the original twelve in the church. Matthew 18.20, with its promise of Christ to be with his own people, comes from the time when the little gatherings of the Christians met to worship.

The argument is that, in the situation of the early church, the church repeatedly had fresh words from the risen Lord to help it to meet them.

It is of interest to see what remains for the form critics, in sayings of this type, of the actual words of Jesus. Bultmann singles out one saying: 'If it is by the Spirit of God that I cast out demons, then the kingdom of God has come upon you' (Matt. 12.28; Luke 11.20). His comment is that this saying 'can, in my view, claim the highest degree of authenticity we can make for any saying of Jesus; it is full of that feeling of eschatological power which must have characterized the activity of Jesus' (p. 162).

(v)   The fifth and last type of story distinguished by the form critics has been given the title *myth*. It is important to understand what is meant by this use of the word myth. In popular language a myth is something entirely fictitious and altogether invented. In this usage a mythical story about a person is a story about something which never happened. This is not what myth means in this context. If we take Bultmann's definition of mythology, we shall arrive at the correct idea of myth. 'Mythology is the use of imagery to express the otherworldly in terms of this world, and the divine in terms of human life, the other side in terms of this side.'[13] Myth, as it has been said, 'is an attempt to state the eternal, the spiritual and the divine in the language and pictures of time, matter, and humanity'. Another definition of myth is 'the attempt to externalize an inner experience'.

Myth, quite simply, is the attempt to state some eternal truth in terms of an earthly picture. So the myths, according to the form critics, are not simply invented and fictitious stories; they are rather the attempt which man has to make to express the eternal in terms of time, for, being man, there is no other way in which he can express it.

To take a very simple and obvious example, it is said of Stephen that
he saw Jesus standing at the right hand of God (Acts 7.55). We know
very well that God is not a manlike figure sitting on a throne with
Jesus standing beside him; we know very well that we cannot take this
as a literal picture. What it does convey is that Jesus is still gloriously
alive and that he is in the most intimate and personal way connected
with God.

So for the form critic a myth is a story into which the supernatural
enters, clothed in terms of an earthly picture. In this sense the baptism
of Jesus is a myth with its picture of the descending dove (Matt. 3.13-
17; Mark 1.9-11; Luke 3.21f.), and the audible voice from heaven.
The temptation narrative is a myth with its visible devil and the
humanly impossible mountain from which all the kingdoms of the
earth can be seen (Matt. 4.1-11; Mark 1.12f.; Luke 4.1-13). This is
very clearly an attempt to externalize an inner experience of Jesus.
The transfiguration narrative is a myth (Matt. 17.1-8; Mark 9.2-8;
Luke 9.28-36), with its resurrected Moses and Elijah, its gleaming
cloud and its audible voice from heaven.

It must be remembered that in calling a story a myth a form critic
does not say that a story is not 'true'. He says that it expresses
spiritual truth in a material picture, that it can therefore not be taken
literally, and that it indeed may use a myth which is no longer
intelligble to the modern man.

There is one other part of the work of Bultmann on the synoptic
material that we would do well to look at. Apart altogether from his
verdicts on its authenticity or non-authenticity, Bultmann's analysis of
the material which includes Jesus' *similitudes, figures, metaphors* and
parables is of the greatest use. In regard to this material he makes the
following points and observations (pp. 166-70).

(i)   The synoptic material which represents the teaching of Jesus
is characteristically *concrete*. An abstract principle is seldom stated
without concrete examples of it in action. The principle of non-
retaliation is stated, and then examples of it are given – the conduct
necessary in the case of the blow on the cheek, of the compulsion to
carry a burden for a mile, of the going to law about the garment (Matt.
5.39-42). It is forbidden to worry about the future, and the definite
example of food and clothes is cited (Matt. 6.25-31). The son's request
to his father is for fish and bread (Matt. 7.9f.). Forgiveness is to be
seventy times seven (Matt. 18.22). John the Baptist does not consider
himself fit to do even the most menial task for Jesus, and that task is
illustrated by the taking off or the carrying of his sandals (Mark 1.7).
There is nothing vague and theoretical about the teaching of Jesus; it
is always tied to definite concrete examples. It is fixed in life.

(ii)   This concreteness makes for vividness, and the vividness is intensified by what might almost be called characteristic *hyperbole*. The offending hand and eye are to be plucked out and thrown away (Matt. 5.29f.). Such is the loving care of God that even the hairs of our head are numbered (Matt. 10.30). God can raise up sons to Abraham out of the very stones of the desert (Matt. 3.9). Not the smallest letter,' and not even part of a letter, of the law will perish (Matt. 5.18). It is as difficult for a rich man to enter the kingdom of God as it is for a camel to go through the eye of a needle (Mark 10.25). A fault-finder can be like a man with a plank in his own eye trying to take a speck of dust out of someone else's (Matt. 7.3-5).

The truth is stated with a kind of unforgettable vividness.

(iii) Besides hyperbole, *paradox* is repeatedly used. The man who saves his life will lose it (Matt. 10.39). The man who has, will receive more, and the man who has not will lose what he has (Mark 4.25). The man who would be greatest must be willing to be the slave of all (Mark 10.44).

The truth is put in such a way that it arrests the mind of the hearer.

(iv) Jesus frequently uses *figures*. It is common in Jewish teaching for the image and the fact to be stated side by side.

> A wooden beam firmly bonded into a building
> will not be torn loose by an earthquake;
> so the mind firmly fixed on a reasonable counsel
> will not be afraid in a crisis (Sirach 22.16).

But in the case of the recorded teaching of Jesus the figure is so clear that it needs no statement of the fact. The city that is set on a hill cannot be hidden (Matt. 5.14). It is the sick who need a doctor (Mark 2.17). If the physician cannot heal himself, no one will trust him (Luke 4.23). You cannot put a new patch on an old coat or new wine into old wineskins (Mark 2.21-22).

The figure itself is so self-explanatory that it does not need to be pointed out.

(v) Sometimes the figure is *doubled*. The two arms of the figure may be joined by 'and'.

> He who is not with me is against me, and he who does not gather with me scatters (Matt. 12.30).

Sometimes they are joined by 'nor'.

> Figs are not gathered from thorns, nor are grapes picked from a bramble bush (Luke 6.44).

Sometimes they are joined by 'or'.

> What man of you, if his son asks for a loaf, will give him a stone?
> Or if he asks for a fish will he given him a serpent? (Matt. 7.9f.)

(vi)   Sometimes a metaphor is expanded into a little picture.

> Can a blind man lead a blind man? Will they not both fall into a pit? (Luke 6.39)

> Salt is good; but if salt has lost its taste, how shall its saltness be restored? It is fit neither for the land nor for the dunghill; men throw it away (Luke 14.34f.).

> No one can enter a strong man's house and plunder his goods, unless he first binds the strong man; then indeed he may plunder his house (Mark 3.27).

These are all cases in which metaphors have been expanded into little cameo-like pictures.

(vii)   Jesus uses the simple *metaphorical phrase*. It is not wise to cast pearls before swine (Matt. 7.6). The narrow way is hard to find and to walk (Matt. 7.13f.). The harvest is great but the labourers are few (Matt. 9.37). The disciple is the man who has put his hand to the plough (Luke 9.62). The Christian must be a man with his loins girt (Luke 12.35).

(viii)   Jesus uses the *simile*, which is a metaphor with the *like* inserted and the likeness spelled out. The disciples are sent out like sheep in the midst of wolves (Matt. 10.16). The Pharisees are like graves which pollute the man who unwittingly walks on them (Luke 11.44). The scribe who has become a follower of Christ is like a householder who brings out of his treasure what is old and what is new (Matt. 13.52).

(ix)   Bultmann (pp. 170-79) identifies three very closely interrelated forms, all of which are more commonly regarded simply as parables.

(a)   There is the *similitude*. The similitude is really an expanded simile; it is a figure or comparison 'worked out in detail'. We take two examples of this:

> Will any of you who has a servant ploughing or keeping sheep say to him, when he has come in from the field, 'Come at once and sit down at table'? Will he not rather say to him, 'Prepare supper for me, and gird yourself and serve me, till I eat and drink; and afterward you shall eat and drink'? Does he thank the servant because he did what was commanded? So also you, when you have done all that is commanded you, say, 'We are unworthy servants; we have only done what was our duty' (Luke 17.7-10).

> Which of you desiring to build a tower, does not first sit down and count the cost, whether he has enough to complete it? Otherwise, when he has laid a foundation, and is not able to finish, all who see it begin to mock him, saying, 'This man began to build and was not able to finish.' Or what king, going to encounter another king in war, will not sit down first and take counsel whether he is able with ten thousand to meet him who comes

against him with twenty thousand? And if not, while the other is yet a
great way off, he sends an embassy and ask terms of peace (Luke 14.28-32).

These are really comparisons worked out in detail; there is no story;
but the points of the comparison are filled in and worked out. Other
such developed comparisons are the children at play (Matt. 11.16-19);
the mustard seed (Matt. 13.31f.); the leaven (Matt. 13.33); the
returning householder (Mark 13.34-37); the treasure and the pearl
(Matt. 13.44-46).

(b) There is the *parable*, and the parable turns the similitude into a
story. It does not deal with a typical or a recurring event, but with one
definite event in a given, particular, interesting situation. The prodigal
son (Luke 15.11-32); the sower (Mark 4.3-9); the barren fig-tree (Luke
13.6-9); the king's supper (Luke 14.16-24; Matt. 22.2-14); the unjust
steward (Luke 16.1-8); the talents (Matt. 25.14-30); the ten virgins
(Matt. 25.1-13); the tares (Matt. 13.24-30); the labourers in the
vineyard (Matt. 20.1-16); the wicked husbandmen (Mark 12.1-9); the
two debtors (Luke 7.41-43); the two sons (Matt 21.28-31) are all like
this. They all deal with a definite story about definite people and not
with some general comparison.

(c) The third type in this group Bultmann calls *exemplary tales*.
The difference in them is that they are not figurative but tell the story
of an actual happening. Such stories are the story of the good
Samaritan (Luke 10.30-37); the rich fool (Luke 12.16-21); the
Pharisee and the tax-collector (Luke 18.10-14). These are, so to speak,
illustrative stories from real life, and not figuratively constructed tales.

Such then is Bultmann's analysis of the form of the sayings, the
similitudes and the parables of Jesus; but Bultmann goes on from
there to list certain characteristics of the parables; and this section of
his work (pp. 188-92) is the most illuminating of all, because from it
there emerge certain principles by which the parables and stories of
Jesus must be interpreted.

(i) We have to note the *conciseness* of the stories. In particular,
only the persons who are absolutely essential to the story appear. For
instance, in the story of the prodigal son (Luke 15.11-32) there is no
mention of the lad's mother. In the story of the friend at midnight
(Luke 11.5-8), there is no mention of the householder's wife. And no
doubt the mother was as involved as the father in the sorrow for the
son, and the wife as involved as the householder in the midnight
disturbance. There are never more than three persons or groups in
these stories. There is the judge and the widow (Luke 18.1-5), the
Pharisee and the tax-collector (Luke 18.9-14), the master and the
servants (Matt. 25.14-30), the father and the two sons (Matt. 21.28-
30). The *dramatis personae* are kept at an absolute minimum, and one
character at a time appears and speaks.

(ii) There is what Bultmann calls *the law of single perspective*. By this he means that there is always one series of events, always told from the point of view of one person. In the parable of the prodigal son, for instance, there is no word of the father's reaction when the son left home; in the parable of the friend at midnight, about anything that the midnight traveller felt or said or did. Everything is focused upon one person's feelings and experience.

(iii) *It is very rarely that anyone in a parable is described by any adjective or any attribute.* The judge is unjust (Luke 18.2); the virgins are wise and foolish (Matt. 25.2); but this kind of description is quite exceptional. The character of the persons involved emerges from their behaviour. They identify themselves for what they are. Or sometimes the character emerges in the address to them. The master says to the unsatisfactory servant: 'You wicked and slothful servant!' (Matt. 25.26). 'Fool!' God says to the rich man whose horizon never stretched beyond this world (Luke 12.20). There is no piling up of adjectives and descriptions; a man is allowed to show himself for what he is.

(iv) *Feelings and motives are only described when they are essential to the point of the story.* We are told of the distress of the fellow servants of the merciless servant (Matt. 18.31), of the joy of the shepherd and the woman who found the lost sheep and the lost coin (Luke 15.6,9), the compassion of the good Samaritan (Luke 10.33); but in stories like that of the prodigal son and the Pharisee and the tax-collector the feelings of the people involved are expressed not in description but in the words and the actions of the characters. There are no psychological studies in these stories.

(v) *There is seldom or never any description of any of the characters in the story, other than the central character.* In the story of the good Samaritan there is no description of either the traveller or the innkeeper; in the story of the unjust judge there is no description of the widow or of the methods which she used to harry the judge into paying attention to her case. There is a strict economy, which leaves only what is essential in the story.

(vi) *There are no studies in motivation.* There is no description of the son's motives in leaving home. There is no reason given why the owner of the vineyard hired the workmen throughout the day right up to the eleventh hour (Matt. 20.1-16). Nothing, however interesting it might be, is allowed to detract attention from the one point of the story.

(vii) *There is often no expressed conclusion to the story*, and it ends, so to speak, in mid-air. We are never, for instance, told that the rich fool died (Luke 12.13-21); we are never told of the result of the wicked steward's deceit (Luke 16.1-8); we do not know what in the end happened to the barren fig-tree (Luke 13.6-9); we are never told whether or not the good Samaritan had to pay more, or whether or not the luckless traveller recovered from his wounds (Luke 10.35); we are not told if the elder brother remained obdurate (Luke 15.25-32). We are not given nicely rounded and completed tales. The point is made – and that is the end.

(viii)   *There is always a bare minimum of event.* We are not told how the wicked steward dissipated his master's money (Luke 16.1), nor what the prodigal son's particular brand of loose-living was (Luke 15.13), nor what the widow did and said when she 'kept coming' to the judge (Luke 18.3). The very things that an imaginary reconstruction would put in are left out, because they would only attract interest away from the main point.

(ix)   In most of the parables there is *direct speech and soliloquy*, which makes for both simplicity and vividness, and speed of narrative. There is a good deal of very effective repetition of key phrases. In the parable of the talents the words of the servants and of the master are repeated (Matt. 25.21-23). The repetition has a kind of underlining effect, giving emphasis to the words.

(x)   There is in these stories and parables what Bultmann calls *the law of end stress*. To put it in modern colloquial language, the punch line comes at the end. So the end of the parable of the sower is the harvest of the good seed (Matt. 13.1-8); the end of the parable of the talents is the condemnation of the lazy servant (Matt. 25.14-30). The end of the story of the Pharisee and the tax-collector is the triumphant vindication of the tax-collector and the praise of humility (Luke 18.9-14).

The principle is of very great importance for the interpretation of the parables, for it will mean that we look for their lesson at the end, and that we must never allow ourselves to be sidetracked by any of the detail which comes before.

(xi)   Lastly, the stories and parables of Jesus are such that they necessarily involve the hearer or the reader, and thus *demand a verdict*. Repeatedly, almost always, they are built on antithesis and contrast. There is the contrast between the faithful and the unfaithful servants (Matt. 25.14-30); between the Pharisee and the tax-collector (Luke 18.9-14); between the two sons (Matt. 21.28-31). Or a human story is told with the implied question, if this is true of man, how much more must it be true of God? Always the reader is being asked to align himself with one side or the other, or he is being asked to draw a certain deduction from the facts. He is not so much being told something as being encouraged to discover something for himself. The stories are such that they cannot be read in detachment. They demand decision. They do not so much say, 'Accept!'; they say, 'Think! and when you have drawn your own conclusion, Act!' These stories and parables are magnificent teaching material, because they do not form a man's conclusions for him, but compel him to form his own.

3

FORM CRITICISM ASSESSED

There are certain scholars, who, even if they pay a tribute of courtesy
to the potential value of form criticism, are nevertheless implacably
opposed to it. Cardinal Bea in his book *The Study of the Synoptic
Gospels* (p. 21) describes it as 'a type of criticism no less destructive
than that of Strauss or Ferdinand Christian Baur of the past century'.
Leonard Johnston in his introduction to Lucien Cerfaux's *The Four
Gospels* (p. xv) writes:

> There are people who claim that it was the faith of the Church which
> created the gospels; that the gospels are wonderful legends, pious
> imaginations in which the Church expressed its devotion to its leader.
> They then dismantle the solid edifice of the gospels in an attempt to get
> back to the Christ of history behind the Christ of faith. And when they
> find that their meddling brings down the building in ruins about their ears,
> they console themselves with the theory that it is after all faith alone
> which counts – like people who would have a roof over their head with
> nothing to support it.

It will be well to set down Cardinal Bea's summary of what form
criticism does and is, for it is one way in which the methods, views and
results of form criticism may be stated.

Form criticism deals, he says, with the forms of the tradition which
lie behind the written gospel; it deals with the *formation* of the gospel.
The gospels are produced within the Christian community. They are
the product of faith, and, so it is alleged, faith and history stand over
against each other, for faith is committed and history to be history
must be detached. The community was very similar to those
'anonymous masses' of people, in which legends are born and flourish.
Further, there is a sense in which this community was creative. It was
deeply impressed with the sayings of Jesus, but it expanded, explained,
imagined, invented, and then inserted its own creations into the gospel
material. Still further, this community necessarily lived in an
environment, and it borrowed from the thought and the practices and
the myths of its environment, and integrated its borrowings into the
gospel material. There is no concern for history. It is all a matter of
faith and worship within the community. Cerfaux (p. 23) quotes –
with disapproval – the verdict of Loisy:

> The Gospels when closely examined are far less the echoes of a tradition

zealous to keep intact the memories of Jesus, than a didactic instrument, we might even say, a catechism of the worship rendered to Jesus.

He follows this up with a quotation from Cullmann:

> We know that every single paragraph was passed by the community before being fixed in writing, and was therefore subjected to the influence of a great many factors. Now, among these there is not found precisely that factor in which the authenticity of a story consists: the concern for history.

So then we are told that form criticism presents us with a view of the gospels as productions of the creative faith of a community, which was the kind of community which produces legends, the kind of community that is deeply influenced by its environment, and which has no concern at all with history.

In answer to all this Bea has certain things to affirm. He insists that the gospel material did not arise in an anonymous community, and that in point of fact we know perfectly well who wrote the gospels and on whose information they depend; nor did they arise in a characteristically legend-forming community, but within the sober society of the church. He insists even more strongly that there is a strong historical interest, even if the gospels are not technical histories. The idea of *witness* occurs more than one hundred and fifty times in the New Testament. The function of the newly chosen apostle is to be a witness to the resurrection (Acts 1.22). 'This Jesus God raised up, and of that we all are witnesses' (Acts 2.32; cf. 3.15; 5.32; 10.39, 41; 13.31). And the very idea of witness involves being witness to an event.

Again, when the New Testament tells of some event, it has a habit of telling of the event, as it were, in time and in eternity at one and the same time. 'This Jesus, delivered up according to the definite plan and foreknowledge of God, you crucified and killed by the hands of lawless men' (Acts 2.23). The divine plan and the event in history, the statement of faith and the statement of fact, are set side by side (cf. 3.13, 15; 4.27f.). The writers are careful to state the historical fact, just as they are certain to affirm the conviction of faith.

Still further, one of the favourite words in the New Testament for the transmission of knowledge is *paradidōmi* with its accompanying noun, *paradosis*. The verb is the verb which Paul uses for delivering knowledge or instruction, and the noun is the word which is translated *tradition*. 'I have received of the Lord what I also delivered to you' (I Cor. 11.23). 'I delivered to you as of the first importance what I also received' (I Cor. 15.3). 'Stand firm and hold to the traditions which you were taught by us' (II Thess. 2.15; cf. II Thess. 3.6). Now this word *paradidōmi* and the noun *paradosis* are characteristically words of accurate, unchanging and unvarying tradition. And Paul's insistence on the maintenance of this tradition is very definite (Gal. 1.9, 12). The atmosphere is not that of legend-making additions but of attested transmission.

So Bea states the view of form criticism as he sees it, and thus adduces his arguments against it. What conclusions then are we to come to and how shall we assess the results and the claims of form criticism? There are certain things which by this time are beyond dispute.

(i)   The identification of the forms which lie behind the written gospels is unquestionably correct. There is no doubt that the classification of the material into pronouncement stories, miracle stories, sayings, legends and myths – using the last two terms in their technical sense – must stand. This was an exercise in literary criticism which has produced permanent results of permanent value.

(ii)   The insistence that the gospels were written out of faith and to produce faith is entirely justified. The gospels are not so much literature as they are preaching. They are written that 'you may believe that Jesus is the Christ, the Son of God, and that believing you may have life in his name' (John 20.31). As Irenaeus in his book *Against Heresies* (3.1.1) puts it, what the gospels give us, and what nothing else can give us, is *the plan of our salvation*. As Tertullian says (*Against Marcion*, 4.2), the evangelical instrument was written by men who had the Christ-given task of *promulgating the gospel*. As the Monarchian Prologue to Matthew has it, Matthew was writing to present the things which are '*necessary for faith*', and which are 'profitable for those who are *yearning for God*'.[1] It cannot be in dispute that it was faith which produced the gospels and the aim was to produce faith.

(iii)   It can hardly be denied that the presentation of the gospel story was influenced by the environment which surrounded it, and to which it was presented. Simply from the point of view of intelligibility it had to be so, for the story had to be told in forms which the hearers could understand. When the Salvation Army began missionary work in India, an Indian said: 'We will believe in your Jesus when he takes off his trousers and his hat.' In other words, the story was, if not meaningless to them, at least remote so long as it was presented in Western forms. Communication involves the presentation of the facts in categories which the hearer can understand. This will not change the content of the material, but it will change the form of it. Further, when any faith meets another faith in collision and in conflict, it will often have to be expanded, explained, developed, and even rethought in order to meet the particular problems of the situation which it is encountering. It would be no compliment to the Christian preachers, and indeed it would be a denial of the work of the Holy Spirit, to insist that the Christian message was never re-expressed to meet new needs.

(iv)   Further, it is in fact quite clear that the Christian message did undergo additions. The stories and the sayings of the apocryphal gospels are proof enough of that, as are the private gospels which the gnostic sects were to produce. Legendary and even fictional material did emerge, and quite soon. Unquestionably, fairly soon things were being put into the mouth of Jesus which he never said. Irenaeus, for instance (*Against Heresies*, 5.33.3), quotes from Papias a saying about the conditions of the millennium, which he attributes to Jesus:

> The days will come, when vines shall grow, each having ten thousand branches, and in each branch ten thousand twigs, and in each twig ten thousand shoots, and in every one of the shoots ten thousand grapes, and every grape when pressed will give twenty-five measures of wine.

This saying is quite obviously part of Jewish apocalyptic rather than of the Christian gospel. That there was development, legendary and even fictional, is quite simply a fact.

(v)   But even allowing for all this, there are certain facts to note. First, there is the fact that this development does not take place within the limits of the first century. The development that we find in the apocryphal gospels and in the gnostic private documents is later than that and does not emerge until the latter half of the second century. It is further true to say that though the gospel writers were writing out of a faith and to produce faith, they did not really doubt that they were telling the story of Jesus. Whatever be true of the others, certainly Luke in his preface is approaching the story as an historian.

It is further true that those who were the researchers and the students and the scholars of the early church did regard the gospel writers as transmitters of a true tradition. Eusebius in his *History* (3.39.1-7) tells us that what Papias was seeking was not strange commandments but the commandments of the Lord, coming from truth itself. Papias certainly thought that he was pressing back to eye-witness accounts. Eusebius also suggests (*History*, 3.24.5-15) that one of the reasons for the writing of the fourth gospel was precisely to supply information about that part of the ministry of Jesus which is not recounted in the other three gospels. Most definite of all is Jerome's criticism of those who have attempted 'to draw up a story rather than to defend the truth of history'.[2] The denial of the historical interest of the gospel writers is not tenable.

(vi)   What is true is this. The gospel writers were writing history, but their main interest was not history. They regarded themselves as transmitting facts, but their main interest was not in facts. Their dynamic was faith, and their main interest was faith. Their aim was missionary – to convert the unbeliever – and pastoral – to provide the Christian community with guidance and courage. But the way in which they proposed to do this was to tell the story of Jesus as they possessed it. They believed that they could not awaken faith by any other method than by placarding Jesus before men (Gal. 3.1).

It is our conclusion that the form critics have done an immeasurable service in enabling us to understand the formation, the genesis and the aim of the gospels, but that their one mistake is their failure to see that the gospel writers sought to awaken faith by showing Jesus as he was. This is not to say that they have the standards and the methods and the accuracy of a modern scientific historian, but it is to say that their aim was to show Jesus as he was in the days of his flesh in order that men might by faith find the risen Lord.

4

THE PEDIGREE OF THE SYNOPTIC GOSPELS

1 · The Priority of Mark

No one can read the first three gospels without seeing how closely similar they are. These three gospels, Matthew, Mark and Luke, are called the synoptic gospels. The word *synoptic* means *able to be seen together*; and it comes from the fact that it is possible to set these gospels down in parallel columns and to look at them together; and when that is done the similarity becomes even more impressive. Let us see how close this resemblance is by setting down the story of the paralysed man who was let down through the roof, and whom Jesus healed. The story is in Matthew 9.1-8; Mark 2.1-12; Luke 5.17-26.

Matthew

And getting into a boat he crossed over and came to his own city. And behold, they brought to him a paralytic, lying on his bed; and when Jesus saw their faith he said to the paralytic, 'Take heart, my son; your sins are forgiven.' And behold some of the scribes said to themselves, 'This man is blaspheming.' But Jesus knowing their thoughts said, 'Why do you think evil in your hearts? For which is easier, to say, "Your sins are forgiven", or to say, "Rise and walk"? But that you may know that the Son of man has authority on earth to forgive sins' — he then said to the paralytic, 'Rise, take up your bed, and go home.' And he rose and went home. When the crowds saw it they were afraid, and they glorified God, who had given such authority to men.

Mark

And when he returned to Capernaum after some days, it was reported that he was at home. And many were gathered together, so that there was no longer room for them, not even about the door. And they came bringing to him a paralytic carried by four men, and when they could not get near him because of the crowd, they removed the roof above him; and when they had made an opening, they let down the pallet on which the paralytic lay. And when Jesus saw their faith, he said to the paralytic, 'My son, your sins are forgiven.' Now some of the scribes were sitting there, questioning in their hearts, 'Why does this man speak thus? It is blasphemy! Who can forgive sins but God alone?' And immediately Jesus perceiving in his spirit that they thus questioned within themselves, said to them, 'Why do you question thus in your hearts? Which is easier, to say to the

Luke

On one of these days, as he was
teaching, there were Pharisees and
teachers of the law sitting by, who
had come from every town of Galilee
and Judaea and from Jerusalem; and
the power of the Lord was with him
to heal. And behold, men were
bringing on a bed a man who was
paralysed, and they sought to bring
him in and lay him before Jesus; but
finding no way to bring him in
because of the crowd, they went up
on the roof and let him down with
his bed through the tiles into the
midst before Jesus. And when he
saw their faith he said, 'Man, your
sins are forgiven you.' And the
scribes and Pharisees began to
question, saying, 'Who is this that
speaks blasphemies? Who can
forgive sins but God only?' When
Jesus perceived their questionings,
he answered them, 'Why do you
question in your hearts? Which is
easier, to say, "Your sins are

paralytic, "Your sins are forgiven"; or to say, "Rise, take up your pallet and walk"? But that you may know that the Son of man has authority on earth to forgive sins' – he said to the paralytic – 'I say to you, Rise, take up your pallet, and go home.' And he rose, and immediately took up the pallet and went out before them all; so that they were all amazed and glorified God, saying, 'We never saw anything like this!'

The resemblance is clear, and the resemblance is so close that it extends even to the little parenthesis, 'he said to the paralytic', in all three accounts. To make this resemblance even clearer, let us take three other parallel passages in which the resemblance is even closer – Matthew 21.23-27; Mark 11.27-33; Luke 20.1-8.

Matthew	Mark
And when he entered the temple, the chief priests and the elders of the people came up to him as he was teaching and said, 'By what authority are you doing these things, and who gave you this authority?' Jesus answered them, 'I also will ask you a question; and if you tell me the answer, then I also will tell you by what authority I do these things. The baptism of John, whence was it? From heaven or from men?' And they argued with one another, 'If we say, From heaven, he will say, Why then did you not believe him? But if we say, From men, we are afraid of the multitude; for all hold that John was a prophet.' So they answered Jesus, 'We do not know.' And he said to them, 'Neither will I tell you by what authority I do these things.'	And they came again to Jerusalem. And as he was walking in the temple, the chief priests and the elders and the scribes came to him, and they said to him, 'By what authority are you doing these things? Or who gave you this authority to do them?' Jesus said to them, 'I will ask you a question; answer me and I will tell you by what authority I do these things. Was the baptism of John from heaven or from men? Answer me.' And they argued with one another, 'If we say, From heaven, he will say, Why then did you not believe him? But shall we say, From men?' – they were afraid of the people, for all held that John was a real prophet. So they answered Jesus, 'We do not know.' And Jesus said to them, 'Neither will I tell you by what authority I do these things.'

forgiven you", or to say, "Rise and walk"? But that you may know that the Son of man has authority on earth to forgive sins' – he said to the paralytic – 'I say to you, Rise take up your bed and go home.' And immediately he rose before them, and took up that on which he lay, and went home, glorifying God. And amazement seized them all, and they glorified God and were filled with awe, saying, 'We have seen strange things today.'

Luke

One day, as he was teaching the people in the temple and preaching the gospel, the chief priests and the scribes with the elders came up and said to him, 'Tell us by what authority you do these things, or who is it that gave you this authority?' He answered them, 'I also will ask you a question; now tell me, was the baptism of John from heaven or from men?' And they discussed it with one another, saying, 'If we say, "From heaven," he will say, "Why did you not believe him?" But if we say, "From men," all the people will stone us, for they are convinced that John was a prophet.' So they answered that they did not know whence it was. And Jesus said to them, 'Neither will I tell you by what authority I do these things.'

The resemblance of the three accounts is clear and unmistakable. When we set it out in figures, the facts are these. Using the versification of the Revised Version, Mark has 661 verses, Matthew 1068, Luke 1149. Matthew reproduces 606 of Mark's 661 verses. That is to say, there are only 55 verses of Mark which are not reproduced in Matthew. But as we can already see from our examples Matthew compresses the material. For instance, the story of the Gerasene demoniac takes 20 verses in Mark and only 7 in Matthew (Mark 5.1-20; Matt. 8.28-34). So the 606 verses from Mark occupy only about 500 verses in Matthew. To put it in a percentage, Matthew has 51% of Mark's actual words. Luke has 320 of Mark's verses, and 53% of Mark's actual words. Finally, of the 55 verses of Mark which Matthew does not have Luke has 24. So of Mark's 661 verses only 31 do not appear somewhere in Matthew or Luke.

These are the facts and we must now go on to seek the explanation of them, and we shall begin with what may be called the standard explanation, although later we shall consider another.

When there is such very close correspondence between the gospels, there are two possible explanations.

First, all three may be going back to some common source which they are all using in their own way. If this is so, then the source which they are using must have been an oral source, for it must have been very early, and there is not one scrap of it left. That it was an oral source is unlikely, because the correspondence is so close. Further, when we set down the three accounts of the healing of the paralysed man, we saw that each of the three gospels had the same little parenthesis, 'he said to the paralytic' (Matt. 9.6; Mark 2.10; Luke 5.24), and this is surely a sign that the common source was written and not oral, for this is the kind of thing that we get in writing rather than in speaking. Of course, each of the gospel writers has his own individual material; and that material may well have been discovered in oral tradition and set down by them, but this explanation will not fit the common material which they all have.

Second, two of the three may have been copying from the third. The work of one of the gospel writers may have been the basis of the work of the other two. Now let us remind ourselves of our figures. Mark has 661 verses; Matthew reproduces the substance of 606 of them and Luke of 320 of them; there are only 31 verses of Mark which are not included in one or other of the other gospels. This would lead us to the strong possibility that Mark was the basis of the other two gospels. We shall shortly adduce other arguments for this, but it may be laid down here and now that the priority of Mark is one of the most widely accepted principles of the modern study of the gospels.

So then, although it is not the only possible view, and although there are scholars who hold other views, it is true to say that, at least among Protestant scholars, the generally accepted view is that Mark is the earliest of the gospels, and that Mark was used as a basis by the other two gospel writers. Let us see what further arguments may be found to confirm this position.

(i)   Purely on general grounds, the shorter gospel is likely to be the earlier gospel. The words and the deeds of Jesus were so precious that it is much more likely that additional material would be added to the tradition than that part of the material would be omitted. It is therefore much more likely that Matthew and Luke would take Mark, and use him as a basis, and add their own information to his account, than that Mark would take Matthew and Luke and abridge and shorten them. The comparative brevity of Mark is therefore a possible argument for the priority of Mark.

(ii)   The textual history of Mark may well be significant. In the earliest days of the church, Mark is the least quoted of the gospels and Matthew is the most quoted. This is so simply because Matthew contains almost everything that is in Mark. Further, as a reference to any of the newer translations of the New Testament will show, the best and most ancient manuscripts of Mark end at Mark 16.8 with the words: 'For they were afraid.' Mark 16.9-20 is a later addition and not originally part of the gospel. Now it is unlikely, even if it is not quite impossible, that Mark's gospel originally ended so very abruptly. The last sheet of Mark's gospel, or the end section of the roll on which it was written, must have got lost, and the additional material must have been inserted as a substitute for the lost page. Now this would mean that at one time there must have been only one mutilated copy of Mark left, from which the later manuscripts were copied. This clearly implies a certain neglect of Mark. It was natural that it should be so, for, as we have seen, all of Mark except a very few verses is contained in the other gospels. The apparent history of Mark's gospel goes at least some way to prove that Mark was the earliest gospel and that it was very nearly lost altogether from neglect when the fuller gospels were written.

(iii)   There is a third general argument which is the most impressive of all. This argument comes from the general structure of the gospel tradition. We have seen that the other gospels take over Mark's material and a high percentage of his actual words. But another very significant fact emerges. The other gospels habitually accept Mark's order of events. So much so is this the case that Matthew and Luke never combine to differ from Mark's order. In cases where one does differ the other always agrees. This is to say that we find Matthew, Luke and Mark all in agreement; we find Matthew and Mark in agreement against Luke; we find Luke and Mark in agreement against Matthew; but we never find Matthew and Luke in agreement against Mark. It does look as if Mark's time scheme for the life of Jesus has been accepted as their basis by the other two.

(iv)   One of the most interesting facts which emerge on a close study of the first three gospels is that Matthew and Mark seem deliberately to 'improve' Mark. They alter certain things in Mark in order to improve Mark's style and Mark's material.

(a)   They sometimes improve his vocabulary. When Mark tells the story of the paralysed man who was let down through the roof at the feet of Jesus he calls the man's bed a *krabattos* (Mark 2.4). This is a colloquial and almost slang Greek word, much like the English *shakedown*; it is a soldier's word. Matthew substitutes the much more polite word *klinē* (Matt. 9.2), and Luke the diminutive of that word, *klinidion* (Luke 5.18). Matthew and Luke refine the colloquial language of Mark.

(b)   They sometimes improve his style. Mark is extraordinarily fond of the historic present. He tells his story as a child might, in the present tense. He tells it as ordinary people do – 'She says to him, and he says to her'. In English we do not see this, because the translators quite properly turned Mark's presents into pasts. There are in Mark 151 examples of the historic present. Matthew retains only 21 of them, and Luke retains only one single instance. Matthew and Luke make more literary Mark's vivid colloquial style.

(c)   Mark has a habit of giving Jesus' words in the original Aramaic. John and James are called Boanerges, sons of thunder (3.17); Jesus says to Jairus' daughter: '*Talitha kumi*, Little girl, I say to you, arise' (5.41); Mark keeps the expression *Corban* (7.11); Jesus says to the deaf and stammering man *Ephphatha*, which means, Be opened (7.34); in Gethsemane Jesus called God *Abba* (14.36); the place where Jesus was crucified is called Golgotha, which means the place of a skull (15.22); in Mark the cry of agony on the cross is *Eloi, Eloi, lama sabachthani* (15.34), which Matthew corrects into *Eli, Eli lama sabachthani* (Matt. 27.46). Apart from the cry of agony, of these Aramaic expressions Matthew retains only Golgotha, and Luke retains none at all. Once again Matthew and Luke seem to be smoothing out the unliterary character of Mark's style.

(d)   Mark's style is marked by repetition, and the habit of saying things twice; Luke and Matthew, so to speak, tidy up his repetitions. Mark 1.32 reads:

| *That evening,* | *at sundown* | they brought to him | *all who were* |
| *sick* | or | *possessed with demons.* | |

In telling of the same incident Matthew (8.16) has:

That evening they brought to him many who were *possessed with demons.*

Luke (4.40) has:

> Now *when the sun was setting* all those who had any that were *sick with various diseases* brought them to him.

Mark stated both the time and the kind of sickness twice; Matthew and Luke each take one of Mark's double phrases.

When Mark is quoting the words of Jesus about David eating the bread of the presence, he has it that David was *in need and was hungry* (2.25). Both Matthew (12.3) and Luke (6.3) have simply *when he was hungry*. Again they both use only one half of Mark's double phrase.

But it is suggested that in the later gospels we have an even more interesting form of improvement than that. It is suggested that besides improving Mark's style and vocabulary, Matthew and Luke made changes in Mark's narrative because they had a more respectful and reverential attitude to the story. We might say that they look at the facts much more theologically than Mark does. Mark is prepared to put things in a way from which Matthew and Luke shrink, because they are more aware of the theological implications than Mark is.

Matthew and Luke tend, so to speak, to 'protect' the apostles. They tend to omit anything that might look like a criticism of the apostles, or anything that might show them in an unfavourable light. At the beginning of the interpretation of the parable of the sower Mark has:

> And Jesus said to them, 'Do you not understand this parable? How then will you understand all the parables?' (Mark 4.13; cf. Matt. 13.18; Luke 8.11)

In Mark there is criticism of the slow minds and the dull understanding of the twelve, and Matthew and Luke omit it.

Matthew and Mark bring to an end the section on the feeding of the five thousand and the walking on the water in quite different ways. Matthew (14.32f.) has:

> And when they got into the boat, the wind ceased. And those in the boat worshipped him, saying, 'Truly you are the Son of God.'

Mark (6.51f.) has:

> And he got into the boat with them and the wind ceased. And they were utterly astounded, for they did not understand about the loaves, but their hearts were hardened.

Matthew's picture is the picture of a company of worshipping men; Mark's is the picture of dull-witted men with impervious minds unwilling and unable to understand.

In the little incident which tells how the disciples had forgotten to bring bread with them (Matt. 16.5-12; Mark 8.14-21) Mark depicts Jesus saying to the disciples:

'Are your hearts hardened? Having eyes, do you not see, and having ears
do you not hear?' (Mark 8.17f.)

Matthew omits this altogether; he will not, if he can help it, show the
twelve in an unfavourable light.

A good example of this kind of thing comes from the incident of the
ambitious request of James and John for the chief places in the coming
kingdom of Jesus (Matt. 20.20-28; Mark 10.35-45). According to
Mark (10.35), it was James and John themselves who made the
request. According to Matthew (20.20), it was their mother. Mark has
no inhibitions about showing the twelve as ambitious men; Matthew
prefers to attribute the request to an ambitious mother rather than to
James and John themselves. There is a difference between a son's
personal ambition and a mother's ambition for a son.

Mark, the argument is, is telling the story simply and naturally,
writing in the early days before reverential conventions had got into
the church; Matthew and Luke are writing in a day when the apostles
had become the legendary princes of the church; and they therefore
'improve' Mark's narrative by 'protecting' the apostles.

A still more interesting suggestion is that Matthew and Luke
'improve' Mark's picture of Jesus. Mark, writing very early, very
simply and very vividly, allows himself to say things about Jesus, from
which a more conventionally reverential and theologically developed
age recoiled. Often this is to be seen rather indirectly and by
implication than directly. Let us set down the ways in which the three
gospel writers introduce John the Baptist:

> Mark 1.4: John the baptizer appeared in the wilderness, preaching a
> baptism of repentance for the forgiveness of sins.

> Luke 3.3: And John went into all the region about the Jordan preaching a
> baptism of repentance for the forgiveness of sins.

> Matthew 3.1: In those days came John the Baptist, preaching in the
> wilderness of Judaea.

Matthew omits the fact that John was preaching *a baptism of
repentance for the forgiveness of sins*. He does so because Jesus is
going to be baptized by John and Matthew cannot contemplate the
involvement of Jesus in a baptism which was obviously for sinners.

In Mark, Jesus is quite simply 'the carpenter' (6.3). But in Matthew
(13.55) and Luke (4.22) Jesus is the carpenter's son. Matthew and
Luke are unwilling so definitely and unqualifiedly to call Jesus a
village tradesman.

Compare Matthew's account of Jesus' experience at Nazareth with
the account of Mark.

> Mark 6.5: And he could do no mighty work there, except that he laid his

hands upon a few sick people and healed them. And he marvelled because of their unbelief.

Matthew 13.58: And he did not do many mighty works there, because of their unbelief.

Mark says quite simply that Jesus *could* do no miracles there; Matthew does not like the implication of the helplessness of Jesus and changes it to '*did* no miracles there'. As Matthew has it, Jesus did no miracles because he *chose* to do none, not because men's faithlessness made it impossible for him to do them.

Both Matthew and Luke omit Mark 3.19-21, the passage in which it is told that Jesus' friends thought that he was mad. This is one of the very few passages in Mark which is not in either of the other gospels. It was not that they doubted its truth, but that they could not bring themselves to say that anyone had actually thought Jesus insane.

Again Matthew makes a significant change in the story of the rich young ruler. The various versions are as follows:

Mark 10.17f.: 'Good Teacher, what must I do to inherit eternal life?" And Jesus said to him, 'Why do you call me good? No one is good but God alone.'

Luke 18.18f.: 'Good Teacher, what shall I do to inherit eternal life?' and Jesus said to him, 'Why do you call me good? No one is good but God alone.'

Matthew 19.16f.: 'Teacher, what good deed must I do to have eternal life?' And he said to him, 'Why do you ask me about what is good? One there is who is good.'

Matthew has clearly rewritten both the question and the answer in order to avoid putting into the mouth of Jesus the startling question, Why do you call me good?

Mark is never afraid to speak of the emotions of Jesus, especially the emotion of anger. In the story of the healing of the man with the withered hand (Matt. 12.9-14; Mark 3.1-6; Luke 6.6-11) only Mark (3.5) has the sentence: 'And he looked around at them with anger, grieved at their hardness of heart.' In the story of the blessing of the children (Matt. 19.13-15; Mark 10.13-16; Luke 18.15-17) only Mark says of Jesus when he saw the disciples keeping the children away, 'When Jesus saw it, he was indignant' (10.14). Matthew and Luke are much less willing than Mark to show Jesus in the grip of strong emotion.

It is significant to note the very slight change that Matthew and Luke make in the narrative of Mark when they relate certain miracle incidents. Compare the following passages:

Mark 1.34: And he healed *many* who were sick with various diseases, and cast out *many* demons.

Matthew 8.16: And he cast out the spirits with a word, and healed *all* who were sick.

Luke 4.40: And he laid his hands *on every one of them* and healed them.

Mark 3.10: He had healed *many*, so that all who had diseases pressed upon him to touch him.

Matthew 12.15: And he healed them *all*.

Luke 6.18: And *those who were troubled* with unclean spirits were healed.

It is significant that regularly Matthew and Luke change Mark's *many* into *all*. Such is their reverence for Jesus that they cannot think of his power as being anything less than totally effective.

We have already noted that there are only 31 verses of Mark which do not occur in Matthew or Luke, and 11 of these verses contain the story of two miracles, the story of the healing of the deaf stammerer (7.32-37), and the story of the healing of the blind man at Bethsaida (8.22-26). What was it about these miracles which made Matthew and Luke omit them? They are unusual miracles and they do stand apart. In both of them Jesus used spittle to effect a cure (7.33; 8.23); and the healing of the blind man is one of the very rare occasions when a miracle had, as it were, two stages. The man's sight came back in two parts, first confusedly, then clearly. It is likely that the other gospel writers did not wish to tell stories in which Jesus used conventional means of healing, for the use of spittle to heal was a common practice, or a story in which Jesus was not immediately successful in the exercise of his healing power. It is significant that in his version of the story of the healing of the Gerasene demoniac (Matt. 8. 28-34; Mark 5.1-20; Luke 8.26-39) Matthew does not tell, as Mark and Luke do, that Jesus began by unsuccessfully commanding the demon to come out of the man (Mark 5.8; Luke 8.29). Matthew will tell no miracle story in which the cure is not immediate.

When we look at the first three gospels, there is a strong case for holding that Mark is the earliest of them, for it certainly does seem that Matthew and Luke consistently improve both Mark's literary style and his theological approach.

5

THE PEDIGREE OF THE
SYNOPTIC GOSPELS

2 · The Hypothesis of Q

We have seen that it is entirely likely that Matthew and Luke used Mark as the basis of their gospels. Let us remind ourselves of the figures. Mark has 661 verses; of these Matthew reproduces the substance of 606, and Luke 320. But Matthew has 1068 verses and Luke 1149. Matthew, who compresses his material, puts Mark's 606 verses into about 500 verses. This is to say that apart from what comes from Mark, there are in Matthew about a further 550 verses and in Luke about a further 830 verses. Now when we examine the parts of Matthew and Luke which are not founded on Mark, we find 250 verses which very closely resemble each other. In many cases the resemblance is so close that it becomes almost identity. Let us set down certain parallel passages taken from these parts of Matthew and Luke which do not come from Mark.

Luke 6.41f.	*Matthew* 7.3-5
'Why do you see the speck	'Why do you see the speck
that is in your brother's eye,	that is in your brother's eye,
but do not notice the log	but do not notice the log
that is in your own eye?	that is in your own eye?
Or how can you say to your brother,	Or how can you say to your brother,
"Brother, let me take out the speck	"Let me take the speck
that is in your eye,"	out of your eye,"
when you yourself do not see	when
the log that is in your own eye?	there is a log in your own eye?
You hypocrite,	You hypocrite,
first take the log	first take the log
out of your own eye,	out of your own eye,
and then you will see clearly	and then you will see clearly
to take out the speck	to take the speck
that is in your brother's eye.'	out of your brother's eye.'

Luke 3.7-9	*Matthew* 3.7-10
'You brood of vipers!	'You brood of vipers!
Who warned you	Who warned you
to flee from the wrath to come?	to flee from the wrath to come?

Bear fruits that befit repentance,	Bear fruit that befits repentance,
and do not begin to say	and do not presume to say
to yourselves,	to yourselves,
"We have Abraham as our father";	"We have Abraham as our father";
for I tell you,	for I tell you,
God is able from these stones	God is able from these stones
to raise up children to Abraham.	to raise up children to Abraham.
Even now the axe is laid	Even now the axe is laid
to the root of the tree;	to the root of the trees;
every tree therefore	every tree therefore
that does not bear good fruit	that does not bear good fruit
is cut down and thrown into the fire.'	is cut down and thrown into the fire.'

Here the similarity is so close that in the Greek 60 out of 63 words are identical in Matthew and Luke.

Let us set out certain shorter passages:

Luke 12.27f.	*Matthew* 6.28-30
'Consider the lilies,	'Consider the lilies of the field,
how they grow.	how they grow.
They neither toil nor spin;	They neither toil nor spin;
yet I tell you,	yet I tell you,
even Solomon in all his glory	even Solomon in all his glory
was not arrayed like one of these.	was not arrayed like one of these.
But if God so clothes	But if God so clothes
the grass which is alive	the grass of the field
in the field today	which today is alive
and tomorrow	and tomorrow
is thrown into the oven,	is thrown into the oven,
how much more will he clothe you,	will he not much more clothe you,
O men of little faith?'	O men of little faith?'

Luke 13.34f.	*Matthew* 23.37-39
'O Jerusalem, Jerusalem,	'O Jerusalem, Jerusalem,
killing the prophets	killing the prophets
and stoning those who are sent to you!	and stoning those who are sent to you!
How often would I have gathered	How often would I have gathered
your children together	your children together
as a hen gathers	as a hen gathers
her brood under her wings,	her brood under her wings,
and you would not! Behold,	and you would not! Behold,
your house is forsaken!	your house is forsaken and desolate.
And I tell you, you will	For I tell you, you will
not see me until you say,	not see me again, until you say,
"Blessed be he who comes	"Blessed be he who comes
in the name of the Lord."'	in the name of the Lord."'

Luke 16.13	*Matthew* 6.24
'No servant can serve two masters; for either he will hate the one and love the other, or he will be devoted to the one and despise the other. You cannot serve God and mammon.'	'No one can serve two masters; for either he will hate the one and love the other, or he will be devoted to the one and despise the other. You cannot serve God and mammon.'

The resemblance between these passages is obvious, a resemblance which in shorter passages becomes identity. Although it is not the only possible conclusion, it is at least a possible conclusion – and it may still be said to be the commonest conclusion – that both Matthew and Luke were drawing their material from some common source, which they both knew and used.

If we accept this conclusion, there is another conclusion to be drawn. Matthew and Luke often quote the same saying of Jesus in a practically identical form, *but in a different context*. It may therefore be deduced that this document which Matthew and Luke were using gave the sayings of Jesus without any context and without any account of the circumstances in which they were spoken. In other words, Matthew and Luke may well both be quoting from a very early handbook of the teaching of Jesus. The distinction is too clear cut, but it could be said in a general way that Matthew and Luke used Mark as their source for the events of Jesus' life, and used this handbook as their source for Jesus' words and teaching.

To this teaching handbook critics have given a symbol; it has been called Q. And about this symbol Q there hangs a mystery. It is commonly said to be the first letter of the German word *Quelle*, which means *a source*, and the name and letter would indicate that it is a source-book of the sayings of Jesus. But R.H. Lightfoot in *History and Interpretation in the Gospels* (pp. 27f.) has a very interesting story to tell. Commonly, the symbol Q is traced back to Wellhausen, who wrote his Introduction to the Gospels in 1903. But Lightfoot tells that in conversation with himself Armitage Robinson claimed to have invented to symbol – and for quite a different reason from that usually given. Armitage Robinson was lecturing on the sources of the gospels. The first source is Mark, and since Mark is said to embody the teaching material of Peter, Robinson designated this material by the symbol P. The second source of the gospels is this hypothetical source book, and since it is the second source, Robinson – so he says – called it by the next letter to P, that is, Q; and thus Robinson claims Q got its name. Robinson thought that some German students had heard his lectures, had taken the Q symbol back to Germany with them, and that then the Germans had provided Q with a new derivation to suit their own language.

Whatever be the source of the symbol Q, it may be said that the Q hypothesis is, at least in Protestant circles, the standard way of explaining the common teaching material in Matthew and Luke.

In his *Students' Introduction to the Synoptic Gospels* (p. 68) Basil Redlich points out that it is Q which contains the many references to nature, to the animal world, and to the happenings of everyday life which make the gospels so vivid and interesting. In Q, he says, we find mention of:

i.   Wheat, harvest, grass, lilies, mustard seed, reeds, figs, thorns, brambles, trees, sycamines, grapes.

ii.   Foxes, serpents, vipers, birds of the air, ravens, lambs, sparrows, nests, wolves, eagles, moths, hens, chickens.

iii.   Lightning, storms, clouds, winds, showers, scorching wind, streams, sand pits, rocks.

iv.   Weddings, feasts, dinners, meals, loaves, fishes, eggs, leaven.

v.   Axes, lamps, purses, millstones, houses, barns, bushels, sawdust, beams, cellars, housetops, money, ovens, threshing, sandals, coats, wallets, cups and platters.

vi.   Children's games, gifts to children, music on pipes.

It is Q which contains the teaching pictures which makes Jesus' teaching live.

It is by no means easy, it is indeed probably impossible, to define either the exact nature or limits of Q. When we examine the parallel passages in Matthew and in Luke, we find three different relationships.

(a) We find passages in which the correspondence is almost verbatim, as it is in Luke 3.7-9 and Matthew 3.7-10 as already quoted; in these two passages there is a 97 per cent identity.

(b) We find passages in which there are very slight, but sometimes significant, differences.

Matthew 7.7-11	*Luke 11.9-13*
'Ask, and it will be given you;	'Ask, and it will be given you;
seek, and you will find;	seek, and you will find;
knock, and it will be opened to you.	knock, and it will be opened to you.
For everyone who asks receives,	For everyone who asks receives,
and he who seeks finds,	and he who seeks finds,
and to him who knocks	and to him who knocks
it will be opened.	it will be opened.
Or what man of you,	What father among you,
if his son asks him for a loaf,	if his son asks for a fish,
will give him a stone?	will instead of a fish
Or, if he asks for a fish,	give him a serpent;
will he give him a serpent?	or if he asks for an egg,

will give him a scorpion?

If you then, who are evil,	If you then, who are evil,
know how to give good gifts	know how to give good gifts
to your children,	to your children,
how much more	how much more
will your Father who is in heaven	will the heavenly Father
give good things	give the Holy Spirit
to those who ask him?'	to those who ask him?'

In a passage like that the differences are very few, but the one difference that there is is significant. Matthew speaks about God giving *good things* to those who ask him, and Luke speaks about God giving *the Holy Spirit* to those who ask him, and this is completely in line with the place which the Holy Spirit holds in Luke's thought, especially in Acts. The little change is a light into the mind of the man who made the change, for the relationship of the passages is so close that they must have come from a common source.

(c) We find passages in which the difference is very wide. The outstanding example of that is the Lord's Prayer:

Matthew 6.9-13	*Luke* 11.2-4
Pray then like this:	When you pray say:
Our Father who art in heaven,	Father,
Hallowed be thy name,	Hallowed be thy name.
Thy kingdom come,	Thy kingdom come.
Thy will be done,	
On earth as it is in heaven.	
Give us this day our daily bread;	Give us each day our daily bread;
And forgive us our debts,	And forgive us our sins,
As we also have forgiven	For we ourselves forgive
our debtors,	everyone who is indebted to us;
And lead us not into temptation,	And lead us not into temptation.
But deliver us from evil.	

The difference there is so wide that we are almost compelled to believe that Matthew and Luke are following different traditions; the surprising thing is that there should be so wide a difference in a prayer which is so central to the life of the Christian. Another case in which there is a very considerable difference is in the following two passages:

Matthew 7.13f.	*Luke* 13.23f.
'Enter by the narrow gate; for the gate is wide and the way is easy, that leads to destruction, and those who enter by it are many. For the gate is narrow and the way is hard, that leads to life, and those who find it are few.'	And some one said to him, 'Lord, will those who are saved be few?' And he said to them, 'Strive to enter by the narrow door; for many, I tell you, will seek to enter and will not be able.'

Once again the passages seem to go back to the same original, but it seems to have reached Luke by a different tradition from that in which Matthew knew it.

There are still further passages which the gospel writers insert into the common material, and which are peculiar to themselves. A clear example of that is Luke's insertion of a short but brilliant summary of John's preaching into the John the Baptist material (Luke 3.10-14).

On the whole it seems that we have to say that there was an area of stereotyped tradition, most likely written down and forming a handbook of the teaching of Jesus; that the gospel writers sometimes at least amended it to suit their own preferences; that there were different cycles of the same tradition, which may well have been connected with different churches; and that there was also a considerable amount of floating tradition, known to one writer and not to another, or at least used by one writer and not by another. It is not claimed that all parallel passages can be neatly assigned to one or other of these categories. It is, for instance, hard to say whether Matthew and Luke had different traditions of the temptation story, or whether each had the same tradition and arranged it as he preferred.

There are still certain things about Q to be noticed.

It is highly unlikely that Mark knew Q, or the Q material, for, if he had known it, he would certainly have used it. But there are certain places where Mark and Q overlap. For instance, both Mark and Q have the narrative of the baptism and of the temptations (Matt. 3.13-17; Mark 1.9-11; Luke 3.21f.; Matt. 4.1-11; Mark 1.12f.; Luke 4.1-13). Both Mark and Q have John the Baptist material (Matt. 3.1-6; Mark 1.1-6; Luke 3.1-6). Both Mark and Q have the missionary address to the apostles (Mark 6.7-11; Matt. 10.1-16; Luke 10.1-12). When this happens, and when Matthew and Luke have the same material both in Mark and Q, they tend to treat it differently. Matthew tends to conflate Mark and Q and to produce a composite version; Luke tends to stick more closely to Q and to neglect Mark. Streeter illustrates this from a short passage in which Mark and Q seem to overlap:

Mark 11.22f.	*Matthew* 17.19-20
Jesus answered them, 'Have faith in God. Truly I say to you, Whoever says to this mountain, "Be taken up and cast into the sea", and does not doubt in his heart, but believes that what he says will come to pass, it will be done for him.'	Then the disciples came to Jesus privately and said, 'Why could we not cast it out?' He said to them, 'Because of your little faith. For truly I say to you, if you have faith as a grain of mustard seed, you will say to this mountain, "Move hence to yonder place," and it will move; and nothing will be impossible to you.'

Here clearly Mark and the common source Q of Matthew and Luke overlap. And if we assume that in Luke we have the form which is nearest the Q version, we find that Matthew has conflated by taking the *faith as a grain of mustard seed* from Q and the *mountain* from Mark. It is characteristic of Matthew to weave his two sources into one composite whole.

Streeter (*The Four Gospels*, pp. 184f.) makes two further observations about Q. We have to be careful both in regard to what we assume have been taken from Q and what we assume not to be from Q.

A passage does not need to be in *both* Matthew and Luke to come from Q. When Matthew and Luke used Mark, each of them took what he wished from it, and they did not take the same things; and we may assume that they used Q in the same way. Each took from Q what he wished to take, and there may well be times when one of them takes a passage from Q and the other does not, and, therefore, even passages of Jesus' teaching which occur in only one gospel may still have been taken from Q.

Conversely, even if a passage, especially a short passage, occurs in both Matthew and Luke, it need not necessarily come from Q. Proverbial sayings, and easily memorized parts of the teaching of Jesus would circulate orally throughout the church, and the fact that a passage is in both Matthew and Luke may mean, not necessarily that it is a Q passage, but rather that it is part of the teaching of Jesus which everyone knew and remembered.

We shall go on to give reconstructions of what Q contained, but it can easily be seen that we cannot be absolutely definite, and it may be that R.M. Grant in his *Historical Introduction to the New Testament* (p. 116) is right when he says that Q is not to be regarded so much as a definite book-like document, but that 'it is no less and no more than a convenient symbol to designate non-Marcan materials common to Matthew and Luke'. That Matthew and Luke did share some common source for the teaching of Jesus seems highly probable; that source

---

Luke 17.5f.

The apostles said to the Lord, 'Increase our faith!' And the Lord said, 'If you have faith as a grain of mustard seed, you could say to this sycamine tree, "Be rooted up and be planted in the sea", and it would obey you.'

may well have been partly oral and partly written; and it will be well
not to insist too closely on its limits.

We have already stressed the fact that it would be unwise and
indeed impossible to delimit Q within narrow limits, but it will none
the less be useful to have a general picture of the material which Q
contained. There is general agreement that the order of the material in
Q is better preserved by Luke than by Matthew. It was Matthew's
habit to assemble and collect material on certain given subjects, as he
does with the material in the sermon on the mount (chs. 5-7) and the
parables of the kingdom (ch. 13). Luke rather gives Q just as it comes.
It is therefore usual to define Q in terms of Luke rather than of
Matthew. A.M. Hunter gives a complete reconstruction of the whole
text of Q as an Appendix to *The Work and Words of Jesus*. But the
most useful and detailed reconstruction, which we set out below, is
given by F.C. Grant in *The Gospels* (pp. 59f.). It is given in terms of
Luke with the Matthew passages which are parallel in brackets.
Sections which are doubtful are enclosed in square brackets.

The ministry and message of John the Baptizer.
 Luke 3. 2b, 3a, 7b-9; John's preaching of repentance (Matt. 3.1-
 10).
 3.16f.: John's prediction of the coming Judge (Matt. 3.11f.)

The ordeal of the Messiah.
 4.1b-12: The temptation (Matt. 4.1-11)

Jesus' public teaching.
 6.20-49: The sermon on the plain (the sermon on the mountain:
  Matt. 5.3-12, 39-48; 7.12, 1-5, 16-27; 10.24f.; 12.33-35;
  15.14)

The response to Jesus' preaching.
 7.2, 6b-10: The centurion's faith (Matt. 8.5-13)
 7.18b, 19, 22-28, 31-35: John's emissaries; Jesus' words about
  John (Matt. 11.2-6, 7-19)
 9.57b-60, 61f. Various followers (Matt. 8.19-22)

The mission of the twelve.
 10.2-16: The mission of the disciples (Matt. 9.37f.; 10.7-16, 40;
  11.21-23)
 [10.17b-20]: The return of the twelve
 [10.21b-24]: The rejoicing of Jesus (Matt. 11.25-27; 13.16f.)

Jesus' teaching about prayer.
 11.2-4: The Lord's Prayer (Matt. 6.9-13)
 11.5-8: The parable of the friend at midnight
 11.9-13: Constancy in prayer (Matt. 7.7-11)

The controversy with the scribes and Pharisees.

> 11.14-23: The charge of collusion with Beelzebul (Matt. 12.22-30)
>
> 11.24-26: The story of the unclean spirit (Matt. 12.43-45)
>
> 11.29b-32: The warning contained in the sign of Jonah (Matt. 12.38-42)
>
> 11.33-36: Jesus' sayings about light (Matt. 5.15; 6.22f.)
>
> 11.39b, 42-44, 46-52: the controversy with the scribes and Pharisees (Matt. 23.4-36)

Jesus' teaching about discipleship: the duties of disciples when persecuted.

> 12.2-12: The testimony of disciples among adversaries (Matt. 10.26-33; 12.32; 10.19f.)
>
> 12.22-31: On freedom from care (Matt. 6.25-33)
>
> 12.33b, 34: On treasure (Matt. 6.19-21)
>
> 12.39f., 42-46: Three parables on watchfulness (Matt. 24.43-51a)
>
> 12.49-53: Messianic divisions (Matt. 10.34-36)
>
> [12.54-56]: Signs of the times (Matt. 16.2f.)
>
> 12.57-59: The duty of speedy reconciliation (Matt. 5.25f.)
>
> 13.18-21: The parables of the mustard seed and the leaven; the steady growth of the kingdom under opposition (Matt. 13.31-33)
>
> 13.24-29: The narrow way (Matt. 7.13f., 22f.; 8.11f.)
>
> 13.34f.: The fate of Jerusalem (Matt. 23.37-39)
>
> 14.11 = 18.14: On self-exaltation (Matt. 18.4; 23.12)
>
> 14.16-23: The parable of the great supper (Matt. 22.1-10)
>
> 14.26f.: On hating one's next of kin and on bearing the cross (Matt. 10.37f.)
>
> 14.34f.: The saying on salt (Matt. 5.13)
>
> 15.4-7: The parable of the lost sheep (Matt. 18.12-14)
>
> [15.8-10]: The parable of the lost coin.
>
> 16.13: On serving two masters (Matt. 6.24)

Sayings about the law.

> 16.16-18: The law and the prophets until John; on divorce (Matt. 11.12f.; 5.18; 5.32)
>
> 17.1f.: On offences (Matt. 18.6f.)
>
> 17.3f.: On forgiveness (Matt. 18.15, 21f.)
>
> 17.5: On faith (Matt. 17.20b)

The coming *parousia*.

> 17.23f., 26-30, 34f., 37b: The *parousia* (Matt. 24.26-28, 37-39; 10.39; 24.40f., 28)
>
> 19.12, 13, 15b-26: The parable of the entrusted talents (Matt. 25.14-30)
>
> [22.28-30]: The apostles' thrones (Matt. 19.28)

These then – about 242 verses – are the main contents of Q.

It remains to indicate briefly the date of Q and the place from which it may have come. As to date, it must be at least contemporary with Mark, and perhaps even earlier. It will certainly not be later than AD 60 and may well be earlier. As to the place of origin, it may well be that each of the great churches had its own edition of Q, which it used for teaching purposes. We cannot say with certainty where Q was first compiled, but an at least probable guess would be Antioch, where the first move was made to the Gentiles, and where such a teaching document would very early become necessary.

6

THE PEDIGREE OF THE
SYNOPTIC GOSPELS

3 · The Special Material of Matthew and Luke

We have been seeing how the different pieces of the pattern of the gospels and their structure fall into place. We have seen how Matthew and Luke have two main sources, Mark and Q. Broadly speaking, Mark is their source for the events of Jesus' life and Q for his teaching. But after we have allocated to their places in Matthew and Luke the sections drawn from Mark and Q, there is still a considerable amount of material unallocated. We may express this as an equation (the figures in brackets represents the total of verses).

$$\text{Matthew } (1068) = \text{Mark } (500) + \text{Q } (250)$$
$$\text{Luke } (1149) = \text{Mark } (320) + \text{Q } (250)$$

This means that there are in Matthew about 320 verses still unallocated and in Luke about 580. This is material which is special to Matthew and Luke. This is, as it were, their own individual contribution to the gospel tradition. For convenience, the symbols M and L have been given to this material in Matthew and Luke respectively. We could now rewrite our equation in general terms.

$$\text{Matthew} = \text{Mark} + \text{Q} + \text{M}$$
$$\text{Luke} = \text{Mark} + \text{Q} + \text{L}$$

This special material will be very significant for finding out the slant of the mind of the gospel writers, for this is the material which they individually chose and which stuck in the memory of each of them. We shall later be discussing the characteristics of each of the gospels as a whole, but the special material itself will give us an insight into the mind of the man who chose to preserve it.

We cannot define this material too closely, for some of it may be no more than a different form of a shared tradition, and some of it may be the adaptation of the common tradition from the individual writer's special point of view. We may generally outline Matthew's special material before we look at any of it in detail.

There are the infancy narratives at the beginning of the gospel. There is a certain amount of new information, especially in connection with the last days in Jerusalem, and with the trial, the crucifixion and the resurrection of Jesus. There are certain new miracles. There are quite a number of new parables. And, above all, there is a large amount of new material about the teaching of Jesus. More than half the sermon on the mount is special to Matthew, and so is by far the greater amount of the material in chapters 18 and 23. Let us then look at the material in some detail.

(i) Some of it may be regarded as what might be called reverential addition. So in 3.14f. Matthew depicts John the Baptist's unwillingness to baptize Jesus, and his sense of unfitness for any such task.

(ii) When we look at the large number of new sayings of Jesus, and the large body of new teachings which Matthew transmits, certain characteristic lines begin to emerge.

(*a*) Matthew is still very interested in the Jewish law. Jesus' function was not the abolition but the fulfilment of the law. So Matthew has much about the Christian interpretation of the ancient laws (5.17-48; 12.5-7, 11-12; 22.23); and the best kind of Christian is a man trained in the Jewish law who has brought his whole Jewish background to be baptized with him into Christianity (13.52).

(*b*) Matthew is equally interested in the correct and Christian way in which the old Jewish acts of piety, religion and devotion may still be carried out. So he has much to say about the Christian way of carrying out the three basic religious actions – almsgiving, prayer and fasting (6.1-18) – and about care in the talk for which we shall one day give account (12.36-37).

(*c*) Matthew is still convinced of the unique place in the plan of God of the Jewish people. Jesus' mission and the mission of the disciples must be first and foremost to them (10.5-8; 15.22-25). The lost sheep of the house of Israel are Jesus' primary concern.

(*d*) It is in a way a corollary of this that Matthew is characteristically the denouncer of those who have made of Jewish piety an ostentatious formalism. The word *hypocrite* occurs more often in Matthew than in any other gospel. The very fact that he sets Jewish religion and piety so high makes his condemnation of the Jewish legalists the sternest of all (6.2,5, 16; 23).

(*e*) Matthew tends to be specially interested in eschatology and the events of the last days (7.21-23; 10.23; 24.10). Even his special parables tend to have an eschatological and a judgment setting.

(*f*) Matthew has a high respect for the apostles. They are the representatives of Jesus, as Jesus is the representative of God (10.40-42), and they will be the judges in the world to come (19.28).

(*g*) Matthew is specially interested in the church and in its leadership and in its life (16.17-19; 18.15-20). He is in fact the only gospel writer actually to use the word church.

(iii) Matthew has three new miracles – the story of Peter walking on the water (14.28-33); the story of the coin in the fish's mouth (17.24-27); the story of the emergence of the saints from their tombs at the time of the crucifixion (27.51-53). The miraculous material in Matthew is specially miraculous, and has the flavour of sacred legend rather than of fact.

(iv)   Matthew has quite a number of additions to the story of the trial, the crucifixion and the resurrection of Jesus.

(a)   He has new material about Judas, including the story of Judas' tragic end and death (26.25, 50; 27.3-8).

(b)   It is only in Matthew that Pilate's wife appears with her dream and her warning to her husband (27.19).

(c)   It is Matthew alone who has the dramatic story of Pilate washing his hands in protestation of his innocence for a decision which he knows to be a travesty of justice (27.24f.).

(d)   As we have already noted only Matthew has the story of the emergence of the dead from their tombs (27.51-53).

(e)   Only Matthew has the stories of the guard at the tomb, of the earthquake which rolled the stone away, and of the bribing of the guard (27.62-66; 28.2-4, 11-15).

(f)   It is Matthew who tells of Jesus' resurrection appearance to the women, and of Jesus' last commission to his disciples (28.9f., 16-20).

There is a considerable amount of additional information here, but the value and reliability of it is not so certain.

(v)   Matthew has a collection of new parables.

> The tares: 13.24-30, 36-43
> The treasure and the pearl: 13.44-46
> The drag-net: 13.47-52
> The unmerciful servant: 18.21-35
> The labourers in the vineyard: 20.1-16
> The two sons: 21.28-32
> The guest without the garment: 22.11-14
> The ten virgins: 25.1-13
> The talents: 25.14-30
> The sheep and the goats: 25.31-46

Certain things stand out unmistakably about this material. It is very interested in Judaism; it is very interested in the church; its main extra information is centred in Jerusalem; it has a strong interest in eschatology and judgment. It would be a fair inference that it had its origin in the Jerusalem church, in days when things were hard for the Christians and when they were eagerly awaiting the release of Christ's coming again.

We turn now to Luke's special material. Let us begin by setting down again our Luke equation:

$$\text{Luke (1149)} = \text{Mark (320)} + \text{Q (250)}$$

Luke then has about 580 verses of special material, as follows:

(i)   There is new sayings material.

3.10-14: John's sayings to certain special classes (the soldiers and the tax-collectors) who came to be baptized

13.1-5: On repentance

14.7-14: On humility and charity

17.7-10: Slaves and wages

17.20f.: The kingdom comes without observation

19.42-44: The destruction of Jerusalem.

(ii)   There are a number of new stories, or stories told in an entirely new way.

4.16-30: The rejection of Jesus at Nazareth

5.1-11: The call of Simon

7.36-50: The story of the woman who was a sinner

10.38-42: Martha and Mary

19.2-10: Zacchaeus.

(iii)   There are a number of new miracles.

5.1-11: The miraculous catch of fishes

7.11-16: The raising of the son of the widow at Nain

13.10-17: The healing of the hunch-backed woman

14.1-6: The healing of the man with dropsy

17.12-19: The ten lepers.

(iv)   There is a Samaritan section of stories.

9.51-56: The refusal of hospitality by a Samaritan village

10.29-37: The story of the good Samaritan

17.12-19: The grateful Samaritan.

(v)   There are a number of new parables, which fall into three sections, two of which are peculiar to Luke.

(a)   There are what we might call normal parables.

7.40-43: The two debtors

13.6-9: The barren fig-tree

14.28-33: The building of the tower and the going to war

15.8-10: The lost coin

15.11-32: The prodigal son

17.7-10: Master and servant.

(b)   The ordinary parable works by analogy. A story is told from nature or from some other source, and from the story the mind has to make the deduction required (e.g. the sower: Matt. 13.1-9; Mark 4.1-9; Luke 8.4-8). But Luke has four passages, which, as J.M. Creed says, are rather cameo-like character studies, in which the chief actors are people whom we ought, or ought not, to follow. They are not so much

analogies as they are illustrations of truth in action. They could be used in complete detachment from their context; they are quite independent and self-sufficient stories. And it is the dramatic brilliance of their character drawing which makes them quite unforgettable.

10.25-37: The good Samaritan
12.13-21: The rich fool
16.19-31: The rich man and Lazarus
18.9-14: The Pharisee and the tax-collector.

(c) Luke has three parables which are unique in that they work by contrast rather than by likeness. They teach a spiritual lesson by citing the conduct of quite unspiritual people, acting in a quite unspiritual way. Two of them go together:

11.5-8: The importunate friend at midnight
18.1-8: The unjust judge

These are both prayer parables, and they tell a story of how two people had their requests granted after repeated and even stubborn asking. They tell of how a churlish and unwilling householder finally answered his friend's appeal for bread, and how an unjust and corrupt judge was finally coerced by persistence into giving a woman justice. These parables do not *compare* God to an unwilling friend and an unjust judge; they *contrast* him with characters like that. They in effect say: 'If a churlish and unwilling householder can be coerced into giving his friend bread, if an unjust and corrupt judge can be coerced into giving justice, *how much more* will God who is a loving father give his children what they need?' This is exactly what Luke goes on to say (Luke 11.9-13).

16.1-12: The unjust steward

This parable is unique in that every character in it is a rascal. It can be seen that it early puzzled its interpreters from the fact that Luke attaches no fewer than three lessons to it (16.8-11). What it in effect says is that Christians would make a much better job of it, if they were as eager to live their discipleship as an unjust steward was to maintain his comfort.

Luke's treasury of new parables would in itself make his gospel beyond price.

There are two other areas in which Luke has a mass of new material. First, there is his *passion narrative*. In it he seems to have had extensive special sources. We list his additional material.

22.15-20: An independent account of the last supper
22.24-30: The dispute about precedence
22.31-34: The prayer for Simon

22.35-38: The two swords
23.2-5: The charge against Jesus
23.6-16: The trial before Herod
23.26-32: The warning to the daughters of Jerusalem
23.34: Jesus' prayer for forgiveness for his crucifiers
23.39-43: The penitent thief
23.46: Jesus' committal of himself to God
24.13-35: The road to Emmaus
24.36-49: Resurrection appearances in Jerusalem
24.50-53: The ascension.

Clearly, Luke had his own sources for the story of the passion and the resurrection of Jesus. It is not necessary to postulate a new document behind Luke's passion and resurrection narrative, for what he has is not so much a new story as a considerable amount of additional detail.

The second case, however, is different. The *infancy narratives* in chs. 1-2 stand alone, and stand self-contained. That they are a self-contained unit is made highly probable by the following five considerations.

(a)   Luke 3.1 with its setting of the emergence of John against the background of world history looks like the beginning of a book; and so it most likely is, and the first two chapters are a preface added later.

(b)   These two chapters almost certainly come from a Hebrew or Aramaic source, for they will readily, as they stand, translate back into the Semitic languages. They are steeped in the language of the Septuagint, the Greek Old Testament.

(c)   They are distinctly parallel to the stories of the birth of Samuel (I Sam. 1 and 2), and the birth of Samson (Judg. 13.1-14). There is the closest possible connection between Hannah's hymn of gratitude (I Sam. 2.1-10) and Mary's *Magnificat* (Luke 1.46-55). This is specially true of the first five verses of Hannah's hymn:

> My heart exults in the Lord;
> My strength is exalted in the Lord.
> My mouth derides my enemies,
>   because I rejoice in thy salvation.
>
> There is none holy like the Lord,
>   there is none besides thee;
>   there is no rock like our God.
> Talk no more so very proudly,
>   let not arrogance come from your mouth;
>   for the Lord is a God of knowledge,
>   and by him actions are weighed.
> The bows of the mighty are broken,
>   but the feeble gird on strength.
> Those who were full

> have hired themselves out for bread,
> but those who were hungry
> have ceased to hunger.
> The barren has borne seven,
> but she who has many children is forlorn.

The parallelism is so close that it can hardly be accidental.

(d) The two chapters are steeped in the idea of the Son of David, the Messiah. The whole atmosphere is intensely Jewish.

(e) It is quite unusual in Luke or any of the gospels to get so long a consecutive narrative. The normal gospel form is a short section, and here we have a narrative that goes steadily on for two chapters. It is very likely that here we have a section which Luke took over from a separate source. If we call this source 'I', standing for Infancy stories, we can now rewrite our equations in general terms:

$$\text{Matthew} = \text{Mark} + Q + M$$
$$\text{Luke} = \text{Mark} + Q + L + I$$

When we look at this material, what are the characteristics of it which are most evident? It has almost none of the apocalyptic and eschatological slant of Matthew. It has nothing of the institutional idea of the church which is beginning to emerge in Matthew. It is instinct with the humanity of Jesus in both senses of the word.

There is literally a certain homeliness about it. Repeatedly we find Jesus as a guest in people's homes; in the home of Simon the Pharisee (7.36); of Martha and Mary (10.38); of Zacchaeus (19.5). A parable like the friend at midnight (11.5-8) turns on the kind of situation which would arise in a village home. Thus the humanity of Jesus is shown, a man among men, and a friend among friends.

But the other kind of humanity, the kindness of Jesus, is abundantly shown. His miracles are miracles of compassion. He is gentleness itself to the woman who was a sinner (7.36-50); sabbath law or not, he will not let the deformed woman suffer one hour more than is necessary (13.16). He responds immediately to the penitent thief (23.39-43).

All through the gospel there runs this compassion and this extension of the love of God to all kinds of people. Streeter in *The Four Gospels* (pp. 219f.) says:

> The desire to represent Christ as the Saviour of the world, but rejected by his own people, is the main theme of Acts. . . . There is throughout the Lucan writings an atmosphere of extraordinary tenderness, somehow made quite compatible with the sternest call to righteousness, sacrifice and effort – an atmosphere which can be felt rather than demonstrated – and finding expression in a unique sympathy for the poor, for women, for sinners, and for all whom men despise.

Finally, we ask where Luke got his special material. Luke was in touch with all the great figures of the church and must have had access to the memories of many; but we may very probably assume that it was during the two years when he stayed with Paul in Caesarea, when Paul was in prison there, that Luke did the research, the investigation and the questioning which rescued from oblivion many of the loveliest things in the gospel story.

7

THE GOSPEL OF MARK

We have now looked at the way in which the gospel tradition was transmitted in the days before it was committed to writing, and at the general development, formation and build-up of the gospels. It is now time to turn to the study of the individual gospels. But before we do so, we may stop to note one very interesting and important fact. There was nothing quite like the gospels before. E.J. Goodspeed in his *Introduction to the New Testament* (p. 125) writes: 'The Gospel is Christianity's contribution to literary types. It is without doubt the most effective literary form of religious expression that has ever been devised.' The gospels are not *biographies*. For instance, they tell us nothing of the physical appearance of Jesus, nothing of his education, nothing except a few detached stories of the first thirty years of his life. Anyone who has ever tried to construct a life of Jesus out of the gospel material will know just how far from being biographies the gospels are. The gospels are not *memoirs*, for in memoirs the story and the events and the characters all centre round the author, while in the gospels the authors might as well be anonymous for all that they tell us about themselves. And yet the fact remains that in the gospels there is a vivid and unforgettable picture of Jesus as he was. It is interesting to note that in Mark we have the earliest surviving example of a type of literature which was the invention of Christianity.

Since Mark is the earliest of the gospels, on the view which we have hitherto been expounding, we shall start with the study of it. When we study a book, it helps to know something of the author who wrote it, so we shall begin by collecting what is known about Mark. For the life and the career of Mark there are two sources. There is the New Testament itself, and there is a fairly large amount of legendary and traditional material, some of which is, as usual, historically useless, and some of which is valuable and may well be true. We shall begin by investigating the New Testament material, and then we shall look at the legendary material and see what part of it can be used.

Mark's full name was John Mark (Acts 12.12, 25; 15.37). In Palestine it was regular practice for a man to have two names, one a Hebrew name, by which he was known to his friends and within the home circle, the other a Greek name, by which he was known in the wider world of business and of commerce and of public life. So we have Simon who is also called Peter and Thomas who is also called

Didymus. In this case John is the Hebrew name, and Markos in Greek
– Marcus in Latin – is the 'public' name.

There were in those days no surnames, and a man was known as A
son of B to distinguish him from others who had the same first name.
We do not know the name of Mark's father, but his mother's name
was Mary. She is known as Mary, the mother of John Mark (Acts
12.12). Normally, we would have known Mark's father's name, and
normally Mary would have been described as Mary, the wife of so-
and-so. It is therefore a reasonable deduction that Mark's father was
dead. Mary must have been comfortably off, for she lived in a house
large enough to have a courtyard with an outer door, and a
maidservant to open it (Acts 12.13). Her house must have been the
accepted centre of the Jerusalem church, for it was to it that Peter
turned when he escaped from prison, and it must have been big
enough to have at least one large room, for there were many
assembled there for prayer (Acts 12.12). Mark's upbringing was
therefore at the very centre of the church in Jerusalem, and no one
would have better opportunities to hear and to discover stories of what
Jesus had done and said.

It has already been noted that it was to the house of Mark's mother
that Peter went when he escaped from prison. There is clearly a very
close connection between Peter and Mark. In the letter which bears his
name Peter refers to Mark as 'my son Mark' (I Peter 5.13). This is not
to be taken literally. It can have either of two meanings. It may mean
that Mark was so close to the older man that their relationship was
like that of father and son. If Mark's own father was dead, then this
becomes even more likely. Perhaps more likely, it may mean that it
was Peter who brought Mark within the Christian faith. It is thus that
Paul can speak of Timothy as being a real and dear son to him, and of
Titus in the same way (I Cor. 4.17; I Tim. 1.2; Tit. 1.4), and it is thus
that he can write to Philemon about Onesimus as 'my child, whose
father I have become in this prison' (Philemon 10). However it came
to be, there was the closest of bonds between Mark and Peter.

Mark first emerges on to the scene in connection with the famine of
AD 45-46. At Antioch the prophet Agabus had foretold a severe
famine, and the Christians of Antioch had determined to contribute to
the needs of their fellow Christians in Jerusalem, which was a poor
church. They sent off Saul and Barnabas with their gift (Acts 11.27-
30). When the gift had been duly delivered, they returned from
Jerusalem bringing with them John Mark (Acts 12.25). Mark was the
cousin of Barnabas (Col. 4.10), although a much younger man, and
Barnabas, who had an eye for seeing the possibilities in any man, no
doubt thought there was scope for his young relative's talents in the
rapidly developing situation at Antioch.

Mark next appears in what was at once his greatest adventure and his greatest failure. It was from Antioch that the great apostolic adventure began, when Barnabas and Saul were sent out on the first mission to the Gentiles, and on this mission 'they had John (that is, Mark) to assist them' (Acts 13.1-5). It is well to see what Mark's status was in this expedition. There are two views of it.

(a) The Greek is: They had John *hupēretēs*. The Greek is a little odd. It is not they had John *as* their *hupēretēs*, but just John *hupēretēs*. By far the greater number of New Testament scholars take *hupēretēs* in the sense of *helper* or *assistant*. The AV has: 'They had John to their minister.' The RSV has: 'They had John to assist them.' The NEB has: 'They had John as their assistant.' It is important to recognize what on this view *hupēretēs* means. It was a word whose meaning had much widened, but originally and literally it meant a rower in the lower bank of oars in one of the great slave-propelled galleys. It therefore described a man who was a helper in a very humble sense of the term. John was the *hupēretēs*, the helper, of Barnabas and Saul, but that does not mean that he was their colleague in preaching and in the specially religious side of the expedition. It means that he helped by looking after the material side of the journey as a kind of secretary or courier. On this view, and it is a view almost universally held, Mark was the organizing secretary of the expedition.

(b) But F.H. Chase in his article on Mark in Hastings' *Dictionary of the Bible* suggested another view, which has never gained acceptance, but which is worth recording. As we have said, the Greek has the rather strange form, 'They had John *hupēretēs*', as if the last word was a kind of title rather than a description of the work and function of Mark. Now *hupēretēs* is a kind of title; it is the Greek translation of the Hebrew word *chazzan*. The *chazzan* was a synagogue official who appears in Luke 4.20, and whom the AV, rather misleadingly nowadays, calls the *minister*, for which the RSV and NEB both have the better modern translation *attendant*. The *chazzan* was the only paid synagogue official. He was responsible for the care of the buildings; for the taking out and putting away of the sacred rolls of scripture; for announcing the coming of the sabbath with the three blasts on the silver trumpet; and he was often the teacher in the synagogue school for children as well. Although he had no direct part in the religious services of the synagogue, the *chazzan* was by far the most important synagogue official. It is in this sense that Chase wished to take the word, and the Greek would bear the meaning: 'They had with them Mark the *hupēretēs*, the *chazzan*, the synagogue attendant.' If this is so, then Mark had the closest possible connection with official and orthodox Judaism, which might go a long way to explain why he left the expedition and went home. But this view has never been accepted, and can only be regarded as a remote possibility.

It was not long before the missionary expedition brought disaster to the young John Mark. After a tour of Cyprus, the home country of Barnabas (Acts 4.36), they took ship for Perga in Pamphylia. There is reason to believe that Paul's thorn in the flesh was a particularly agonizing kind of malarial fever. The low-lying plain of Pamphylia was notoriously a malarial region. So they did not halt to preach there, but they decided to take the steep and dangerous mountain road which led to the clean air of the central table-land, on which Pisidian Antioch stood. It was there at Perga that John Mark left them and went back home to Jerusalem.

We can only guess why he did so. Perhaps the journey into the interior by that dangerous and brigand-infested road was more than he had bargained for. Perhaps his orthodox Jewish scruples brought him doubts about this deliberate ministry to the Gentiles. Perhaps he had been softly brought up in a wealthy home and did not care for the privations of the journey. Perhaps he resented the downgrading of his kinsman Barnabas at which the story hints. When the expedition had set out from Antioch Barnabas was clearly the official leader, for his name comes first (Acts 13.2, 7); but after the events of Cyprus the expedition is described in terms of Paul and his companions (Acts 13.13). Maybe Mark objected to the way in which Paul had inevitably acquired the leadership. Or, perhaps, as Matthew Henry quaintly says, Mark 'either did not like the work, or wanted to go to see his mother'. Whatever the reason Mark turned and went home.

That was something which Paul did not easily forget. It was to be the thing which finally came between him and Barnabas and split their partnership for good. The first missionary journey ended. The Council of Jerusalem was called to discuss the position of the Gentiles in the church, and decided to throw the door wide open. Paul and Barnabas decided to take to the road again and to see how their young churches were faring. Barnabas, loyal to his kinsman, wished to take Mark with them again. Paul utterly refused to have with him the man who had played the deserter at Perga. So bitter was the quarrel that Barnabas took Mark and sailed for Cyprus, and Paul took Silas and set out inland (Acts 15.38-42), and so far as we know, Paul and Barnabas never worked together again.

There follows a fairly lengthy period in which Mark vanishes from history. There is legendary material for that period, but we shall postpone looking at it until we have looked at all the New Testament evidence. Towards the end of Paul's life, when Paul was in prison and in trouble, without warning Mark re-emerges as one of Paul's closest friends and most valued helpers.

There is a glimpse of Mark in Colossians 4.10. Mark is apparently intending to come to Colosse, and Paul sends word to the church there to make him welcome when he comes. Paul wrote the little Letter to

Philemon when he was a prisoner in Rome, and there are in it greetings from Mark, Aristarchus, Demas and Luke 'my fellow-workers' (Philemon 24). The deserter has become the fellow-worker. And at the very end of his life Paul writes to Timothy: 'Pick up Mark and bring him with you, for I find him a useful assistant' (II Tim. 4.11). The AV is in modern times a little misleading. It has in the latter half of the verse: 'He is profitable to me for the ministry', which sounds as if it referred to the ministry of the church in the modern sense of the term. But the word is *diakonia*, which means both practical and personal service. It is as his personal helper and assistant that Paul values Mark. J.B. Phillips has it: 'I can certainly find a job for him.'

This completes the New Testament picture of Mark, and there are two things which stand out clearly and unmistakably about him. First, Mark is the man who redeemed himself; he is the despised quitter who became the fellow-worker and the valued helper. There was a time when Paul wanted nothing more to do with him, but later he set him high in the list of men he could not do without. Second, this picture of Mark tells us that he must have had a very wonderful character. He had to undergo scathing criticism, and yet his missionary enthusiasm was not destroyed. Paul publicly and unmercifully humiliated him and yet at the end of the day he was still willing to serve under Paul. Mark's ability to accept criticism and retain his enthusiasm and harbour no bitterness shows him as truly great in Christian character.

We now come to the legendary material about Mark. Legend makes very many of the New Testament figures who were not members of the twelve, and who were not apostles, members of the seventy whom Jesus sent out (Luke 10.1). So Epiphanius in his book *Against Heresies* (20.4; 51.6) says that Mark was one of the seventy, and that, when Jesus refused to become king, Mark was one of those who turned back and followed him no longer (John 6.66). It is extremely unlikely that either of these statements is true, because Mark was too young to be actively involved in the ministry of Jesus.

But young as Mark was, he may have had his part in the ministry of Jesus, as three closely interrelated legends tell. Theodosius the Archdeacon (about AD 525), writing about sacred sites in the Holy Land, reports what is clearly an already accepted tradition that it was in the house of Mary, Mark's mother, that the last supper was eaten, and that it was she who supplied the upper room. The fact that her house was clearly the centre of the church in Jerusalem (Acts 12.12) makes that suggestion likely, and even probable.

Second, both Mark and Luke record a vivid detail in connection with the arrangements for the last supper. They both record the instruction of Jesus to the disciples who were to make the preparations to go into the city and to look for a man carrying a pitcher of water, and to follow him, and so be led to the house where the room had been prepared (Mark 14.13; Luke 22.10). That this was a prearranged signal can hardly be doubted. To carry water from the well was in Palestine a woman's duty and a man carrying a pitcher would be a most conspicuous sight, who would stand out in any crowd. A sixth-century Cypriot writer called Alexander, in a eulogy of St Barnabas, records the tradition that Mark was the man with the pitcher to guide the disciples to the upper room. And, if the upper room was in his mother's house, this is likely enough. If this is so, at that time Mark's father must still have been alive, for Jesus speaks of the owner of the house (Mark 14.13).

Third, there is in Mark a rather mysterious statement:

> And a young man followed him, with nothing but a linen cloth about his body; and they seized him, but he left the linen cloth and ran away naked (Mark 14.51f.).

It seems an extraordinarily trivial and irrelevant incident to insert into the high tragedy of the events in the Garden. The suggestion has been made that the Garden of Gethsemane was also the property of Mary and her husband and it was through them that Jesus had received the right to use it, and that the young man was none other than Mark himself, who had been present at the last supper almost unnoticed and who had slipped out after Jesus and his disciples to see what was going to happen. Zahn says: 'Mark paints a small picture of himself in the corner of his work.' This is the tradition which is likeliest of all to be true.

If Mark redeemed himself it must have been in the years between the split from Paul before the second missionary journey and the last days of Paul, when Paul was in prison in Rome. Now there is a strong tradition that it was Mark who founded the church in Alexandria in Egypt, and, if he did so, it must have been in these years.

Eusebius in his *History* (2.16.1) writes: 'They say that this Mark was the first that was sent to Egypt, and that he proclaimed the gospel that he had written, and first established churches in Alexandria.' The same tradition is handed down by Jerome in his book *On Famous Men* (8):

> So, taking the gospel which he himself had composed, Mark went to Egypt, and, first preaching Christ at Alexandria, he formed a church so admirable in doctrine and continence of living, that he constrained all followers of Christ to his example.

Like all legends, the legend begins to develop. Epiphanius (*Against Heresies*, 51.6) adds to it the information that Peter sent Mark to Alexandria as his substitute, when he was unable to go himself. The final touches are put to the legend by the fourteenth-century writer Nicephorus Callistus, who also compiled an *Ecclesiastical History* in which (2.43) he describes the martyrdom of Mark in Alexandria. On the Festival of Serapis the mob broke into the church where Mark was preaching. They seized him, bound his feet with cords, and dragged him through the streets to the place called Bucellus. They did not kill him that day but threw him into prison overnight. The next day they again dragged him through the streets 'until his flesh being torn off, and his blood run out, his spirit failed and he expired'. The story goes on to say that the Egyptians burned Mark's dead body, but the Christians rescued the ashes and the bones, and interred them near where he used to preach. (The final episode in the story is that the bones and ashes were taken to Venice to the famous church which bears Mark's name.)

It is a vivid story, but there are insuperable difficulties about it. First, it is very odd that none of the great Alexandrians, such as Origen or Clement, ever mention any connection of Mark with Alexandria, and, if they had known of it, they would surely have told of it. Second, Eusebius later says in his *History* (2.24) that in the eighth year of Nero's reign 'Annianus succeeded Mark the evangelist in the administration of the parish in Alexandria'. This would be in the year AD 62; but the strong tradition is that Mark wrote his gospel to enshrine the teaching of Peter after Peter's death, and Peter did not die until about three years later than this. The dates of the tradition which connect Mark with Peter and Rome do not agree with the dates of the tradition which connect Mark with Alexandria. In spite of the apparently strong tradition which connects Mark with Alexandria the difficulties are such that we must regard it with suspicion, at best to be left in suspense.

We shall have to be content to say that Mark was the man who redeemed himself, but we cannot tell how.

There is one further additional scrap of traditional material about Mark. Hippolytus in his *Refutation of Heresies* (7.30) describes Mark by the adjective *kolobodaktulos*, and he uses the word in such a way that it is clear that it is a generally accepted and widely known description. *Kolobos* means either 'stunted' or 'maimed', and *daktulos* means 'a finger'. *Kolobodaktulos*, therefore, describes either a person whose finger or fingers were naturally stunted or misshapen or deformed, or a person whose fingers had been in some way injured or mutilated. There have been many suggestions as to how this word is to be applied to Mark.

(i) It has been suggested that the word is not so much a description of Mark as it is of his gospel. The style of the gospel is rough and unpolished; and, what would be even more relevant, the gospel, as we shall see, has lost its original ending, and might therefore quite naturally be described as mutilated.

(ii) It has been suggested that the word quite literally describes some congenital deformity from which Mark suffered. The *Codex Toletanus*, a tenth-century manuscript of the Vulgate, has a note that Mark's fingers were undersized in proportion to the rest of his body. The word could be simply a physical description.

(iii)   There is a series of prologues to the gospels called the Monarchian Prologues which may go back to the third century. Acts 4.36 tells us that Barnabas was a Levite by birth, and, since Mark was related to Barnabas, it is to be assumed that Mark also belonged to the priestly tribe. It is doubtless with this in mind that the Monarchian Prologue to Mark states: 'Mark is said to have amputated his thumb after he had embraced the faith, so that he might be counted unfit for the priesthood.' It was true that any physical defect disqualified a man from the priesthood (Lev. 21.1623). Psalm 137 tells of the impossibility of singing the Lord's song in a strange land, and there is a rabbinic commentary on the Psalm which says that the Levites who had been transported to Babylon deliberately bit off their thumbs with their teeth, so that they would never again be able to play the harp, and thus accompany the singing of the Lord's songs, as it was the duty of the Levites to do. In early Christian history there is the story of a monk called Ammonius who cut off his left ear in a deliberate act of self-mutilation to make his election as a bishop impossible. The idea, then, is that Mark deliberately mutilated himself to make quite sure that he would never serve as a priest.

(iv)   Tregelles, the great English textual critic, produced the strangest of all theories. In the ancient world *kolobodaktulos* could be used of a soldier who deliberately injured himself in order to avoid military service, or to escape being sent on some campaign. This kind of thing has been done in all armies. Such men are in essence deserters, and so the word came to mean a cowardly creature who has run away from battle. Tregelles then goes on to suggest that the word was applied to Mark after his 'desertion' at Perga, and that it stuck to him afterwards. But we have seen that Mark was pre-eminently the man who redeemed himself, and it is highly unlikely that he would be known as Mark the deserter.

If any author is giving an account of any person or of any series of events, it is all-important to see what the sources of his information were. If the sources were good, the account will be trustworthy; if the sources are unsatisfactory, then the reliability of the account must also be called in question. We have already said, and it will become increasingly plain that it is so, that Mark was not writing a biography of Jesus, and that the main aim of the gospel writers is not to write history; but, even accepting that, we must still believe that Mark was aiming to give his readers a portrait of Jesus. Therefore, Mark's sources will have to be examined.

On general grounds it must be said that few people were in a better position than Mark to learn the facts about Jesus. If his home was the place in which the last supper was held, then he had first-hand knowledge of the last events of Jesus' life. If his home became the centre of the Christian church, as the narrative of Acts makes highly probable, then from his earliest days he was in contact with all the great figures of the church, and must have continually met those who had actually been with Jesus in the days of his flesh. Mark's home circumstances must have given him every chance to gather first-hand evidence for the life and the teaching of Jesus.

But the tradition of the early church was unanimous that there is something more than that, for there is an early, widespread and unanimous tradition which connects the written gospel of Mark with the preaching of Peter. This tradition is so important that we must obviously examine it in detail.

It begins with the evidence of Papias, who was bishop of Hierapolis, which is in South Phrygia and within the province of Asia, in the first thirty years of the second century. Papias was a man who spent his life collecting all the information he could about the early traditions of the church. No one has ever questioned Papias' honesty although Eusebius questioned his intelligence. He was, says Eusebius in his *History* (3.39.13), a man of very limited intelligence. But Eusebius may well have been prejudiced, because he did not at all like Papias' millenarian views, and it suited him to belittle Papias. Papias wrote a work consisting of five books on *The Exposition of the Oracles of the Lord*. The work itself is lost, and our knowledge of it is confined to the fragments of it which Eusebius preserves in quotations in his *Ecclesiastical History*. Papias states his own methods of investigation (op. cit., 3.39.3-4):

> I will not hesitate to give a place for you, along with my interpretations, to everything that I learned carefully and remembered carefully in time past from the elders, guaranteeing their truth. For, unlike the many, I did not take pleasure in those who have so very much to say, but in those who teach the truth; nor in those who relate foreign commandments, but in those who record such as were given from the Lord to the faith, and are derived from the truth itself. And again, whenever I met a person, who had been a follower of the elders, I would enquire about the discourses of the elders – what was said by Andrew, or by Peter, or by Philip, or by Thomas or James, or by John or Matthew, or any other of the Lord's disciples, and what Aristion and John the elder say. For I did not think that I would get so much profit from the contents of books as from the utterances of a living and abiding voice.

Although there has been considerable argument about what exactly Papias means, it is fairly clear that he means that he took every opportunity to talk to those who had actually been companions of the disciples of Jesus. By the elders he means much what we would mean by the fathers of the church, and in this case that means those who had been in direct living touch with Jesus. If this is so, then his sources were good.

Let us then set down what he says about Mark's gospel. He tells us that his source for what he says is John the elder. There are many things in the information which Papias gives which we shall have to discuss in detail, but at the moment we shall set it down in a more or less literal translation and leave the discussion until we have cited the evidence.

> The elder said this too: Mark who was (or, who became) Peter's interpreter wrote down accurately though not in order (or, without orderliness) all that he remembered of what Christ had said or done. He did not hear the Lord, nor was he a follower of his; but at a later date, as I have said, he followed Peter, who adapted his teaching to meet the needs of his hearers (or, who gave his teaching in *chreia* form), but not as if he was giving a systematic compilation of the Lord's oracles. Mark therefore made no mistake, but he wrote down some things as he remembered them, for he had one purpose in mind, not to omit anything he had heard, and not to falsify anything in it (op. cit., 3.39.15-17).

We shall have to examine this statement of Papias very closely and carefully, but before we do so it will be convenient to cite the rest of the evidence for the connection of Mark and Peter.

(i)   Justin Martyr (*c.* AD 150) in his *Dialogue with Trypho* (106) refers to the fact that Jesus called James and John 'sons of thunder', and then goes on to say that the information comes from what he calls the *Memoirs of Peter*. That particular story is told only in Mark (3.17). Justin must therefore be thinking of Mark as the reminiscences of Peter.

(ii)   Irenaeus (*c.* AD 170) writes: 'After their death [that is, the death of Peter and Paul] Mark, the disciple and interpreter of Peter, also handed down to us in writing the things preached by Peter' (*Against Heresies*, 3.1.1).

(iii)   Clement of Alexandria (*c.* AD 180) says: 'When Peter had publicly preached the word in Rome, and had by the Spirit declared the gospel, those who were present – they were many – urged Mark, since he had followed Peter for a long time, and since he remembered the things which had been spoken, to write out the things which had been said; and, when he had done so, he gave the gospel to those who had asked him. When Peter later learned of it, he neither obstructed nor commended it.'

(iv)   Origen (*c.* AD 200), again writing in Alexandria, says: 'The second gospel is by Mark, who composed it according to the instructions of Peter, who in his catholic epistle acknowledges him as his own son.'[1]

(v) Tertullian (*c.* AD 200), in North Africa, writing his book *Against Marcion*, says (4.5): 'That gospel which Mark edited may be affirmed to be of Peter, whose interpreter Mark was.'

(vi) Jerome (*c.* AD 400), the great Latin scholar whose work produced the Vulgate, has two accounts of Mark's gospel. The first is in the preface to his *Commentary on Matthew*:

> Mark, the interpreter of the apostle Peter, and the first bishop of the church of Alexandria, who himself had not seen the Lord, the very Saviour, is the second who published a gospel; but he narrated those things he had heard his master preaching more in accordance with the trustworthiness of the things performed than in order.

The other is in his book *On Famous Men* (8):

> Mark, the disciple and interpreter of Peter, when asked by his fellow Christians at Rome, wrote a short gospel, according to what he had heard Peter reporting. When Peter heard of this he approved it, and authorized it to be read in the churches.

There are certain things which have to be said about this tradition which connects Mark's gospel with Peter. It is *early*; it goes back very probably to the first quarter of the second century. It is *widespread.* Papias knew it in Asia Minor, as did Irenaeus who took it to Gaul with him. Clement of Alexandria and Origen knew it in Egypt, and the catechetical school of Alexandria was one of the greatest centres of scholarship in the church. Tertullian knew it in North Africa. If Jerome knew it, it must have been known in Rome.

It is quite true that it develops. Irenaeus says that Mark was written after the death of Peter – and this is far the likeliest account. Clement of Alexandria says that it was written during the lifetime of Peter, but that Peter's attitude was quite neutral to it. Origen says that it was written on the instructions of Peter. Jerome says that Peter authorized it to be read in churches. This is exactly the kind of development and elaboration that might be expected, but the basic fact of the connection of the gospel with Peter remains unshaken and unvarying.

It has been pointed out that, even without the Papias tradition, there are certain facts which might well connect the gospel of Mark with Peter. The call of Peter coincides with the beginning of Jesus' public ministry and the early events centre on Peter's house (1.16-18, 29, 36), and the gospel ends with a private message to Peter from the risen Christ which is not in any other of the gospels (16.7).

A.E.J. Rawlinson, following B.W. Bacon, has pointed out in his commentary on Mark (p. xxviii) that Peter is hardly ever mentioned in Mark's gospel other than in terms of rebuke and disgrace. Peter is sternly rebuked at Caesarea Philippi for being nothing less than the agent of Satan (8.31-33); his blundering intervention on the mount of transfiguration is recorded (9.5f.); his demand as to what he and the other disciples were to get out of their loyalty to Jesus is set down (10.28-30); his boastful self-confidence, so soon to be proved an illusion, is exposed (14.27-31); he is shown asleep in Gethsemane at the time when his master needed help and support most of all (14.37); the story of his denial of Jesus is told in all its tragic detail (14.66-72).

It might well be held that no one but Peter would have produced such a picture of Peter. There may be three intertwined reasons for this portrait of Peter. First, if Mark's gospel was written soon after the death of Peter, then the heroism of the martyr's death would atone for all. Second, it may well be that the disciples are depicted at their weakest and their worst to show the difference that the resurrection and the presence of the risen Lord made to them. Third, it may well be that Peter deliberately drew this picture of himself, as if to say: 'Look what I was – and he still loved me. Look what I was – and see what he has done for me.' Peter may have wished to show himself as the best advertisement for the grace of Jesus Christ.

We must now turn to the detailed examination of the tradition as it is in Papias himself (p. 120 above). It reads with deceptive simplicity, but in point of fact it abounds with words and phrases of which the meaning is ambiguous and perhaps even in the end doubtful. Let us then examine the difficulties.

The first phrase can either mean 'Mark who was the interpreter of Peter', or, 'Mark who became the interpreter of Peter'. *Genomenos* is the ambiguous Greek word in question, and *gignesthai*, the verb from which it comes, can at this stage in the Greek language equally well mean 'to be' or 'to become'. There are three real possibilities.

(i)   If we take *genomenos* in the sense of 'became', then the simplest way to take it will be to assume that it does not refer to Mark's connection with Peter during Peter's life-time, but that it means that Mark became the interpreter of Peter, *when he wrote the gospel*. In this case Mark's *interpretation* of Peter is the gospel which he wrote.

(ii)   It is on the whole rather more likely that we should take *genomenos* rather in the sense of 'was'. Mark *was* Peter's interpreter. The word for 'interpreter' is *hermeneutēs*, and the difficulty now is to decide just in what sense this word is being used, for as in English it can have two related senses.

It can be taken quite literally that Mark was Peter's translator. No doubt Peter knew Greek in addition to his native Aramaic; but it could also well be the case that, while his Greek was good enough for anything that Palestine required, it was not good enough to preach in public in Rome. Of course, the native language of the Romans was Latin, and it is not quite impossible that the translation referred to is translation into Latin, which it is highly unlikely that Peter would know. But it is not likely that Mark knew Latin either, and, even in Rome, at this time the language of cultured communication was Greek. When Paul wrote to the church in Rome, he wrote in Greek, and when Clement of Rome wrote to the church of Corinth, it was Greek he used. When Marcus Aurelius, the Roman Emperor, wrote his *Meditations*, he wrote them in Greek. When Plutarch of Chaeronaea came to Rome on an embassy from his native town, he knew no word of Latin, but Greek served him very well. If this is to be taken literally, then we must think of Mark as translating Peter's Aramaic sermons into Greek, as Peter preached.

A closely parallel practice was regularly used in the synagogue. The readings in the synagogue were in Hebrew, which was even by that time an archaic language no longer used. The Jew of New Testament times spoke either Aramaic or Greek, or most likely both. In the synagogue there was an official called the *targumist* or *methurgeman*, and it was his task to translate the Hebrew of the reading, one verse at a time, into whatever language the congregation most readily understood. In this case Mark would be acting as Peter's targumist. So E.J. Goodspeed in his *Introduction* (pp. 133f.) reconstructs what may have happened:

> They must have listened with rapt attention as the old apostle told of his walks and talks with Jesus in Galilee, and of the swift tragedy of the betrayal and crucifixion which had followed in Judaea. Then Peter is snatched from them and suffers martyrdom ... It must have filled the Roman congregation with grief. No more would they hear the old man uttering his inimitable reminiscences of Jesus, for with his death a priceless treasure of such memories perished from the earth. But not entirely. For, as the old man had preached, there stood beside him of course now one, now another of them, who could understand his Aramaic speech and immediately translate it into Greek for his Roman hearers. He had used these memories only to illustrate and strengthen his own preaching, and, from hearing these incidents over and over a number of times, and putting them into Greek, a capable and alert interpreter would come to have a very definite memory of their wording. Out of such memories, Papias means to say, one of these interpreters named Mark composed his gospel.

(iii)   But there is another sense in which the word 'interpreter' can equally well be used. If someone writes a book in which he expounds the philosophy or the thought of some thinker, we will call him that thinker's interpreter. An interpreter can be a person who communicates, transmits or disseminates the thought of someone to a wider circle. If the word is used in that sense, it could mean that Mark understood Peter's thought so well, had entered into Peter's mind so fully, that, when Peter was gone from this earth, he was able to communicate to others all that Peter had said and taught about Jesus. In this case he was not so much translating Peter's words as expounding Peter's thought.

We do not really need to decide between these two uses of the word 'interpreter'. We may well believe that during Peter's lifetime Mark was his interpreter in the sense of his translator, and that after Peter's death Mark was still Peter's interpreter in that in his gospel he communicated Peter's teaching to a still wider circle.

There is another possible ambiguity. Papias says that Mark who was Peter's interpreter, wrote down . . . all that he remembered of what Christ had said or done. Then Papias goes on to say: He wrote down some things as he remembered them. Who is the 'he' in 'he remembered'? The general assumption is that it is Mark, that Mark wrote down all he remembered of what Christ had said or done, that Mark wrote down some things as he remembered them. But it has been suggested that 'he' is not Mark, but *Peter*. So the meaning would be that Mark, who was Peter's interpreter, wrote down all that *Peter* remembered of what Christ had said or done, that he wrote down some things as *Peter* remembered them. It is perhaps less natural to take Peter as the subject of 'remembered', but it is a possibility, and, if that is the translation, it brings Mark's gospel even nearer to Peter.

But a far more important question arises when we come to the phrase which is usually translated 'accurately but not in order'. The phrase for 'in order' is *en taxei*, and this is usually taken of *chronological* order. Mark, it is then said, is accurate enough in his information, but he has no chronology. Peter, the idea is, used these incidents and sayings of Jesus as illustrations in his sermons. They were quite detached; where they came in the life of Jesus was not the point. Therefore, it is said, you do get accuracy in Mark, but you do not get chronology.

It is not in question that *taxis* can and often does mean chronological order. But is it fair to say of Mark that he has no *taxis* in his gospel in that sense of the term? In one sense it is true to say that Mark has this *taxis*. His gospel has a dramatic pattern; his gospel does show the life of Jesus in terms of preparation, conflict, tragedy, and, no doubt in the lost ending of his gospel, triumph. It is true that we cannot follow Jesus from day to day and from week to week and from year to year, but the dramatic pattern is clear. And it is surely relevant to remember that Matthew and Luke found Mark's chronological order so satisfactory that they both used it as the basis of their gospels, and that they never combine to differ against him. It would surely be true to say that many criticisms may be made of Mark's work, but the one criticism that cannot be made of it is in fact just this criticism that he has no chronological order. J.B. Lightfoot says[2] that 'the leading idea in the extract is the absence of strict historical sequence in St Mark's narrative', but Plummer says in his edition of Mark in the *Cambridge Bible for Schools and Colleges* (p. xxiii): 'The statement of the Presbyter in Papias that Mark wrote "accurately but not in order" is perplexing, because, with all his defects, his order is remarkably good.' We cannot help feeling that the idea that *en taxei* means *chronological order* has been too easily accepted. But if it does not mean that, what are the alternatives? There are two alternatives.

(i) J. Kleist in his book called *Memoirs of St Peter* (pp. 17-42) points out that *taxis* can be used in the sense of 'a list, an inventory, a detailed enumeration'. He therefore suggests that what Papias is saying is that Mark wrote accurately, but not with the fulness of a detailed account, and indeed the extract goes on to say that Peter's teaching did not aim to give a systematic compilation of the oracles of Jesus. This is certainly possible; it would be a much truer verdict on Mark, but whether this is a natural meaning of *taxis* is not so sure.

(ii) F.H. Colson[3] offers another explanation. *Taxis* is a technical word of Greek literary criticism. In an author's work there are three spheres. There is *heuresis*, the discovery of his material; there is *taxis*, the orderly marshalling and arranging of it, by the proper laws of rhetoric and art; there is *phrasis*, the expressing of the material in a correct literary style.

Here is a definite and known use of the word *taxis*; it is the literary and artistic arrangement of the author's material. Clement of Alexandria wrote a work called the *Stromateis*, which means the *Miscellanies*, and at the end of the seventh book he remarks that the *Miscellanies* do not aim at *taxis* or *phrasis*; they do not aim at artistic arrangement and good literary style. A miscellany in its nature is a disjointed and haphazard collection. Lucian in his book *On how to Write History* (48) tells his author to collect his material first.

> When all or nearly all is collected, draw up a rough sketch, as yet without beauty, and unorganized. Then introduce *taxis*, then add beauty, the colouring of style and figures and rhythm.

Taxis again is the artistic arrangement of the material.

Now Dionysius of Halicarnassus, one of the greatest of the Greek literary critics, has a work on *The Criticism of Thucydides*, and he says (10-20) that there are some who criticize Thucydides' *taxis* on the ground that he neither begins nor ends his history, as it were, in the right place. If Papias only knew Mark in the version which ends at Mark 16.8 he could certainly say that Mark did not end in the right place. Further, Theon, another literary critic, in his *Progymnasmata* (190) says that any proper history must give 'the ancestor and parentage of the personages, and many such things'. This is exactly what Mark does not do; therefore, from the literary point of view, like Thucydides, he is deficient at the beginning as he is at the end. His *taxis* is at fault. Still further, two other parts of *taxis* are *grouping* and *proportion*. Mark certainly does not group his material as Matthew does (cf. Matt. 5-7, 13). And Mark does expand his narrative with vivid detail, but could be said to get it out of proportion. As we have seen (p. 000 above), in Matthew the cure of the Gerasene demoniac takes seven verses and in Mark twenty (Matt. 8.28-34; Mark 5.1-20). For all his vividness Mark can be said to be out of proportion.

From all this it can be clearly seen that it is perfectly just to charge Mark with having no *taxis* in the sense of orderly and artistic arrangement, but it is not just to charge him with having no *taxis* in the sense of chronology. It would be better to translate the phrase by some such English form of words as 'accurately but artlessly'. It is not Mark's order that is in question but his orderliness, not his chronology but his arranging of his material.

When we have got this length with the Papias quotation, another very interesting possibility emerges. So far we have seen that there is a distinct possibility that *taxis* does not mean chronological order, but order in the literary sense of the term. This further possibility is discussed by R.M. Grant in *The Earliest Lives of Jesus* (pp. 15-20). There is a phrase in the Papias quotation which is commonly translated in some such way as: 'Peter adapted his teaching to meet the needs of his hearers.' In the Greek there is nothing about *hearers*; this is supplied by the translators. The phrase is that Peter made his teaching *pros tas chreias*. There is no question that *chreia* can mean 'need'. A literal translation of this sentence would be: 'Peter made his teaching to the needs.' Moffatt in his *Introduction to the Literature of the New Testament* (p. 186) translates: 'Peter adapted his instructions to practical needs', thereby supplying the word *practical*. This makes good enough sense, but taken in this way the word *chreias* is oddly up in the air, and always something has to be supplied to fill it out.

Now *chreia* has another meaning, a literary meaning. A *chreia* in Greek literary language is defined as 'a brief declaration or action, referred to some definite person or something like a person'. It is a kind of very brief anecdote. It is not a proverbial saying, for a *chreia* always refers to a definite person; it is not a general statement as a proverbial saying is; it does not need to give a moral lesson; and it often has more than speech in it: it may also have incident. If in the Papias extract we take *chreia* in this sense, we get the translation: 'Peter gave his teaching in *chreia* form.' That is to say, Peter's teaching consisted of little detached anecdotes and stories about Jesus. This suits, because a *chreia* cannot be criticized for not having chronological order; it was never meant to have that; but it can be criticized because its literary style is rough and artless.

As it happens, we can go even further than this. A *chreia* is, so to speak, the shortest and most primitive unit of tradition. But Greek has another closely related word, the word *apomnēmoneuma*. An *apomnēmoneuma* is a memory about someone. Xenophon wrote his book the *Apomnēmoneumata* of Socrates, which is usually called the *Memorabilia*; it is Xenophon's memoirs or reminiscences of Socrates. An *apomnēmoneuma* is a kind of developed and worked-up *chreia*, a *chreia* in fuller and more literary form. Now this is precisely what the gospels were called. When Justin Martyr speaks about the gospels he calls them the *apomnēmoneumata* of the apostles (*First Apology*, 66) or of Peter (*Dialogue with Trypho*, 106), the memoirs, the reminiscences of the apostles or of Peter.

Now it is the verb of this noun which Papias uses of Mark when he says that Mark wrote down some things as he *remembered* them. Mark, as it were, turned Peter's simple *chreia* into more developed *apomnēmoneumata*. In Mark's hands Peter's little anecdotes become more developed memoirs or reminiscences.

But we can go even further. The *chreia* is the simple, short, basic story; the *apomnēmoneumata* are the fuller reminiscences and memoirs; but material composed of these elements will not be orderly and systematic; and we have the further word *suntaxis*, which means a *systematic compilation*. *Chreia, apomnēmoneuma, suntaxis* form a ladder in development. And once again the verb from *suntaxis* meets us in the Papias extract, when Papias says that Mark was not *giving a systematic compilation*. It may well be, it is indeed probable, that Papias is defending Mark from a comparison with the fuller and more systematic gospel of either Matthew or John, either of which could be called a *suntaxis*, or systematic compilation.

So then it seems to us that what Papias is saying is that Mark took the *chreiai* of Peter, Peter's little short stories, and made them into *apomnēmoneumata*, into reminiscences or *memorabilia* or memoirs, but he neither aimed to produce, nor did produce, a *suntaxis*, a systematic compilation to compare with either Matthew or John. The Papias extract is not a criticism of Mark for a failure in chronology. It simply says of Mark that he took Peter's short illustrative stories and developed them into reminiscences, although he did not produce a finished and systematic book. Mark, then, in the opinion of Papias, is an accurate but artless reproduction of the simple teaching material of Peter.

There is in our opinion no good reason for rejecting the tradition of the connection of Mark's gospel with Peter. It was a tradition which was widespread in the ancient church; Papias got it on good authority; and, as we shall go on to see, it fits the character of the gospel itself. Since this is so, the importance of Mark's gospel is immense, for as Rawlinson writes in his commentary (p. xxi), we have in it, 'a record in writing of that fundamental apostolic tradition upon which from the first the spoken message of "the Gospel" was based'. Let us then go on to see the characteristics of this earliest gospel.

There are two views of Mark's gospel, and we shall begin with the simpler of them. Of this A.B. Bruce, writing in *The Expositor's Greek Testament* (I, pp. 32-4), is the typical exponent. To him Mark is the simplest of all the gospels. Mark, he holds, has no conscious didactic aim. 'The purpose of the writer seems to be mainly just to tell what he knows about Jesus.' There is in Mark the quality of simple, dramatic, vividness. It is a rapid sketch of the ministry of Jesus in a series of graphic tableaux from the commencement in Galilee to the tragic close in Jerusalem. E.J. Goodspeed in his *Introduction* (p. 139) reminds us that R.F. Horton wrote a book called *The Cartoons of Saint Mark*, and Goodspeed himself says that the gospel is a series of great pictures boldly and simply drawn.

> A situation is sketched. Jesus appears in the midst of it, or says something or does something that relieves it. His words flash through the scene like a bright sword.

It is for this reason that almost all commentators, no matter what their standpoint, stress the vivid realism of Mark's gospel. J.H. Ropes in *The Synoptic Gospels* (p. 32) speaks of Mark's 'incomparable touch of reality'. It is for this reason that more than one commentator holds that in Mark we are in the closest possible touch with the actual historical life of Jesus. Goodspeed (pp. 145f.) writes:

> Mark brings us nearer the immediate circle of Jesus' followers than any other record of him that we possess. It is as though Mark felt that he was in the presence of something far too great for him to master or control, which he must just record as simply as he might. This is why we get in Mark this strange, vague sense of great things close at hand – conflicts, insights, purposes, decisions.

A.B. Bruce says:

> In Mark we get nearest to the true human personality of Jesus in all its originality and power ... One who desires to see the Jesus of history truly should con well the pages of Mark first.

We have already noted that simplicity in Mark which the later gospel writers tend to improve and to correct and to tone down. This very simplicity adds to the vividness and the realism of Mark. A.B. Bruce speaks of

> the unreserved manner in which Mark presents the character and the person of Jesus and the disciples. He takes facts as they are, when one might be tempted not to state them at all, or to exhibit them in a subdued light. Luke writes from the view-point of reverential faith, Mark from that of loving vivid recollection.

In Mark we can hear Peter speaking from 'the indelible impressions made on his eye and ear'. The material in Mark comes from 'fondly cherished past memories', written down 'before the feeling of decorum had become controlling'. All this is to say that Mark, according to this view, is the nearest approach to a factual report and an eyewitness account of the earthly life of Jesus. It is true that there are certain features of Mark in which this quality of vivid realism comes out.

(i)   There is no gospel which gives what might be called such a flesh-and-blood life of Jesus as Mark does. Mark has no hesitation in attributing human feelings and emotions to Jesus. In his weariness Jesus falls asleep (4.38). In face of suffering he is moved with compassion (1.41), and the word (*splagchnistheis*) is the strongest emotional word in Greek and means that he was moved to the depths of his being. He can speak with sternness (1.43). He can know anger and indignation (3.5; 10.14). He can be surprised at the turn of events (6.6). He can feel a wave of love at the sight of an attractive personality (10.21). He can be distressed and in agony of mind (14.33f.). In the most natural way he can ask questions and seek for information (5.30; 8.5; 9.16). There are certain ultimate things which are not known to Jesus, but only to God (13.32).

In Mark, Jesus is a man among men, deeply involved in the human situation, completely identified with men, knowing the heights and the depths, the light and the dark of human experience.

(ii)   There are in Mark certain vivid touches which indeed look as if they were the product of the recollection of an eyewitness. In the storm at sea Jesus was asleep on a cushion in the stern of the boat (4.37). Only Mark speaks of the Gerasene demoniac shrieking and cutting himself with stones (5.5). When Mark tells the story of the feeding of the five thousand, he tells how the people were made to sit down in rows and groups on the grass, and the word he uses for the groups is the word for flower-beds (6.40). Only Mark tells the story of the blind man whose sight came slowly back, and who at first saw men like trees walking about (8.24). Only Mark tells us that, when Jesus saw the young ruler, he loved him as he looked at him (10.21). Only Mark in the stories of the children tells us that Jesus took them up in the crook of his arm (9.36; 10.16).

It is difficult to explain touches like that other than as eyewitness memories coming back unbidden to the mind and lodging in the narrative. These are exactly the things that Peter might well remember.

(iii)   Mark frequently gives the words of Jesus in Aramaic (3.17; 5.41; 7.11, 34; 14.36; 15.22, 34). This is not because Mark was writing for an Aramaic-speaking public, for he always gives the Greek explanation and translation. The natural explanation is that when

Peter was telling these stories he heard again in his memory the voice
of Jesus speak, and unconsciously slipped again into the language in
which the words were first spoken, the language which in any event
came first to his tongue.

(iv)   Mark has certain habits of speech which make for simplicity,
realism and vividness.

(a)   Mark is characteristically fond of diminutives. Most Greek
diminutives end in *-ion* in the singular and *-ia* in the plural. In Greek,
as in most languages, diminutives are affectionate, familiar and a little
colloquial. Jairus' daughter and the daughter of the Syro-Phoenician
woman are both in Mark *thugatrion* (5.23; 7.25), while in Matthew
and Luke the word is *thugatēr* (Matt. 9.18; 15.22; Luke 8.42; Luke
does not have the story of the daughter of the Syro-Phoenician
woman). As a Scot would put it, the girl is 'a wee lassie'. To Mark the
children are *paidia* (10.13), in Scots, 'wee bairnies'. In the miracle of
the loaves and the fishes, in Matthew the fish are *ichthues* (Matt.
15.36), but in Mark they are *icthudia* (8.7). The boat in which Jesus
sailed is not *ploion* (Matt. 8.23), the usual word for boat, but *ploiarion*
(3.9), in Scots again, 'a wee boatie'.

Mark's use of diminutives brings to the story a kind of homely
intimacy.

(b)   Mark has a number of words which are simply Latin words
transliterated into Greek. He speaks of a *kenturiōn* (15.39, 44) which
is the Latin for a centurion; of a *spekoulatōr* (6.27), which is the Latin
speculator; of the *kēnsos* (12.14), which is the Latin *census*. He uses the
strange Greek verb *phragelloun* in the sense of 'to scourge', which is a
formation from the Latin *flagellare* (15.15). No doubt Mark was
writing in Rome, and he is never afraid to say things in a way that his
readers would understand, however uncouth the Greek sounded.

(c)   Mark is abnormally fond of the historic present; he has no
fewer than 151 examples of it. In colloquial language as used by
simple people a story is often told in the present tense, and so Mark
keeps it.

(d)   Mark is very fond of the Greek word *euthus*, which means
'immediately'. It occurs in his gospel 41 times. In the first chapter
alone it occurs some 10 times (1.10, 12, 18, 20, 21, 23, 28, 29, 30, 42).
In Mark the events come almost tumbling over each other. It is
sometimes said of a story that it marches; but Mark's narrative tends
not so much to march as to gallop at breathless speed.

(e)   Mark is very fond of the word *palin*, 'again'; it occurs in his
gospel over 25 times, as when he says of Jesus: 'Again he entered the
synagogue' (3.1).

(f)   Mark tends to tell a story as a child tells it. He does not
subordinate his clauses to each other; he simply goes on adding
statement to statement joined by 'and . . . and . . . and'. In ch. 3 of his

gospel 29 out of the 35 verses begin with 'and'. Mark was much more concerned with intelligibility than elegance, and the result is that even the English translations of his gospel tend to 'improve' its style and so sometimes to obscure its characteristics.

Of Mark's simplicity and vividness there is no doubt. It is not difficult to believe that in Mark we have a simple and straightforward story of an eyewitness.

The second view of Mark is very different; it is that, so far from being an artless and a simple story, Mark is a highly theological document. This is unquestionably true. Mark is certainly not a biography of Jesus. There is nothing about Jesus' antecedents; there is nothing about his early life; there is no description of him; it is quite impossible to follow him from day to day and from month to month in Mark. There is no systematic and complete account of the teaching of Jesus. Jesus' teaching is summed up in one sentence: 'The kingdom of God is upon you; repent and believe the gospel' (Mark 1.14f.), and it is a summary of which almost every word requires a commentary.

The very first sentence of Mark is a highly theological statement: 'The beginning of the gospel of Jesus Christ the Son of God' (Mark 1.1). A glance at any of the new translations will show that it is doubtful if the phrase 'Son of God' is part of the original text; but even if it has to come out, there is a theological affirmation still left. 'Christ' is not really a proper name; it is the Greek for 'Messiah'. The gospel therefore begins with the highly theological statement that Jesus is the Messiah. This is not the way an artless story begins; this begins with the vastest and most far-reaching theological presuppositions and implications.

In any event, as we have already fully seen, the gospels are not literary works. They are not written as such and they are not meant to be such. As A.E.J. Rawlinson has it (p. 11): 'The New Testament, considered broadly, is the literature of a missionary movement – the mightiest missionary movement the world has ever known.' Therefore, always 'behind the literature stands the preaching'. The gospels are the substance of the apostolic preaching, and surely that is truest of all in regard to Mark. The gospels are preaching, and preaching is always preaching for a verdict in favour of Jesus Christ. The gospels are not simple narratives. They begin with a theological conviction about Jesus Christ which it is their intense desire that all men should accept and share. We shall therefore expect to find that the gospels are highly theological documents. Two writers have made very acute analyses of the motives behind Mark.

As Rawlinson says,[4] Goguel has found three motives behind the writing of Mark, or for that matter behind the writing of any gospel. There is the *theological* motive. The church was bound to ask and to

enquire what part the human and earthly life of Jesus Christ the Son
of God had played in the divine drama of redemption. The incarnation
and the significance of it must remain of primary importance for any
expression of the Christian faith. There is the motive of *human
interest*. No one who had known Jesus could ever forget him, and no
Christian could fail to wish to know more about what Jesus was like in
the days of his flesh. Such an interest is inevitable. There is the *moral*
motive. Life continually confronts the individual and the church with
the necessity of choice and of decision. Clearly the words and the
example of Jesus Christ are of essential importance in the solution of
all such problems. What Jesus had said and done and been must be
the guide to what the church and the Christian must say and do and
be. The individual and the Christian must follow the pattern of Christ,
and must have that pattern to follow. These aims will operate in any
gospel.

Allan Menzies in his commentary on Mark (pp. 14-18), finds three
other motives which will be operative in any gospel. First, there is the
aetiological motive. *Aitia* is the Greek for a *cause*, and the science or
the study of aetiology seeks to find the origins and the causes of the
rites, the practices and beliefs which have become standard and
accepted in any community. So a gospel will naturally try to explain
the origin of baptism, the origin of the Lord's Supper, the place that
the apostles hold in the Christian community. A gospel will wish to
show how the practices of the church began, and it will be specially
interested to trace them, if possible, back to Jesus himself. Second,
there is the *apologetic* motive. Any gospel will wish to defend the faith
of the church and the faith it expounds, especially if it is written and
produced at a time when that faith is under fire. So the gospels are
interested to show that Jesus was not a revolutionary, that the
Christians are neither lawless rebels nor haters of mankind, and that
the slanders of the Jews and of the heathen are alike untrue. A gospel
will wish to commend the faith which begat it to the age to which and
for which it is written. There is the *devotional* motive. When love is
threatening to grow cold, when hope is burning dim, and when faith is
losing its grip, there can be no better way to revive them than to go
back to the beginning and to see Jesus in action again. Any gospel will
either consciously or unconsciously have an aetiological, an
apologetic and a devotional aim.

J.H. Ropes in *The Synoptic Gospels* (pp. 12-30) has expounded the
view that Mark is fundamentally 'the discussion of a theological
problem in the form of a dramatic historical sketch'. The theological
problem is: *If Jesus was the Messiah, why did he die a criminal's
death upon a cross?* Mark's gospel is not a biography of Jesus. It may
even be right to say that it is not a chronological account of the life of
Jesus. But it is the dramatic grappling with the problem of the death of

the Messiah.

Before we look at any of them in detail, let us set down the three broad lines along which Mark sees the answer to this problem. Mark sees three reasons for the death of Jesus. First, Jesus died because of the enmity of the leaders of orthodox Judaism. Their enmity was not an embittered and small-minded thing; it was born of the genuine conviction that the teaching and example of Jesus were destructive of all true religion. Second, Jesus died quite simply because he chose to die. Third, Jesus died because his death was in accordance with the scriptures, and therefore in accordance with the purpose and the plan of God.

So Mark begins by bringing Jesus on to the scene full grown, and showing us his baptism by John and the descent of the Spirit on him. At once a dramatic element is introduced into the story. Now we, the readers, know that Jesus is the Messiah, but the other people involved in the actual story do not know this. The conjunction of our knowledge with their unawareness makes the story all the more dramatic. We then see Jesus becoming widely and publicly known. Then in chs. 2 and 3 there comes the first clash of conflict. Hints are dropped. The day will come when the bridegroom will be taken away (2.18-22). Judas is already branded as the traitor (3.19). In ch. 4 there comes a series of parables in which the lesson is that in spite of apparent failure and disaster the harvest is sure. In chs. 5 and 6 there follows a series of messianic acts. In ch. 8 there comes the hinge of the gospel, Peter's confession of Jesus as Messiah at Caesarea Philippi. Two things follow. Jesus begins privately to instruct his disciples about the events which lie ahead. Death and resurrection become the theme of his teaching to his disciples. And second, Jesus takes the offensive. He goes to Jerusalem, enters the city in a blaze of publicity, cleanses the temple, engages his opponents in public debate and defeats them, with all the time the undertone that there is nothing political or seditious in his activity. Then come his arrest and his trial, and it is made clear that his messianic claim is in fact the basis of the charge against him. And in the end there comes the cross – which is also the way to glory. The dramatic pattern is clear, though we have still to look at some of the detail of it.

(i) *The death of Jesus was due to the opposition of orthodox Judaism.* There is no kind of antisemitism in this statement. It is a statement which many today would deny. But that Mark's story says this is not open to question. Mark sees this hatred rising very early. After the healing in the synagogue of the man with the withered hand Mark says: 'The Pharisees went out, and immediately held counsel with the Herodians against him, how to destroy him' (3.1-6). Towards the very end Mark writes that Pilate was well aware that it was out of envy that the chief priests had delivered Jesus to him (15.10).

Since this enmity is there from almost the beginning, it is possible to see Mark as a series of controversies between Jesus and his Jewish critics. F.C. Grant in *The Gospels* (p. 81) identified no less than fifteen controversies on the following subjects:

i. Healing (2.1-12)
ii. Eating with sinners (2.13-17)
iii. Fasting (2.18-22)
iv. Keeping the sabbath (2.23-3.6)
v. The source of Jesus' 'power' (3.22-30)
vi. The external requirements of the law, the scribal traditions and the food regulations (7.1-13)
vii. 'Signs' (8.11f.)
viii. Elijah's coming (9.11-13)
ix. Remarriage and divorce (10.2-12)
x. Jesus' authority (11.27-33)
xi. Civil obedience, and the payment of tribute (12.13-17)
xii. The resurrection (12.18-27)
xiii. The interpretation of the law, i.e., the chief commandment (12.28-34)
xiv. The Messiah's descent from King David (12.35-37)
xv. Scribal ostentation and greed (12.38-40).

Within these controversies the rejection of Jesus works itself out.

The nature of these controversies and of this whole situation must be clearly understood. The opposition of the Jewish leaders did not come from unreasonable hatred and from embittered and selfish prejudice. Nothing could be further from the truth than that. What was at stake here was a conflict between two different ideals of religion, and it was a conflict which was already centuries old. In the days of Jesus Pharisaic religion expressed itself in an endless series of outward observances, in a rigid code of what could and could not be done on the sabbath day, of what was and was not clean, of what might and might not be eaten, of ritual cleansings and washings which a devout Jew must observe.

But the matter cannot be left there. The Jew saw the very essence of the demand of God in the saying of God: 'You shall be holy, for I the Lord your God am holy' (Lev. 19.2). Basically, the meaning of the word holy is *different*. The Jewish nation was under obligation to be different from other nations, and that difference had to be expressed in a rigid adherence to the demands and rules and regulations of the law. In essence this is not legalism; it is simply the determination to express the difference of the holy people in a special way of life. But it is also clear that this does run the very real and serious danger of turning religion into the rigid observance of outward rituals and practices.

But it is to be noted that the great prophets like Isaiah and Hosea and Amos said things every bit as hard as Jesus said about a religion which expressed itself in ceremony and ritual instead of in social justice and human compassion. In other words, the clash between Jesus and orthodox Judaism is the final culmination of the centuries-old tension between prophet and priest which runs all through Jewish religion. The consistent attempt had been to silence and to eliminate the prophets, and the very same thing happened to Jesus. The controversy is as old as Amos, and it is a controversy between two views of religion, the view of religion as expressed in ritual and law and the view of religion as expressed in social responsibility and in mercy.

The supreme tragedy of the situation was that the opponents of Jesus were men who loved God passionately, who saw with insistent clarity Israel's obligation to be different, who were prepared to accept a discipline and a sacrifice to make that difference visible, and who genuinely believed that Jesus was out to wreck all that they regarded as so precious. To say that envy was their motive in seeking to remove Jesus is a misreading of the situation. The crucifixion of Jesus was at least as much a tragedy as it was a crime, because it came from the clash between two views of religion, both sincerely and intensely held.

To say all this is not to say that the Jewish leaders were guilty of a unique sin of which other people are not guilty; it is simply to say that they did what men have done in every age and generation — they preferred their idea of religion to the idea of religion which Jesus Christ brought to men. The certainty is that any generation in any country, including our own, would crucify Christ.

(ii) But the death of Jesus was not due simply to the opposing forces; Jesus was not simply an heroic figure caught up in an inevitable situation. *The death of Jesus was also the result of his own self-chosen action.* In the human sense of things Jesus need not have gone to Jerusalem; and, if he did go, he did not need to enter the city in such a way that a glare of publicity surrounded him. He could either have stayed away in Galilee where he would have been quite safe; or, if he did come into Jerusalem, he could have slipped in unseen, deliberately lost in the Passover crowds. What he did, he did deliberately, open-eyed, and fully aware of the consequences.

It is clear from the story that he had to force himself to go. On the way to Jerusalem he walked alone, and there was that about him which made men hesitate to intrude into his private conflict (10.32). 'The Son of man,' he said, 'came not to serve but to be served, and to give his life a ransom for many' (10.45). From Mark's story it is quite clear that he knew what he was doing and chose to do it, in the certainty that the cross was the way to the completing of the work he had been given to do, even although, humanly speaking, he could well have avoided it.

(iii)   There is another way to put this. *Jesus chose to die because he knew that his death was an integral part of the will of God for him.* Into his language there comes the word *must*. 'The Son of man *must* suffer many things' (8.31; 9.31; 10.33). He is going the way appointed for him in the scriptures (14.21). His agonized prayer is that he may be enabled to accept the will of God (14.36). And this is not the *must* of the involvement in circumstances; it is the *must* of necessary obedience to the will of God.

In the pattern of Mark's gospel the Messiah died because of the opposition of the religious leaders of his day, because of his own conscious choice, and because it was for him the will of God.

There are certain large questions of aim in the gospel of Mark at which we still have to look, but before we turn to them we note certain subsidiary aims which F.C. Grant identifies (pp. 84f.). These are practical aims arising from the situation within the early church.

(i)   There was the question, Who are the real leaders of the church? Mark's answer is that the leadership of the church is put into the hands of the twelve by the choice of them by Jesus (3.13-19).

(ii)   There are signs that in the early church there was a certain problem in connection with those who were flesh-and-blood relations of Jesus. Their physical connection with Jesus might well be used as an argument for assigning to them a special place within the church. James, Jesus' brother, very early became the head and leader of the Jerusalem community. Eusebius in his *History* (3.32.6) quotes a report of Hegesippus that by the time of Domitian, towards the end of the first century, those who were of the Lord's family had acquired a leading position in every church, which is obviously an exaggeration, but which is none the less a significant statement. Mark deals with this in 3.20f., 31-35 and in 12.35-37, passages in which he makes it quite clear that physical connection with Jesus and participation in the lineage of David confer no special privileges on anyone, and that the true kin of Jesus are those who do his Father's will. Mark intends to show that in the church there is no aristocracy of leadership dependent on physical relationship to Jesus.

(iii)   There are signs that in the early church there were times when John the Baptist was given too high a place, and that there was even a sect which took him as their leader. This is specially clear in John (1.8, 15, 19-34) and in Acts (19.1-7). Mark makes it quite clear in his gospel that John is the great forerunner, but nothing more, that his greatness is not in himself but in the one to whom he pointed.

There are two modern views of Mark at which we must look, the first of which has had a very great influence on the interpretation of Mark's gospel, and the other of which is interesting, although it has not met with very general acceptance.

Vincent Taylor in his commentary (p. 121) has written:

The sheer humanity of the Markan portrait [of Jesus] catches the eye of the most careless reader; and yet it is but half seen, if it is not perceived that this Man of Sorrows is also a Being of supernatural origin and dignity, since he is the Son of God ... Mark has no theory of the incarnation, but his assumption appears to be that Jesus is *Deus absconditus*, the Hidden God ... Behind a fully human life Deity is concealed, but is visible for those who have eyes to see, in his personality, teaching and deeds.

Taken by itself, this is a view which no one would be likely to dispute.

> Veiled in flesh the Godhead see;
> Hail the Incarnate Deity!

It makes sense to see Jesus as the one in whom the mind and heart of God became flesh, and at the same time the one who was not recognized, except by those who had the eyes to see and the heart to understand.

But this theory was taken much further, and the idea behind it was radically changed in a book by Wrede published in 1901, and now at last translated as *The Messianic Secret*. Few books have been more influential for the study of the gospels in this century.

Let us then set down Wrede's view. If Mark is taken to be historically accurate, then the hinge of the gospel is unquestionably the passage in 8.27-30 with Peter's confession of Jesus as Messiah. Up to that point the messiahship has been known only to Jesus himself. After that point, the secret is shared with the disciples, but they are pledged to secrecy (8.30). It is only at the very end, at the trial before the Sanhedrin (14.61f.), that Jesus openly and publicly asserts his claim. The usual explanation of this is that the crowds were incurably obtuse, that the disciples had to be gradually and secretly educated into recognition, and that even after recognition secrecy had to be imposed, until the disciples could be led to see the true meaning of messiahship. This meaning Jesus expounded on the journey south when he repeatedly told them of his coming sufferings and death. Thus the disciples were slowly educated and slowly prepared.

To Wrede this whole picture is unintelligible and this view is untenable. He begins by analysing the material.

(i)   The demons recognize Jesus, but they are ordered to be silent (1.23-25, 34; 3.11f.; 5.6f.). The demons are themselves part of the supernatural world and therefore recognize the supernatural in Jesus, when they see it, even when it is hidden from others. But in spite of that, they are consistently told that they must not make their knowledge known.

(ii)   Those who are healed are repeatedly told not to tell anyone of what has been done for them (1.43-45; 5.43; 7.36; 8.26).

(iii)   Even after the disciples themselves have discovered the messiahship of Jesus they are forbidden to make it public and sternly enjoined to keep it secret (8.30; 9.9).

(iv)   More than once, both in Syro-Phoenicia and in Galilee, Jesus follows a policy of deliberate concealment of himself (7.24; 9.30).

(v)   On occasion the injunction to silence can even come from the crowd (10.48).

(vi)   Repeatedly Jesus is depicted as withdrawing to teach his disciples (4.10-13, 33f.; 7.17-23; 9.28f.), or as giving them esoteric teaching when they are by themselves apart from the crowd (9.30f., 38-41; 13.3-41).

As Wrede sees it, in Mark the messiahship of Jesus is a secret, and during his lifetime is meant to be a secret. It is known only to his nearest disciples, and it is only after the resurrection that the secrecy is to be removed. They are charged to tell no one what they have seen 'until the Son of man should have risen from the dead' (9.9). And to Wrede this picture simply does not make sense. He sees the following difficulties in it.

(i)   If the demoniacs were continually shouting that Jesus was Messiah, how could the messiahship be kept secret? They repeatedly spoke before they could be silenced.

(ii)   How could the miracles be kept secret? It was surely impossible to keep secret the fact that Jesus had worked these wonderful cures. And in any event it is plainly said that the people who were ordered to keep them secret repeatedly broke the command and in fact told everyone about what had been done for them (1.45; 7.36).

(iii)   If the secret of the coming death and resurrection was in fact told to the disciples in advance, as Mark says it was (8.31, 32; 9.31; 10.32-34; 9.9-13), why were they so shocked by his death, even to fleeing in terror (14.50), and why did the resurrection come to them as such a total surprise? According to Mark, they had been warned over and over again about what was going to happen, and yet, when it came, they were totally unprepared for it.

As Wrede sees it, Mark's explanation is that the disciples simply did not understand (4.13, 40f.; 6.50-52; 7.18; 8.16-21; 10.24; 14.37-41). They were suffering from a supernatural hardening of the heart such as came to Pharaoh (Ex. 9.12), and such as Isaiah saw in the people of his day (Isa. 6.9, 10).

To Wrede the whole situation is quite unhistorical and is the product not of facts but of theological construction. The Marcan position is that Jesus was Messiah from the beginning, but that during his days on earth this was a secret. He never revealed himself generally, but only to his disciples, and they were by divine action kept from seeing the truth. But although at the time they did not see the truth, the words and deeds remained in their memories, and the full significance was seen by them after the resurrection. Over against that, the demons are told not to speak and yet do speak; those who are healed are told to be silent, but the cures are seen and the story is told and Jesus' fame as a wonder-worker is not to be hid.

To Wrede the whole contradictory picture does not make sense. What, then, is the real situation?

Wrede's view involves the almost complete abandonment of Mark as an historical document. It is Wrede's view that no one ever thought of Jesus as Messiah until *after the resurrection*, and that Jesus never in fact made any claim to be the Messiah. It was only after the resurrection that Christian theology began to see in Jesus the Messiah. The idea of Jesus as Messiah is not the product of history, but the product of theology. Mark 9.9 with its injunction not to speak of these things until after the death of Jesus supplies the necessary hint and clue to the situation.

Once the discovery had been made that Jesus was Messiah, his messiahship was read back into his earthly life. But it had then to be explained why during his lifetime Jesus did not appear to men as he now does to Christian faith. So the whole motif of secrecy is introduced to explain this, and is complete invention on the part of Mark, or on the part of the sources from which he takes his picture. So then the steps may be set down like this. (i) Jesus never claimed to be Messiah. (ii) During his lifetime no one thought of him as Messiah. (iii) The resurrection gave men the idea that he was the Messiah. (iv) The problem then arises why he was not recognized as such during his life. (v) A whole series of passages and sayings are constructed to make it appear that during Jesus' lifetime the fact of his messiahship was kept deliberately secret, except from the disciples, who were supernaturally blinded, and who only saw the truth in the light of the resurrection. (vi) Therefore none of the secrecy passages come from the life and the lips of Jesus at all; they are the construction of the church. And thus there emerges the completely self-contradictory narrative of Mark.

What then are we to say about this position of Wrede? It is examined sympathetically in R.H. Lightfoot's *History and Interpretation in the Gospels* (pp. 16-22). It is examined with hostility in W. Sanday's *Life of Christ in Recent Research*.[5] Sanday declares that the whole theory is 'not only very wrong but distinctly wrong-headed', and says of it: 'I cannot easily conceive anything more utterly artificial and impossible.' It is examined critically but temperately in Rawlinson's commentary on Mark (pp. 258-62).

Certain things about Wrede's view may at once be allowed.

It is obviously true that Mark had a theory about the demons and the demoniacs and their relationship to Jesus and his messiahship. But this theory was common enough in the ancient world. In the ancient

world there was a line of thought which had a kind of reverential awe
for insanity. It was said that sometimes the gods took away a man's
own mind to give him the divine mind; and the recognition of Jesus by
the demons is fully in line with that idea.

We do not need to doubt that Mark exaggerated the 'supernatural
stupidity' of the disciples. Nor do we need to doubt that the disciples
were indeed changed men after the experience of Pentecost, and that
they inevitably did see new things in the life of Jesus when they looked
back upon it. Mark may well exaggerate it, but the closed mind did
become the open mind, and the blind eye did become the seeing eye,
and the ununderstanding heart did become the understanding heart.
Nor do we need to doubt that in setting down the story in the light of
the events the sayings of Jesus may well have been made more definite
and clear-cut than they originally were. Into the saying there would
inevitably be put the meaning and the content which it was not
originally realized that the saying possessed. It may well be that
teaching is ascribed to Jesus which arose out of the experience of the
church (e.g. 4.10-12, 34; 7.18-23).

But there are certain comments to be made on Wrede's contention
that the whole Marcan picture is unintelligible and untenable.

(i)   There is nothing either impossible or unnatural in the fact that
Jesus told people to say nothing about his miracles and that in fact
they did. It may well have been the case that Jesus wanted to avoid
being primarily regarded as a wonder-worker, and that he did not
want himself publicized as such. In that case he would try to avoid
publicity for his miracles. And it is equally quite intelligible that, even
when he asked them not to talk, people did talk. It may well be that
Mark has turned this into a kind of general rule, but at the back of it
there is a perfectly intelligible situation.

(ii)   In regard to the disciples, it is quite easy to think of a situation
in which they were so wedded to their own idea of what the Messiah
should be that their minds refused to grasp the idea of a Messiah
whose destiny was suffering and death. The very violence of Peter's
reaction to the idea (8.32f.) shows how utterly alien and intolerable the
idea was to the minds of the disciples. There is nothing in human
nature to preclude the supposition that to the end of the day they
refused to understand.

(iii)   There is nothing more natural than that Jesus should sternly
instruct his disciples not to declare his messiahship broadcast. It must
be remembered that in Palestine there was a background of violence,
with the fanatical Zealots following their career of assassination and
ever ready to explode in rebellion and revolution if they could find any
leader round whom to assemble. The claim that Jesus was Messiah
would unquestionably have provoked violence. John tells how Jesus
had to avoid a movement to make him king almost by force (John

6.15). It was quite inevitable that Jesus should wish to educate his disciples into understanding what messiahship meant, before he could allow them to proclaim it. To claim to be Messiah was to play with fire. Premature proclamation of a mistaken form of messiahship would have been nothing less than disastrous. Jesus' prohibition of the open declaration of his messiahship was not only not unnatural, it was in the political circumstances of Palestine inevitable.

(iv) Long ago Weiss pointed to the basic weakness in Wrede's theory. The resurrection could not have produced a theory that Jesus was Messiah; *it could only vindicate that claim if it had already been made.* The resurrection would not make Jesus' followers claim that he was Messiah; but it would appear to them to be the complete guarantee of a claim which had already been made, and which the disaster of the cross had rendered doubtful.

We have said nothing about the fact that the reminiscences of Peter lie behind Mark. That fact would make us slow to question the basic historicity of the gospel. Even without that fact, Wrede's contention must be rejected, on the grounds that it produces more problems than it solves, and that it is not the necessary explanation of the facts.

Before we leave Mark's gospel, there is one other theory of its origin at which we may briefly look. That is what is called *the calendrical theory of Mark*. In its full form it is a highly elaborate theory and we can do no more than state it in its barest outline. It was first fully propounded by Philip Carrington in his book *The Primitive Christian Calendar*. Archbishop Carrington provided a short summary and defence of it in an article on it in the *Expository Times* of January 1956.

It is a fascinating theory in many ways. Its originator states it summarily in the Foreword (p. xi) of his book:

> The Gospel (of Mark) consists of a series of lections for use in the Christian *ecclesia* on the successive Sundays of the year, and of a longer continuous lection which was used on the annual solemnity of the Pascha (Passover) at which the Passion was commemorated. The series of lections for the year are numbered 1 to 48 (or 49) in *Codex Vaticanus* (B), and the remaining lections (49-62) constitute the Passion lection.

We can at least see how Carrington arrived at this conclusion. He was investigating the seed parables in Mark with their accompanying element of mystery. The mystery is stated in Mark 4.11f.; 8.17f.; which is connected with the Feeding of the Five Thousand, and 8.31f.; which follows the confession at Caesarea Philippi. Now in the last case in Mark 8.32 there comes after the prophecy of the death and the resurrection the statement: 'And he said this plainly.' That which was mysterious has now been plainly stated. The inevitable conclusion is that the mystery is nothing other than the death and the resurrection of Jesus.

Now this mystery had already been connected with the seed parable of the sower (4.3-9). Carrington holds that it is Mark's consistent custom to arrange things in triads, in groups of three; and there are two other seed parables, the parable usually called the parable of the seed growing secretly (4.26-29), and the parable of the mustard seed (4.30-32). Now what is the point of these parables? They all talk of the seed falling into the ground (4.8), or being cast upon the earth (4.26), or being sown upon the earth (4.31). And they all speak of the rising of the seed, springing up and increasing (4.8), springing up and growing (4.27), growing up and becoming greater than all herbs (4.32). The motif is casting into the ground and rising again, exactly the death and resurrection motif. Carrington holds that these parables are death and resurrection parables.

Now this death and resurrection, secrecy and revelation motif has three stages, connected with three mountains (for the mountains cf. 3.13; 6.31, 46 [cf. John 6.3]; 9.2). At the first mountain in the parable of the sower the motif is told in a mystery; at the second, it is enacted in the feeding; at the third, it is openly declared (9.32). So we have this death and resurrection motif increasingly revealed.

The death and resurrection motif naturally takes the mind to the cycle of the year, spring, summer, autumn, winter. Is it then possible that the whole gospel is made to fit the cycle of the year? Carrington experiments in order to see. We can place the feeding of the five thousand at the Passover time (John 6.4). If we place the feeding of the five thousand of Passover time, then the feeding of the four thousand will fall exactly at Pentecost, the transfiguration at the midsummer festival, and the teaching at Jerusalem at the Feast of Tabernacles. Further, if we work back we will find that the gospel will begin exactly in mid-September precisely at the time of the Jewish New Year. So with no difficulty we get a scheme like this:

i.   New Year: the preaching of John
ii. Spring sowing: parable of the sower
iii. Passover: five thousand
iv. Pentecost: four thousand
v.   Midsummer: the transfiguration
vi. Tabernacles: entry into Jerusalem, as far as the discourse on the Mount of Olives.

Is there anything which supports this? We turn to the manuscripts. In regard to chapter headings we find the manuscripts in three classes. (i) *Sinaiticus, Washington* and *Chester Beatty* have no chapter divisions. (ii) The Greek manuscripts headed by *Alexandrinus* have what is clearly a standard system of chapter headings used in the

Greek church from the fourth century onwards. (iii) But there is one manuscript, *Vaticanus*, which has its own divisions. The ordinary division of Mark is into 48 or 49 sections which suits the lunar year, but *Vaticanus* has 62 sections which exactly fits the calendar year plus the Passion lection. The division of *Vaticanus* are exactly what we are looking for. The actual divisions which emerge are as follows:

1.1-8	14-29	11.1-11
9-11	30-44	12-19
12-13	45-52	20-12.12
14-20	53-56	12.13-40
21-28	7.1-16	41-44
29-34	17-23	13.1-31
38-45	24-30	
2.1-12	31-37	*The Passion*
13-14	8.1-9	*Lection*
15-17	10-12	13.32-14.2
18-22	13-21	14.3-9
23-28	22-26	10-16
3.1-6	27-9.1	17-26
7-13	9.2-27	27-42
14-35	28-29	43-52
4.1-9	30-32	53-72
10-34	33-50	15.1-15
35-5.1	10.1-16	16-23
5.2-20	17-45	24-37
21-43	46-52	38-41
6.1-6		42-47
7-13		16.1-8

Certainly this theory of Mark is of the greatest interest. If Mark was from the very beginning designed to be a series of lections for reading on each Sunday at the worship of the church and culminating in the passion narrative, then it has a double importance, for it becomes at one and the same time the personal witness of Peter and the public handbook of the church.

It must be said that Carrington's theory demands consideration, although it cannot be said that it has commanded anything like universal acceptance. And, although on a general statement of it, it appears to have a certain possibility, it is not so certain that it will stand up to detailed investigation.

There remains one problem connected with Mark. The reader of a modern translation of the New Testament is likely to be a little surprised when he reaches the end of Mark, for he is liable to find himself confronted by no fewer than three different endings; and most modern translations will indicate to him that the best authenticated ending of the gospel is at 16.8 with the words, 'For they were afraid', and that what follows is a later and not original addition. Let us then look at the three endings, and let us examine the facts about them.

(i) There is the ending in 16.9-20 which is printed in the Authorized Version. This is known as the *Longer Ending* or the *Canonical Ending*.

(ii) Following 16.8, there is an alternative ending printed in many of the modern translations; we give the translation of the New English Bible:

And they delivered these instructions briefly to Peter and his companions. Afterwards Jesus himself sent out by them from east to west the sacred and imperishable message of eternal salvation.

This is known as the *Shorter Ending*.

(iii) In the Moffatt translation the reader will find a fairly lengthy insertion between 16.14 and 16.15, which runs as follows:

But they excused themselves saying, 'This age of lawlessness and unbelief lies under the sway of Satan, who will not allow what lies under the unclean spirits to understand the truth and power of God; therefore,' they said to Christ, 'reveal your righteousness now.' Christ answered them, 'The term of years for Satan's power has now expired, but other terrors are at hand. I was delivered to death on behalf of sinners, that they might return to the truth and sin no more, that they might inherit the glory of righteousness which is spiritual and imperishable in heaven.'

This is known, after the manuscript which contains it, as the *Freer Logion*.

We will begin by simply setting down the facts. First, we set down the position in the various translations. It may first be noted that only Moffatt prints the Freer Logion. The Revised Standard Version in the text stops at 16.8, and then in the lower margin prints first the Longer Ending, then the Shorter Ending. The New English Bible has a note to the effect that the most ancient witnesses bring the gospel to an end at 16.8, and then in separate paragraphs in the text prints first the Shorter Ending, then the Longer Ending. Moffat prints 16.8 as if it broke off in the middle of a sentence – 'They said nothing to anyone for they were afraid of —'; he then prints in separate paragraphs the Longer Ending with the Freer Logion inserted between 16.14 and 16.15, and then the Shorter Ending. In a note he says that these two endings are 'a couple of second century attempts to complete the Gospel'. He goes on to say that apparently the Freer Logion, between verses 14 and 15, originally belonged to the gospel, but that it was excised from it at an early date, for some unknown reason. Weymouth and Kingsley Williams give only the Longer Ending, but enclose it in square brackets. The Twentieth Century New Testament gives first the Longer Ending, then the Shorter Ending, heading them respectively A Late Appendix and Another Appendix. E.J. Goodspeed gives first the Shorter Ending, then the Longer Ending, heading them respectively An Ancient Appendix and Another Ancient Appendix. The Amplified New Testament gives only the Longer Ending, and does not enclose it in brackets, but notes in a footnote that two of the most ancient authorities do not include this passage. Almost alone of the modern translators Kenneth Wuest prints the Longer Ending in the text, without comment and without alternative, as if it was unquestionably an original and integral part of the text.

Let us now go on to see what the evidence for these various endings is in the original manuscripts.

(i)   The two greatest and most important manuscripts of the New Testament, *Codex Sinaiticus*, and *Codex Vaticanus*, stop at 16.8, although in *Vaticanus* there is a blank space after 16.8, as if the scribe knew that there was other material which ought to go in there, but which he himself did not know or possess. In the oldest translations the gospel stops at the same place. It stops there in the oldest of the Syriac translations, in three of the oldest Armenian manuscripts, in the Ethiopian translation, and in one important Latin manuscript. Two of the greatest scholars of the early church, Jerome who produced the Vulgate, and Eusebius the church historian, both say that the most accurate manuscripts of Mark stop at 16.8.

In the ancient manuscripts the text is often divided into sections suitable for reading at the public worship of the church. Two of these manuscript divisions systems are known as the Ammonian and the Eusebian Sections; neither includes 16.9-20; it cannot therefore have been in the text from which they made their divisions.

On the other hand Irenaeus, who lived and wrote in the second half of the second century, uses 16.9-20 without comment as part of the gospel. About the middle of the second century Tatian produced the first harmony of the gospels, in which he wove together the material of the four gospels into one composite narrative, and he includes 16.9-20 in his harmony, called the *Diatessaron*. (The word means *through four*, and indicates that the harmony is a composite document based on the four gospels.) All this must mean that, though there were those in the early church who knew that 16.9-20 was not part of the original gospel, it had none the less established itself in the gospel by the middle of the second century.

(ii)   The Shorter Ending is in *Codex Regius* and *Codex Laurensis*, which are eighth-century manuscripts. It is also in certain Egyptian, Syriac and Ethiopian manuscripts, and in the one Latin manuscript which lacks the Longer Ending. With the single exception of the one Latin manuscript, the Shorter Ending is always given as an alternative ending *along with* the Longer Ending. In the Greek manuscripts it never exists alone but always as an alternative, and the word *telos*, which means *the end*, is in these manuscripts usually inserted after *both* 16.8 and 16.20. The Shorter Ending is therefore regarded as an *alternative ending*, not as the only ending.

(iii)   The Longer Ending is in all the later Greek manuscripts. It quite certainly did become the standard ending in later times, but it could not have become standard until after the fifth century or Jerome would have known it better.

(iv)   The Freer Logion, the addition between 16.14 and 16.15, and printed only by Moffatt, exists only in the Freer manuscript, discovered by C.L. Freer in 1906. It also must be early, for Jerome knew it and quotes at least part of it.

This then is the evidence, but there remains an interesting fact to add to it. In 1891 F.C. Conybeare discovered an Armenian manuscript in Etchmiadzin. In it there is a note that Mark 16.9-20 is the work of Ariston the Presbyter. Now we have already seen (p. 119 above) that when Papias tells of the sources which he had for discovering facts about the gospels and the life of Jesus one of these sources is Aristion. Ariston and Aristion are interchangeable names. This means that if the Aristion of Papias and the Ariston of the Etchmiadzin manuscript are the same person, 16.9-20 may not go back to Mark and Peter, but it does go back to the circle of the original disciples, and is therefore very early. But this, although possible, cannot be regarded as certain.

What then are our conclusions to be?

(i)   16.9-20 is almost certainly not a part of the original gospel of Mark. This must mean that at one time there must have existed only one copy of Mark which had lost its last section. This is perfectly possible, for Mark was so neglected after the emergence of Matthew, that right down to the fourth century no commentary on Mark exists. It is also remotely possible that what happened was that Mark died before he was able to complete his gospel, or was otherwise prevented from finishing it.

(ii)   It is obvious that Mark 16.8 is an impossibly abrupt ending. It is therefore likely that when the four gospels were collected and edited, the missing material was filled in and became the Longer Ending, while the Shorter Ending is another attempt to 'finish' the gospel. There is a possibility that the Longer Ending was the work of Aristion who was a disciple of Jesus, but this is only a possibility and far from a certainty.

(iii)   The last – and the most important – question is, In view of all this can Mark 16.9-20 be regarded as scripture? There are two answers to that. First, there is what we might call the standard Roman Catholic answer, as given by Wikenhauser in his *New Testament*

Introduction. He writes (pp. 172f.):

> Even if the longer ending of Mark is not by Mark himself, it is an integral
> part of Holy Scripture (hence the name 'canonical ending' of Mark, as
> opposed to the shorter ending), and it contains dependable ancient
> tradition.

In other words, Mark 16.9-20 is to be regarded as fully scripture.
Second, there is the view of which R.A. Cole in the Tyndale
Commentary (pp. 258f.) is an able representative. He likens his part of
Mark to the story of the woman taken in adultery in John 8.1-11. It is
undoubtedly early and quite likely genuine. Its content is undoubtedly
evangelical and it belongs to the gospel tradition. It might well be an
'official' ending subjoined to a 'second edition' of Mark. 'However,'
Cole goes on, 'it would be unwise to build any theological position
upon these verses alone; and this no responsible Christian group has
done.' This is a sane verdict. We can accept the position that these
verses are not part of the original gospel of Mark but that they are
part of the early tradition. We shall therefore not reject them, but we
shall remember that they are secondary, and not primary, in their
evidence.

The Collect for St Mark's Day

O Almighty God, who has instructed thy Holy Church with the heavenly
doctrine of the evangelist Saint Mark; give us grace that being not like
children carried away with every blast of vain doctrine, we may be
established in the truth of thy holy Gospel; through Jesus Christ our Lord.
Amen.

8

THE GOSPEL OF MATTHEW

When we turn to Matthew, we turn to the book which may well be called the most important single document of the Christian faith, for in it we have the fullest and the most systematic account of the life and the teaching of Jesus. And yet to turn to Matthew is to turn to a book beset by problems to which there is no certain answer.

The early traditions about Matthew are clear, consistent and unanimous. Three things are consistently said about this gospel.

i.   It is said to be the earliest of the gospels.
ii.   It is said to be the work of the apostle Matthew.
iii.   It is said originally to have been written in the Hebrew tongue.

Since this is a matter of such importance, we shall set down the evidence in full.

Irenaeus in his book *Against Heresies* (3.1.1) writes: 'Matthew also published a book of the gospel among the Hebrews, in their own dialect, while Peter and Paul were preaching the gospel in Rome and founding the church.'

Eusebius in his *History* (6.14.5) quotes Clement of Alexandria as saying that the gospels which contain the genealogies of Jesus, that is, Matthew and Luke, were written first.

He also (6.25.4) quotes Origen as saying that he has learned that 'the first gospel was written by Matthew, who was once a tax-collector, but who was afterwards an apostle of Jesus Christ, and it was prepared for the converts from Judaism, and published in the Hebrew language'.

In his own account of the origins of the gospels (3.24.5) Eusebius writes: 'Matthew, who preached earlier to the Hebrews, committed his gospel to writing in his native tongue, and so compensated by his writing for the loss of his presence.'

Augustine in his work *On the Agreement of the Evangelists* (1.2.4) writes: 'Of these four it is certain that only Matthew is regarded as having written in the Hebrew language, while the others wrote in Greek.' And he says that Mark 'followed closely in his footsteps, as his imitator and epitomizer'.

The Monarchian Prologues say in the Argument to Matthew's Gospel: 'Just as Matthew from Judaea is placed first in order, so he also wrote his gospel first in Judaea.'

Both Eusebius in his *History* (5.10.3) and Jerome in his book *On Famous Men* (36) pass down a story about Pantaenus. He was said to have gone to India, 'where, the story goes, he found the gospel according to Matthew, which had arrived there before him, among certain people who had learned about Jesus'. He heard a story that 'Bartholomew had preached to them, and that he had left the writing of Matthew in Hebrew letters, and that it existed there when Pantaenus was there'.

Jerome has two further references to Matthew's gospel. The first is in the preface to his commentary: 'Matthew, the tax-collector, with the cognomen Levi, is the first of all to have published a gospel in Judaea in the Hebrew language. It was specially produced for the sake of those Jews who had believed in Jesus and who were serving the truth of the gospel at a time when the shadow of the law had by no means disappeared'. In *On Famous Men* (3) he writes:

> Matthew who is also called Levi, and who was changed from a tax-collector into an apostle, was the first in Judaea to write a gospel of Christ in Hebrew letters for those of the circumcision who believed. But who afterwards translated it into Greek is unknown.

Jerome says that he had actually seen a copy of this gospel in the library at Caesarea.

As we have said, and as we have now seen, the tradition of the early church is clear, consistent and unanimous. It was believed that Matthew wrote the first gospel, that he wrote it first of all the gospels and that it was originally written in Hebrew.

On the face of it Matthew *must* have had something to do with the production of the gospel which bears his name. It is certainly true that in the ancient world books did tend to get themselves connected with famous names. No one felt that there was anything wrong in giving a book the protection of a famous name. It was in fact a compliment and act of scholarly devotion for a disciple to write a book in his master's name. Between the Testaments there were books issued under the names of Moses, Isaiah, Baruch, Enoch. It was in fact the normal thing at that period for books to be in the technical term pseudonymous, that is to say, attributed to a writer who did not actually write them. There is a kind of humility in this way of doing things. The later writer did not feel that his name meant anything, and so he wrote in the name of the intellectual and spiritual giants of the past.

Further, it was common for writings of a particular kind to get themselves attached to the acknowledged master of that kind of literature. So dialogues get themselves attached to the names of Lucian and Plato, the masters of the dialogue, and essays get themselves attached to the name of Plutarch, the great essayist. This was normal, accepted practice with which no one thought there was anything wrong. In the New Testament there is one book like that, the letter to the Hebrews. As Origen said, God only knows who the author of that letter was.[1] But it was clearly much too great a letter to be lost and abandoned. It was therefore covered with the mantle of Paul, the great letter-writer, and no one saw anything wrong in this.

But the whole point is that Matthew was not one of the great figures of the church. Nothing is known of him; he has no history. He plays a very small part in the gospel story, and, apart from legend, there is nothing about him in the history of the early church. He is not in the same class as Peter or John or Paul or even Barnabas. He is not one of the princes of the early church, either in action or in writing. In other words, if Matthew did not actually have something to do with the writing of the first gospel, it is very difficult, it is even impossible, to see how it got itself attached to his name. He had, so to speak, no claim to it, if he did not at least share in its writing. Why, then, not simply accept the tradition of the early church as it stands? Why question it?

(i) We have seen that it is one of the foundation pillars of the criticism of the gospels that Mark is the earliest gospel. True, there are still those who question this, and we shall later look at their work; but it can be said to be the standard view of the gospels that Mark is the earliest. It is difficult to accept the view that Matthew was the first to write.

(ii) We have seen that Matthew and Luke both use Mark as their framework, or at least as one of their principal sources. Now this is quite intelligible in the case of Luke; but it is not intelligible in the case of Matthew. It is hard to see how an apostle who was an actual eye-witness of the events narrated should base his work on the writings of one who was not an eyewitness. If Matthew was an eyewitness and an original member of the twelve, it is difficult to see why he should use Mark as a basic document, and not base his gospel on his own memories and experiences.

(iii) There may be some possibility of argument in regard to these first two claims, but in regard to the third there seems to be none. Whatever else is true or not true, Matthew's gospel as it stands was not originally written in Hebrew. For one thing, Matthew uses 51 per cent of Mark's actual words; it is not the case of a man writing in Hebrew; it is the case of a man using Mark's Greek. For another thing, when Matthew quotes the Old Testament, as he so often does, it is the Greek Old Testament he quotes usually, not the Hebrew Old Testament. Matthew as it stands is not a translation from Hebrew; it was written in Greek.

Here then is our problem. It is almost impossible totally to reject the early tradition of the connection of Matthew with the first gospel, and it is equally impossible totally to accept it as it stands. We must then try to find a connection of Matthew with the first gospel which will cover both the tradition and the facts. Three suggestions have been made.

(i) We have already seen (p. 120 above) that Papias gives us certain information about Mark and its connection with Peter. In the some passage Papias has also given us some information (preserved by Eusebius in his *History*, 3.39. 16) about Matthew:

> Matthew wrote the *Logia* in the Hebrew language, and everyone interpreted them as he was able.

Logia, which is connected with *logos*, which means 'a word', is usually translated 'oracles'. What then are these *Logia*, and what relation do they have to the gospel which bears Matthew's name?

When we were discussing the build-up of the gospels, we saw that Matthew and Luke, apart from the material which they drew from Mark, have about 200 verses in common. These verses contain the teaching of Jesus. To these verses the symbol Q is attached. Q, then, is the symbol for a now lost primitive handbook of the teaching of Jesus. It is argued that such a book might well be called *The Oracles of Jesus*. It is also argued that it is highly probable that such a book would first exist in Aramaic and would be translated into Greek as and when necessity arose. It is then suggested that Matthew was the compiler of this book, this handbook of the teaching of Jesus called Q. And since Q is a very important part of the gospel of Matthew, since it is the independent contribution of that gospel to our knowledge of Jesus, and since Matthew was the compiler of Q, his name naturally came to be attached to the whole gospel.

There is a simple, intelligible and attractive theory. It cannot be totally written off; but, as we shall come to see after we have looked at the next suggestion, there are difficulties in it.

(ii) We have only to glance through Matthew's gospel to see that one of his main interests is the fulfilment of prophecy. His characteristic phrase is: 'This happened to fulfil what the Lord spoke through the prophet . . .' (1.22; 2.15, 23; 4.14; 8.17; 12.17; 13.35; 21.4; 26.56). To a Jew the prophets were the great foretellers of the future; and therefore to a Jew the unanswerable proof that Jesus was truly the Messiah would be the demonstration that in him and in his life all the messianic prophecies were fulfilled. It would therefore be the case that one of the most valuable books that the early church could possess would be a collection of Old Testament prophecies with the corresponding events in Jesus' earthly life in which they were fulfilled. There is evidence that the church did possess such a book. It has been called the *Testimonia*, the collection of Old Testament witnesses to Jesus.

In his valuable book *According to the Scriptures* (pp. 107f.) C.H. Dodd has identified four groups of passages which he subdivides into primary and secondary, as follows:

Primary sources	*Subordinate or supplementary sources*
i. Joel 2-3	Mal. 3.1-6
Zech. 9-14	Dan. 12
Dan. 7	
ii. Hosea	Isa. 29.9-14
Isa. 6.1-9.7; 11.1-10; 28.16; 40.1-11	Jer. 7.1-15
	Hab. 1-2
Jer. 31.10-34	
iii. Isa. 42.1-44.5; 49.1-13; 50.4-11; 52.13-53.12; 61	Isa. 58.6-10
Pss. 69; 22; 31; 38; 88; 34; 118; 41; 42-43; 80	
iv. Pss. 8; 110; 2	Pss. 132; 16
Gen. 12.3; 22.18	II Sam. 7. 13f.
Deut. 18.15, 19	Isa. 55.3
	Amos 9.11f.

It is suggested that this invaluable book of *Testimonia* must have been compiled by someone, and that that someone may well have been Matthew. It is then suggested that this book is so integral to the first gospel, and that the gospel is so written round about it, that it came to be known as Matthew's gospel, as if the whole gospel was a kind of expanded commentary on the *Testimonia*.

Again this is a very attractive theory, but it suffers from the same difficulty as the first theory, and at that difficulty we must now look, before we consider the third suggestion.

The difficulty with these two suggestions lies in the meaning which they both attach to the word *Logia*. They both assume that *Logia* must mean 'words', since it is so closely connected with *logos* which does mean a word. So it is assumed that, when Papias says that Matthew 'wrote the *Logia* in the Hebrew language', he must be referring to a book of the *sayings* of Jesus or the *sayings* of the prophets, either to the material in Q or in the *Testimonia*. But J.B. Lightfoot[2] examined the use of the word *Logia*, and it cannot be held that *Logia* can only describe a book of sayings.

Ephraem of Antioch said that he recognized as scripture the Old Testament, the *Logia*, the oracles, of the Lord, and the preaching of the apostles. Quite clearly, by the *Logia*, the oracles, of the Lord, he means the gospels, which contain far more than sayings of Jesus. Paul says that one of the great privileges of the Jews is that they possess the oracles of God (Rom. 3.2), and from the context it is quite clear that he means the Old Testament scriptures in general, not just the sayings of the prophets, but the books of history as well. Clement of Rome in his *First Epistle* (53) writes to the church at Corinth: 'You know well the sacred scriptures and have studied the oracles of God,' and he clearly means the whole Old Testament. Irenaeus (*Against Heresies*, 1.8.1) speaks of the heretics distorting the oracles of God, and then goes on to deal with what they say about the story of Jairus' daughter. Amongst the *Logia,* the oracles, he clearly includes events and deeds as well as sayings.

We cannot therefore assume that Matthew's *Logia* was a handbook of the teaching of Jesus, or of the sayings of the prophets. It is much more likely to mean something like the gospels, which dealt with deeds and events as well as words.

(iii)   We must therefore look at the third suggestion which was made by E.J. Goodspeed in his *Introduction* (pp. 174f.).

The New Testament material quite certainly began by being oral tradition. The common words both for transmitting it and for receiving it are technical words for the receiving and the handing on of such material. Paul introduces his account of the last supper by saying: 'I received from the Lord what I also delivered to you' (I Cor. 11.23). He begins his account of the evidence for the resurrection by saying: 'I delivered to you as of first importance what I also received' (I Cor. 15.3). The word for 'receiving' is *paralambanein*, and the word for 'delivering' is *paradidonai*. These are the two technical words for giving and receiving oral tradition, and these sayings in the letter to the Corinthians make it quite clear that in the early church as soon as AD 55 there existed a fixed and standard oral tradition which Paul had received and was now passing on.

When Luke (1.1-4) speaks about Theophilus being 'informed' about the gospel story, he used the word *katēchein*, which means 'to din into someone's ears', and which is the word from which 'catechumen' comes. Here again is the proof that in the beginning the gospel material was orally transmitted.

The same fact emerges when we see how the writers of the early church quote and use scripture. It is their habit to begin their quotations: 'Remember the *words* of the Lord Jesus', not, 'Remember what is written in the records'.

In point of fact this is precisely what we would have expected in a Jewish community. Jewish teachers did not approve of writing things down. 'Commit nothing to writing,' the rabbis said. It is told that Gamaliel I (about AD 50) once came on a written targum or translation of Job and immediately ordered it to be destroyed. This is the very opposite of the Greek point of view. A Greek teacher once said: 'If you have found a saying of one of the great philosophers and have nothing to write it on, write it on your garments.' The Greek instinctively wrote; the Jew instinctively did not write.

But although the Jew did not write, he transmitted his oral tradition with the greatest accuracy. The Jewish oral law was never written down until the third century AD; but the memory of a good student was 'like a well-plastered cistern which never loses a drop', and if every word of the oral law was lost, any twelve rabbis, so it was claimed, could have supplied it all from memory.

Oral tradition does more than simply grow; it needs someone to mould it into its fixed stereotyped forms, as the great rabbis did with the Jewish tradition. It is Goodspeed's suggestion that it was mainly by Matthew's teaching work that the oral tradition was finally stereotyped into the form in which it was passed down. Perhaps in Jerusalem, perhaps in Antioch, it may be that Matthew put the gospel material into fixed teaching form, while it was still in Aramaic and before it had been translated into Greek – and, if he did that, there is no difficulty in seeing how a fixed gospel came to bear his name.

It is not possible to be certain just what Matthew's share in the writing of the gospel which bears his name was; but, whatever it was, we can be sure that he had some share, or it is impossible to see how he ever became so unanimously connected with it.

It will be well at this point to collect what we know about Matthew. In each of the three gospels the story of his call is told, and in each case the story is slightly different.

> And as Jesus passed on, he saw Levi the son of Alphaeus sitting at the tax office, and he said to him, 'Follow me.' And he rose and followed him (Mark 2.14).

> As Jesus passed on from there, he saw a man called Matthew sitting at the tax office; and he said to him, 'Follow me.' And he rose and followed him (Matt. 9.9).

> After this Jesus went out, and saw a tax-collector named Levi, sitting at the tax office; and he said to him, 'Follow me.' And he left everything, and rose and followed him (Luke 5.27f.).

In two of the accounts the name is Levi and in the third it is Matthew. It was perfectly normal for a Jew to have two names in those days, one the Hebrew or Aramaic name by which he was known at home and by his friends, the other a Greek name by which he was known at business and in the outside world. Often the two names had the same meaning. So Cephas is the Hebrew and Peter is the Greek for a rock, and Thomas is the Hebrew and Didymus is the Greek for a twin. But in this case the difficulty is that both names are Hebrew. There are two possibilities. It is possible that Jesus gave Matthew a new name, as he did when he called Simon by the new name Peter (Mark 3.16; Luke 6.14; John 1.42). In that case the name Matthew would not be inappropriate for Matthew means *the gift of God*. It is possible that Matthew was Matthew ben Levi, Matthew the son of Levi, and that he was a Levite. If this is so, it would explain the characteristically Jewish slant of his gospel.

Mark calls him the son of Alphaeus. In the list of the twelve there is a James the son of Alphaeus (Mark 3.18; RSV correctly so; AV *brother* of Alphaeus is much less likely). If this is so, then Matthew and James were brothers. This opens a fascinating possibility. At the end of the apostolic lists there come as a group James the son of Alphaeus, Thaddaeus, Simon the Zealot, and Judas Iscariot (Matt. 10.3f.; Mark 3.18f.; Luke 6.15f.; in Luke, Judas the son of James for Thaddaeus). What is the connection which makes these four into a group? Simon was a Zealot; that is, the most fanatical kind of nationalist, sworn to violence against the Romans and to the assassination of any Jew who collaborated with the Romans. It is likely that Judas Iscariot belonged to the same party, for the name Iscariot may well be connected with the name *sikarios* or *sicarius*, a dagger-bearer, which was the name by which the most violent of these violent nationalists were called. This makes it at least possible that the connecting link between these four disciples is that they were all ex-Zealots, all former violent Jewish nationalists, pledged to the murder and assassination of the Romans and of any of their countrymen suspected of collaboration with the Romans. Now Matthew was a tax-collector in the service of Herod, who was a Roman vassal king, and Matthew was therefore a collaborator. If any of these four nationalists had met Matthew before they met Jesus, they would have plunged a dagger into him with the greatest pleasure. Even James would willingly have murdered his brother. We may well have here an extraordinarily vivid instance of the power of Jesus Christ to reconcile men to each other as well as to God. In the circle of Jesus the old enmities were forgotten.

The salient fact about Matthew was that he was a tax-collector. The word 'publican' is now misleading. Tax-collectors were called *publicani* because they dealt with public money. In the ancient world tax-collectors were bitterly hated. Stapfer calls them 'a class of despised pariahs'. When Cicero is talking about the trades and professions in which no gentleman will engage, he includes that of the tax-collector and usurer. In his vision of the underworld Lucian sees a long line of men destined for special torment and judgment – 'adulterers, procurers, tax-collectors, toadies, informers . . . millionaires and money-lenders, pale, pot-bellied, gouty'.[3] The Jews classed together 'murderers, robbers, and tax-gatherers'. A tax-collector could not be a witness in a law case, and was even debarred from the synagogue and its services. That is why the tax-collector in the parable had to stand 'far off' (Luke 18.13).

The hatred of the tax-collector stemmed from two causes. First, there was the basic fact that the tax-collector had taken employment with his country's masters, and, therefore, with his country's enemies. The tax-collector, at least to the nationalist, was a quisling and a traitor. Second, the Roman method of collecting taxes made the matter very much worse. The Roman government did not collect its own taxes. It farmed out the right to collect taxes within a certain area, usually to tax-collecting companies. They in turn farmed out the right to collect taxes in smaller areas to individual tax-collectors. The real seriousness of this situation lay in the fact that the tax-collector could retain for himself anything he managed to extract over and above the agreed total for the area. Since there was no way of issuing mass announcements, as can now be done through the newspapers or radio, the provincials did not ever know just what they ought to be paying, and therefore the door to extortion was wide open.

There were two kinds of taxes. There were stated taxes in which the room for extortion was much more limited, for in this case the people did know what they had to pay. There was a ground-tax, which consisted of one-tenth of a man's grain crop, and one-fifth of his crop of wine, fruit, and oil. Part of this could be commuted for a cash payment, but the greater part of it went to Rome to be doled out there to the idle population, for these were the days when it was beneath the dignity of a Roman citizen to work. There was a poll tax, which everyone had to pay, men between the ages of fourteen and sixty-five, women between the ages of twelve and sixty-five. It was probably a *denarius* – the basic silver coin, which used to be equated with our shilling – per year. There was income tax which worked out at one per cent of a man's income per year. All this must be evaluated in the light of the fact that a working man's wage was a *denarius* a day, and even allowing for the difference in purchasing power, one shilling a day was little on which to live and support a family.

These taxes were burdensome but were not necessarily unjust, and there was little opportunity in them for extortion. The other taxes were in the nature of customs duties. There was a tax on everything imported and exported. There was a tax to use a main road, a market, a harbour, to enter a walled town. There was a tax on animals, on carts, on wheels, on axles. It was here that there was infinite scope for extortion, for it was here that the people did not know what they had to pay, and the tax-collector could extract as much as he could get out of them.

It was in this second kind of tax-collecting that Matthew was engaged. His work was in Galilee on the great road that led from

Damascus in Syria to Egypt. His office was on the road that led out of Galilee into Samaria, and would be very busy. It is true that in Galilee he was not directly in the service of the Romans. He was employed by Herod Antipas, king of Galilee, but Herod was no more than a Roman vassal, and to all intents and purposes Matthew was a Roman civil servant. Matthew was one of these hated officials, cashing in on the misfortunes of his own countrymen. No wonder the tax-collectors were classed with Gentiles, sinners and prostitutes (Matt. 21.31f.; 18.17; 10f.; 11.19; Mark 2.15f.; Luke 5.30; 7.34; 15.1).

Luke's version of what happened after Matthew's call is very significant. Matthew invited Jesus to a meal and a reception in his house, and there was no one but tax-collectors and sinners there (Luke 5.29-32). These were the only people with whom Matthew was friendly, and it was with them that he wished to share his new found discovery. There is both pathos and courage here, the pathos of the man who is an outcast from respectable society, and the courage of the man who will witness to the change in his life amongst those who know him best.

There was doubtless one special thing that Matthew did bring with him. To the rest of the disciples, to the men who worked on the fishing-boats, a pen and a book would be strange and unfamiliar things; but Matthew's work would make him familiar with the act of writing and reading and recording. He left all, but he brought with him a talent that one day in some way he would use for his new Master.

The legends which attached themselves to the name of Matthew are bizarre and fantastic, and they are complicated by the fact that he tends to be confused with the Matthias of Acts 1.26. They cannot be history, but they may be briefly outlined.

Matthew, so Eusebius tells us in his *History* (3.24.5), preached first in Judaea to the Jews and it was for them that he wrote his gospel. There was a legend that the disciples met and, so to speak, partitioned the world amongst themselves for the purposes of missionary work. According to this legend, which is recorded by Socrates in his *Ecclesiastical History* (1.19), Matthew went to Ethiopia. Ambrose connects him with Persia; Paulinus of Nola with Parthia; Isidore with Macedonia. Clement would imply that Matthew died a natural death, and hands down the odd bit of tradition that Matthew was a vegetarian and 'ate seeds, nuts and vegetables, without flesh'.[4] In the Talmud there is a tradition that he was condemned to death by the Jewish Sanhedrin.

The most famous work on Matthew is the apocryphal *Acts of Andrew and Matthew*, famous because it was put into Anglo-Saxon verse, perhaps by Cynewulf. It is a fantastic story. Matthew, it says, went to the land of the Anthropophagi, the man-eaters, 'who ate no bread and drank no wine, but ate the flesh and drank the blood of men'. It was the custom of the Anthropophagi to put out the eyes of strangers, give them a drug which took their senses away, and keep them in prison for thirty days before eating them. This they did to Matthew, but the drug was powerless to affect him, and the Lord, unknown to the gaolers, gave him back his sight. For twenty-seven days Matthew lay in prison.

Word came to Andrew of Matthew's plight. After a miraculous voyage in a ship manned by angels and piloted by Jesus, all unbeknown to him, Andrew arrived in the land where Matthew was. At Andrew's prayer the seven guards fell dead, and at the sign of the cross the prison doors opened. So Matthew escaped. Later he returned to the land of the Anthropophagi to convert and civilize them. The king was jealous of the mighty deeds he did. He took him and bound him, rolled him in papyrus soaked in dolphin's oil, poured brimstone, asphalt and pitch on him, heaped up tow and wood, and surrounded him with the images of the country's twelve gods and proceeded to burn him. But the fire turned to dew, and the flames melted the images of the gods, but left Matthew unharmed. Finally, the fire changed to a dragon which pursued the king and kept him in his palace. Then Matthew rebuked the fire, and prayed, and so died. In the end the king was converted and became a priest, 'and with two angels Matthew departed to heaven'.

This is fantasy and fiction, but somewhere at the back of it there is the basic truth that Matthew had something to do with the writing of a gospel, and preached and witnessed unto death for Jesus Christ. Let us now turn directly to the gospel which bears his name.

In the order of the gospels Matthew's gospel comes first, and that is a place which it deserved to hold. Renan called Matthew's gospel the most important book ever written.[5] E.F. Scott says in *The Literature of the New Testament* (p. 65) that it may not be the oldest or the most beautiful of the gospels, but it is by far the most important. It is 'the authoritative account of the life of Jesus', 'the fundamental document of the Christian religion', 'the standard presentation of the faith'. J.H. Ropes in *The Synoptic Gospels* (p. 33) says that in all ages Matthew's gospel is 'the favourite and most constantly read gospel'. Apart from any such subjective judgments, it is certainly true, as Wikenhauser points out in his *Introduction* (p. 198), that in and from the time of Irenaeus, in the second half of the first century, both the early church and Christian literature in general were more deeply influenced by the gospel of Matthew than by any other book.

Why should this gospel occupy this unique place in the written record of Christianity? It does not possess the vivid realism of Mark, or the sheer moving beauty of Luke, or the lofty mysticism of John, and yet it rightly occupies this foremost place. Why? To answer that question we must look at the characteristics of this gospel. out- standing

(i)   Its first characteristic is also its main claim to pre-eminence. As E.F. Scott says (p. 65), we must begin with the simple fact that Matthew's gospel is 'the most comprehensive of the gospels'. It is, as Filson says in the introduction to his commentary (pp. 2f.), the 'completest' gospel. It shows us Jesus through his earthly life – his birth, his days in Palestine, his death, his resurrection, his commission to his disciples. And in addition to that it has 'a remarkably comprehensive account of the chief themes of his teaching'.

J.H. Ropes (p. 45) has an interesting comment to make. Most lives of Jesus are laid out in the same pattern. They give in alternate sections an account of some part of the life of Jesus, and an account of some part of the teaching of Jesus. They alternate life and teaching. This is exactly what Matthew does, and Ropes says:

> Of the many books, chiefly quite modern, which treat in alternating chapters of the life of Christ, and of the biblical theology of the synoptic gospels, Matthew is the earliest, and in the series this earliest one stands without a later rival.

So deliberately comprehensive is Matthew's gospel that it might be called the *representative gospel*. It seems so determined to represent all points of view of the Christian teaching that it can at times seem inconsistent and self-contradictory. For instance, there are times when Matthew seems to be narrowly nationalistic and to confine salvation to the Jews (10.5-8), and there are times when it is the most universalistic of all the gospels, thinking in terms of a world for Christ (28.19). It seems that Matthew made a deliberate attempt to include all points of view, as if to show that the church is big enough and catholic enough to include them all.

Matthew is as comprehensive in his aim as he is in his material. R.V.G. Tasker in his commentary (pp. 15-19) finds three aims in Matthew (*a*) Matthew is defending the Christian faith against the attacks of Jewish opponents. (*b*) Matthew is instructing converts from paganism in the ethical implications of the religion which they have accepted. (*c*) Matthew is seeking to help those inside the church to live a disciplined life of fellowship, based on the record of the deeds and words of their Lord and Master, and that record is in an orderly and systematic form which they could read week by week at the services of the church and the meetings of its congregation. To put it briefly, at one and the same time, Matthew aims to be an apology for the faith, a handbook of instruction, and a lectionary for church worship.

There can be no doubt that on the score of its sheer comprehensiveness Matthew deserves its premier position.

(ii)   There is a second reason why Matthew fittingly stands first in the New Testament. As Filson says on the opening page of his commentary:

Matthew is the gospel which persistently emphasizes the deep dependence of the New Testament on the Old Testament, and yet asserts that in the New Testament there is a plus, a new element, so that the gospel is no mere continuation or improvement of the Old Testament, but rather a decisive new word of God. It links the New Testament with the Old Testament, and at the same time insists that God's central act in Jesus Christ brings the new age.

Moffatt in his *Introduction* (p. 244) sees in Matthew's gospel a deliberate claim that the three most precious and unique possessions of Judaism are fulfilled and transcended in the gospel. (*a*) The announcement of the angel is: 'You shall call his name Jesus, for he will save his people from their sins' (1.21). Here the idea of the chosen people, the holy nation is transcended. The holy people is no longer the Jewish nation; the holy people consists of all those whom Jesus Christ will save from their sins, through faith in his name. The new Israel has come into being, and membership of it depends, not on nationality, but on relationship to Jesus Christ. (*b*) The claim of Jesus to the critical Pharisees is: 'I tell you, something greater than the temple is here' (12.6). To the Jews there was nothing in the world more sacred than the temple, and yet even that is transcended in Jesus Christ. (*c*) In the sermon on the mount the very essence of the teaching is that the new transcends the old, and the assumption is that Jesus had the authority to alter, change and develop the ancient law (5.17, 21, 27, 31, 33, 38, 43). Jesus quotes the old commandment and replaces it with a commandment of his own. To the Jew the law was the very voice of God, and yet in Jesus it is both fulfilled and transcended.

The three most cherished possessions of Israel, the three things that made Israel what it was, are all overpassed and transcended, and at the same time completed and fulfilled, in Jesus Christ. No gospel sees more clearly the connection between the Old Testament and the New Testament, and yet no gospel is more certain that the New is a new and decisive action of God.

(iii)   Matthew is the most Jewish gospel, written by a Jew for Jews. It implies a knowledge of the Jewish way of life and belief. It knows that the great religious acts of the Jewish religion are almsgiving, prayer, and fasting, and that, when they are done in the wrong spirit, they become acts of ostentatious pride rather than of selfless devotion (6.1-8; 23.5). It knows of the prayer-boxes, the phylacteries, worn at prayer, and of the fringes on his garments which every orthodox Jew wore (23.5). It knows of the eager search for proselytes, converts to the Jewish faith (23.15). It knows how meticulously an orthodox Jew would tithe even the smallest things (23.23). It knows how the scribes tended to desire the highest and the most prominent places (23.6). It knows of the distinction between greater and lesser commandments

(5.19), and of the way in which the rabbis spoke of binding and loosing for forbidding and permitting (16.19). Jerusalem is called, as the rabbis called it, the holy city (4.5; 27.53). The other gospels speak regularly of the *kingdom of God*; Matthew regularly speaks of the *kingdom of heaven*, for Matthew, being a devout Jew, preferred a reverential periphrasis to the using of the actual name of God. The other gospel writers tend to explain Jewish words and practices, as for instance in Mark 7.1-13, but Matthew assumes that such words and customs will be familiar to his readers, and do not need to be explained.

Matthew's gospel is clearly written by a Jew for Jews.

(iv)   It is then, as Moffatt says (p. 244), a main aim of Matthew's gospel 'to show that Christianity is the true consummation of Judaism'. From beginning to end its dominant aim is to show that Jesus is 'the true Messiah, born and trained under the Jewish law, and yet Lord of a Church whose inward faith and organization, procedure and world-wide scope, transcended the legal limits of Judaism'. As Filson puts it (pp. 10f.), Matthew is written to show that Jesus is 'the perfect expression of the real teaching of the Law', and it has 'an unequalled interest in the promise and fulfilment theme'.

To this end Matthew has a very special interest in the life of Jesus as the fulfilment of prophecy. One of the characteristic phrases of his gospel is that such and such an event in the life of Jesus took place in order to fulfil what the prophet had said (1.22; 2.15, 17, 23; 4.14; 8.17; 12.17; 13.35; 21.4; 26.56; 27.9). To a Jew the surest way to prove that Jesus was the Messiah was to demonstrate that he fulfilled the prophecies of the Old Testament, and this Matthew consistently attempts to do. But in Matthew's use of prophecy two things are to be noted.

(a)   He uses prophecy, and he uses the Old Testament, in a way in which we cannot now honestly use them. Let us take three instances.

In 2.15 he takes the words of Hosea 11.1, 'Out of Egypt have I called my son', as a forecast of the flight into Egypt of Jesus and his family and of his subsequent return. But let us set down the Hosea word in its context:

> When Israel was a child, I loved him,
>   and out of Egypt I called my son.
> The more I called them,
>   the more they went from me;
> they kept sacrificing to the Baals,
>   and burning incense to idols.

In the Hosea passage the saying has nothing whatever to do with the calling of the Messiah out of Egypt. It is a complaint that God in his mercy and power called the nation of Israel out of their slavery in Egypt, but afterwards in their forgetful ingratitude they refused to answer his call and went their own mistaken way.

In 2.17f. he takes the words of Jeremiah 31.15 as a forecast of the mourning consequent on the slaughter of the children of Bethlehem by Herod. Let us set down the Jeremiah passage again in context:

> Thus saith the Lord:
> 'A voice is heard in Ramah,
>   lamentation and bitter weeping.
> Rachel is weeping for her children;
>   she refuses to be comforted for her children,
>   because they are not.'
>
> Thus says the Lord:
> 'Keep your voice from weeping
>   and your eyes from tears;
> for your work shall be rewarded, says the Lord,
>   and they shall come back from the land of the enemy.
> There is hope for your future, says the Lord,
>   and your children shall come back to their own country.'

The context of this passage is this. Judaea had been conquered by the Babylonians; the people are to be taken into exile; and for the journey into exile they are assembled at Ramah (Jer. 40.1). Rachel's tomb was near there (I Sam. 10.2f.), and Rachel from her tomb is depicted as weeping, as she sees the finest flower of the people taken away into exile, and she is bidden to be comforted, for the time will come when they will come back. The Jeremiah passage refers to the historical incident of the taking of the people into exile, and has nothing to do with the slaughter of the infants at Bethlehem.

The thirty pieces of silver and Judas' return of them (Matt. 27.3-10) is said to be forecast by a word of Jeremiah. There is a mistake here, for the prophecy referred to is in Zechariah 11.12f. Let us set it down:

> Then I said to them: 'If it seems right to you, give me my wages; but if not, keep them.' And they weighed out as my wages thirty shekels of silver. Then the Lord said to me: 'Cast it into the treasury' [or, to the potter: RSV margin] – the lordly price at which I was paid off by them. So I took the thirty shekels of silver and cast them into the treasury in the house of the Lord.

The Zechariah passage is obviously obscure. But the general sense of it is that the unsatisfactory shepherd asks for his wages and gets his thirty shekels of silver. The 'lordly price' is sarcasm, for that was the price of a slave (Ex. 21.32). He is then told to cast it into the house of the Lord. In all probability that means that he is told to deposit it in the house of the Lord for safe keeping, for the Jerusalem temple, like all temples, was used by the ancient peoples as a bank and a safe deposit. Whatever the passage means, it is clear that it has no connection whatever with Judas and with his action.

What are we to say about this use of prophecy? We can say at once that however impossible it may be for the twentieth century it was both valid and convincing for a Jew of the first century. For any Jewish student and scholar any portion of scripture had four meanings. It had the meaning called *peshat*, which is the simple meaning, the first-sight meaning. It had *remaz*, which is the suggested meaning, that which the passage implies and leads on to. It had *derush*, which is the meaning after investigation, after all the resources of lexicography and history and geography and archaeology have been brought to it. It had *sod*, which is the inner, the spiritual, the allegorical meaning, which was the most important of all. The initial letters of these four words are P R D S, which are the consonants of the word *paradise*, and to enter into these four meanings of scripture was said to be equivalent to entering into paradise. With this view of scripture and this method of interpreting scripture Matthew was only doing what Jewish teachers regularly did, when he used prophecy in this way.

(b) A much more serious question than that has been raised about Matthew's use of prophecy. It has been argued that there are events written into the life of Jesus not because they happened, but because some prophecy indicated that they should have happened. The event is, so to speak, created to suit the prophecy. In this case prophecy is not simply a guarantee and confirmation of the significance of an event which did happen; it is what F.C. Grant in *The Gospels* (p. 147) calls 'determinative and productive', in the sense that the prophecy begat the story of the event. To take one of the examples that we have already quoted, it is suggested that the story of the flight into Egypt was produced, not because there ever was a journey by the family of Jesus into Egypt, but because of the Hosea word. Similarly it is suggested that the thirty pieces of silver have their origin, not in any historical event, but in the Zechariah prophecy.

This line of thought has been specially applied to the passion narrative. It is suggested that the story of the division of Jesus' garments (27.35) was produced by the saying in Psalm 22.18:

> They divide my garments among them
> and for my raiment they cast lots.

So the mockery of the passers-by (27.39) is said to have been produced on the basis of Psalm 22.7f.:

> All who see me mock at me,
> they make mouths at me, they wag their heads;
> 'He committed his cause to the Lord; let him deliver him,
> let him rescue him, for he delights in him!'

The cry of dereliction (27.46) is said to come from Psalm 22.1:

'My God, my God, why hast thou forsaken me?'

Similarly, the prayer in Luke 23.46 would be traced to Psalm 31.5;

'Into thy hands I commit my spirit.'

The giving of the vinegar (27.48) is traced to Psalm 69.21:

> They gave me poison for food,
>   and for my thirst they gave me vinegar to drink.

In each case the argument is that the prophecy produced the story, on the ground that, if the event was prophesied, then it must have happened. This seems strange to a western twentieth-century mind, but to a Jewish mind this is not impossible, and the idea cannot be discarded without consideration. F.C. Grant sets down the Jewish-Christian point of view: the Old Testament is not only the *proof*, but also the *evidence* of what happened. He goes on (p. 149):

> For Matthew, as for many another student of the Old Testament at that early time (before the New Testament writings had come into general use), the Old Testament was a book of divine revelation in which everything relating to Christ and his church had either been openly or secretly described in advance. Indeed, the Old Testament, had the question been asked, would have been reckoned among the valid sources for the life of our Lord. As a divine prediction and foreshadowing of it it was equally as reliable as the testimony of eyewitnesses.

We may find this a strange point of view, we may find ourselves unable to accept it, but there is no doubt that it was thoroughly Jewish. It is quite certain that Matthew deliberately searched the Old Testament for passages which could be interpreted as foretellings of the life of Jesus in the days of his flesh, in order to convince the Jews that he was indeed the Messiah.

We need not feel compelled to accept the point of view that the Old Testament prophecies produced stories of the life of Jesus to fit them. The close resemblance between the words of the Old Testament and the way in which the gospel writers tell the story of Jesus is far more likely to be due to the simple fact that the New Testament writers were so steeped in the thought and the language of the Old Testament that, when they themselves wrote, they could hardly help reproducing it.

(v)   There is no gospel which seeks to conserve the place of the Jews in the purpose and the plan of God as Matthew does. Jesus did not come to destroy the law and the prophets, but to fulfil them; and so long as heaven and earth last, not the smallest letter, not even the smallest part of a letter, of the law will pass away (5.17f.). The Pharisees and the experts in the law are the inheritors of the work of Moses. Even if their practice is to be rejected, their teaching is still to be obeyed and observed (23.3). To Matthew the best kind of Christian would be a converted expert in the law, for such a man could bring out of his treasure things old and new (13.52). To the old riches he already possessed, Christianity had added new wealth and new lustre. According to Matthew, when the twelve were sent out, they were told to go neither to the Gentiles nor to the Samaritans, but only to the lost sheep of the house of Israel (10.5). The appeal of the Canaanite woman for help was at first met with the same principle, that the objects of Jesus' search were those who belonged to the house of Israel, and who had got lost, and that it was not right to take the food which belonged to the children and to give it to the dogs (15.24-26). There is in Matthew what at first sight looks like a narrow and exclusive Jewish interest.

So much is this so that there are those who have discerned in Matthew an attack on Paul. Two anti-Pauline references have been suggested. In 5.19 Jesus is recorded as having said: 'Whoever then relaxes one of the least of these commandments and teaches men so, shall be called least in the kingdom of heaven; but he who does them and teaches them shall be called great in the kingdom of heaven.' It is claimed that this is a counterblast to the Pauline attitude to the law. In the parable of the tares, of the sowing of the tares among the wheat, it is said: 'An enemy has done this' (13.28). And it is claimed that the enemy is Paul, who made men think less of the law.

It is in the last degree improbable that there is any attack on Paul there; but it is true that there are things in Matthew that only a devout Jew would and could say. But, as so often, there are two sides to this in Matthew.

(vi) There is no gospel which so unsparingly condemns the Jews, and especially the Pharisees. In the parable of the wicked husbandmen the conclusion is that the vineyard will be taken away from them and given to others (21.40-43). Many will come from the ends of the earth to be guests in the kingdom of God, while the children of the kingdom themselves will be shut out (8.12). The invited guests refused the king's invitation, and therefore others, who never expected to be guests, are brought in to take their places (22.1-10). The Jews have come to a state in which they are incapable of seeing or hearing or understanding (13.11-17).

The attack is concentrated on the orthodox leaders, and especially on the Pharisees. They are the spawn of vipers (3.7). The disciples must beware of their evil influence (16.6, 11f.). The righteousness of the Christian must exceed theirs (5.20). Even the ordinary people recognized the difference in the teaching of Jesus (7.29).

The Jewish leaders are repeatedly shown in an evil light in their attitude to Jesus. They accuse him of being in league with the prince of devils (9.34; 12.24). They repeatedly find fault with him in regard to the keeping of the law (9.11, 14; 12.2; 15.1). They repeatedly set malicious traps for him with their loaded questions and their envenomed arguments (19.3; 22.15). They plot to arrest him and to kill him, and they bring Jesus to Pilate on a charge which they know to be untrue (12.14; 21.45; 27.62). The culmination comes in the terrible indictment of ch. 23.

The very sternness and intensity of Matthew's condemnation of the Jewish leaders shows his sense of the poignancy of the tragedy that somehow the chosen people had missed their destiny.

(vii) We noted in Matthew such a desire to maintain the place of the Jewish nation in the purpose and the plan of God that he could sometimes record things which sound like narrow and exclusive nationalism. But equally in Matthew there is a universalism in which the gospel is for the whole wide world.

It is the faith of a Gentile centurion which receives the highest commendation (8.10). Many will come from the east and the west to be fellow guests with Abraham and Isaac and Jacob at the messianic feast in the kingdom of heaven (8.11). The servant of God will proclaim justice to the Gentiles, and in his name the Gentiles will hope (12.18, 21). The gospel of the kingdom is to be preached throughout the whole world as a testimony to all nations (24.14). In the end all nations are to be gathered without distinction in the presence of the King to be sent to their reward or to their punishment (25.32). The lovely story of the anointing is to be told wherever the gospel is preached throughout the whole world (26.13). The ultimate commission and command is to go and make disciples of all nations (28.19).

Matthew has a deep consciousness of the place of the Jewish nation in the purpose of God, but he has also a deep awareness that the kingdom of God is a kingdom without boundaries and without distinction of race or birth or country.

(viii) It may well be that the most important characteristic of Matthew is that it is *the teaching gospel.* J.H. Ropes in *The Synoptic Gospels* (p. 35) describes it as 'a systematic compendium or handbook of what was known about the deeds and words of the Founder of the Christian Church'. E.F. Scott in *The Literature of the New Testament* (p. 65) calls it 'the fullest and most succinct account of Jesus' teaching'.

So much so is this the case that Matthew habitually cuts down on the narrative material to make more room for the teaching material. When we compare the narrative material in the three synoptic gospels we often find that Matthew is shortest, as we see from the following examples:

The healing of the paralytic man (Matt. 9.2-8; Mark 2.1-12; Luke 5.17-26).

The healing of Jairus' daughter and of the woman with the issue of blood (Matt. 9.18-26; Mark 5.21-43; Luke 8.40-56)

The healing of the Gerasene demoniac (Matt. 8.28-34; Mark 5.1-20; Luke 8.26-37).

Vincent Taylor in *The Gospels* (p. 77) points out that in the story of the healing of the Gerasene demoniac Matthew uses two words for every five of Mark's (Matthew 136 words; Mark 328 words; Luke 284 words). In the story of the healing of Jairus' daughter and of the woman with the issue of blood Matthew uses one word for every three of Mark's. In his anxiety to give Jesus' teaching Matthew sometimes reduces the narrative material to less than half the length which it occupies in Mark. Matthew may well be said to be fulfilling Jesus' command to go and teach.

The most notable thing about Matthew's recording of the teaching of Jesus is that Matthew is the great systematizer. J.H. Ropes (pp. 39f.) says of him that he has 'a singular fondness for system and uniformity'. He describes Matthew as having 'a deep and sympathetic understanding of Jesus' own main ideas, and, secondly, a trained and systematic habit of mind'. This is best of all seen in the way that Matthew assembles his material into five great discourses.

i.   The sermon on the mount, or the law of the kingdom (chs. 5-7)
ii.   The charge to the twelve, or the ambassadors of the kingdom (ch. 10)
iii. The chapter of parables, or the parables of the kingdom (ch. 13)
iv.   The discourse about greatness and forgiveness, or the personal relationships of the members of the kingdom (ch. 18)
v.   The eschatological discourses, or the coming of the kingdom (chs. 24-25)

In these great discourses Matthew gathers under these headings the teaching of Jesus. That Matthew is collecting and systematizing can be seen from the fact that passages which come together in Matthew are often widely separated in Luke, as in the following instances:

> Matthew 5.13 = Luke 14.34f.
> Matthew 5.15 = Luke 8.16
> Matthew 5.18 = Luke 16.17
> Matthew 7.1-5 = Luke 6.37-42
> Matthew 7.7-12 = Luke 11.9-13.

Matthew's discourses always end with a kind of summing-up formula: 'When Jesus finished these sayings the crowd were astonished at his teaching, for he taught them as one who had authority, and not as their scribes' (7.28f.; cf. 11.1; 13.54; 19.1; 26.1). We are not meant to regard the discourses in Matthew as sermons preached on one particular occasion; they are rather Matthew's summaries of the substance and quintessence of all the sermons and all the preaching and teaching of Jesus.

It is further characteristic of Matthew that he does everything possible to help his readers to remember the teaching he is transmitting. There are five discourses, five blocks of the teaching of Jesus, just as there are five books of the Pentateuch, five books of the old law. Just as the five books of the Pentateuch lay down the laws binding on the life of the Jew, so the five discourses lay down the laws binding on the life of the Christian.

It has always to be held in mind that Matthew was writing in an age long before printing had been invented, and therefore in an age when very few people would ever possess a book. If they were to possess any teaching it had to be in the memory. So Matthew frequently uses aids to memory. He begins by setting down the genealogy of Jesus (1.2-16). Jesus for him is Messiah, and it is all-important to him to prove that Jesus is the son of David. The names are divided into three groups of fourteen names each. In Hebrew there are no signs for figures; the letters of the alphabet do duty for figures also. Hebrew, properly speaking, has no vowels, and the vowel signs are later inventions. The consonants of the name David are in Hebrew D W D. When these consonants are taken as numbers their equivalents are D = 4, W = 6, D = 4, and their total is 14. This is Matthew's way of helping his readers more easily to memorize the genealogy.

In his commentary on Matthew in *The International Critical Commentary* (p. 1xv) W.C. Allen points out that Matthew habitually arranges things in threes, fives and sevens. There are three divisions in the genealogy of Jesus (1.17); three incidents from the childhood of Jesus (2); three temptations (4.1-11); three illustrations of righteousness (6.1-18); three prohibitions (6.19-7.6); three commands (7.7-20); three miracles of healing (8.1-15); three miracles of power (8.23-9.8); three miracles of restoration (9.18-34); three prayers in Gethsemane (26.39-44); three parables of sowing (13.1-32); three denials of Peter (26.69-75); three questions of Pilate (27.17-23); five discourses, and five illustrations of the fulfilment of the law (5.21-48); seven woes (23). Just as Matthew collected the sayings of Jesus in chs. 5-7, he collected his miracles in chs. 8 and 9, arranged, as we have seen in three groups of three.

The church's debt to Matthew as a teacher is immense. As F.V. Filson says in his commentary (pp. 4f.): 'The Church needed a document which leaders of limited ability and understanding could use in guiding the worship, teaching, life, and witness of the Church.' And Matthew gave it to them supremely well. It became the gospel which above all others the church consistently used. And, to quote Filson again (p. 2), 'its strength lay not in its narrative power, literary appeal, or mystical depth, but in its proved and persistent capacity to shape Christian thought and Church life'. With his love of system and of clarity Matthew gave the church not only a gospel, but a gospel which, as J.H. Ropes says (p. 39), is 'singularly easy to refer to and to use as a work of reference'.

(ix) In view of this the next characteristic of Matthew emerges naturally. Matthew is *the ecclesiastical gospel*, the gospel of the church. It is clearly written both *in* and *for* the church. F.V. Filson says that the aim of the writer was not to invent episodes or sayings, but to present the common message of the church. He was not an imaginative idealist; he was the voice of the church. The book is designed to be used within the church. It is written not so much for private reading as for the guidance of Christian teachers in their work. G.D. Kilpatrick thinks that Matthew's gospel was deliberately written to be read aloud at meetings of the church. He believes that the great discourses were meant to be read within the Christian congregation, and that the formula which ends them (7.28; 11.1; 13.53; 19.1; 26.1) means in effect: 'Here endeth the first, second, third, fourth, fifth, book of the oracles of Jesus the Messiah.'

In the circumstances of the early church, when converts were coming straight out of paganism, and when it was not possible to put anything like a handbook of Christian teaching into their hands, the teachers (I Cor. 12.28; Eph. 4.11) must have been amongst the most important and essential officials in the church, for it was to them that converts must have been handed over for instruction. In the hands of these teachers, as Filson says (p. 5), Matthew's gospel must have proved 'a powerful and useful tool for the Church's common life and mission'. Matthew's gospel must have been one of the main teaching instruments of the early church.

Matthew has much to say about the life and practices of the church. It speaks about the right way of fasting, of almsgiving and of praying (6.1-18). It lays down the Christian rule for marriage and divorce (5.27-32; 19.3-9). It has much to say about the conduct necessary toward children and brothers in the faith (18.10-22). It stresses the power of the church to make its own decisions (18.18f.) It gives encouragement in time of persecution (10.17-39). It gives the authority for baptism (28.19f.) It assures the smallest group of worshipping Christians of the presence of their Lord (18.20). It lays down the pre-eminence of Peter and of the apostles within the church. Peter was the first man to discover who Jesus really was, and this makes him in a real sense the foundation stone of the church (16.13-20). The apostles are to be the princes and the judges in the messianic kingdom (19.28).

It is significant that Matthew is the only gospel which uses the word *church*. Peter is the foundation member of the church, and no power can prevail against the church (16.18). It is within the church that all personal differences must be settled, and in such decisions the decision of the church is final and binding (18.15-17).

It is in and for the church that Matthew's gospel is written.

(x)   Of all the gospels Matthew has *the strongest eschatological emphasis.*

(a)   Matthew is very interested in the second coming, and on occasion he slants sayings of Jesus in such a way that they refer much more definitely to the second coming than do the parallel sayings in the other gospels. We take two examples:

> Mark 9.1: Truly, I say to you, there are some standing here who will not taste death before they see the kingdom of God come with power.

> Luke 9.27: But I tell you truly, there are some standing here who will not taste death before they see the kingdom of God.

> Matthew 16.28: Truly, I say to you, there are some standing here who will not taste death before they see the Son of man coming in his kingdom.

Matthew has quite clearly made this a much more definite second coming saying than Mark or Luke does. The second example is the answer of Jesus at his trial:

> Matthew 26.64: I tell you, hereafter you shall see the Son of man seated at the right hand of Power, and coming on the clouds of heaven (cf. Mark 14.62).

> Luke 22.69: From now on the Son of man shall be seated at the right hand of the power of God.

Once again, Matthew has made the saying refer much more definitely to the second coming. The second coming was clearly very much in the forefront of Matthew's mind.

(b)   Matthew has a habit of using standard and technical apocalyptic language, that is, the language in which writers usually spoke of the events of the last days. The word *parousia* became the technical Christian word for the second coming of Jesus, and only Matthew uses it (Matt. 24.3, 27, 37, 39). The word *paliggenesia*, literally 'rebirth', was the technical word for the coming into being of the new world when the old world vanished in judgment and destruction, and only Matthew uses it (19.28). One of the standard descriptions of the terrors of the last times is that there will be weeping and wailing and gnashing of teeth. Matthew uses that phrase five times (8.12; 13.42; 22.13; 24.51; 25.30), and outside Matthew it only occurs once elsewhere in the New Testament (Luke 13.28). Clearly Matthew's mind runs in these apocalyptic terms.

(c)   Only Matthew has a series of parables which turn on judgment and which can be interpreted in terms of the second coming. Only he has the parable of the wise and the foolish virgins and the shut

door (25.1-13); the parable of the sheep and the goats and the final judgment (25.31-46); the parable of the talents and the casting out of the unsatisfactory servant (25.14-30). This again is the kind of material which Matthew instinctively records and preserves.

(d) Even in instances in which the other gospel writers record such material (Mark 13; Luke 17.22-37) Matthew inserts extra material. Matthew 24 and Mark 13 are largely parallel, but Matthew has extra verses:

> Then will appear the sign of the Son of man in heaven, and then all the tribes of the earth will mourn, and they will see the Son of man coming on the clouds of heaven with power and great glory; and he will send out his angels with a loud trumpet call, and they will gather his elect from the four winds, from one end of heaven to the other (Matt. 24.30f.).

Whenever Matthew can bring in material about the second coming he does so, and whenever he can interpret material in terms of it he also does so. No doubt he lived in a time when persecution was so violent and agonizing that he seized on any word of Jesus which promised relief in a blessed future from a terrible present.

(xi) When we are looking for one final characteristic of Matthew's gospel, a characteristic which will in some sense contain and sum up all the others, it may well be that we will find Tasker right when he claims (p. 19) that Matthew is supremely *the royal gospel*. It is the gospel which more than any other stresses the sheer royalty of Jesus.

More often than in any other gospel Jesus is the royal son of royal David (1.1; 9.27; 12.23; 15.22; 20.30; 21.9, 15). The Davidic descent of Joseph is stressed (1.16, 20). The child who is born is king of the Jews (2.2), and is the destined ruler from Bethlehem who is to govern God's people (2.6).

This royalty gives him sovereign authority over the law. He alone can tell what it really means (5.21, 27, 31, 33, 38, 43). The law and the prophets point to him and are consummated in him as the appearance of Moses and Elijah on the mount of transfiguration shows (17.1-8). He takes it upon himself to condemn the tradition of the elders which by that time was even more reverenced than the written law (15.3-6).

Even in the closing scenes, rather, especially in the closing scenes, Jesus moves through his trial, his humiliation, his crucifixion like a king. Legions of angels are his for the asking (26.52-54). His enemies may think that they are eliminating him, but he will come again with a glory before which the whole universe will bow (26.64). At his death the temple veil is rent in two, the centurion is reduced to wondering admiration, and even the gates of the underworld are burst and the dead come forth (27.51-53). And in the last glimpse of all he is declaring that all authority is his, and visualizing a whole world in which men will be his disciples (28.16-20).

But the divine one is also the human one in Matthew's gospel, and the royal one is also the servant. In his manhood he is a 'Galilaean provincial' (2.23). He is the carpenter's son (13.55). He is gentle and humble in heart (11.28f.), and, when he comes, he comes riding upon an ass, the beast of peace (21.5).

No gospel-writer paints such a picture of the kingliness of Jesus as Matthew does, but the royalty is the royalty of the Servant of God and of men.

It is little wonder that Matthew in the order of the gospels comes first. It may not have the vivid, quick-moving realism of Mark; it may not have the sheer tender beauty of Luke; it may not have the eagle's wings of John. But for all that it is irreplaceable. No gospel so sees the connection between the old and the new, in which the value of the old is never forgotten and the wonder of the new is never underrated. Nowhere is there such a full account of the teaching of Jesus. And nowhere is Jesus so vividly shown as King and Servant.

Before we leave Matthew's gospel we must look at a quite different view of it, the view that it is the earliest of the gospels. This view is seldom stated by Protestant scholars. The strength of the case of the priority of Mark is considered to be so powerful that it is not necessary to investigate any other view. But the importance of this view is that it may be said to be the orthodox and standard Roman Catholic view. The two outstanding Roman Catholic books on it are *Matthew, Mark and Luke*, by Dom John Chapman, and *The Originality of St Matthew*, by B.C. Butler. It is the argument of Chapman that we mainly expound, because it is easier to follow. But it is worth noting that this view is by no means dead because in 1965 there appeared a full-scale examination of it in *The Synoptic Problem*, by William R. Farmer. We shall examine this view as fully as we can within our limits, for there is more to be said for it than Protestant scholars will usually allow, and it certainly cannot be answered by ignoring it, nor can it be dismissed out of hand.

There may be said to be four main views of the growth of the gospels.

(i) It has been argued that all three arise independently from oral tradition. The parts which are the same come from what may be called a standardized oral tradition; the parts which are the same, but in which there are differences, are the result of each author's individual handling of the oral tradition; the parts which are different, the material which appears only in one gospel or another, are either parts of oral tradition which one author chose to preserve and another did not, or they are due to the fact that certain oral traditions had come to the knowledge of one writer and not to the knowledge of the others.

There will always be an attraction about this theory, for, on the face of it, it seems the simplest and the most natural. But it does not explain the differences which occur, for instance, in the Lord's Prayer; it does not explain the verbatim agreement which occurs in, for instance, the accounts of the preaching of John the Baptist; and, above all, it does not explain the kind of agreement which extends even to a parenthesis as in Mark 2.10 = Matthew 9.6 = Luke 5.24.

No one doubts that there must have been oral tradition, but oral tradition by itself is not enough to explain the growth and development of the first three gospels.

(ii)   It has been argued that everything goes back to one original written gospel, composed as early as, say, AD 35; and that all subsequent differences and divergences are due to copying, to transmission, and to successive revisions of the original document. On this theory all three synoptic gospels stem from one original gospel, which grew and developed as the years went on. If there was such a gospel, it would be odd that there is no trace of it. When we study the quotations of the very early period of the church, in the writings of the apostolic fathers, the one thing which strikes us is the looseness of quotation, and the variation in quotations. The impression which any such study gives is that it was a long time before there was in fact anything like a standard text. The evidence is all against the very early existence of a written gospel, for such a gospel would have stereotyped the account of the works and words of Jesus much earlier than it was fixed.

(iii)   The third view, and this may be said to be the standard Protestant view, is the view that we have already previously expounded, the view that there are two basic documents, Mark and Q, and that on them the later gospels were built. The obvious question in regard to this view is why Q vanished without trace. It is never referred to, never quoted in any way that would identify it. Even gospels which did not achieve canonicity, as, for example, the *Gospel according to the Hebrews*, left some trace. They are occasionally quoted; of their existence there is not any doubt; but Q must remain for ever an hypothesis, without one fragment of actual quotation to prove that it ever existed. It is true that a document has been conjured up out of a deduction, even if it is claimed that it is possible to hold that the deduction has a very high degree of probability in light of the finished product.

(iv)   So, then, we come to the last view, the view that we are at present examining. According to it the process was as follows:

(a)   Matthew wrote a gospel in Aramaic.
(b)   Out of that gospel Mark produced his gospel. How it was produced we shall in a moment see.
(c)   Matthew's gospel was then translated into Greek. There are

supporters of this view who would reverse the order of (*b*) and (*c*).

(*d*) Luke then used Greek Matthew plus Mark to produce his gospel.

On this view the order of the gospels is Matthew in Aramaic, Mark, Matthew in Greek, Luke. On this view Q vanishes, for that which is common to Matthew and Luke was simply material which Luke borrowed from Matthew.

Butler succinctly sets out the relationship between the gospels, a relationship which we have already seen, but Butler from the same facts draws quite other conclusions. Let us remind ourselves of the relationship.

i.   Nearly all Mark is contained in Matthew, and, except for a very few verses, that which Matthew omits from Mark is in Luke.

ii.   The order of Mark is midway between Matthew and Luke. Matthew sometimes varies Mark's order of events, Luke practically never; either Matthew or Luke always agrees with Mark in matters of order.

iii.   When all three agree in *matter* (as distinct from *order*), Matthew and Mark tend to agree in *wording* against Luke; and Luke and Mark tend to agree in wording as against Matthew; but very seldom do Matthew and Luke agree against Mark.

The inevitable conclusion is that *Mark is the mean between Matthew and Luke.* Now if this is so, the connection can be expressed in four possible ways, one of which must express the right relationship.

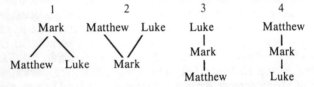

On general grounds, 2 is unlikely, for there seems to be no reason why Mark should set out to make one shorter gospel out of two fuller gospels. 3 is still more unlikely, for it would mean that the Gentile gospel preceded the two Jewish ones, which is so historically improbable as to be next door to impossible. We are therefore left to choose between 1 and 4, and, as we have already shown in detail at the beginning of our study of Matthew, 4 is the unanimous and unbroken verdict of the early church. The patristic evidence is solid for the priority of Matthew. The question is, can this very reasonbly be held?

But we are faced now with the problem of explaining something which we have already noted. Matthew looks like an *improvement* of

Mark. Mark is often longer in his description of an incident, as, for instance, in his description of the incident of the Gerasene demoniac. Mark is much more vivid, but he is also much more diffuse. Further, Mark's style is much more colloquial and much less polished. This has made scholars deduce that Matthew used Mark, but improved and tidied up his material. But is this the only possible explanation of the facts?

Chapman brings forward a possible – and, let it be said, an attractive – explanation. Chapman accepts as unquestioned facts two things – first, Peter's connection with Mark's gospel, and, second, Peter's connection with Rome. His explanation is this. Peter preached in Rome. He used as the 'textbook' of his preaching Matthew's gospel. As he read Matthew aloud, and as he taught from it, he added his own vivid, impetuous, eyewitness memories, in high colloquial language and with an impulsive speaker's complete disregard for things which could be theologically misunderstood. To take only one instance, the Marcan story of the healing of the Gerasene demoniac, which is three times as long as the Matthew version, is nothing other than the Matthew version used as a 'textbook' with Peter's memories and recollections vividly and impulsively superimposed upon it. It was this preaching of Peter with Matthew as a background 'textbook' that Mark wrote down, perhaps in shorthand. Granted the supposition of the situation, this will certainly explain the difference between Matthew and Mark. As for Luke, with regard for propriety, he toned down Mark in terms of Matthew. On this argument the priority of Matthew is quite as probable as the priority of Mark.

Is there then any proof that this was the course of events, and that Matthew is prior to Mark? It would be better if we rephrased this question. There cannot in the nature of things be *proof* of a contention like this. But is there any indication or hint which supports it?

Chapman takes and sets beside each other the material in Matthew 13 and Mark 4. Since Matthew is so characteristically systematic, and since Mark writes so quickly that he would not take time to construct an invisible join, there ought to be some sign of a gap, if Matthew does come first, and if Mark was using him. The Matthew passage has fourteen sections:

i.   The sower, 1-9
ii.   The disciples ask for an explanation, 10-13
iii. The prophecy from Isaiah, and the blessing on him who sees and hears, 14-17
iv.   The explanation of the sower, 18-23
v.   The wheat and the tares, 24-30
vi.   The mustard seed, 31f.
vii. The leaven, 33

Of this material Mark has sections i, ii, iv, vi and viii, to which are added (21-25) certain verses found elsewhere in Matthew, and one short parable (26-29) which is peculiar to himself. The question is, does Mark show any signs of having omitted any material which he knew to be there? Does his narrative imply the existence of material which he knew, but deliberately did not include?

Matthew's introduction (13.3) reads:

> And he (Jesus) told them many things in parables, saying . . .

Mark's introduction reads (4.2):

> And he (Jesus) taught them many things in parables, *and in his teaching he said to them* . . .

That is to say, what follows was said *in the course of Jesus' teaching*, and this can very well mean that Mark is deliberately saying that what follows is to be regarded as a selection from a larger body of teaching. In effect Mark is saying: 'Included in Jesus' teaching was the following . . .'. This would fit exactly, if when Mark wrote he had the Matthew material before him and selected from it. There are seven parables in Matthew; he is going to give only three.

Let us take another passage later on, as it stands in Matthew and Mark. Matthew 13.34f. reads:

> All this Jesus said to the crowd in parables; indeed he said nothing to them without a parable: 'I will open my mouth in parables, I will utter what has been hidden since the foundation of the world.'

And immediately after that Matthew moves to the private explanation of the parable of the wheat and the tares. Mark's version (4.33f.) is:

> With many such parables he spoke the word to them, as they were able to bear it; he did not speak to them without a parable, but privately to his disciples he explained everything.

So then Mark says that Jesus spoke with *many such parables*. Here again is the indication that he, Mark, is making only a selection. Matthew goes on to give the private explanation of the wheat and the tares; Mark omits the explanation, but says that Jesus explained everything privately to his disciples, thereby making it quite clear that he knew of the existence of the explanation which he chooses to omit. There is no doubt that at least a possible explanation of Mark's narrative is that he is making a selection from a larger body of material, and that the larger body of material is in fact Matthew's much fuller account.

Chapman chooses another illustration. In Matthew 23.1-39 Matthew gives us the long discourse against the scribes and Pharisees, ending with the appeal to Jerusalem. Mark 12.38-40 compresses the whole passage into two and a half verses. But let us again see the respective introductions. Matthew 23.1 runs:

> Then said Jesus to the crowds and to his disciples,

and the whole long passage follows. Mark begins (12.38):

> And in his teaching he (Jesus) said.

What teaching? Chapman asks. Once again Mark gives a passage as occurring *in the course of Jesus' teaching*, thereby implying, if not saying, that he knew there was far more than he had selected. It is almost as if he said, You know where to go for further information, if you want it, thus pointing them to the fuller account available in Matthew. Once again, it is a possible explanation that Mark is selecting from Matthew.

In this case it may even be possible to suggest a reason for Mark's omission of this material. We remember that the suggestion is that Mark is the Roman preaching of Peter, on the basis of Matthew as a textbook. Matthew 23 is one of the greatest and most moving chapters in the gospels, but it is also one of the most 'Palestinian' chapters. Its whole background would be foreign and alien and even unintelligible to Rome. Therefore Peter does not use this material in Rome, and therefore Mark does not transmit it, although by his introduction he hints that he knows very well of its existence.

We may take still further examples of passages in which Mark seems to presuppose a knowledge of Matthew, and even if the further examples are based on arguments which are more subtle and hints that are more tenuous, they are for that very reason even more convincing.

Let us take the three passages which are parallel, Matthew 17.22–18.5; Mark 9.30-37; Luke 9.43-48. All three begin with Jesus' second prediction of his passion and death; then Matthew alone inserts the story of the temple tax and the coin in the fish's mouth; then the three gospels come together again for the passage about the dispute about greatness and importance. Each of the three gospels introduces the last section differently.

> Matthew 18.1: At that time the disciples came to Jesus saying: 'Who is the greatest in the kingdom of heaven?'

Luke 9.46: And an argument arose among them as to which of them was greatest.

Mark 9.33: And they came to Capernaum; and *when he was in the house* he asked them: 'What were you discussing on the way?'

Mark has the phrase *when he was in the house.* Why does he insert this, and where does he get it? We go back to the incident of the coin in the fish's mouth which is in Matthew and which is not in Mark, and which immediately precedes this passage (Matt. 17.24-27). And there we find that the incident of the coin into the fish's mouth is introduced with the saying: When he came *into the house* (RSV: came home), Jesus spoke to him (Peter) first. It is at least a possible conclusion that Mark knew from the Matthew narrative, although he did not include it, that this happened *in the house*, and so he correctly inserted it at the point at which he took up the story.

Let us look at the long passage which is in Matthew 21.23-22.46; Mark 11.27-12.37; Luke 20.1-44. This passage has eight sections in it, and can be tabulated as follows:

i.   The question about authority (Matt. 21.23-27; Mark 11.27-33; Luke 20.1-3)

ii.   The two sons (Matt. 21.28-32)

iii. The wicked husbandmen (Matt. 21.33-46; Mark 12.1-12; Luke 20.9-19)

iv.   The marriage feast (Matt. 22.1-14; elsewhere in Luke in 14.16-24)

v.   Tribute to Caesar (Matt. 22.15-22; Mark 12.13-17; Luke 20.20-26)

vi.   The resurrection of the dead (Matt. 22.23-33; Mark 12.18-27; Luke 20.27-40)

vii. The great commandment (Matt. 22.34-40; Mark 12.28-34; elsewhere in Luke 10.25-28)

viii. David's son (Matt. 22.41-46; Mark 12.35-37; Luke 20.41-44)

Here then is a section which is very closely parallel in all the three gospels. But within it Matthew has a series of three parables of which Mark and Luke give only one. Let us set down the introduction to that common parable in the three gospels:

Matthew 21.33: Hear another parable.

Mark 12.1: And he began to speak to them in parables.

Luke 20.9: And he began to tell the people this parable.

Matthew speaks about *another parable*, for to him this is simply one parable in a series of three; Luke speaks about *this parable*, for he does not connect any other parables at all with this situation; but

Mark says that Jesus began to speak *in parables*, and then gives one. One perfectly possible explanation is that Mark was well aware of Matthew's three parables, and is in effect intimating that out of the three he has chosen one. That explanation certainly fits the facts.

Let us look at another kind of passage, one from which we may be able to draw some conclusion from the passage as a whole rather than from hints within it. Let us look at the passage which tells of the healing of the Gerasene demoniac (Matt. 8.28-34; Mark 5.1-20; Luke 8.26-40). The first thing which strikes us is that Mark's account is three times as long as Matthew's. If Matthew was using Mark, we would have to find some reason why he deliberately and purposely cut out vivid, interesting, and lifelike detail. The second thing we note is that the general impact of the story is different. In Matthew the final impression is an astonishment at the destruction of the pigs; but in Mark's story attention is concentrated on the man. Mark is always characteristically interested in demon possession, and in Mark the impact of the story is concentrated on the extraordinary change in the man. It is at least possible that the explanation is that Peter was using Matthew as his basic teaching document and was adding to it as he went along his own vivid personal recollections of the incident, which for him culminated in the restoration of the man to sanity, a miracle to which the destruction of the pigs was no more than incidental. It may well in this case be easier to think of Mark as built on Matthew than of Matthew as summarizing Mark.

Let us look at one more story, the story of the healing and raising from the dead of Jairus' daughter (Matt. 9.18-26; Mark 5.21-43; Luke 8.40-56). In Mark this story together with the story of the woman with the issue of blood takes 316 words to tell; in Matthew it takes 135 words. Now let us see the additions which Mark's story has. It has six main additions:

i. Jesus took Peter and James and John with him.
ii. When he had put the rest of the people out, he kept the girl's father and mother with him in the room.
iii. Mark has the words of Jesus to the girl in Aramaic: *Talitha cumi*.
iv. The girl was twelve years old.
v. When she was cured she rose, and walked about.
vi. Jesus gave instructions for her to be given something to eat.

She rose – *and walked about*. Can that last phrase be anything but the eye of memory seeing the scene again? Every detail which is added to Matthew is precisely the kind of detail that an eyewitness would remember and add to a summary narrative. It certainly makes sense to regard the Mark story as Peter's personal and expanded version of

Matthew's shorter and more detached version.

The order of production of the gospels on this hypothesis is, first, Matthew in its Aramaic form, then Mark, then Matthew in its Greek form, then Luke. This view involves another radical departure from what may be called the normal and orthodox position. It involves the disappearance of Q, for now the resemblances between Matthew and Luke are due quite simply to the dependence of Luke on Matthew. Let us then see the arguments which are advanced for the elimination of Q.

Q is the general name for the material common to Matthew and Luke apart from that which is said to come from Mark. There is no agreement at the beginning or the end of Matthew and Luke; it may therefore be said that Q did not contain an account of either the birth or the death of Jesus. Q is very largely a collection of the sayings and sermons of Jesus.

(i)   One of the main arguments used for the priority of Mark, and for the dependence of Matthew and Luke on Mark, is that basically Matthew and Luke accept Mark's order of events; the pattern of events in Matthew and Luke is said to be based on the pattern of events in Mark. But, if Q did exist, and if Matthew and Luke did use it, then the case is very different, for there is no agreement at all between Matthew and Luke as to the order of Q. If Q did exist, then Matthew and Luke cut it up quite differently. Both Matthew and Luke have long sermons of Jesus, and Matthew has longer sermons than Luke. Now the characteristic of these sermons is that, if Q exists, they are highly composite. None is wholly Q; all consist of bits of Q, bits of Mark, and bits of special Matthew and Luke material. There is no agreement as to the order and the division of Q. If Q did exist, and if Matthew and Luke used it, there is no parallel at all to the way in which they are said to have used Mark.

(ii)   The parallels between Matthew and Luke differ widely in character.

(a)   There are passages which are almost identical in language (e.g. Matt. 3.7-10, 11f.; Luke 3.7-9, 16f.).

(b)   There are passages in which the general sense of Matthew and Luke is the same, but in which there are wide divergences of language, so wide that they cannot be, for instance, different translations of the same Aramaic original (e.g. the sermon on the mount [Matt. 5-7] and the sermon on the plain [Luke 6.20-49]; the parable of the wedding feast [Matt. 22.1-14; Luke 14.16-24]).

(iii)   There are passages in which there is wide divergence of material with at the same time close resemblance in language, sometimes even identity of language (e.g. The Lord's Prayer [Matt. 6.9-15; Luke 11.2-4]; the centurion's servant [Matt. 8.5-13; Luke 7.1-10]; the parables of the talents and the pounds [Matt. 25.14-30; Luke 19.12-27]).

So then, even if we assume the existence of Q, there is no kind of agreement between Matthew and Luke in either the order in which they quote it or in the method in which they quote different passages of it.

There are further points to meet. According to Streeter, who may be said to express the generally accepted view of Q, Q is very early; it was written in Palestine by people who as yet needed nothing to remind them of the deeds and actions and life of Jesus, but who did want to possess a record of his teaching. That view ends in several paradoxes.

(a) Q has none of Matthew's proofs by prophecy, none of the familiar, 'This was done that it might be fulfilled. . .'

(b) Apart from Matthew 5.18 = Luke 16.17, the saying that not the slightest part of the law will pass away, Q has nothing about Jesus' relation to the law. It has, for instance, nothing of the section contained in Matthew 5.21-48 in which Jesus states the law only to recreate its meaning and significance.

(c) The relation of Jesus to the Jewish sects is clear in Mark and Matthew, and is a very prominent and significant part of the story. Q has little about scribes and Pharisees and nothing at all about Sadducees and Herodians. Even the debates with the different sects which characterize the last days of Jesus' ministry come from Mark and not from the alleged Q material.

(d) Luke and Mark have phrases which betray an underlying Aramaic original and Matthew more so, but Q has fewer of such phrases.

Now the initial supposition was that Q was a very early Palestinian document, and yet the whole evidence we have cited would prove that the document which is alleged to be the most Palestinian in origin is the least Palestinian in language and in content.

There does seem reason to suspect the existence of Q, and all the more so when there is no clear and definite way of settling either the content or the order of Q. If we discard the Q hypothesis, what have we? We may note certain facts.

(i) When Matthew and Luke agree in Greek words they generally do so more closely than Matthew and Mark, or Luke and Mark agree. Sometimes the agreement of Matthew and Luke is so close that interdependence in one direction or another is a safer assumption than a common source. The agreement is such that one of them seems to depend on the other rather than both on a common source. And it can usually be shown that Luke is the borrower.

(ii) When the substance of a story is different in Mark and in Luke, and when there is yet resemblance in wording, the reasonable explanation is that they received the story from different sources, but that Luke corrected his source by Matthew.

(iii) When the matter is the same but the wording is widely

different, as in the case of the sermon on the mount and the sermon on the plain, and in the case of the two versions of the Lord's Prayer, then the natural conclusion is that the two accounts came from different sources and have no immediate contact.

The argument from all this is that Matthew wrote his gospel in Aramaic for Jews, Peter used it as a textbook in Rome, and, as he read it and preached from it, added his own memories and reminiscences. This preaching of Peter was put into writing by Mark. Matthew was then translated into Greek, and very naturally in this translation Mark was used. Luke in the meantime had written a gospel out of his own recollection together with the material Mark supplied. He then came upon Matthew, and added Matthew's extra teaching material into his gospel.

There are two further lines of thought at which we may briefly look.

(i) If Mark is the spoken teaching of Peter, if Mark represents Peter's spontaneous, and, as it were, unconsidered additions to the narrative of Matthew, then we would expect Mark to show the characteristics of colloquial speech as opposed to the characteristics of literary care. Is this in fact the case? There is no doubt that Mark does have the characteristics of conversation rather than of writing.

(a) *Parataxis* is a characteristic of Mark. That is to say, Mark tends to join clause to clause by the word 'and', rather than to subordinate one clause to another. Mark is only about half the length of Matthew or Luke; and yet in Mark the word *kai* 'and', occurs 400 times, as against 250 in Matthew and 380 in Luke. In the short passage Mark 8.6-9 the word *kai* 'and', occurs no fewer than 10 times:

> *And* he commanded the crowd to sit down on the ground; *and* he took the seven loaves, *and* having given thanks he broke them *and* gave them to his disciples to set before the people; *and* they set them before the crowd. *And* they had a few small fish; *and* having blessed them, he commanded that these also should be set before them. *And* they ate, *and* were satisfied, *and* they took up the broken pieces left over, seven baskets full. *And* there were about four thousand people.

In Mark 3, out of 35 verses 20 begin with *kai* 'and'. This is the way in which speech runs on rather than the way in which writing is done.

(b) As we noted when we were studying the characteristics of Mark's style, Mark is abnormally given to using the historic present. He does so (according to Chapman) no less than 151 times. He tells the story in the present instead of in the past tense, and this is exactly the way in which a simple person tells a story in colloquial language. It is normal speaking, but it is hardly normal writing.

(c) Mark has no fear of the repetition of words, where someone more conscious of literary style would have found a synonym or some other way of avoiding the repetition.

The Spirit immediately drove him *into the wilderness*. And he was *in the wilderness* forty days, tempted by Satan (1.12f.)

And the scribes of the Pharisees, when they saw that he was eating with *sinners and tax-collectors*, said to his disciples, Why does he eat with *tax-collectors and sinners*? (2.16).

For many *bore false witness against him*, and their witness did not agree. And some stood up and *bore false witness against him*, saying . . . (14.56f.).

This kind of thing makes for unmistakable clarity in everyday speech, but it does not make for good written style.

(d) Mark has a way of saying things twice unnecessarily.

That evening, at sundown, they brought to him all who were sick or possessed with demons (1.32).

He led them up into a high mountain *apart by themselves* (9.2).

And other seeds fell into good ground, *growing up and increasing*, and yielding thirtyfold and sixtyfold and a hundredfold (4.8).

This is the kind of way in which a speaker speaks, but it is also the kind of thing that a writer eliminates.

There is ample evidence of the colloquial character of Mark.

(ii) The second point which would be significant is this. On the theory which we are at present examining Matthew began as an Aramaic document, and was later translated into Greek. Is there any hint or evidence of this to be found in Matthew as it stands? Chapman produces certain alleged evidence.

(a) Right at the beginning of the gospel in 1.21 we have the instruction:

You shall call his name Jesus, for he will save his people from their sins.

Now in Greek the point of this is quite obscure; in fact in Greek the point is not made at all. The point is that Jesus is the Greek form of the name Joshua – Jeshuah and Jehoshuah – which means *God saves*. That point is quite unintelligible to anyone who does not know Hebrew, and it is not explained. It is at least possible to argue that it must originally have occurred in a document which was written in Aramaic for those who understood Aramaic, and who therefore needed no explanation.

(b) Chapman argues that there are Aramaisms in the other gospels, but they are *occasional*, whereas the Aramaisms in Matthew are *habitual*. Of this he produces certain examples.

There is in Matthew an extraordinary use of the Greek word *tote*, which in English means 'then'. It occurs in Matthew 89 times, 51 times in passages which have parallels in Mark and 38 times in passages which have no parallels in Mark. The comparable figures are that *tote* occurs 6 times in Mark, 15 times in Luke, and 10 times in John. Matthew seems to have an addiction for *tote*, and the constant use of it is something that no ordinary Greek writer could have tolerated. What is the explanation? *Tote*, 'then', in Hebrew is *'az*, and is common enough, but in Aramaic it is *edhayin* or *bedhayin*, and is extraordinarily common. In the Greek translation of the Hebrew parts of the Old Testament, which, of course, form by far the greater part of the Old Testament, a sample of the occurrence of *tote* is as follows: Genesis 4 times; Exodus 0; Leviticus 4; Numbers 1; Deuteronomy 0; Joshua 7. But in the Aramaic parts of the Old Testament in the Greek translation, translating the Aramaic words we have mentioned, the occurrences are as follows: Daniel 2.14-39, 9 times; Daniel 3, 6 times.

The conclusion seems clear: the extraordinary frequency of *tote* in Matthew seems to point to an Aramaic original. Otherwise, if Matthew used Mark we have to assume that he inserted a *tote* into Mark in 45 different places.

The word for 'heaven' in Greek is *ouranos*, which is singular; the plural is *ouranoi*; in normal Greek the word is almost always used in the singular, and hardly ever in the plural. It so happens that the word for 'heaven' or 'the heavens' is in Hebrew plural in form (*shamayim*). In the Greek Old Testament the singular *ouranos* is much commoner than the plural *ouranoi*. Only in the Psalms is the plural common. In the Psalms the singular occurs 56 times, and the plural 22 times; but in the rest of the Old Testament the figures are 10 occurrences in the plural to 370 in the singular.

Now Matthew has *ouranoi* in the plural 55 times, Mark 5 times, Luke 4 times, John not at all, Acts twice, Paul 10 times. Matthew's *ouranoi* in the plural is quite unusual, and it, too, is characteristically Aramaic.

Matthew speaks of the *kingdom of the heavens* instead of the *kingdom of God* 33 times, and Mark, Luke, John, Acts and Paul never speak of the *kingdom of the heavens*, but always of the *kingdom of God*. Just so, Matthew speaks of the *Father in the heavens* 13 times.

Once again Matthew's odd use of the plural where the singular would be expected points to an Aramaic background and original.

Such then is the argument that Matthew wrote his gospel in Aramaic; that Peter used it as his basic textbook, and amplified and illustrated it with his own reminiscences in colloquial and quite unliterary form, that the Peter version was written down by Mark, that Matthew was then translated into Greek, a process in which Mark was used, that finally Luke, having already put together Mark and his own material, came upon Matthew and used him as a quarry for the teaching of Jesus. And it is claimed correctly that this is in accordance with the unanimous tradition of the early church.

That there is a case to present there is no doubt; that that case has been unduly neglected there is also no doubt. Whether the case is strong enough to overturn the widely accepted arguments for the priority of Mark must remain in doubt. It may in the end be safest to say that the view that Mark is the earliest gospel still holds the field, but that it cannot be regarded as a totally closed question.

And one thing is certain – whatever the origin of Matthew's gospel, it is the gospel which the Christian teacher cannot do without.

The Collect for St Matthew's Day

O Almighty God, who by thy Blessed Son didst call Matthew from the receipt of custom to be an Apostle and Evangelist; Grant us grace to forsake all covetous desires, and inordinate love of riches, and to follow the same thy Son Jesus Christ, who liveth and reigneth with thee and the Holy Ghost, one God, world without end. Amen.

9

THE GOSPEL OF LUKE

When we turn to the gospel of Luke we may straight away say two things about it.

First, it is one of the loveliest books in the New Testament. In a famous phrase Renan called Luke's gospel 'the most beautiful book in the world',[1] and, though all superlatives are dangerous, this is a verdict with which few would wish to disagree.

Second, it is one of the most important books in the New Testament. It is a notable fact that Luke, the only Gentile writer in the New Testament, wrote more of the New Testament than anyone else. In the Revised Standard Version of the New Testament there are 552 pages. Luke's gospel takes up 78 pages and Acts take up 71 pages, that is, 149 pages together. This is to say that Luke wrote about 27 per cent of the New Testament. Put together, Paul's Letters take up 121 pages of the New Testament, which is considerably less than Luke's two books. Luke is, therefore, the principal contributor to the New Testament in terms of the sheer amount of material.

Still further, although this is a matter to which we shall have to return, it may well be claimed that for biographical purposes for the life of Jesus, Luke's gospel stands alone. It is said that once a student asked James Denney to recommend a good life of Jesus, and that Denney replied: 'Have you tried the one that Luke wrote?' F.C. Grant writes in *The Gospels* (p. 133): 'If we had to choose between them – God forbid! – there is little question which of the gospels many would prefer to keep, and let the others pass into oblivion.' Luke, he says, is 'the most valuable writing in the New Testament'. He ends: 'If a final personal estimate may be hazarded, it is Luke who brings us closest of all the gospel writers to the Jesus of history, who is also the Lord of the church's faith.'

Let us begin our study of the third gospel by examining the church's tradition of its origin and character. The evidence is comprehensively set out by H.J. Cadbury in the second volume of *The Beginnings of Christianity*, in the chapter on 'The Tradition' (pp. 209-64).

(i) In the tradition there are two strands which it is impossible to separate, for they consistently occur together. These two strands are that the third gospel is by Luke, and that it has the closest connection with the gospel of Paul. When Luke is mentioned, very often it is in connection with Paul that the mention is made.

The earliest tradition is in the Muratorian Canon, which represents the view of the church in Rome about AD 170:

> The third book of the gospel, according to Luke, Luke that physician, ... after the ascension of Christ, when Paul had taken him as companion of his journey, composed in his own name on the basis of report.

The last phrase, as we shall later see, is simply a way of saying that Luke's gospel is not, and does not claim to be, an eyewitness account of the words and deeds of Jesus. Right from the beginning the Lucan authorship is asserted, and the connection with Paul is noted.

Irenaeus says in his book *Against Heresies* (3.1.1): 'Luke the follower of Paul recorded in a book the gospel that was preached by him.' And again (3.14.1): 'Luke ... preached with Paul ... and was entrusted with handing on the gospel to us.'

Eusebius in his *History* (6.25.6) reports Origen, when he is describing the process of the formation of the gospels, as writing: 'Third came that according to Luke'. He describes the gospel as 'Luke's words'.

Eusebius himself (3.4.6) writes:

> Luke, being by birth one of the people of Antioch, by profession a physician, having been with Paul a good deal, and having associated himself intimately with the rest of the apostles, has left us examples of the art of curing souls that he obtained from them in two divinely inspired books.

We shall now look more closely at the Pauline connection of Luke's gospel. Tertullian, writing *Against Marcion* (4.2), describes Luke's gospel as the gospel of his master, that is, of Paul.

So close was this connection taken to be that there were those who held that, when Paul used the words 'my gospel' (Rom. 2.16; 16.25; II Tim. 2.8; Gal. 1.11), it was Luke's gospel of which he was speaking. Eusebius (3.4.7) writes:

> They say that it was actually the gospel according to Luke that Paul used to mention whenever, as though writing about some gospel of his own, he used the expression 'according to my gospel'.

Jerome writes (*On Famous Men*, 7): 'Some suspect that whenever Paul says in his letters "according to my gospel" he means the volume of Luke.'

Another New Testament phrase became connected with this relationship between Luke and Paul. In II Corinthians 8.18 Paul writes to the Corinthians that he is sending to them with Titus 'the brother whose praise is in the gospel throughout all the churches'.

That translation – and it is the meaning which the early writers take out of it – means 'the brother who is praised throughout the churches for the gospel that he wrote'. It is true that the modern translations do not accept this meaning. The RSV speaks of 'the brother who is famous through all the churches for his preaching of the gospel', and the NEB has, 'one of our company whose reputation is high among our congregations everywhere for his preaching of the gospel'. The modern versions take it that the fame of the brother comes from his services in preaching and in evangelism; the ancient writers took it to mean that the fame of the brother came from the gospel that he wrote. We cannot say that the ancient writers must be wrong, for after all they spoke Greek as their native language, and, if they thought that the Greek could mean that, it certainly could. Certainly they regularly take this brother to be Luke, and take the phrase as a complimentary reference by Paul to Luke and his gospel.

Origen in the passage just quoted speaks of Luke's gospel as 'the gospel praised by Paul'. In the first of his *Homilies on Luke* he says:

> Luke is justly praised by the apostle who says, 'whose praise in the gospel is in all the churches', for this is said about no one else, nor accepted as said, except about Luke.

Jerome (*On Famous Men*, 7) is equally definite:

> The follower of the apostle Paul and comrade of all his travels, Luke wrote the gospel of which the same Paul says, 'We have sent together with him the brother whose praise is in the gospel through all the churches.'

And again in the preface to his *Commentary on Matthew* Jerome speaks of 'the third [gospel writer], Luke the physician, by birth a Syrian of Antioch, "whose praise is in the gospel"'.

The ancient writers so stressed the connection between Luke and Paul that they went the length of saying that Paul describes Luke's gospel as 'my gospel', and that he picks out Luke and his gospel for special praise. Even if we do not accept this point of view, the fact that it existed shows how close the connection of Luke with Paul was taken to be.

(ii)   The second strand in the tradition implies something further – the consistent recognition that Luke's gospel is not an eyewitness account, together with the equally consistent claim that in spite of that Luke's method of writing it makes it an apostolic document.

The Muratorian Canon says: 'However, Luke himself did not see the Lord in the flesh, and therefore, as he could trace the course of events, so he set them down.'

Irenaeus (*Against Heresies*, 3.14.3) writes:

> So the apostles, plainly and grudging no man, delivered to us those things which they had heard from the Lord. So Luke, also grudging no man, delivered to us those things which he had heard from them.

Tertullian writes (*Against Marcion*, 4.2):

Our faith is based on John and Matthew, it is built up on Luke and Mark, followers of the apostles . . . Luke indeed was not an apostle, but a follower of the apostles, not a master, but a disciple.

Jerome (*On Famous Men*, 7) distinguishes between the gospel and Acts: 'The gospel he wrote as he had heard; but the Acts of the Apostles he composed as he had seen.' Eusebius in his *History* (3.24.15) writes that Luke wrote 'aided by his continuous and intimate fellowship with Paul, and by his intercourse with the rest of the apostles'.

Luke himself, then, was not an eyewitness, but for all that his material is thoroughly apostolic.

(iii) The third strand of the tradition stresses the Greekness of Luke's gospel and holds that it was specially for Greeks and for Gentiles that Luke wrote. Origen in the passage quoted from Eusebius (6.25.6) writes: 'And third came the gospel according to Luke, who had made for converts from the Gentiles the gospel praised by Paul.'

Jerome writes in his *Commentary on Isaiah* (3.6):

The ancient writers of the church say that the evangelist Luke was very learned in the art of medicine, and that he knew Greek better than Hebrew. And, therefore, too, his language in the gospel, as well as in the Acts of the Apostles, that is in both volumes, is more eloquent and smacks of secular eloquence, and he uses Greek quotations more than Hebrew.

In one of his letters (20.9, to Damasus) Jerome gives an example of this:

With regard to the word *hosanna*, because they could not translate it into the Greek language, just as we see was done also in the case of *hallelujah* and of *amen* and in most other words, they put down the Hebrew itself, saying *hosanna*. Luke therefore who was the most learned in the Greek language among all the evangelists, since he was a doctor and wrote the gospel among the Greeks, because he saw that he could not translate the proper meaning of the word, thought it better to omit it, than to put down what would raise a question in the reader's mind.

In the Monarchian Prologue to Luke we read:

The principal object of his toil was that he should labour that the Greek faithful might, by the manifestation of all the perfection of God coming in the flesh, be prevented from giving themselves to the study of Jewish fables, and from being held by the desire of the law only, and that they might not be seduced by heretical fables and foolish questions, and so depart from the truth.

The early tradition held that Luke, himself a Greek, wrote specially for the Greeks.

Before we look at the attack on this tradition, it will be convenient at this point to collect what we know about Luke, both from the New Testament and from the tradition.

Our definite knowledge of Luke is very limited, for in the New Testament there are only three brief mentions of him. We know that he was one of Paul's fellow-workers (Philemon 24). We know that in the last days of Paul's imprisonment Luke alone was with him (II Tim. 4.11). Most important of the New Testament passages is Colossians 4.10-14. From that passage we learn that Luke was a doctor – the beloved physician, Paul calls him. And further, it is from this passage that we can deduce with certainty that Luke was a Gentile. In vv. 10f. Paul lists Aristarchus, Mark and Jesus Justus. These he says are the only men of the circumcision, that is, the only Jews, among his fellow-workers for the kingdom. Then he goes on to list another little group, Epaphras, Demas and Luke, who are clearly Gentiles.

But there is another part of the New Testament from which information may be gathered about Luke. There is in Acts a phenomenon which any reader will notice. The narrative will continue for a time in the third person plural – they did this, and they did that; and then it will change to the first person plural – we did this, and we did that. These latter passages are called the 'we passages' of Acts, and they are in Acts 16.10-17; 20.5-15; 21.1-18; 27.1-28.16. We shall consider these passages much more closely in connection with Luke's sources for Acts in Volume 2 ch. 14 (pp. 000ff.); but on the face of it, if Luke was the author of Acts, as we believe he was, then these passages represent times when Luke was actually present and a participator in the events which they describe. This will mean that Luke was with Paul on this first European journey from Troas to Philippi, that he was with him on the journey to collect the money for the offering to Jerusalem, that he went with Paul to Jerusalem, and that he finally accompanied Paul on his journey to Rome.

This last section of the journeys opens one interesting possibility. When a man was travelling to Rome under arrest, he was, if he had them, allowed to take two slaves with him as his personal attendants. It may well have been that Luke and Aristarchus enrolled themselves as Paul's slaves in order not to be separated from him on his last journey. If that is true, then devotion to friendship can go no further, and it makes Luke's determination to stay with Paul to the end even more dramatic.

That Luke was a doctor is noted by many of the ancient writers, and that he was also an evangelist makes him the doctor alike of the body and the soul. Jerome in a letter (53.8) says of him that his words are 'medicine for the sick soul'. And Zahn[2] says: 'Luke's professional calling might well open the way for him to many homes and hearts that remained closed to others.' It is said that a clergyman sees men at their best, a lawyer at their worst, and a doctor as they are. In a good doctor there is a vein of deep compassion. And so in his compassion Luke may well in the course of his work as a doctor have taken men as they are to make them physically and spiritually what they might become.

Before we leave the New Testament there is one other interesting speculation which we may note.

There are two passages in II Corinthians which speak of an unnamed *brother*. We give three different versions of each, for the significance of these passages involves a matter of translation. The first passage is II Corinthians 8.18:

AV: And we have sent with him [Titus] the brother whose praise is in the gospel throughout all the churches.

RSV: With him we are sending the brother who is famous through all the churches for his preaching of the gospel.

NEB: With him we are sending one of our company whose reputation is high among our congregations everywhere for his service to the gospel.

In the Greek the word is *adelphos*, which means 'brother'. It means brother in the family sense of the term, but Christians have always used it in the sense of 'fellow Christian', and it is definitely in this way that the NEB, perhaps mistakenly, takes it.

The second passage is II Corinthians 12.18:

AV: I desired Titus and with him I sent a brother.

RSV: I urged Titus to go and sent the brother with him.

NEB: I begged Titus to visit you, and I sent our friend with him.

Now of these three translations it is the RSV which is literally correct. The Greek is *the* brother. But as Souter has pointed out,[3] it is very possible that it is the church use of the word 'brother' which has confused the translation of these two passages. If anyone came on the second passage in ordinary Greek, he would certainly translate it, for it is the natural translation:

I urged Titus to go and sent *his* brother with him.

And the first passage would perfectly naturally mean:

With him [that is, Titus] we are sending *his* brother who is famous through all the churches for his preaching of the gospel.

This is to say that these two passages present us with the very interesting possibility, if not indeed the probability, that Luke was the brother of Titus.

So very little was known about Luke that it was inevitable that there should be speculation about his identity, and several identifications have been made. He has been identified both with the Lucius of Romans 16.21 and the Lucius of Cyrene of Acts 13.1. But the two names are not the same. Lucas, which is Luke in English, is the abbreviated form of the Latin Lucanus, and has nothing to do with the name Lucius. In these searches for identifications ingenuity replaces sense at times. Luke has been identified with Silvanus on a fantastic piece of exegesis. *Silva* and *lucus* are Latin words which both mean 'a wood, grove or forest', and so it is suggested that Luke and Silvanus both mean the same thing and refer to the same person!

When the early church wished to find some place for a great figure who had not been a member of the twelve, they frequently declared that he had been a member of the seventy sent out by Jesus (Luke 10.1-7). So it has been claimed that Luke was one of the seventy, but the fact that Luke was a Gentile makes that impossible, for the seventy would certainly all be Jews. It has been suggested that Luke was one of the Greeks who came to Andrew with the request to see Jesus (John 12.20). The most beautiful suggestion was made by Theophylact, that Luke was the unnamed companion of Cleopas on the walk on the way to Emmaus when the risen Christ appeared to them. Much as we would like to believe this, it is impossible, for quite certainly that companion was a Jew; and equally certainly Luke was not a follower of Jesus by that time, for it is repeatedly asserted that Luke was not an eyewitness of the events which he narrates.

There has been much argument as to where Luke came from. When the early writers speak about this they usually say that Luke came from Antioch. Eusebius in a passage already quoted (p. 000) describes Luke as 'being by birth one of the people of Antioch'. Jerome (*On Famous Men*, 7) speaks of 'Luke the physician, an Antiochene'. And in the preface to his *Commentary on Matthew* he describes Luke as 'by birth a Syrian of Antioch'. The Monarchian Prologue calls him 'a Syrian of Antioch by nation'.

Basilides and Cerdo, the Gnostic heretical writers, came from Antioch, and Luke's is the only gospel that they quote. From the narrative of Acts it is clear that Luke had a great deal of information about Antioch and considerable interest in it (11.1-27; 13.1-3; 14.19, 21, 26; 15.22f., 30, 35; 18.22).

There is one other fact to be added to this. *Codex Bezae*, a fifth-century manuscript with special characteristics of its own, has a 'we' passage in Acts 11.27f. In this it differs from most other manuscripts, but, although in the minority, it may possibly be right. The story tells how prophets came to Antioch from Jerusalem and how Agabus spoke. In this manuscript there come the extra words: 'There was great rejoicing, and, *when we had all assembled*, one of them called Agabus said . . .'. If this reading is accepted, then Luke's first personal appearance on the scene is in Antioch.

There is certainly evidence to connect Luke with Antioch, but it could well be that the statement that he came from Antioch is no more than a deduction from the fact that Luke does speak so much about Antioch.

Sir William Ramsay has made an interesting case to connect Luke with Philippi. In the great majority of manuscripts the first 'we passage' begins at Acts 16.10. The scene is Troas; Paul was undergoing a time of indecision, not knowing where to turn. Just at that time there appeared to him the man from Macedonia, in which Philippi was, with the appeal to come over and help them. Then the narrative continues: 'When *he* had seen the vision, immediately *we* sought to go into Macedonia.' In the mass of the manuscripts that is Luke's first appearance on the scene.

Ramsay then exercised his historical imagination. At that moment Paul had been quite uncertain where to go. Perhaps he met Luke then; perhaps he called him in as a doctor to help to treat the thorn in his flesh; perhaps he had known Luke already, for Tarsus was the most famous medical university in the ancient world at that time. Luke may have trained there, and Paul may have met him then. That night Paul had his dream and saw the man from Macedonia appealing for help. Ramsay then asks the question, how did Paul know that this man was from Macedonia, for Macedonians were like all other men? Ramsay's answer is that the man in the dream may well have been Luke himself. Maybe Luke had been pleading with Paul for days to come to Macedonia, and then Paul dreamed about him still pleading, and knew that the sign for action had come. It is speculation, but the picture makes sense.

Further, when Luke writes about Philippi, he does so with a kind of ringing pride. 'Philippi,' he writes, 'which is the leading city of the district of Macedonia and a colony' (Acts 16.12). But it was by no means as simple as that. There were other colonies in Macedonia, and, as for Philippi being the leading city, there was at that time bitter debate as to which was the chief city. Here speaks civic pride. In fact, as Ramsay says, no one but a Philippian would have spoken of Philippi in terms of such unqualified admiration. We may add that in Acts 17 the third person plural begins again, and the necessary deduction is that Luke stayed on in Philippi when Paul left.

We may note finally that a few late manuscripts connect Luke with Alexandria, but for that there is no firm evidence at all and no probability.

There is evidence to connect Luke with Antioch. Later tradition even declared that there was a wealthy citizen of Antioch named Theophilus. But the odd thing is that Antiochene tradition itself lays no claim to Luke. There is evidence to connect Luke with Philippi. But in the end we shall have to say that it is quite uncertain where Luke came from.

Little as it is, and comparatively useless as it is, we must collect the last fragments of the tradition about Luke.

There is a tradition about where he composed his gospel. Jerome in the preface to his *Commentary on Matthew* says: 'Luke . . . composed his book in the districts of Achaea and Boeotia.' An alternative reading has 'Bithynia' for 'Boeotia'. The Monarchian Prologue to Luke repeats this information:

> When gospels had already been written, by Matthew in Judaea and by Mark in Italy, at the instigation of the Holy Spirit Luke wrote this gospel in the parts of Achaea.

This may well be no more than a development of the belief that Luke wrote primarily for the Greeks.

As for Luke's death, the Monarchian Prologue seems to imply that he died a natural death: 'He never had a wife or children, and died at the age of seventy-four in Bithynia full of the Holy Spirit.'

Still later tradition makes him a martyr, crucified upon an olive tree, some said in Thebes. And Jerome (*On Famous Men*, 7) tells us that his relics and those of Andrew were translated to Constantinople in AD 357. His calendar day is 18 October.

There is one last tradition which is of interest. This tradition comes from a fourteenth-century historian, Nicephorus Callistus, who may be quoting from a sixth-century writer Theodorus the Reader. This is the tradition that Luke was a painter. The story goes on to say that the Empress Eudoxia found in Jerusalem a picture of Mary the mother of Jesus painted by Luke, and that she sent it to Constantinople to her daughter Pulcheria, the wife of Theodosius the Second. From there it was, so the story goes, brought to Venice. And to the present time there is in the church of Santa Maria Maggiore in Rome, in the Capella Paolina, a picture of Mary which is ascribed to Luke and which dates at least to AD 847.

Such then is the tradition about Luke. The later tradition may well be valueless, but the tradition of his connection with the third gospel and with Acts is early and consistent; and we must go on to see just what has been used to throw doubt upon it in modern times.

The attack on the Lucan authorship of the third gospel and of Acts is connected with the name of F.C. Baur and with the Tübingen school of theology. Its real point of attack is Acts and we shall deal with it more fully in the section on Acts in Volume 2, especially in chs. 11 and 12. But we must give some account of it here, because if it can be proved that Acts is not Lucan, then neither is the third gospel, for the two are inextricably connected. Although we cannot here enter into the detailed examination of the attack, we can lay down its general principles and that will be enough to see its methods and its results, and to judge how far they are to be accepted.

The Tübingen school accepted unreservedly the Hegelian view of history. This view sees history in terms of thesis, antithesis and synthesis. That is to say, one point of view, the thesis, emerges; the opposition point of view, the antithesis, equally emerges; between the thesis and the antithesis there is conflict, often bitter conflict; but the end of the process is a new situation, the synthesis, in which the thesis and the antithesis are blended or moulded or welded into one new whole. A much simpler way to put this in ordinary language would be to say that history consists of a series of swings of the pendulum.

To translate the Tübingen Hegelian view into New Testament terms, the situation is said to be this. In the beginning the church was a Jewish institution, and to this view all the original apostles subscribed; that is the thesis. Into this situation, which is typified and exemplified in Peter, there enters a new point of view which sees Christianity as a universal religion in which the Jews have no special rights, and in which the claims of the Jewish law are obliterated, and this situation is typified in Paul. That is the antithesis. Between these two points of view there comes an inevitable and violent clash, a clash between Petrine and Pauline Christianity. Thus there was a quite prolonged period of violent conflict. But finally there emerged the Catholic Church in which the conflict is resolved and unity and conciliation achieved; that is the synthesis.

The Tübingen claim is that in Acts we have a picture of the conciliation; we have a picture of a time when there is no real conflict between the two views. On the one hand, from the Jewish point of view, the original apostles plan missions to the Gentiles; it is actually Peter who baptizes the first Gentile, Cornelius. The work among the Gentiles is accepted and officialized, with only a few food regulations insisted upon (Acts 15) which Paul willingly and obediently accepts. On the other hand, from the Pauline point of view, Paul is a true Jewish Christian with all the hopes and the expectations of his people; he is recognized as an apostle by the original apostles; he is so much of a Jewish Christian that he guarantees his orthodoxy by undertaking to pay the expenses of the Jewish men who were engaged in the Nazirite vow (Acts 21).

There is in Acts, so it is claimed, a kind of deliberate equalization of Peter and Paul. What one does the other does. Peter heals a lame man at the gateway of the temple (Acts 3.1-10); Paul heals a lame man at Lystra (Acts. 14.8-10). The sick are healed by Peter's shadow passing over them (Acts 5.15); the sick are healed by the touch of articles of clothing which Paul had worn (Acts 19.12). Peter raises Tabitha from the dead (9.36-41); Paul restores life to Eutychus (Acts 20.9-12). The achievements of Peter and Paul are meticulously equalized.

All this presupposes a situation of conciliation in which there is no conflict at all. But was this the real situation? Was this the situation at the period which Acts purports to describe, or is this a reading back of a situation which did not arise until the conflicts had been synthesized into the Catholic Church?

For the Tübingen school there were certain documents which were certainly and unquestionably genuine. These were the four great Pauline letters, Galatians, Romans and I and II Corinthians. In them, so they believed, we will find the facts, the reflection of the actual historical situation as it was. And in them what do we find? Unquestionably, we find conflict. Paul is the anti-Judaist; the mission to the Gentiles was resented by the original church; it is Paul's and Paul's alone, and he was allowed to go on with it because they cannot do anything with him or stop him. In these letters we find Paul continuously under bitter attack by the Jewish opposition; the attack is both personal and is also a deliberate attempt to undo his work and to undermine his teaching. And the attack comes, not as it does in Acts from racial and religious Jews, but from Jewish Christians. The impression that Acts leaves is that there was no opposition within the church; the impression that the four unquestioned letters leave is that Paul was continuously subjected to bitter and active hostility. And, it is claimed, there can be no doubt that the evidence of the letters is to be accepted, for they are the account of the situation by Paul himself.

So, the argument runs next, Acts cannot be an accurate account of the situation which it purports to relate. It is rather an account written by a man after the conflicts were all ended and the synthesis of the Catholic Church had come; he reads back the era of conciliation into an era which was in fact an era of conflict. From this there follows an inevitable conclusion, Acts must be a work written some time in the first quarter of the second century, by which time the synthesis had come. And if Acts is a second-century work, it is certainly not by Luke, and, therefore, the third gospel cannot be Luke's work either. Is there an answer to this? Or must this view of Acts be accepted as the only possible view of the facts?

(i)	Before we begin to look at the general answers to this point of view, there is one particular point which must be noted. It is an odd fact about Acts that from it no one would ever have known, or even deduced, that Paul ever wrote a letter at all. Now, suppose there was a late second-century writer who was trying to make an account of the Pauline situation, if Paul's letters were available, then it is incredible that he would not have used them, and that he would not have had the skill to bring his account into line with them.

It would almost seem to be an inevitable conclusion that *Acts was written before Paul's letters had become common property*. In the first instance Paul's letters *were* letters; they were not originally regarded as scripture; it took time before the greatness of the man and his letters were discovered and the letters were collected and edited and issued as a book of the church. When did this happen? Paul's letters are first quoted by Clement of Rome; by his time it is clear that the letters are accepted and authoritative documents. Clement's date is midway through the last decade of the first century, about AD 95; but, even after the letters were edited and published, it must have taken some time for them to circulate and to establish themselves. They cannot have become public property much later than AD 90 or even AD 85. Now, if the writer of the Acts did not know about Paul's letters, he must have been writing prior to that, and therefore Acts cannot be a second-century document; it must come from a time between the years AD 85 and 95. This is a strong argument against a late date for Acts.

(ii)   But this does not in itself explain the apparent discrepancy between the picture of the situation in Acts and the picture of the situation in the letters. Can these two pictures be reconciled?

(a)   It is perfectly possible for a matter to be settled in *principle* and yet for a period of considerable difficulty to elapse before it is settled in *practice*. It would be perfectly possible for the church to accept the mission to the Gentiles in principle and for very serious difficulty to arise before the principle became accepted practice. We could argue that Acts sees the picture in principle; Paul in the nature of things sees it in practice.

(b)   It is still more possible for the leaders of a movement to accept a principle while the rank and file do not. To take a very modern example, responsible trades union leaders are all against wildcat and irresponsible strikes in industry, but that does not stop such strikes occurring. Trades union leaders may say one thing while shop stewards do another; and it is difficult for the leaders to find any workable way to impose their authority.

This seems an excellent analogy to the situation in the early church. It is perfectly possible that the leaders of the original church accepted the mission to the Gentiles and accepted Paul, while the rank and file Jews continued to hate him. This would in fact be the likeliest situation of all. The responsible leaders accepted the situation; the irresponsible rank and file refused to accept it, and there are always enough fanatics to lead the opposition.

There is no good reason why we should not believe that the leadership of the church accepted and backed Paul, while fanatical Jews still did everything to frustrate him. And this would mean that from their respective standpoints both Acts and the letters describe the same situation.

(c)   There is another point of view in this matter in which a necessary difference would arise.

There is always a difference in the point of view of the man who is more or less detached from the situation and the man who is deeply involved in it. Luke, writing from the position of the historian who looks at the events from the outside, sees them quite differently from Paul who is in the middle of them. True, Luke was involved in them also, but nothing like to the same extent as Paul.

It is perfectly possible that to a man with a volcanic and impatient temperament like Paul, the opposition and the frustrations seemed much more serious than they seemed to Luke. Paul was a man with a fire in his bones; he was driven by an internal compulsion; and opposition which to another would seem niggling seemed to him nothing less than the work of the devil and all his angels.

It is perfectly possible that Acts and the letters tell the same story from different points of view.

It is our conclusion that the arguments against the Lucan authorship of Acts and the third gospel are not sufficient to overturn their traditional connection with Luke.

We must now go on to try to see how Luke composed and put his gospel together. From his preface we may be sure that he would seek out all possible sources, that he would carefully test their accuracy, and that he would arrange his material in what seemed to him the best possible order.

To begin with we must go back to the place where we started our investigation of the gospels. If we accept the priority of Matthew, then Luke simply drew much of his material from there; but if we accept what may be called the more orthodox view, the priority of Mark, we can set down again the equations with which we started, in which the figures in brackets are the number of verses involved.

It will be remembered that the orthodox view of the connection between the gospels is that there are for Matthew and Luke two basic documents. There is Mark and there is a hypothetical document containing a collection of the sayings of Jesus to which the sign Q (*Quelle* = source) has been given. On this view Matthew and Luke used Mark and Q and added to these two documents their own special information, denoted by the symbols M and L respectively. The original equations therefore read:

Matthew (1068) = Mark (500) + Q (250) + M (320)
Luke (1149) = Mark (320) + Q (250) + L (580)

From these equations certain facts emerge.

i.   Luke does not use nearly so much of Mark as Matthew does, and he has much more material of his own than Matthew has.

ii.   When we examine Luke we find that he has two lengthy passages which do not depend on Mark at all. These are the 90 verses from 6.12-8.3 and the 349 verses from 9.51-18.14. Here are two long sections, the second the central section of the gospel, which are quite independent of Mark.

iii.　We next find that Luke completely omits one section of Mark. He has nothing at all from Mark 6.53-8.10.

iv.　When we study how Luke uses his material, we find that he has a quite different method from that of Matthew; they use their sources quite differently. Matthew interweaves his sources, drawing the different strands together into one new pattern. Luke does not interweave at all; he sets down his sources in alternating blocks. If we for the moment omit Luke 1 and 2, which are a special section, we find that Luke can be divided into 13 sections. Let us set these sections down, with its source letter beside it, 'M' for Mark and 'L' for Luke's own special source.

i.	3.1-4.30	L
ii.	4.31-44	M
iii.	5.1-11	L
iv.	5.12-6.11	M
v.	6.12-8.3	L
vi.	8.4-9.50	M
vii.	9.51-18.14	L
viii.	18.15-43	M
ix.	19.1-28	L
x.	19.28-36	M
xi.	19.37-48	L
xii.	19.49-22.13	M
xiii.	22.14-24.53	L

Here then is the way in which Luke built up his gospel, and it is quite different from Matthew's method. Matthew integrates his sources, until they become one new, composite whole; Luke sets down his sources in alternating slabs or blocks.

There could, of course, be more than one explanation of this shape of Luke's gospel; but the simplest explanation is that Luke had already written the first draft of his gospel *before* Mark came into his hands, and then simply inserted Mark's material in six different blocks at the appropriate points in his own gospel. This would mean that Mark was *not* one of the sources with which Luke started, but was rather extra material with which Luke completed and filled in that which might well have been composed some time before. The simplest explanation is that Luke inserted the Marcan material into his gospel without any attempt to interweave it into the original version. As Vincent Taylor says in *The Gospels* (p. 39): 'Mark for Luke is a quarry from which stone is obtained to enlarge an already existing building.'

If this view is correct, we might reconstruct the process as follows. During his two years' stay in Caesarea Luke discovered a copy of Q, the handbook of the teaching of Jesus. Caesarea was the headquarters of the Roman government of the province. Jerusalem was no great distance away. There would still be many left who had seen Jesus and who had talked' with him and listened to him. Luke collected all the material about Jesus which he could discover in his investigations. And out of this material, to which, as we remember, the symbol L is given, plus Q, he constructed a book. F.C. Grant in *The Gospels* (p. 118) calls it 'a small *vade-mecum*, most likely used by Luke himself and by the teachers in the Palestinian church'. This book of course does not now exist, but to it scholars have given the name of Proto-Luke, that is, the original form of Luke, the first version of Luke. It consisted of the following passages: 3.1–4.39; 5.1-11; 6.12–8.3; 9.51–18.14; 19.1-28, 37-44, 47f.; 22.14–24.53. If this reconstruction is so far accurate then the interesting fact emerges that this Proto-Luke material, which no other gospel has, is very early, at least as early as Mark, and perhaps earlier. We would be in this material as close to the earthly ministry of Jesus as it is possible to be.

Later, it would almost certainly be when he was with Paul in prison in Rome, Luke acquired a copy of Mark. Mark has just the material which Luke lacked. Luke lacked material about the time of Jesus' ministry spent in Galilee, for Galilee was far from Caesarea; Luke lacked the nature-miracle stories and the kingdom parables. This material Mark had. So Luke incorporated the Marcan material into his own book; but he did not interweave it; he simply inserted it in solid panels at certain places in his own work.

As a reconstruction this makes sense, and it explains the particular pattern that Luke has in relation to Mark. If this is true we have to rewrite one of the general equations with which we began. Our two general equations were:

$$\text{Matthew} = \text{Mark} + Q + M$$

and this equation can still stand.

$$\text{Luke} = \text{Mark} + Q + L$$

This equation must be altered to read:

$$\text{Luke} = (Q + L) + \text{Mark}$$

and we shall have to develop that equation a little further before we reach its final form.

If we accept the fact that Luke used Mark in this way, we have another question still to ask. Why did Luke completely omit the whole section Mark 6.53–8.10? Why is it that he takes nothing at all from it? That is obviously a question to which we can give no certain answer. The simplest answer to that question would be that Luke's copy of Mark was mutilated and that it did not contain that section because it was missing. But the trouble about that suggestion is that it is not difficult to conceive of the beginning or the end of a document being missing, but it is hard to conceive of the middle being missing, especially when in all probability the document was not a book but a roll. It may be that Luke felt that either the material was adding nothing new to what he had, or that some of it did not fit in with what he was trying to do. The feeding of the four thousand, the cure of the deaf and dumb man, the sayings about the traditions of the elders could be paralleled from elsewhere in the narrative. The story of the Syro-Phoenician woman was not a story that a writer with a special interest in the place of the Gentiles in the ministry of Jesus would choose to tell. And we have to remember that the maximum working length of a papyrus roll was 30 feet, and Luke's gospel, as it stands, would take all that space. Something in any event had to be missed out. There is more than one quite adequate reason why Luke should have omitted this section.

There are still certain other things which have to be fitted into Luke's pattern. Luke 3.1 reads as if it was intended as the beginning of a book:

> In the fifteenth year of the reign of Tiberius Caesar, Pontius Pilate being governor of Judaea, and Herod being tetrarch of Galilee, and his brother Philip tetrarch of the region of Ituraea and Trachonitis, and Lysanias tetrarch of Abilene, in the high priesthood of Annas and Caiaphas, the word of God came to John.

This elaborate sixfold dating reads like the initial sentence of a book which proposed to relate certain historical events. It gives a fixed point in time for the start. There can be little doubt that Luke did originally mean that sentence to be the opening sentence of his book. But as the gospel now stands there are two chapters before it.

The first two chapters of Luke's gospel stand alone. They are unique in their story of the birth of Jesus; unique in the human and the divine characters they bring on to the stage; unique in their great Christian hymns, the *Benedictus,* the *Magnificat*, the *Nunc Dimittis*, the *Gloria in Excelsis*. These chapters have no parallel in any of the other gospels.

They even stand alone in style, a difference that can be felt even in the English translation. They are almost certainly skilful translations of a Hebrew original, made by a man who was himself steeped in the Greek of the Septuagint, the Greek version of the Hebrew Old Testament. J.H. Ropes in *The Synoptic Gospels* (p. 69) writes of these two chapters that they are

> not improbably the translation of a little Hebrew book, charming in the

poetry which pervades it everywhere, as well as in the familiar canticles, and breathing a piety strikingly Jewish, and yet perfectly congenial to the Gentile-Christian gospel.

Luke, Ropes thinks, discovered this little book, skilfully translated it and used it as the beginning of his gospel. In these two chapters we are in touch with the poetry which makes theology look drab. That Luke rescued them from oblivion is something for which we should be profoundly grateful.

One last suggestion has been made about the Lucan pattern. It has been suggested that Luke had not only a special birth and infancy source, but that he had also a special resurrection source. Once again, there is no parallel in the other gospels to the walk to Emmaus story (24.13-35), which has been called 'the greatest recognition scene in history'. If we give the first two chapters the symbol 'I', to stand for infancy, and the resurrection stories the symbol 'R', we can now complete the Lucan equation:

$$\text{Luke} = (Q + L) + \text{Mark} + I + R.$$

We must now turn to the characteristics of Luke's gospel, and the consideration of the characteristics will also give us an insight into the aim of the gospel.

(i)   We have already seen that more than one ancient writer noted the fact that *Luke is the most Greek of the gospels*. Eusebius in his *History* (6.25.6) quotes Origen as saying that Luke's gospel was made 'for converts from the Gentiles'. Jerome in his *Commentary on Isaiah* (3.6) noted that in Luke's two volumes the style 'is more elegant and smacks of secular eloquence'. The Monarchian Prologue says that the object of the gospel is that the Greek believers might be kept steadfast in the faith. There are certain things in the gospel in which this is obvious.

(a)   Luke's vocabulary is more Greek than that of the others. Luke regularly substitutes a good Greek word for a Hebrew word, or for a Latin word, or for a colloquial word. He substitutes the Greek title of respect *epistatēs* for the Hebrew title *rabbi* (Mark 9.5; Luke 9.33). Instead of the Aramaic *rabbouni* he has the Greek *kurie* (Mark 10.51; Luke 18.41). He does not repeat Mark's Aramaic *Abba*, in the phrase *Abba*, Father (Mark 14.36; Luke 22.42). Simon in Luke is not *Kananaios* but *Zēlōtēs* (Mark 3.18; Luke 6.15; Acts 1.13). The first word is the Aramaic, the second the Greek, for a member of the sect of the Zealots.

In New Testament times Greek had borrowed certain Latin words; Luke frequently changes them back into their proper Greek equivalents. Mark will quite happily call a centurion *kenturiōn*, which is a straight transliteration of the Latin word; Luke calls that rank of soldier *hekatontarchēs*, which is Greek meaning literally commander of a hundred men (Mark 15.39; Luke 23.47). Mark uses *kēnsos*, which is the Latin word *census*, for tribute; Luke uses the correct Greek word *phoros* (Mark 12.14; Luke 20.22). In Matthew too (5.26, from Q) we find a Latinism, *kodrantes*, which is the Latin *quadrans* in Greek dress (meaning a very small coin); Luke (12.59) uses the much more Greek *lepton*. Luke instinctively changes colloquial Latinisms into good Greek.

Luke corrects some of Mark's colloquial words. In Mark the paralytic's bed is a *krabattos*, which is a colloquial word meaning a 'shakedown'; in Luke it is *klinidion*, a much more correct word for a bed (Mark 2.11; Luke 5.24). In Mark the little girl is a *korasion*; in Luke, more elegantly, she is *pais* (Mark 5.41; Luke 8.51). Luke is instinctively more fastidious in his choice of words.

In one particular sphere this argument has been specially stressed. In 1882 W.K. Hobart[4] published a book in which he claimed to prove by an examination of their vocabulary that only a doctor could have written the third gospel and Acts. It is now generally held that Hobart overstated his case, and that he reckoned as distinctively medical terms words which any educated layman would know and use. Here, for instance, is an invented paragraph, which is replete with medical terminology and which nevertheless any layman might have written:

> It was abundantly clear to any wise diagnosis that the body of the nation was labouring under grievous sickness. A fever of excitement had raised the national temperature, and it was clear that there were certain evils eating like a cancer into the life of the country. It was not a sedative, an opiate, or a tranquillizer that was needed. The people were in fact anaesthetized to the seriousness of the situation. Clearly there was need of drastic surgery to remove the disease which had invaded the national life. The health of the body politic was in the hands of the country's ministers of state.

It is perfectly true that a man does not need to be a trained doctor to have in his vocabulary many medical terms which have become part of the general vocabulary of any educated man.

But even when allowance is made for that, there are still indications that Luke did think in technical medical language. In the story of the demon-possessed man in the synagogue in Capernaum, the word which Mark uses for the demon throwing the man into convulsion is *sparassein*, which is a perfectly general word; Luke uses the word *riptein*, which is the technical medical word for such a seizure (Mark 1.26; Luke 4.35). Mark says simply that Peter's mother-in-law was 'sick with a fever'; Luke says that she was 'ill with a high fever' (Mark 2.30; Luke 4.38). Thus Luke shows that he knows the technical medical distinction between greater and lesser fevers. In Mark 1.40 Mark describes the suffering man as simply a leper; Luke says that he was full of leprosy (Luke 5.12). In Luke 9.38 the father of the epileptic boy asks Jesus to 'look upon' his son, and the word he uses is the word *epiblepein*, which is technical for a doctor's examination of his patient. In the story of the raising of the widow's son at Nain (7.15) and in the story of the raising of Tabitha (Acts 9.40) the word that Luke uses for 'sitting up' is *anakathizein*, which is the technical word for a patient sitting up in bed.

There are occasions when Luke uses medical language with technical precision. In the story of the healing of the man at the Temple gate, Luke uses the rare medical word *sphudra* for ankle-bones; literally the word means the condyles of the leg-bones. In telling of the cure of Paul's blindness (Acts. 9.18) Luke uses two technical medical terms, the word *lepides* for the scales that were on Paul's eyes, and the word *apopiptein* for their falling off. In telling of the blindness of Elymas Luke uses the word *achlus*, which is translated 'mist'; and it is the technical word for a certain kind of eye disease (Acts 13.11). Perhaps the most interesting case is in the parallel passages Matthew 19.24 = Mark 10.25 = Luke 18.25. This is the verse which talks about a camel going through the eye of a *needle*. For 'needle' both Matthew and Mark use the word *raphis*, which is the ordinary word for a domestic needle; Luke uses *belonē*, which is the word for a surgeon's needle. Apparently it was the medical word which came first to Luke's mind and tongue.

In telling of the paralysed man who was brought to Jesus by his friends Mark (2.3) describes him as *paralutikos*, which is a popular and colloquial term; Luke (5.18) calls him *paralelumenos*, which is the correct medical term, the word which a doctor would naturally use. When Luke tells the story of the man with the withered hand, he adds the information that it was the man's *right* hand (Mark 3.1; Luke 6.6); and in the story of the events of the Garden Luke adds the information that it was the *right* ear of the high priest's servant which was wounded and healed (Mark 14.47; Luke 22.50, 51). In telling the story of the woman with the issue of blood Mark (5.26) says that 'she had suffered under many physicians, and spent all she had, and she was no better but rather worse'. Luke (8.43) says simply that she had had a flow of blood for twelve years, 'and could not be healed by anyone', thus removing the implied jibe against doctors.

We may agree that Hobart overstated his case and found technical medical language where there was none; but in spite of that there is still enough evidence left to show that Luke did use medical language in a way that reveals the expert.

(b) There are at least two instances in which Luke uses the accepted literary conventions of his day, as H.J. Cadbury points out and illustrates in his book *The Making of Luke-Acts* (pp. 194-209). The first instance is in his preface. 'The preface of Luke,' says

Overbeck,[5] 'is the one place in the New Testament of which one may say that in it the world shines through most plainly.' Luke's preface is carefully written, in the best Greek in the New Testament.

In contemporary secular literature the preface was a regular feature. Cadbury writes that in their prefaces 'even the most incapable of writers made an effort at style for the frontispiece', and it was almost universally the case that the preface was different from the rest of the work, with choice and elegant words, carefully balanced sentences, and a good cadence at the end. Even in writers the rest of whose writing is almost barbarous the preface was always in carefully wrought Greek. In the prefaces there was usually some reference to past writers on the same subject, some reference to the writer's special qualifications, some indication of his decision to write and his aim and purpose in writing, and often a dedication to some particular person. Sometimes the preface was so carefully wrought and so lengthy that it was altogether out of proportion, 'the head of a colossus', as Lucian said,[6] 'on the body of a dwarf'.

When Luke chose to begin his gospel with such a preface as he used, he was following the established literary convention of his day. We may cite two prefaces from secular writers to show how closely Luke did follow the conventional custom. The first, interestingly enough, is from a medical work, the *Materia Medica* of a writer called Dioscorides:

> Although not only many ancient but also many modern writers have composed works on the preparation, the power and the testing of drugs, my dearest Areios, I shall try to prove to you that no empty or unreasonable impulse has moved me to undertake this work.

Josephus begins his work *Against Apion* thus:

> It is my intention by composing a work on ancient history, Epaphroditus best of men, to give clear information to those who meet with it, about the nature of the Jews. Since I see that many disbelieve our claims, I thought it necessary to write briefly to convict the deliberate falsification of some, to correct the ignorance of others, and to teach all who wish to know the truth.

The pattern of all the prefaces is the same, the carefully wrought Greek, the implication that the previous writers have not been adequate, the statement of purpose, and the name of the person to whom the work is addressed or dedicated. In the preface Luke, by the very act of writing it, shows us that he intended to produce a literary work for cultured Greeks to read.

(ii) There could be, and there probably is, one far-reaching reason for the Greekness of the third gospel. An author's style and method will obviously be largely determined by the audience for which he is writing. Both Luke's books are written to a man called Theophilus (Luke 1.3; Acts 1.1). If we could find out just who Theophilus was and for what he stood, it would be a great help in deciding the purpose and the aim of Luke's books. This is, of course, a matter about which we can only speculate, and it is obviously the kind of matter on which speculation was bound to be busy. It is at this point therefore that we must turn to look at Theophilus, and at some of the theories which have been advanced about him.

(a) It has been suggested that Theophilus is not really a proper name, but rather a general title for the Christian. It is compounded of two Greek words, *theos*, which means *God*, and *philein*, which means 'to love'. It could therefore mean 'lover of God', a title which could describe any Christian, and this is what Epiphanius, for example, says in his *Heresies* (51.7) that it means. He takes the gospel to be addressed 'to every man who loves God'. The second part of the word could be derived not from the verb *philein*, which means 'to love', but rather from the noun *philos*, which means 'friend'. Theophilus could therefore be a general title for anyone who is a friend of God, and it is in this way that Ambrose takes it in his *Commentary on Luke*. Origen in the first of his *Homilies on Luke*, accepting the second derivation, takes it to mean not so much 'one who loves God', but 'one whom God loves'. In Jerome's Latin translation of Origen we read:

> You all, who hear us speaking, if you are such as to be loved by God, are Theophiluses, and to you the gospel is written. If anyone is a Theophilus he is best and strongest. This is what is clearly meant by the Greek word *kratistos*.

(*Kratistos*, which is translated 'excellent', can also commonly mean 'most strong' or 'most powerful'.) So, says Origen, 'No Theophilus is weak', that is, no one loved by God can be weak.

Attractive as these suggestions are, it is much more likely that Theophilus really was a definite individual, and that the name is not just a general title for a Christian. Let us, then, look at some of the suggestions which take Theophilus to be an individual.

(b) We may first of all note that the fact that a book is dedicated to one particular individual is no proof at all that it was meant to be read only by him. As we have seen, Dioscorides dedicated his *Materia Medica* to Areios, and Josephus his *Against Apion* to Epaphroditus, and Seneca dedicated his *Quaestiones Conviviales* to Sossius Senecio. In modern times a book is not meant only for the person whose name appears on the dedication page.

As Cadbury points out, there could be many reasons for such a dedication. The person to whom the book was dedicated might be a friend of the author; he might be the person who inspired, or asked for, the book; he might be a famous name which would add prestige to the book; he might be a patron who had guaranteed or provided the costs of publication; he might simply be an authority in the field on which the book was written and thus a fitting person to receive such a dedication. The fact that a book is dedicated to someone is not even a guarantee that the person so addressed is specially interested in its contents. As Cadbury says in *The Making of Luke-Acts* (pp. 203f.), in the second century alone books were dedicated to reigning Roman emperors on word accents (in twenty volumes) by Herodian; on military strategy by Aelian and Polyaenus; on the sayings of kings and generals by Plutarch; on geography by Arrian; a dictionary by Pollux; and of course all the early defences of the Christian apologists were addressed to emperors or influential men in the state.

Dedications were common in the Hellenistic world just as they are common now, and could be either a compliment to some great one whom the author did not even know personally, or an attempt to gain some prestige for the book. But we would judge from the tone of Luke's addresses that he had a closer connection with Theophilus than that.

(c) We may dispose of the less likely suggestions first. The *Clementine Recognitions* (10.71) speak of a Theophilus who was a wealthy and influential citizen of Antioch, and who was so moved by the preaching of Peter that he turned his house into a church. Still later tradition makes him a bishop of Antioch. The *Apostolic Constitutions* (7.46) have a story of a Theophilus who was the third bishop of Caesarea after Cornelius and Zacchaeus. These are highly improbable traditions.

(d) Luke calls Theophilus 'most excellent Theophilus' (1.3). The Greek is *kratiste*. This could simply mean 'best of men'; but *kratiste* is the normal title which in modern English would be rendered 'Your Excellency'. It is the title for a high government official. If this is so, then Luke's gospel and Acts may well have been written in defence of Christianity. They may have been written to prove to some Roman governor or high official that Jesus was not revolutionary, that Christianity was not politically dangerous, and that in fact Paul had received nothing but courtesy and even protection from Roman officials. Some have gone so far as to suggest that Luke's two books are nothing other than the material for the brief for the defence of Paul. To this we shall return. At the moment we simply note that this is a perfectly possible view of the identity of Theophilus and of the nature of the third gospel and Acts.

(e) As the RSV has it, Luke writes to Theophilus 'concerning the things of which you have been informed'. The word which is translated 'informed' is a part of the verb *katēchein*. This word can have two meanings each of which would give good sense.

It is, first, the word from which the English word 'catechumen' comes; in this case Theophilus would have had instruction as a catechumen and Luke would be giving him fuller information. This would bring Theophilus definitely within the Christian church, or would at least infer that he was very interested in Christianity and was an enquirer.

But, secondly, this word *katēchein* can and does mean to 'misinform', to give malicious and twisted information (cf. Acts 21.21, 24; 24.1; 25.2; 25.15). In this case Luke would be writing to correct the inaccurate and probably damaging information which Theophilus had received about Christianity. Thus Luke's two books would be an attempt to counteract falsified accounts of Christianity which had reached the ears of Theophilus, and, if Theophilus was a high government official, such correction would be very necessary and valuable.

(f) There is one romantic possibility. Luke was a doctor. Many doctors began by being slaves. It is possible that Luke was the doctor of Theophilus, that he had been of signal service to him, perhaps even saving his life, and that then Theophilus had given Luke his freedom, and that in gratitude Luke gave to Theophilus the only thing of value he had to give, the story of Jesus and of the church.

That this could happen is certain. Pliny was the governor of Bithynia during the reign of Trajan. He was personally on terms of close friendship with Trajan and he wrote him a long series of letters on all kinds of things during his governorship. One of the letters (10.5) runs like this:

> Last year I was attacked by a severe and dangerous illness. I employed a physician, whose care and diligence, Sir, it is not in my power to reward, except with your gracious help. I entreat you therefore to make him a citizen of Rome, for he is a freedman belonging to an alien.

It is just possible that Theophilus did the same for Luke as Pliny did for his doctor, and that Luke's two books are the token of his gratitude to Theophilus.

(g) The last possibility in regard to Theophilus is the most dramatic, but, even if it itself were to be rejected, that which it stands for will take us a very considerable distance into the aim and the purpose of the third gospel. The possibility with which we now go on to deal is well set out in B.H. Streeter's *The Four Gospels* (pp. 535-39).

In its early days Paul could say of the church that not many in it were wise according to worldly standards, not many powerful, not many of noble birth (I Cor. 1.26). Such a situation could not continue to exist indefinitely, if the church was to be the universal church, and by the last quarter of the first century there were signs in Rome that this situation was in fact changing.

The era of Domitian was an era of persecution; Domitian was the first of the emperors to insist on and delight in the title, *kurios kai theos, dominus et deus*, lord and god. An emperor governing from such a point of view was bound to be a threat to Christianity. But the astonishing thing is that by the time of Domitian Christianity seems to have reached the very highest level of society. In AD 91 the former consul Acilius Glabrio was compelled to fight against the beasts in the arena 'as an innovator', and there is at least the possibility that he was a Christian.

An even more startling event happened in Rome in AD 95 just eight months before Domitian himself was assassinated. This was the execution of Titus Flavius Clemens for 'atheism', and the banishment of his wife Domitilla to the little island of Pontia.[7] Titus Flavius Clemens was Domitian's cousin; he was married to Domitilla, who was Domitian's niece, the only daughter of his only sister. Domitian had associated him with himself as consul; he had bidden him to name his two sons Domitian and Vespasian. Domitian himself was childless, and it is certain that he meant Flavius Clemens and his sons to succeed him in the imperial power. And then, to the shocked astonishment of Rome, in AD 95 Flavius Clemens was executed and Domitilla was banished. Domitilla has always been claimed as a Christian martyr, and, although the claim in the case of her husband has never been so definitely made, it is at least possible and even likely that he died as a Christian.

Streeter would go as far as to claim that it is within the bounds of possibility that Theophilus to whom Luke wrote was none other than Titus Flavius Clemens himself. But, whether or not we accept this identification, what is clear is that by this time Christianity had reached the highest level of Roman society.

For this new kind of clientèle Christianity clearly needed a new kind of literary approach. Something must be written which would not jar on the literary taste of educated and cultured Romans and Greeks. As Streeter points out, the chances are that the upper class Roman would see three objectionable things about Christianity. It was sordid in its origin, for it came from the hated Jews. Luke shows Christianity, not as a Jewish production, but as a world religion, universal in its scope. It would seem newfangled in its teaching. Luke goes to the prophets and shows Christianity to be as ancient as the eternal purpose of God. It would seem politically dangerous; it was as a political danger that Nero had attacked Christianity. Luke shows that the teaching of Jesus is the reverse of revolutionary in this political sense, and in Acts he shows that the Roman government was often the best protector of Christianity. Three times Pilate declares that he finds no fault whatever in Jesus (Luke 23.4, 14, 22).

Luke's work, Streeter says, is an attempt, and an extraordinarily successful attempt, to meet this new situation. It is the first of the

'Apologies' which were in the following centuries to be so often presented to the Roman power.

Luke's work in its Greekness and in its elegance and beauty is an attempt to present Christianity to a new audience without at the same time ever forgetting the ordinary people.

(iii)   Wikenhauser in his *Introduction to the New Testament* (p. 213) called Luke 'the historian evangelist', and it has often been claimed, although now the view is disputed, that of all the gospel writers Luke comes nearest to being an historian, and of all the gospels his comes nearest to being a biography of Jesus.

As far back as 1797 Herder wrote of Luke's gospel that it is 'the first Christian history'. It is 'no collection of gospel stories, like Mark; no Jewish demonstrative argument, like Matthew. Luke wrote his history like a pure Greek.'[8] Zahn writes:

> Luke does not, like Matthew, write an apology on behalf of Christ and his Church in order to meet objections of a national character. Nor does he, like Mark, present, from a single point of view, narratives which have been impressed upon his memory by frequent hearing and repetition. His design is rather, as a Greek historian, to set forth the history of Christianity from its beginnings to the completion which it had reached in his own time, and he aims to do this in such a way that his exposition, based upon thorough investigation and presenting the whole development of Christianity connectedly, shall impress, with a sense of the trustworthiness of the Christian traditions, a cultured Gentile who has heard much about the facts which are current in the Christian Church and held to be the basis of its faith, and whose relations to individual Christians, like the author, are friendly.[9]

The traditional view of Luke's gospel does regard it as being at least in aim history. Lucien Cerfaux writes in *The Four Gospels* (p. 57):

> With the work of St Luke, the gospel tradition embarks on its career as literature . . . Matthew and Mark are not historians but evangelists, St Luke claims to write as an historian of Christianity.

That Luke intended to write a work of history is certainly indicated by certain things in the gospel. The preface (1.1-4) is an historian's preface, and is a claim to historical research within the limits of Luke's day. The sixfold dating in 3.1f. is a setting of the Christian story in the context of world history. Thucydides, the Greek historian (2.2.1), has a precisely similar dating for his basic event, the attack on Plataea, which began the Peloponnesian War, about which he wrote his history:

> In the fifteenth year of the armistice, in the priesthood at Argos of Chrysis, then in her forty-eighth year of service, in the ephorship of Ainesias at Sparta, in the archonship among the Athenians of Pythodorus

with two months still to serve, in the sixth month after the battle at Potidaea, at the beginning of spring, came men from Thebes....

This is exactly the way in which Luke, too, works out his date. It is further significant that Luke is the only New Testament writer to mention a Roman emperor by name. He mentions Augustus, Tiberius and Claudius (Luke 2.1; 3.1; Acts 11.28; 18.2). It is Luke who sets the whole matter in its historical perspective, and who writes as an historian wrote.

But we would do well to remember just what an ancient historian was trying to do. It is in fact a matter of interest to see what any historian regards himself as trying to do. Lucian in his book *On how to Write History* (39) says: 'The one task of the historian is to describe things exactly as they happened.' Streeter in *The Four Gospels* (p. 543) says: 'History is the endeavour to find out what actually happened.' We shall have to leave the full consideration of Luke as an historian for a separate work on Acts, but we can at least see something of what history meant in his day. Is this idea of history as a narrative of events either the legitimate or the best view of history?

T.R. Glover has an essay on 'The Study of Ancient History'.[10] In it he quotes certain verdicts on history and the writing of it. Dr Johnson once said:

> Great abilities are not requisite for an historian; for in historical composition all the greatest powers of the human mind are quiescent. He has facts ready to his hand; so there is no exercise of invention. Imagination is not required in any high degree ... Some penetration, accuracy and colouring will fit a man for the task, if he can give the application which is necessary.

'There is but a shallow stream of thought in history,' he said on another occasion. On still another occasion he said: 'That certain kings reigned, and certain battles were fought, we can depend upon as true; but all the colouring, all the philosophy is conjecture.' Boswell answered: 'Then, sir, you would reduce all history to no better than an almanack, a mere chronological series of remarkable events.' And the extraordinary fact is that Gibbon was present on this occasion and made no protest! Even Aristotle in the *Poetics* (1451b) said that history merely tells us 'what Alciabiades did or suffered'; poetry is therefore a 'more philosophic and serious' thing than history.

This, as Glover points out, is in any event an inadequate view of history. 'History is movement', and movement implies direction. Therefore history requires perspective. If the only object is the discovery and recovery of bare facts, then one fact tends to become as important as another fact. There is need of both perspective and proportion to make any kind of sense of the picture.

This, of course, involves the fact that in historical writing there is evaluation, and this in turn involves both a standpoint and an aim on the part of the historian. Glover quotes Carlyle as saying that the two necessary qualities in an historian are Stern Accuracy in discovering the facts and Bold Imagination in interpreting them.

The ancient historians openly and admittedly had their aims. It may be well to remember that originally in the ancient world history was a branch of rhetoric. Herodotus read his histories to his audience. It would, then, be not unfair to say that history had an entertainment value. But this is not very different from saying that the historian, like any writer, must master the art of communication, and the art of communication is quite simply the art of awakening the interest of the hearer or the reader. It is difficult to imagine any writer writing a completely 'aimless' book.

Ancient history was on the whole moral in its aim. Lucian in his book *On how to Write History* (42) says that one of the great aims of history is *usefulness*. The purpose of good history is that 'if ever again men find themselves in a like situation they may be able from a consideration of the records of the past to handle rightly what now confronts them'. Herodotus in his opening chapter tells us that he wrote his history 'in order that the memory of the past may not be blotted out from among men by time, and that great and marvellous deeds done by Greeks and foreigners and especially the reason why they warred against each other may not lack renown'. Thucydides (1.22) wrote the history of the Peloponnesian war because he believed that 'this was the greatest moment that had ever stirred the Greeks'. Livy in his Preface tells us that he had two reasons for writing. He wished to have the joy of perpetuating the memory of the premier people of the world, the Romans. Second, he wrote to provide real examples of every kind of behaviour. 'From these you can take, both for yourself and for the state, ideals at which to aim; you can learn also what to avoid because it is infamous either in its conception or in its issue.' This is not far off the saying that 'history is philosophy teaching by examples'. Tacitus in his *Annals* (3.65) says much the same: the aim of history is to see to it that 'virtues are not passed over in silence, and to make sure that from their consequences and their ill-fame wicked words and deeds are dreaded'.

That is the moral view of history, but there were more philosophic views. Polybius (5.21.6) took it to be the task of history to explain why what happens follows and must follow from what has happened. Cicero in one of his letters to his friend Atticus (9.5) says that his main interest is not in events but in their causes.

What must be quite clearly seen is that it does not damn a history out of hand to say that it had an aim and a purpose, and that it set out to show that something was or was not the case. A man need not be a bad or dishonest historian because he was writing for a verdict.

Luke is not the less an historian because he is trying to commend

Christ and Christianity to the audience for which he writes.

In regard to this matter of the historicity of Luke, we may select one aspect of it, on which different writers have had quite different opinions based on exactly the same facts. This is the matter of Palestinian geography in Luke and Acts.

Harnack in his book *The Acts of the Apostles* (pp. 71-87) comes to the conclusion that Luke had at least a tourist's personal knowledge of Palestine, and claims that it is possible to see this from the way in which he writes. If we accept the fact that Luke did write Acts, and if we accept the fact that the 'we' passages of Acts represent occasions when Luke was personally present, then in Acts 21 we find the information that Luke accompanied Paul to Jerusalem, and it may well be that he spent the two years of the Caesarean imprisonment with Paul. From this we can deduce with certainty that Luke had at least been in Palestine.

His knowledge in certain places, both in the gospel and in Acts, seems vivid and detailed. He knows that Caesarea is not part of Judaea, but the headquarters of the Roman government (Acts 12.19; 21.10). He knows that Mount Olivet is a sabbath day's journey from Jerusalem (Acts 1.12); that the field in which Judas Iscariot died was called Akeldama, the Field of Blood (Acts 1.19). He knows the road that goes from Jerusalem to Gaza (Acts 8.26). He knows about the upper room where the disciples met in the house of Mary (Acts 12.12). His description of the prison of Peter is curiously vivid. 'When they had passed the first and second guard, they came to the iron gate leading into the city' (Acts 12.10); and if we add between the two clauses the addition of the Western Text, 'and when they had gone down the seven steps', it becomes even more vivid. It even looks as if Luke might have visited the place and seen it for himself. He knows of the beautiful gate of the temple (Acts 3.10) and of Solomon's colonnade (Acts 3.11). He knows of the official called 'the captain of the temple' (Acts 4.1), and about the auxiliary cohort stationed in Jerusalem (Acts 21.31). He knows about the steps which lead up to the tower of Antonia (Acts 21.40). He knows that the Sanhedrin contained Pharisees and Sadducees, and that they differed violently about the resurrection from the dead (Acts 23.6f.). He knows that Caesarea is two days' journey from Jerusalem; it was 62 miles away (Acts 23.31f.).

The Emmaus story begins: 'That very day two of them were going to a village called Emmaus, about seven miles from Jerusalem' (Luke 24.13). Harnack (p. 81) says that one does not write like that, 'unless one has been oneself on the spot'.

It might well seem that here we have a very strong case for holding that Luke has vivid and accurate geographical knowledge of Palestine and Jerusalem. But precisely the opposite point of view is taken by Hans Conzelmann in *The Theology of St Luke*. His view is that it is useless and pointless to try to identify Lucan geographical references, for geography in Luke is not literal and physical but symbolic and theological. So the Jordan is the region of John the Baptist and therefore the region of the old era (p. 20). The temptation happens in the desert, but 'it is pointless to attempt to locate it', because the desert is not geographical; it marks the symbolic separation between the Jordan and Galilee (p. 27). Galilee itself is not a region; it is simply the place of the people who were later to become the orginal witnesses; 'Galilean' is not a geographical description at all; it stands for those who were these witnesses (pp. 41, 47). The mountain in Luke has become entirely stylized as the place of prayer. So much so is this the case that in Luke 4.5, in the story of the temptations, the word 'mountain' vanishes from the story and it is not said that Satan took Jesus into a high mountain and showed him the kingdoms of the world (as in Matt. 4.8).

> There is no question of locating 'the' mountain. It is a mythical place to which 'the people' cannot come. . . . It has become the type of the place of prayer and heavenly proclamation (p. 44).

The transfiguration is 'the classical mountain-scene' (p. 57). Similarly the plain is 'the place of meeting with the people' (p. 44). In the same way the lake is also stylized. 'The lake is more a "theological" than a geographical factor. It is the place of manifestations which demonstrate the power of Jesus' (p. 42). 'The lake is the given setting for the manifestation of power' (p. 49).

As Conzelmann sees it, there is no physical geography in Luke. Luke is not even clear as to where places are. He, so Conzelmann would say, visualizes Galilee as being directly north of Judaea.

Here we have two exactly opposite ideas, the idea of Luke as an historian who knows at least something of the area in which the events are taking place, and the idea of Luke as a theologian, to whom the meaning of everything is symbolic.

The decision between the two viewpoints cannot be other than a subjective judgment. No one will deny that Luke had theological interests and aims, for all the gospel writers were seeking to confront men with Jesus Christ as Saviour and Lord, but in our judgment Luke's writings read in such a way that they are the writings of a man who was writing history, in the sense of history with a purpose, as the ancient writers understood history.

We can now turn to the characteristics of Luke's gospel which are not matters of controversy, but on which all would be agreed.

(iv)   From the point of view of the sweep of its material Luke is *the most comprehensive of the gospels*. It begins with the events which are the prologue to the life of Jesus and it does not leave him until it has told of the ascension. If the material in all three gospels is put together, it can be divided into 172 sections. Of these sections Luke contains 127; Matthew 114; Mark 84. Of these sections 48 are peculiar to Luke; 22 to Matthew; 5 to Mark. This is to say that between one-third and one-quarter of the material in the gospel is special to Luke.

Luke has at least five miracle stories which are his own:

The miraculous catch of fishes (5.1-11)
The raising of the widow's son at Nain (7.11-17)
The healing of the bent woman (13.10-17)
The healing of the man with dropsy (14.1-6)
The healing of the ten lepers (17.11-19).

Luke's contribution to the stock of parables is even richer. He has at least thirteen parables which are his own:

The two debtors (7.40-43)
The good Samaritan (10.29-37)
The friend at midnight (11.5-8)
The rich fool (12.13-20)
The barren fig-tree (13.6-9)
The rash builder and the reckless king (14.28-32)
The lost coin (15.8-10)
The lost son (15.11-32)
The unjust steward (16.1-9)
The rich man and Lazarus (16.19-31)
The farmer and his servant (17.7-10)
The unjust judge (18.1-8)
The Pharisee and the tax-collector (18.9-14).

Here the church's debt to the research of Luke is obvious.

Luke has also a certain amount of narrative material which is his own. We may cite as examples:

The story of the Samaritan village (9.51-56)
The story of Zacchaeus (19.1-10)
The story of the trial before Herod (23.6-12)
The story of the penitent thief (23.39-43)
The walk to Emmaus (24.13-35).

In sheer amount of material Luke's gospel takes a foremost place.

(v)   We have already noted that Luke is the most literary of the gospels; but we may select two literary characteristics which are specially characteristic of it.

(a)   Certain of its stories have *a cameo-like quality*. Such stories are the story of the raising of the widow's son at Nain (7.11-17); the incident in the house of Simon the Pharisee of the woman who was a sinner (7.36-50); the story of Martha and Mary (10.38-42). The story of the final dénouement of the walk to Emmaus has been called 'the greatest recognition scene in literature' (24.13-35). Whether or not the legend that Luke was a painter is true, he certainly saw things with an artist's eye.

(b) Many writers have noted Luke's masterly use of *contrast*. He has a habit of placing two contrasting things side by side so that the one illumines the other.

He shows us the unwilling priest and the willing maiden (1.18, 39); the self-abasing tax-collector and the self-righteous Pharisee (18.9-14); the coldly contemptuous Pharisee and the passionately loving sinner (7.36-50); the thankless Jewish lepers and the grateful Samaritan leper (17.11-19); the practical Martha and the mystical Mary (10.38-42).

Luke was a master of the art of dramatic juxtaposition.

(vi) Perhaps the most obviously outstanding characteristic of Luke's gospel is that it is *the universal gospel* and that it thinks in terms of *the universality of salvation*. Matthew traces the genealogy of Jesus back to Abraham (Matt. 1.2), the founder and father of the Jewish nation; Luke traces it back to Adam (3.38), the father of all men. All four gospels quote the passage from Isaiah (40.3) as a foretelling of the coming of the herald of the Messiah. Matthew (3.3), Mark (1.2f.) and John (1.23) have:

> The voice of one crying in the wilderness:
> Prepare the way of the Lord,
> make his paths straight.

Only Luke (3.4-6) continues the quotation:

> Every valley shall be filled,
> and every mountain and hill shall be brought low,
> and the crooked shall be made straight,
> and the rough ways shall be made smooth;
> *and all flesh shall see the salvation of God.*

Luke deliberately continues the quotation to include the universal promise.

It is not without significance that Luke is the only gospel writer to record the great claim of Jesus: 'The Son of man came to seek and to save the lost' (19.10). (As the RSV and the NEB show, this verse is wrongly included at Matthew 18.11 in the AV. In the best text it occurs only in Luke.)

Luke has a picture of God with arms outstretched wide enough to hold the whole world in their embrace, and with a heart great enough to love all men.

(vii) In this universalism *the Samaritans* are included. They are not only included, they are praised. Jesus refuses to destroy the Samaritan village which will not give him hospitality (9.51-56). The hero of the parable is the kindly Samaritan whose conduct far surpasses that of the orthodox Jewish ministry (10.30-37). Of the ten lepers only the Samaritan returns to give thanks (17.11-19). The Jewish hatred and contempt for the Samaritans is overpassed in the universal love of God in Jesus.

(viii)   In this universalism *the Gentiles* are included. It is quite true that at its highest Jewish thought conceived of the Jewish nation as being a light to the Gentiles (Isa. 42.6; 49.6). But far more often, at least in popular thought, the choice of Israel implied the rejection of the Gentiles, and the dream of the future was that of a situation in which the Gentiles would either be enslaved or destroyed. A mission to the Gentiles is not a normal part of Jewish thought. But in Luke (2.32) the aged Simeon sees in the baby Jesus one who is destined to be:

> A light for revelation to the Gentiles,
> and for glory to thy people Israel.

In Luke (3.6) it is all flesh which is to see the glory of God. When Jesus was rejected in Nazareth, he pointed out that it was to a widow of Zarephath in Sidon that Elijah was sent, and it was Naaman, a Syrian, whom Elisha healed (4.25-27). It was in a Gentile centurion that Jesus found a faith the like of which he had never found in Israel (7.1-10). Many will come from the east and the west and the north and the south to be guests at the table of God (13.29). God's invitation is not to a nation but to a world. Repentance and forgiveness of sins is to be preached to all nations, beginning from Jerusalem (24.47).

Further, what Luke omits is as significant as what he includes. He omits the saying in Matthew that that which is holy must not be given to dogs and pearls must not be cast before swine (Matt. 7.6). Luke does not tell of the sending out of the twelve, but he does tell of the sending out of the seventy (Luke 10.1-16). The accounts are closely parallel, but Luke does not include the command not to go to the Gentiles or the Samaritans (Matt. 10.5). He omits the saying that many are called but few are chosen (Matt. 22.14). He does not tell the story of the Syro-Phoenician woman, which he must have known, since he knew Mark's gospel (Matt. 15.21-28; Mark 7.24-30), lest it be hurting to some Gentile.

It is not to be thought that Luke regarded these stories as untrue, or these sayings as unauthentic; he knew they had their place in the teaching of Jesus. But he had to select and he omitted that which could be misinterpreted or misunderstood. He would use no material which might be used to lessen and limit and narrow the universal love of God.

(ix)   Luke's gospel has a very special place for *the poor*. It has been said that Luke is the first Christian socialist. But Luke's interest in the poor is not politically based. In a society in which a working-man's wage was less than a shilling a day men could never have been far above the hunger-line. Even one day's unemployment would bring a situation where there was not enough to eat. And who knows what goes on inside a home better than a well-loved and trusted doctor? It is most likely that what Luke saw as a doctor gave him his passionate concern for the poor.

Twice Jesus presents it as part of his messianic credentials that the gospel is preached to the poor (4.18; 7.22). Luke does not spiritualize the Beatitudes as Matthew does; for Luke it is not: 'Blessed are the poor *in spirit*' (Matt. 5.3). It is quite simply: 'Blessed are you poor, for yours is the kingdom of God. Blessed are you that hunger now, for you shall be satisfied. . . . But woe to you that are rich, for you have received your consolation. Woe to you that are full now, for you shall hunger' (Luke 6.20f., 24f.). It is the rich and the well-to-do who refuse the King's invitation, and it is the poor, the lame, the maimed, and the blind who become the guests, collected by the King's servants from the streets and the lanes (14.12-24). The parable of the rich man and Lazarus shows how little wealth riches have against the background of eternity and how rich godly poverty can be (16.19-31).

It has been said that the *Magnificat* (1.46-55) is one of the most revolutionary documents in all literature. It contains three separate revolutions.

> He has shown strength with his arm,
> he has scattered the proud in the imagination of their hearts.

That is a *moral* revolution.

> He has put down the mighty from their thrones,
> and exalted those of low degree.

That is a *social* revolution.

> He has filled the hungry with good things,
> and the rich he has sent empty away.

That is an *economic* revolution.

But the passage in which Luke tells most beautifully of humble and godly poverty is when he tells of Mary. He tells how after the birth of Jesus Mary went to the temple to offer the requisite sacrifice for her purification, and the sacrifice she brought was two young pigeons (2.24). It is in Leviticus 12 that the regulations for such a sacrifice are laid down. The normal sacrifice was a lamb a year old and a young pigeon or a turtledove (Lev. 12.6); but the regulations go on: 'If she cannot afford a lamb, then she shall take two turtledoves or two young pigeons' (Lev. 12.8), and this sacrifice was known as the offering of the poor. It was the offering of the poor that Mary brought to the temple for her purification.

(x)   Luke's interest in the poor gives him a strong sense of *social justice*. He tells of John the Baptist's instructions to the tax-collectors to collect only the correct sum (3.13), for tax-collectors were notorious for overchanging, which was easy, for people did not know what they had to pay, and, of course, the extra money found its way into their own pockets. He warns against covetousness (12.15). He shows Jesus pressing home the truth that a man's life cannot be evaluated in terms of his material possessions (12.13-21). He shows us Jesus speaking about the unrighteous mammon and comparing it with the true riches (16.11).

It has often been pointed out that many of Luke's parables turn on the right attitude to, and the right use of, money. He has the parable of the two debtors (7.40-43); of the rich fool (12.16-21); of the rash builder of the tower (14.28-30); of the unjust steward and his astute financial manipulations (16.1-9); of the rich man and Lazarus (16.19-31); of the servants and the pound (19.11-27). It was clearly Luke's opinion that there are few better tests of a man than the way in which he uses his money.

He has his own sayings about almsgiving (11.41; 12.33). He has the feeling that a man's true wealth consists in what he gives away.

Luke is deeply concerned about the material things of life. He knows well how grim life can be without them, and he knows how wrong life can be when they usurp too large a place, and he knows that the use of them is an excellent test of any man.

(xi)   Luke sees the universal love embracing *the outcast, the disreputable, and the sinner*. Of all men in Palestine tax-collectors were the best hated, for they had taken service with their country's masters in order to line their own pockets at the expense of cashing in on the misfortunes of their fellow countrymen. Yet we see Jesus calling Matthew from the tax-collector's table; and then we see Matthew making a feast for people as bad as himself and inviting Jesus to it; and we see the orthodox Jews shocked that Jesus should have anything to do with people like that; and we hear Jesus saying that it is precisely people who are ill who have most need of a doctor (5.27-32). We see Jesus dealing gently with the woman who was a notorious sinner, and who revolted the soul of the self-righteous Simon (7.36-50). We see the proud Pharisee and the penitent tax-collector, and we learn that it was the tax-collector's prayer which was more acceptable to God (18.9-14). We see Jesus staying with Zacchaeus, the best hated man in Jericho (19.2-10). We hear the complaint of the scribes and Pharisees: 'This man receives sinners and eats with them' (15.1). We read of the glad welcome home of the son who had done his best to break his father's heart (15.11-32). And we listen to the promise of paradise, made on the cross to the penitent brigand (23.39-43).

When the scribes and the Pharisees and the orthodox Jews made it
a charge against Jesus that he welcomed people with whom no
respectable person would have had anything to do, to Luke they were
citing Jesus' greatest glory.

Yet Luke does not present us with a picture of a kind of inverted
snobbery. Jesus had friends at the other end of the scale too. Three
times we see him as a guest in a Pharisee's house (7.36; 11.37; 14.1).
Amongst his friends is the wealthy and distinguished Joseph of
Arimathaea (23.50-53). Among his followers was Joanna, the wife of
Chuza, Herod's steward, and she must have been a member of what
we call high society (8.2).

As Luke sees him, Jesus welcomes rich and poor, distinguished and
disreputable, saint and sinner alike. Never was a man who had such a
varied circle of friends as Jesus of Nazareth had.

(xii)   Another mark of Luke's characteristic universalism is *the
place he gives to women* in his gospel. There are certain spheres in life
in which a woman must always be supreme. The mother will always
be queen in her own family, and the good wife will always be the help
and the support of her husband. But both among the Greeks and the
Jews in public life the woman had no place at all. She had no legal
rights; if ever she was involved in anything to do with the law her
guardian had to act for her. She was not educated. To educate a
woman, so the Jewish rabbis said, was to cast pearls before swine. In
the normal form of Jewish morning prayer a man thanks God that he
has not made him a Gentile, a slave, or a woman. Xenophon in the
Oeconomicus (7-10) paints one of the most charming pictures in
literature of marriage and love. Ischomachus has just married the girl
wife who loved him and whom he loved. Socrates asks him if the girl
came to him trained in her duties, or if she had to be instructed. Had
she the knowledge to run a house? 'How could she have sufficient
knowledge when I took her,' answers Ischomachus, 'since she came to
my house when she was not fifteen years old, and had spent the
preceding part of her life under the strictest restraint, in order that she
might see as little, hear as little, and ask as few questions as possible?'
In the ancient world a woman lived the most secluded of lives.

But in Luke's gospel women play a large part. If Luke came from
Philippi, he was a Macedonian, and in Macedonia women were more
emancipated than anywhere else in Greece. But it is more likely that
Luke is simply describing a situation in which the love and the
graciousness of Jesus went out to women too.

It is in Luke's gospel that we read of Elizabeth, the wife of
Zachariah, the mother of John the Baptist, and the kinswoman of
Mary (1.5, 24f., 27, 58). It is in Luke that we get the loveliest picture
of Mary the mother of Jesus (1.26-56). It is in Luke that we meet
Anna the prophetess, who in the temple rejoiced to see the baby Jesus

(2.36-38); the widow of Nain to whom Jesus gave back her son (7.11-17); the woman in the house of Simon the Pharisee whose great love atoned for her sin (7.36-50); Mary Magdalene out of whom twelve devils had been ejected (8.2); Susanna, and Joanna, the wife of Chuza, Herod's steward, and therefore a member of high society (8.2); the woman with the issue of blood (8.42-48); Martha and Mary in all the vividness of their contrasting natures (10.38-42); the woman with the two mites (21.1-4); the weeping daughters of Jerusalem (23.27-31); the women at the tomb (23.55–24.11); all these move across the pages of Luke's gospel.

It is an amazing gallery of saint and sinner, dreaming mystic and practical housewife, lady of society and woman of the streets, sick and well, dedicated prophetess and ordinary person. There was none whom Jesus did not welcome and understand, and there was no level of society or morality which did not give its love to him.

When we think of the universality of the mind of Luke, when we see how he draws all classes and conditions of men and women into the circle of the love of Jesus, we can understand Dante's title for him, *scriba mansuetudinis Christi*, the recorder of the gentleness of Christ.

But equally there are things in Luke's portrait of Jesus which forbid us to sentimentalize the picture. There is more to this than a picture of the 'gentle Jesus, meek and mild'. It was this same Jesus who said: 'He who denies me before men will be denied before the angels of God' (12.9). It was this same Jesus who said: 'When you have done all that is commanded you, say, "We are unprofitable servants; we have only done what was our duty"' (17.10). And it was this same Jesus who made the unsurpassable demand for loyalty: 'Whoever of you does not renounce all that he has cannot be my disciple' (14.33), and who in his demand for the first place in life could say: 'If anyone comes to me and does not hate his own father and mother and wife and children and brothers and sisters, yes and even his own life, he cannot be my disciple' (14.26). The universal love has not taken away the universal authority.

(xiii) There are still other characteristics of Luke's gospel at which we must look before the picture is complete.

H.J. Cadbury in *The Making of Luke-Acts* (p. 271) has pointed out how *domestic* Luke's gospel is, how many incidents happen in private houses, and how many references there are to inns and feasts and eating and drinking and entertaining.

In Luke we enter the house of Simon the Pharisee (7.36-50); of Zacchaeus (19.1-10); of the two travellers on the road to Emmaus (24.28-32); of Martha and Mary (10.38-42). We find Jesus dining with two other Pharisees in addition to Simon (11.37; 14.1). We have the picture of the persistent visitor in the middle of the night (11.5-8); of the woman baking (13.20f.); of the woman sweeping the house (15.8-

10); of the father's vigil for the son who had left home (15.11-32).

There is no room for Joseph and Mary in the inn (2.7). The kindly Samaritan leaves the wounded traveller in the inn (10.34). The crowd in the lonely place are sent away to find food and lodging (9.12).

We hear of those who ate and drank in the presence of Jesus (13.26). We have the picture of the messianic banquet to whom people from the ends of the earth will come as guests (22.30). We hear of the luxurious meals of Lazarus and of the poor man getting the scraps that fell from his table (16.21). We read of the unjust steward taking steps to see that he will at least have somewhere to stay when he is dismissed from his post (16.4). We watch the risen Christ eating a meal with his disciples (24.41f.).

Luke 14.1-24 is made up entirely of incidents and parables which have to do with meals and with entertaining. It begins with Jesus dining at a Pharisee's house (1-6); it goes on to tell of the foolishness of conceitedly pushing oneself forward at a banquet (7-11); it goes on to say that, when a feast is given, it should be given not to those who can return the hospitality but to those who cannot (12-14); finally it tells of the man who gave the banquet to which the invited guests refused to come and to which the poor and the outcasts were brought in (15-24).

A very great deal of Luke's story moves in ordinary houses and on ordinary occasions.

(xiv) Luke's gospel might well be called *the gospel of prayer*. In particular, it often shows us Jesus at prayer. There are occasions when all the gospels show Jesus at prayer. They show him at prayer in Gethsemane (Matt. 26.39; Mark 14.35; Luke 22.41). Matthew and Mark show him retiring to pray after the feeding of the five thousand (Matt. 14.23; Mark 6.46). But there are seven occasions when only Luke shows Jesus at prayer. He shows us Jesus at prayer before his baptism (3.21); before his first conflict with the Jewish leaders (5.16); before he chose the twelve (6.12); before his first foretelling of his sufferings and death (9.18); at the transfiguration (9.29); before he taught his disciples his own prayer (11.1); and on the cross (23.46). Luke shows us Jesus at prayer at each great moment of his life.

Only Luke tells us that Jesus prayed for Peter, that Peter's faith might stand the test (22.32). Only Luke tells of Jesus' instructions to his disciples to pray for themselves that they might not enter into temptation (22.40). Only Luke adds the injunction to pray to the injunction to be watchful: 'Watch at all times, praying that you may have strength to escape all these things that will take place' (Luke 21.36; cf. Matt. 25.13; Mark 13.33). It is in Luke that we find the two prayer parables, the parable of the friend at midnight (11.5-8), and the parable of the unjust judge (18.1-8). For Luke prayer was clearly one of the pillars of Jesus' life and one of the pillars of the life of the Christian.

(xv) Luke's gospel is characteristically *the gospel of praise.* The phrase 'praising God' occurs oftener in Luke's writings than in all the rest of the New Testament put together. The verb *chairein*, to rejoice, occurs in Matthew and Mark 8 times, and in Luke and Acts 19 times. The corresponding noun *chara*, joy, occurs 7 times in Matthew and Mark and 13 times in Luke and Acts.

There are three main words involved.

(a) There is *doxazein*, 'to glorify'. It is used of the shepherds (2.20); of the paralysed man after he is healed (5.25f.); of the people at Nain (7.16); of the bent woman (13.13); of the one grateful leper (17.15); of the blind man who received his sight (18.43).

(b) There is *ainein*, 'to praise'. It is used of the angels (2.13); it also is used of the shepherds (2.20); of the crowd when Jesus rode into Jerusalem at the triumphal entry (19.37).

(c) There is *eulogein*, 'to bless'. It is used of Zachariah after his cure (1.64); of Simeon when he saw the baby Jesus (2.28); of the disciples in the temple after the ascension of Jesus (24.53).

It is to be noted that Luke's gospel begins and ends in the temple with people praising God (1.9; 24.53).

The pages of Luke's writings are scattered with people praising God.

(xvi) There is one last great characteristic of Luke's gospel. It is pre-eminently *the gospel of the Holy Spirit.* The Holy Spirit is referred to 5 times in Matthew, 4 times in Mark, and 53 times in Luke and Acts.

The first two chapters of Luke's gospel are a continuous narrative of the action of the Spirit. Zachariah is told that his son John is to be filled with the Spirit (1.15). Gabriel's greeting to Mary is that the Holy Spirit is with her (1.35). At the sight of Mary, Elizabeth is filled with the Spirit (1.41). Zachariah prophesies, filled with the Holy Spirit (1.67). It was the Spirit who told Simeon that he would not die until he had seen the Messiah, and who led him into the temple on the day when the baby Jesus was brought there (2.25-27).

After his baptism Jesus was full of the Spirit, and it was by the Spirit that he was led into the desert to undergo the ordeal of temptation (4.1). It was in the power of the Spirit that he went into Galilee (4.14). Jesus rejoiced in the Holy Spirit (10.21). If a parent in his ignorance and weakness and sin will give good gifts to his children, how much more will God give the Spirit to those who ask him (11.13)?

Luke's story in the gospel and in Acts is the story of Spirit-filled men in a Spirit-filled world. It is always the record of the action of God.

Each man has his own favourite gospel and it is well that it should be so, and there are many for whom Luke's gospel comes first of all. It may be that it speaks to us and our condition for two reasons.

First, it is the gospel, not of a Jew, but of a Gentile, and that in itself brings it nearer to us.

Second, we have stressed the fact that Luke was deliberately writing literature and deliberately writing history, and that he did with diligence and efficiency the necessary investigation and research. But there is another thing that shines through this gospel. It is clearly the product of Luke's own experience of the love of God. A.H. McNeile writes:

> The aspects of Christianity revealed in the gospel are those of a personal and spiritual religion, resulting from the experience of God's love and forgiveness. . . . While Luke writes with a purpose, he is himself absorbed in the beauty of the fairest human life.[11]

Luke could tell of the love of Jesus to others for he had known it himself, although his knowledge came by faith and not by sight.

The Collect for St Luke's Day

> Almighty God, who calledst Luke the Physician, whose praise is in the gospel, to be an Evangelist and Physician of the soul; May it please thee, that by the wholesome medicine of the doctrine delivered by him, all the diseases of our souls may be healed; through the merits of thy Son Jesus Christ our Lord. Amen.

10

THE DEVELOPMENT OF GOSPEL CRITICISM

We can distinguish certain definite stages in the criticism of the gospels, in the development of the approach to them, from the time of the early church until the present day.

(i) The development began with the time when it was never questioned that the gospels were historical accounts of the life of Jesus, and when it was a basic assumption that everything in them was an accurate statement of fact. At that stage the only problem was the problem of harmonization. Nothing could be omitted; nothing could be questioned. If, therefore, there were apparent differences, the only problem was to fit together the various pieces of the jigsaw. What was required was not judgment but ingenuity. So Augustine can say:

> Whenever we find the evangelists inconsistent in their accounts of anything said or done by our Lord, we are not to suppose them to be speaking about the same thing but of some other, very like it, said or done at a different time. For it is a sacrilegious vanity to calumniate the gospels rather than to believe the same thing to have been twice performed, when no man can prove that it could not really be so. Therefore when this rule fails, the reader's next direction is to take up with any solution rather than allow it as consequence that any of the evangelists had been guilty of an untruth or a mistake.

Thus if John records the cleansing of the temple at the beginning of Jesus' ministry and the other three gospels record it at the end, the explanation is that the incident happened twice (John 2.13-22; Matt. 21.12f.; Mark 11.15-17; Luke 19.45f.). If there were two versions of a parable, it was because Jesus used the parable on different occasions, and told it slightly differently. Harmonization was not always as easy as that. According to Mark (15.25) it was 9 a.m., the third hour, when they crucified Jesus; according to John (19.14) it was about the sixth hour, twelve o'clock midday, when Pilate finally passed sentence. The difference is explained, as Augustine tells us in his book *On the Agreement of the Evangelists* (3.14.43), by saying that Jesus was really crucified when the mob shouted: 'Crucify him! Crucify him!

It is easy to see that there are limits to the length to which harmonization can go, but there were no limits to the length to which ingenuity would go to achieve it.

(ii) This attitude to the gospels lasted for centuries, but bit by bit there came into being 'scientific history'. The rigorous assessment of evidence, the checking of every report, the examination of contemporary official documents all became part and parcel of the approach to history. Thus Hume wrote to Robertson, who was contemplating a history of Greece:

> What can you do in most places with these (the ancient) authors but transcribe and translate them? No letters or state papers from which you could correct their errors, or authenticate their narration, or supply their defects exist.[1]

It has been claimed that the ancient historians, whether the writers of the gospels or the classical historians, knew nothing of scientific history. In point of fact this is less than fair to the great historians. Thucydides (1.22) writes of his own efforts and aims:

> But as to the facts of the occurrences of the war, I have thought it my duty to give them, not as ascertained from any chance informant nor as seemed to me probable, but only after investigating with the greatest possible accuracy each detail, in the case both of the events in which I myself participated and of those regarding which I got information from others. And the endeavour to ascertain these facts was a laborious task, because those who were eyewitnesses of the several events did not give the same reports about the same things, but reports varying according to their championship of one side or the other, or according to their recollection. And it may well be that the absence of the fabulous from any narrative will seem less pleasing to the ear; but whoever shall wish to have a clear view both of the events which have happened and of those which will some day, in all human probability, happen again in the same or a similar way – for these to adjudge my history profitable will be enough for me. And, indeed, it has been composed, not as a prize-essay to be heard for the moment, but as a possession for all time.

This is obviously the statement of an historian who, according to his lights, was both rigorous and conscientious.

T.R. Glover in his essay 'Polybius at Rome', tells us that Polybius who was bred in politics, uses the word *autopatheia* to express what he regards as a necessity in a historian. Glover says:

> The historian must himself have done things, seen things, . . . and taken part in some measure in great counsels and great actions. Otherwise he is exposed to the danger of what Polybius caustically calls the *bibliakē hexis*, the 'document habit', we might call it, or, worse still the habit of mind that depends on other men's books, the failing of Timaeus, who did his work on a sofa at Athens for fifty years. . . . Polybius had been a hunter in Arcadia . . .; and when he compares Timaeus to the painter who painted only stuffed animals, his meaning is clear. The painter needs to know the living animal, and so does the historian.[2]

Polybius himself said (1.14.6) that in writing history all favour, prejudice, sympathy, hatred must be banished, and must never be allowed to affect the presentation of the facts.

> For just as a living creature which has lost its eyesight is wholly incapacitated, so if History is stripped of her truth all that is left is but an idle tale.

So we are told that Polybius studied and translated original treaties and inscriptions; travelled to Libya, Spain, Gaul and beyond; measured the plan of Carthagena; walked Hannibal's route across the Alps.

In his essay *On how to Write History* (chs. 39, 41 and 61) Lucian says:

> The historian's one task is to tell the thing as it happened; he must sacrifice to no god but truth . . . He must be fearless, incorruptible, independent, a believer in frankness and veracity; one who will call a spade a spade, make no concession to likes and dislikes, nor spare any man for pity or respect or propriety; an impartial judge, kind to all, but too kind to none; a literary cosmopolitan with neither suzerain or king, never heeding what this or that man may think, but setting down the thing that befell . . . May it be said of you: 'This was a man indeed, free and free spoken; flattery and servility were not in him; he was truth all through.'

It cannot be said that the ancient writers were without their ideals regarding the writing of history. But it is also true that they did not approach their subject with the stringency, and what might even be called the suspicion, of the modern scientific historian.

So we come to a situation in which the gospel records are subjected to the most merciless scrutiny; but none the less the approach is still basically historical and the aim is still to save and to preserve the few nuggets of gold that may still be buried in the dross of myth and legend. The article by P.W. Schmiedel in the *Encyclopaedia Biblica* on the gospels is a typical example of that approach.[3] Before we begin to look at his approach to the gospels, let us again remind ourselves that he is thoroughly historically minded; he is not trying to abolish history; he is trying to rescue such history as can still be salvaged from the wreckage.

First, let us look at Schmiedel's attack on the historicity of the gospels.

(a) The framework is quite unreliable. Mark's favourite word *euthus*, 'immediately' (seven times between 1.12 and 1.30), cannot be taken literally. It is not possible literally to cram so much into so short a time. Matthew's equally favourite *tote*, 'then', is quite vague and indefinite. Schmiedel gives eleven examples from Matthew:

15.1:   Then the Pharisees and scribes came to Jesus.
15.12: Then the disciples came and said to him.
16.20: Then he strictly charged the disciples.
16.24: Then Jesus told his disciples.
17.19: Then the disciples came to Jesus privately.

18.21: Then Peter came up and said to him.
19.13: Then children were brought to him.
20.20: Then the mother of the sons of Zebedee came up to him.
21.1:   Then Jesus sent two disciples.
22.15: Then the Pharisees went and took counsel.
23.1:   Then said Jesus to the crowds.

It is quite clear that from the point of view of working out a chronology this sort of use of 'immediately' or 'then' is of no help at all. There is just no real chronological framework.

(b) Schmiedel now proceeds to look at certain historical difficulties. One of the dates by which Luke fixes the emergence of John the Baptist (3.1) is when Lysanias was tetrach of Abilene. The year that Luke means is AD 28, but Lysanias had been executed by Mark Antony in 34 BC. It is to be noted that Josephus tells how twice, in AD 37 and AD 53, Abilene came into Jewish hands, and in each report he identifies it as having been ruled by Lysanias.[4] It may be that the name of Lysanias stuck to Abilene, although the only Lysanias known to history died in 34 BC.

(c) Luke in the same passage says that John emerged in the high priesthood of Annas and Caiaphas. There never were two high priests. Annas was high priest only from AD 6-15, however influential he may have continued to be. The text here should mention only Caiaphas.

(d) The incident of Jesus' mother and brothers seeking to see him, and his rejection of them, follows the saying about the sin against the Holy Spirit in Matthew (12.46-50) and Mark (3.31-34), while in Luke (8.19-21) it comes after the parable of the sower and the lamp sayings.

(e) Of the sayings in Matthew 5-7, some are collected up in Luke 6; others are scattered throughout Luke.

Matthew	Luke
5.3-12	= 6.20-23
5.13-16	= 14.34f.; 11.33
5.17-24	; no parallel
5.25f.	= 12.57-59
5.27-30	; no parallel
5.31f.	= 16.18
5.33-37	; no parallel
5.38-42	= 6.29f.
5.43-48	= 6.27f., 32-36

A consecutive passage in Matthew is found all over Luke's gospel.

(f) Are we really to believe that all who wished to follow Jesus came to him at the same time? And in Matthew these offers of discipleship were made when Jesus and the disciples had crossed, or were about to cross, to the other side of the lake (8.18-22), while in

Luke they were made after the hospitality had been refused to Jesus and his disciples in a Samaritan village (9.51-62).

(g) It is quite clear that there are groups of sayings collected together because of a common word, rather than because they were spoken at the same time. For example, Mark 9.42-48 collects sayings around the word *skandalizein*, to cause to sin, while Mark 9.49f. collects sayings around the word 'salt'.

These groupings are for mnemonic purposes, rather than because the sayings were originally said together.

(h) There are times when the command to silence does not make sense. Mark (5.43) says: 'He strictly charged them that no one should know this', while of the same incident Matthew (9.26) says: 'The report of this went through all that district.' The two sayings contradict each other.

(i) Luke (9.18-20) apparently knows nothing about Caesarea Philippi being the scene of Peter's confession of faith.

(j) Which is the correct wording of the Lord's Prayer, that in Matthew 6.9-13, or that in Luke 11.1-4?

(k) Was the sermon on the mount delivered to the disciples (Matt. 5.1) or to the crowds (Matt. 7.28)?

(l) In the miracle in the country of the Gadarenes Matthew (8.28) has two demoniacs, Mark (5.2) and Luke (8.27) have one.

(m) There are divergences in the stories of the healing of the blind man at Jericho. Mark (10.46-52) has one blind man, named Bartimaeus, and the incident takes place as they *leave* Jericho. Luke (18.35-43) has one unnamed man and the incident takes place as they *enter* Jericho. Matthew (20.29-34) has two unnamed men and the incident takes place as they leave Jericho.

(n) It could be argued that certain sayings in the gospels are not intelligible except in the light of later happenings. So, it is asked, is the demand to take up a cross (Matt. 10.38; 16.24; Mark 8.34; Luke 14.27) intelligible *before* the crucifixion? Are sayings about sufferings (e.g. Matt. 10.16-23) really intelligible *before* the age of the persecutions? Would Jesus really speak about the church (Matt. 16.18; 18.15-17)? Or rather, would anyone understand these sayings before there was a church?

(o) In Matthew (28.19) the command is to baptize in the name of the Father, and the Son, and the Holy Spirit; in Acts (2.38; 10.48; 19.5) and Paul's letters (e.g. Rom. 6.3; Gal. 3.27) baptism is always in the name of Jesus alone.

(p) In the story of Jairus' daughter in Mark (5.23) and Luke (8.42) she is said to be at the point of death; in Matthew (9.18) she is said to be dead.

Schmiedel further held that there were two other factors which affected the historical value of the New Testament. First, he believed that the literalizing of figurative and poetical language produced alleged miracles where no miracle was intended. Thus the rent veil (Mark 15.38; Matt. 27.51; Luke 23.45) stands for the revelation of God, the opening of God's presence and God's truth to all. Matthew's strange story of the opening of the tombs (27.52) is a vivid way of describing the defeat of death. The darkness which came over the land (Mark 15.33; Matt. 27.45; Luke 23.44) is a pictorial way of describing the darkness of sorrow. So Schmiedel suggests that pictures and metaphors have been turned into facts and events.

Second, Schmiedel suggested that in the gospels, Old Testament incidents have so to speak given birth to New Testament incidents, on the principle that, whatever the prophets did, the Messiah must do with even more power when he came. So the stories of the raising to life of the son of the widow at Zarephath by Elijah (I Kings 17.17-24) and of the Shunammite woman's son by Elisha (II Kings 4.17-37) are the begetters of the stories of how Jesus raised the dead to life again. The story of how Elisha's twenty barley loaves fed a hundred men (II Kings 4.42-44) produces the stories of the feeding of the crowds in the gospels. The stories of Jesus walking on the water, says Schmiedel, are based on passages like the following:

> Thy way was through the sea,
>   thy path through the great waters;
>   yet thy footprints were unseen (Ps. 77. 19).

> Thus says the Lord,
>   who makes a way in the sea,
>   a path in the mighty waters (Isa. 43.16).

> God is he
> who alone stretched out the heavens,
>   and trampled the waves of the sea (Job 9.8).

The story of the walking on the water is traced to Psalm 107.29f.:

> He made the storm be still,
>   and the waves of the sea were hushed.
> Then they were glad because they had quiet,
>   and he brought them to their desired haven.

The story of Judas throwing down the money in the temple is said to come from Zechariah 11.12f.:

> Then I said to them, 'If it seems right to you give me my wages; but if not keep them.' And they weighed out as my wages thirty shekels of silver. Then the Lord said to me, 'Cast it into treasury' – the lordly price at which I was paid off by them. So I took the thirty shekels of silver and cast them into the treasury in the house of the Lord.

The healing of the withered hand has as its source the restoration of

Jeroboam's hand (I Kings 13.1-6). Thus the Old Testament events become a series of sources of the stories of the New Testament.

As we have already stressed, in spite of this radical treatment of the gospel narrative, Schmiedel's interest is basically historical. His aim is to rescue what is undoubtedly historical from the accretions and inventions which have almost submerged it. So he examines the gospels, and he emerges with nine 'foundation-pillars', nine uninventable sayings which must be the basis of any scientific life of Jesus. The 'pillars' (§§139f., cols. 1881-3) are as follows:

i.   Mark 10.18, where Jesus asks, 'Why do you call me good?' No one would put such a question into Jesus' mouth, unless he had actually asked it.

ii.   Matthew 12.31f., where Jesus says that, while a word against the Holy Spirit will never be forgiven, a word against the Son of Man will be forgiven. No one would ever invent a saying which makes a sin against Jesus a less serious sin than some other sin.

iii.   Mark 3.21, where Jesus' family say of him, 'He is beside himself.' Unless the incident really happened, it would be intolerable for anyone to put into the mouths of his own flesh and blood a statement that he was mad.

iv.   Mark 13.32, where Jesus says that the day and the hour of his second coming are unknown to him, and known to God. It is incredible that anyone should attribute ignorance to Jesus about such a matter as this.

v.   Mark 15.34, where Jesus cries, 'My God, my God, why hast thou forsaken me?', which is the most uninventable saying in the whole gospel story.

vi.   Mark 8.12, which is developed in Matthew 12.39; 16.4; Luke 11.29f. The sign of Jonah is the opposite of a sign; it stands for preaching.

vii.   Mark 6.5f. which says that in his own country Jesus *could* do no mighty work, because of the unbelief of the people, a saying of which Matthew 13.58 is 'a manifest weakening'. Helplessness is not something which any inventor would readily attribute to Jesus.

viii.   Mark 8.14-21 combined with Matthew 16.5-12. Schmiedel interprets that incident as follows. When Jesus rebukes them, the disciples first take it as a rebuke for forgetfulness in not bringing bread. Jesus rebukes them for their lack of understanding and reminds them of the feeding. Then he asks them how they could fail to see that he was not talking to them about bread. They then see that 'the leaven of the scribes and Pharisees' means their false teaching. Now, says Schmiedel, this only makes sense if the bread that Jesus was speaking of was *the bread of truth* which he gave them, a truth which satisfied them, and a truth that was so abundant that there was more of it than they could ever appropriate (the baskets of fragments left over).

Schmiedel therefore concludes that by the feeding with bread Jesus did not mean a material miracle with material food, but the food of truth. But it is quite clear that the gospel writers did relate and understand the miracle of the feeding as a physical miracle. So if they include a passage which equally clearly reads that miracle as a spiritual feeding with truth, then they must have found it in their tradition, and certainly did not invent it.

ix.   Matthew 11.5 = Luke 7.22, where we have Jesus' answer to John:

> Go and tell John what you hear and see: the blind receive their sight and the lame walk, lepers are cleansed and the deaf hear, and the dead are raised up, and the poor have good news preached to them.

The poor have good news preached to them. This is the culmination, *and it is not a physical sign.* Schmiedel says: 'It would be impossible to counteract the preceding enumeration more effectually than by the simple insertion of this clause.' It means that the people enumerated in the early part of the saying are the *spiritually* blind and lame and leprous and deaf and dead. This Schmiedel says, fits well with the succeeding verse: 'Blessed is he who is not offended at my unpretentious simplicity.' But since the gospel writers are again clearly thinking in physical terms they would not have included this saying unless they had found it in their source, even if they do turn the spiritual into the physical.

Here then is the meagre store with which Schmiedel is left when he applies 'scientific' historical methods to the gospel story. But the significant thing about Schmiedel and those like him and of his generation is not so much the result with which they emerged as the fact that they were still interested in history; they were still determined to find some basis of history, however much they felt forced to discard.

(iii)   To sum up so far: first there was the period of unquestioning and uncritical acceptance, with no problem but the problem of harmonization to solve. Second, there was the period when the rigorous tests of scientific history were applied to the gospel material. Now we come to the third stage. Of it we need here say less, for a good deal was said about it in the first chapter of this book, the chapter entitled 'The Nature of the Gospels'. This third point of view fully agrees that it is not possible to regard the gospels as technical history; it is not possible to view them as biography; but it is none the less still true that their picture of Jesus is real, authentic and sufficient. This line of thought is clear that historical questions always demand an historical answer. Deissmann writes:

> If I stand before a great cathedral in a town, and say to an old inhabitant:

'Who built this cathedral?', and he answers solemnly: 'We must thank God's grace for this wonderful building', that is a good answer, but it has not answered my historical question. I want to know something of the men who built the cathedral, its date, its further fortunes.[5]

To use the well-used analogy again, there are different ways in which the attempt may be made to indicate what a person is like; there is the photograph, there is the portrait, there is the way of the impressionist artist. And this point of view would hold that we do not have a photograph of Jesus, a completely detailed representation; we do not have a biography of Jesus, but 'what the Gospels do give us is not sufficient to form a biography, but they give us the main outline of his character'.[6]

Before we leave this line of thought there are two things to notice. Suppose it was possible to discover a series of events each of which was fully authenticated and supported by irrefragable evidence, and then suppose that these events were set down one after another, this still would not be history. It might be a chronicle; it might be a set of annals; it would not be history. History has to show connection and development. It has to show how one event grew out of the previous event and led to the next event. If the record is the record of a person, it has to show how that person was affected by the events and how the events were affected by him. A bare narrative of events, even if they are in the correct order, is less than history. Growth and development have to be shown. It will therefore often be better to open a series of windows looking on to significant events, even if the chosen events are quite few, than to try to chronicle every single thing that happened in a disconnected way.

Second, even if we do apply the test of rigorous scientific method to the contents of the New Testament, it may well be that we will find more history there than we thought there was. It is in fact true to say that, if the critic comes to the gospels determined not to find history, he will not find it; but if he comes determined to find history, he will find it. Take the case of the stories of Jesus' infancy. Guignebert writes:

> Neither the visit of the Magi, nor the appearance of the miraculous star, nor the massacre of the innocents has any other basis than the imagination of the hagiographer who put the whole story together.[7]

E. Stauffer, however, has constructed the following not inconsiderable case for the star.[8] There is ample proof that the ancient Babylonian astronomers could calculate the movement and conjunction of the planets in advance. The 'Berlin Table' is a papyrus copy of a list drawn up in 17 BC and covering planetary movements until AD 10. The Star Almanac of Sippar (on some of the latest cuneiform tablets) drew up a year beforehand the planetary movements for 7 BC. In the spring of 7 BC Jupiter crossed the path of Venus in the sky. And in the summer and autumn of that same year Jupiter and Saturn met in the Sign of the Fishes, a meeting called the *conjunctio magna*, the great meeting, a meeting which occurs only once in every 794 years. There is no doubt at all that the ancient astronomers could and did forecast these meetings. So much for astronomy; but what did astrology make of these meetings? Jupiter was regarded as the star of the world ruler; the constellation of the Fishes was regarded as the sign of the last days; Saturn was regarded as the star of Palestine. So then when *Jupiter* meets *Saturn* in the constellation of the *Fishes*, this means: There will appear in *Palestine* in this year the *ruler* of the *last days*. And this is exactly what brought the Magi to Palestine (Matt. 2.2). So Stauffer writes: 'It is clear that the Matthaean account stands on solid ground, and agrees perfectly with the original documents of the time . . . The star of Bethlehem is a fact of history.' Does it matter? To this extent it does. If this is true and the inferences are valid, it means that the gospel writers were not inventing fairy-tales but were transmitting facts.

So at this third stage we are at a situation when, although we cannot call the gospels either history or biography, they contain quite enough material to give us an authentic picture of Jesus, and may well contain more history than the more radical critics would allow.

So we can say that at the first stage there was uncritical and unquestioning acceptance of the gospels as historical documents; at the second stage there was an attack on their historicity in the name of the scientific method, but the aim was still to salvage such history as was left; at the third stage, although no claim was made for technical historicity, it was still maintained that the over-all portrait of Jesus was both trustworthy and adequate. At all three stages there was a firm grasp on history. So Westcott can write of Mark: 'In substance and style and treatment the gospel of St Mark is essentially a transcript from life.'[9]

(iv) So we come to the fourth stage. It cannot be said that at this stage history is entirely discarded. Austin Farrer, as he begins his book *A Study in St Mark*, can still say: 'Bare history is of inestimable importance.' R.H. Lightfoot could begin his Bampton Lectures with the words:

> The four canonical Gospels are the most valuable part of the literary treasure of the Christian Church. They seem to have reached their unique position by the best of all possible methods, the test of use and time, in the course of the second century.

Lightfoot called his book *History and Interpretation in the Gospels*. It is nevertheless true to say that this fourth approach, which by and large is the commonest approach today, starts from the principle that the gospels are primarily *theological* and not *historical* documents.

In any event we would need to ask just what history is. In answer to that question let us summarize the opening pages (pp. 1-9) of Farrer's *Study in St Mark*. A pile of anecdotes is not history, even if arranged in the right order. There must be continuity 'in theme as well as in time'. There must be a 'ground-plan' of the life of the person involved. His effect on circumstances, and the effect of circumstances on him, must be unfolded.

> Even a well-articulated account of a man's ideas would not be history, if it were statically presented. To make history of it we should want to show how his ideas unfolded, and in what relation the process of thought stood to the sequence of circumstances and the policy of action.

Have we got that in Mark? Have we got the continuity and development which makes history? Or, if we do not have that, have we at least got a disconnected narrative out of whose *disiecta membra*, disconnected incidents, we may construct a continuous story? Is Mark an adequate source book for history? Can the *disiecta membra* be assembled into organic history? Is there in Mark at least 'the virgin material' of history? Can we 'unpick' and 'reassemble'? Or have we material which is not historical at all, but which is theological, material which to begin with would need to have its theological 'bias' recognized, admitted and removed – what may well be impossible? 'Must we let go the *history* of Christ and content ourselves with St Mark's ... presentation of the *meaning* of Christ and of his saving acts?'

In Mark there is a double testimony. There is the testimony of Jesus Christ and the testimony of the Spirit. 'The Redeemer had acted and spoken among the Jews, the Spirit spoke and worked in the Church.' There was no kind of tension, because 'Christ had given the Spirit to continue his redeeming work, and to unfold his saving gospel'. So the writer of Mark is controlled by the traditional facts about Jesus Christ, who possessed his mind. The 'shaping, the patterning, the unfolding of symbol and doctrine' are the work of the Spirit. So Mark 1.1-11 is not simply – if at all – the historical account of certain events in the life of Jesus; it is a statement that he is Son of God and Messiah. We are confronted with the theological truth, not the historical truth – truth known to us, but not to the original participants in the events.

So then the new principle is that in the gospels we have theology rather than history. But while the older scholars did search for history, the newer scholars abandon it – and they make a virtue out of a necessity by holding that we are more or less well rid of history. As far back as 1730 Lessing said: 'The contingent truth of history can never serve as a demonstration of the eternal truths of reason.' D.F. Strauss said: 'The infinite grudges the pouring out of the fulness of its being into one particular instance.' And – to express the same thought in different words – Bornkamm in *Jesus of Nazareth* (p. 9) said: 'Faith cannot and should not be dependent on the change and uncertainty of historical research.' This much can be said – history is no longer primary. Let us see what happens when the gospels are approached thus, and let us take as our examples D.E. Nineham's Introduction to his Pelican Commentary on Mark (pp. 15-29) and R.H. Lightfoot's *History and Interpretation in the Gospels*.

Nineham begins by laying it down that the gospels cannot be understood at all 'without some knowledge of the long and rather complicated process by which they were written'. This is not true of a modern book. We can pick up, read, understand and enjoy, say, a detective novel of Agatha Christie's, or a text-book of geometry, without any knowledge of *how* they were written. But, argues Nineham, if the gospels are read by a modern reader with no knowledge of the process of construction and formation, he will almost certainly misunderstand. If, for example, he approaches them as biographies, he will almost certainly find things which are not there, and he will equally miss the insights that are there. (In passing one may well ask, one will have to ask, if this means that it is unsafe to put the gospels into the hands of those who have no equipment in the critical introduction to the New Testament, and that readers thus unequipped are bound to get wrong ideas from their unassisted reading.)

But what is the knowledge which is required? What is the 'correct' approach? The correct approach is that of form criticism. Form criticism has already been described in chapter 2, and here we need only very briefly recapitulate. Originally form criticism was concerned only to identify and distinguish the 'forms' in which the gospel material was stereotyped in its preliterary age, before it was written down; originally it was not concerned with historical judgments or any kind of judgments at all. Form criticism identified:

The *pronouncement story* in which everything is subordinated to the saying of Jesus which it enshrines and in which it culminates.

The *tale* in which everything is subordinated to the story of something which Jesus did.

The *saying* which is a piece of Jesus' teaching not set in any particular context.

The *legend* which is a story about an individual person.

The *myth* which is an attempt to put into pictorial and concrete forms abstract and spiritual truths which are not expressible in human language at all.

So far so good; the identification of such forms was interesting but innocuous. But the form critic went further. And it may well be that the most important thing he said was that each of these units was complete in itself and totally detached; that therefore the order in which they happen to be arranged and the links which connect them are quite artificial; that they have no more connection than pearls on a string. If that be so, then the gospels are formed of a series of utterly discontinuous and unconnected units. And if that be so, there can be no study of chronology or of development, and therefore no history. This then is the background and this is the beginning of the process which has to be understood.

The process begins with a time when the transmission of the story was completely oral and completely Christian. No one but Christians had anything to do with the transmission. There is no kind of detached impartiality about the Christian story. It is from the beginning told by people who are prejudiced; it is not history; it is propaganda.

Further, at no time in the early days was this considered to be telling and transmitting stories about a man who was dead and gone; Jesus the central figure was the risen Lord, a living contemporary. The earthly Jesus and the risen Lord at God's right hand were one and the same.

Still further, at this stage Christians lived in the hourly expectation of the second coming. They strove to tell others about that and to fit themselves for it. There was no inclination for historical research, for there was not going to be any history. So R.H. Lightfoot (p. 23) gives us the three principles, which had been already set down by Julius Wellhausen long before the form critics had ever been heard of:

i. Mark is largely made up of little narratives or sections, each of which had at first a separate existence and which were later joined together more by theme than by chronology.

ii. Mark has been subject to revision or revisions until it reached its present form.

iii. Mark gives information not only about Jesus, but also to some extent about the beliefs and circumstances of the early church, at the time when it was written.

What this is saying is that the dominating interest in the life of Jesus is in its effect as salvation. In the case of modern biography we expect intimate, gossipy, spicy, personal detail. In the case of Jesus this personal interest is not there. The only interest in any incident is, how did it contribute to the total action of the play? In what way had Jesus' life on earth contributed to man's salvation and to the coming of the kingdom of God? The only history that mattered was salvation history.

Thus the concentration is on the death of Christ, for that death interpreted as the great sacrifice for sin was the greatest contribution to the divine drama. So in the gospels the passion narrative gets by far the greatest space. Paul shows no interest in any aspect of Jesus'

earthly life except his death. But, as Nineham points out (p. 19), the
letters were written to those who were already Christian. At the very
first contact, when the name of Jesus was first mentioned, and the
claims of Jesus first made, the obvious question was, Who was he?
Are his claims justifiable? That is to say, there must from the
beginning have been a cult story. Any convert would have certain
needs.

> They would require a living, concrete picture of the one to whom they
> were now committed. If they were to enter into relationship with him, they
> must be able to envisage him, his demands, his attitude towards them, the
> attitude he expected from them, the way he wanted them to live and so
> forth.

So here is the motive for memories of Jesus – but for memories of a
certain sort.

The necessary memories were memories such as would convince
non-believers of Jesus' supernatural status; such as would help
converts to realize him as a living person; such as would help them to
discover the implications of their discipleship; and, since the initial
work was very largely among Jews, memories in which the life of
Jesus was seen as the fulfilment of Old Testament prophecy.

It is obvious that the memories preserved will be highly selective.
For example, the sinlessness of Jesus will never be doubted; the
complete truth of all he said will never be in question. His humanity
will necessarily be accepted, but none the less it will be as a
supernatural figure that he will be presented. They did not think of him
as receiving anything from his humanity, nor did they think of his
environment having any effect on him. They would not think in the
modern terms of 'self-consciousness' or 'self-understanding'.

There are two further considerations which enter into the matter.
First, they never doubted that the heavenly Christ was still revealing
further truth about himself to his followers. 'We have the mind of
Christ' writes Paul (I Cor. 2.16). 'I think,' he says, 'that I have the
Spirit of God' (I Cor. 7.40). Jesus has many things to say which at the
time he cannot say, but the Spirit will say them for him; the Spirit will
take of what is his and show it to his followers (John 16.12-15). And
since the glorified Christ was the same person as the earthly Jesus, it
was natural, it was inevitable, that the memories of his earthly life
should be not merely transmitted, but also interpreted, modified,
added to in the light of continuing revelation. Revelation was not static
but dynamic, not closed but continuing, for Christ was alive, and
through his Spirit was still communicating with men.

Second, the Old Testament was nothing less than a source for the
life of Christ. It was accurate in every detail, and everything it
predicted of Christ must have been fulfilled. And since it was inerrant

and infallible, it was actually a better source than the fallible memories of men, however well informed they were. There are passages about which we cannot be sure whether they came from witnesses, or whether they are deductions from Old Testament prophecies, which were bound to be fulfilled. For instance, Nineham suggests (*Mark*, p. 423) that Jesus' saying in Luke 24.39, 'See my hands and my feet', may derive from Psalm 22.16: 'They have pierced my hands and my feet.' It was not normal to nail the feet of the criminal to the cross (in the story of Thomas in John 20.24-29 there is no mention of the feet).

Further, the circumstances of the transmission had their effect on both the substance and the form of the tradition. At the very beginning all kinds of audiences would be addressed; but before long the transmission of the tradition would be very largely in the context of public worship and of the instruction of catechumens. This had certain consequences. On such an occasion the preacher or teacher would take an event or a parable or a group of sayings and expound it. And, as Nineham very soundly points out (p. 22), the kind of passage he chose would depend on the needs of the congregation. If the congregation needed instruction in good neighbourliness, then the teacher might choose the story of the good Samaritan (Luke 10.29-37). If the congregation needed a word about citizenship and the duty of paying their taxes, he might well take the incident in which Jesus was asked if it was right to pay taxes to Caesar (Mark 12.13-17). The order in which the material was used would vary from congregation to congregation. Local needs were more demanding than the necessity to remember the order of events in Jesus' life. And so, Nineham says, the tradition would take the form of numerous separate stories, each with its lesson, but with no generally agreed over-all order. Stories would be collected, but usually by theme and for practical preaching and teaching purposes, for instance, the stories of controversy (Mark 2.1-3.6) or the injunctions to watchfulness (Mark 13.28-37). (We might well ask if this was not more likely to happen *after* the general over-all cult story was told and known.)

The one exception to this was the passion narrative. There a coherent and connected narrative was essential. The death of Christ was central for missionary preaching, and it was an astonishing fact that divine honours were being claimed for a man executed on a cross, after he had been charged with blasphemy and insurrection by the acknowledged leaders of the Jewish people, and after full examination by Roman law. It had to be shown, first, that the accusations were false and the product of malice and hatred on the part of the Jewish leaders, but also that all had happened as the Old Testament said it would, and that it was therefore part of the plan and purpose of God. For that reason a connected narrative was a necessity. Nor was it ever an objective account of events; it was from the beginning constructed to support the Christian interpretation of it.

Furthermore, as Nineham points out, the way in which the tradition was handed down mainly at public worship and in official instruction did affect the form of it. Personal detail was out of place in a context like that. It had to be transmitted in the way in which the point was most directly made, and in which it best led up to the application and exposition. If the point is a saying of Jesus, the saying is given in full, but the context is kept to a minimum, for all it has to do is to lead up to the saying. In the case of a healing, the story is told in such a way that the supernatural powers of Jesus will be stressed. The chronic and long-lasting nature of the trouble is emphasized; the ease of the cure; the astonishment of the spectators; the completeness of the new health – the story stresses them all.

There would be a natural and inevitable development. At first the stories would be told by eyewitnesses, and there would be a wealth of the kind of detail that an eyewitness naturally introduces. But as time went on the stories were told by preachers who had never been eyewitnesses, even by people who had never seen Palestine and who knew nothing of the background of events. So, as Nineham puts it (p. 24), the stories were increasingly 'streamlined'. They were stereotyped into a form where nothing but the religious significance remained, and were told in such a way as to be fixed in their most 'economical' form.

Nineham notes three further points. First, ancient historians did not write like modern historians. If an ancient historian was himself convinced that Jesus was the Son of God, he might well tell the story in terms of Jesus having claimed and having been given that title, although there was no actual information that this had been so. He might even feel that it was wrong to do anything else, for, if Jesus really was the Son of God, an account of his life which did not make that clear would be nothing less than misleading, in that it did not convey the true meaning of the facts it was describing.

Second, clearly if Jesus was the Son of God his significance was universal, he was for all men. What he said must mean something to every man of every nation. Now Jesus had worked and taught in Palestine, and what he had said did not apply, in the form he had said it, to some Hellenistic congregation twenty, thirty, forty years later. But, it would be argued, what he really meant must have relevance for everyone. Therefore the original tradition was bound to be unconsciously modified to meet 'the circumstances and preoccupations of the various little communities scattered over the Mediterranean world'. The form was modified to bring out the meaning for those who came from a different background.

Nineham supports these two points with quotations from three earlier writers, A. Menzies, H.A. Guy and Martin Dibelius:[10]

'The formulation of the tradition regarding Jesus was a work of enthusiasm and devotion, carried on by men on whom he had made an overmastering impression, and in whom his spirit was alive and active . . . Their heart was in the work of making their Master live and act again in the world, as they now knew he had lived and acted when in the flesh.' 'It was in this enthusiasm that the teacher or preacher could not be restrained from adding his own comment to the narrative.' . . .

Dibelius . . . stresses the remoteness of such enthusiastic, uncultured preaching from the 'critical conscience of a historian, guarding with meticulous exactness the very words which had been spoken'.

There was a kind of 're-inspiration'.

So Nineham concludes (p. 27):

In the first place it means that what the Evangelist had to work on, apart from an outline Passion narrative and perhaps one or two short collections of material relating to special subjects, was a series of essentially disconnected stories. This at once explains an otherwise puzzling feature of the Gospel, the way it consists of a number of unrelated paragraphs set down one after another with very little organic connexion, almost like a series of snapshots placed side by side in a photograph album.

The units are sometimes connected by little phrases at the beginning and the end, but there is no real connection. Each is essentially complete in itself. There is no real mention of time or place; characters are very briefly described, and are almost never named. In Mark 3, for example, the paragraphs are so essentially separate that they could be interchanged into any order without making any difference. The order, says Nineham, is the evangelist's, and by the time he wrote the historical order was unknown, except in the most general terms. The evangelist may well not even have been interested in historical order, for his interest was not historical; it was practical and religious.

So Nineham sums up (p. 29):

The older view that the Gospels were attempted biographies of Jesus, as adequate as the education of the Evangelists and the circumstances of the time would allow, has given place to the recognition that each of them was produced to meet some specific and practical needs in the church of its origin, and that it is those needs which have very largely controlled each Evangelist's choice, arrangement, and presentation of material, and distribution of emphasis.

On this view the gospels are neither history or biography; they are an anthology of preaching and teaching, with reference to the local situation.

So the story starts with an age when there was unquestioning and uncritical acceptance of the gospels as history. This was followed by a time when the criteria of scientific historical method were applied to the gospels, not with a view to denying that they were basically history, but with the aim of rescuing the historical gold from the legendary dross. This gave place to a time when it was agreed that the gospels were neither technical history nor technical biography; but it was held that they did present an authentic and adequate and sufficient portrait and characterization and impression of Jesus. Finally, there came the time – still largely with us – when the gospels were taken to be documents which are not and were never meant to be primarily historical, but are rather theological.

In the mind of anyone trained under the older approach to the gospels one question must long since have arisen – what has happened to Papias? The Papias tradition, preserved by Eusebius in his *History* (3.39.15f.), had handed down two pieces of information: first, that Mark's gospel was in effect the preaching material of Peter, and, second, that 'Matthew composed the oracles in the Hebrew language, and each one interpreted them as he could'. (See pp. 120, 151 above.) This made Mark into something that was next door to an eyewitness account – but now there is not even a mention of Papias. What we might call 'The Passing of Papias' has been complete. The devaluation of Papias has been total.

In 1908 Vernon Bartlett could write:

> There is no early evidence as to our Gospels comparable to that of Papias, Bishop of Hierapolis, even in the fragmentary and obscure form in which it has reached us through the pages of Eusebius.[11]

Even though it could go down on two octavo sheets of notepaper, the Papias evidence was considered top-class material. But in 1934 R.H. Lightfoot in *History and Interpretation* (pp. 28f.) could write:

> Nor does it seem on the whole probable that the Papias tradition will bear the weight which it is sometimes sought to lay upon it. The character of this Gospel (Mark), at any rate for the greater part of its contents, points to a different kind of origin. Internal evidence suggests that many sections of the narrative have passed through a 'moulding' process, as it were, before they reached their present form.

This is to say that R.H. Lightfoot, like Nineham, would regard Mark as a community rather than as an individual production. In 1951 Austin Farrer took the matter even further; in *A Study in St Mark* (pp. 11, 20f.) he writes:

> We will endeavour to show that it is possible to decide exactly what the Papias tradition means, and that what it means is nothing about which we need trouble our heads . . . The Papian tradition must be simply given up, as someone's ingenious but false construction . . . Papias has given us neither a prescription to be followed, nor an oracle to be interpreted, but only a false theory to be set aside.

Finally, in 1963 W.G. Kümmel wrote in his *Introduction to the New Testament* (pp. 43f.):

> It can easily be shown that Papias had no clear knowledge which allows us to understand more certainly the origin of Matthew and Mark than does the investigation of the Gospels themselves ... It is therefore advisable to leave Papias' notions, in spite of their great age, out of consideration with respect to the investigations of the literary connections of the Synoptic Gospels.

In a little more than fifty years the evidence of Papias has been downgraded from something which was of primary importance to something which may well be discarded.

Before we finally consign Papias to oblivion, let us take one look at an argument which finds his evidence confirmed by the gospel of Mark itself. J.B. Lightfoot wrote in 1889: 'The Gospel [of Mark] is just what we should expect, if the author had derived his information in the way reported by the Presbyter.'[12] One of the most impressive attempts to prove the correctness of the Papias information was made nearly fifty years ago by C.H. Turner. Turner speaks in his commentary (pp. 6-9) of 'the unique historical importance of the Gospel according to St Mark'. In the early church the need was increasingly felt for 'a record in permanent written form of the life and teaching of Jesus Christ'. And Mark is 'the unique record, objectively stated, of the experience of an eyewitness, an intimate companion of Jesus throughout His Ministry'. 'We may hold the connection of the Gospel as a whole with Peter to be undeniable.'

Turner finds in Mark a very suggestive form of narration. 'In strong contrast to Matthew and Luke,' he says, 'Mark's Gospel may be called autobiographical. They write lives of Christ; he records the experience of an eyewitness and companion.' Turner goes on to say:

> It is crucial in this respect to note the predominant use of the plural in the narrative of Mark. Time after time a sentence commences with the plural, for it is an experience which is being related, and passes into the singular, for the experience is that of discipleship to a master.

Take as an example the story in Mark 1.29-31:

> And immediately they[13] left the synagogue, and entered the house of Simon and Andrew with James and John. Now Simon's mother-in-law was sick with a fever: and immediately they told him of her, and he came and took her by the hand.

Matthew (8.14f.) has no plurals:

> And when Jesus entered Peter's house, he saw his mother-in-law lying sick with a fever; he touched her hand and the fever left her.

Luke (4.38f.) has altered two of the three plurals:

> And he arose and left the synagogue, and entered Simon's house. Now Simon's mother-in-law was ill with a high fever, and they besought him for her. And he stood over her and rebuked the fever, and it left her.

Now let us suppose that Mark had heard Peter tell the story again and again. How would Peter tell it?

> Immediately *we* left the synagogue and went into our house with James and John. Now my mother-in-law was sick with a fever; and immediately *we* told him about her, and *he* came and took her by the hand.

Mark's 'they' corresponds to Peter's 'we', as Peter told the story; but the others have no 'we' to look back on, and so go straight into a narrative with 'he'. It is perfectly true that this change from plural to singular is a feature of Mark's narrative, and the change is perfectly intelligible, if the plurals go back to Peter's *we*, as he told the story. Mark (5.1) says:

> *They* (we) came to the other side of the sea, to the country of the Gerasenes, and when *he* had come out of the boat there met him out of the tombs a man with an unclean spirit.

Matthew (8.28) begins:

> And when *he* came to the other side, to the country of the Gadarenes . . .

Other instances in Mark are:

> And they (we) came to Bethsaida. And some people brought to him a blind man (8.22).

> They (we) went on from there and passed through Galilee. And he would not have had anyone know it (9.30).

> And they (we) came to Capernaum; and when he was in the house . . . (9.33)

> And they (we) were on the road going up to Jerusalem, and Jesus was walking ahead of them (us) (10.32).

> And they (we) came to Jerusalem. And he entered the temple (11.15).

> And they (we) came again to Jerusalem. And as he was walking in the temple . . . (11.27).

> And they (we) went to a place which was called Gethesemane, and he said to his disciples . . . (14.32).

It is true that the plural-singular combination is characteristic of Mark; and it is also true that the explanation that Mark's *they* goes back to Peter's *we* does make sense. So it could be claimed that, if there is internal evidence to discredit the Papias story, there is also internal evidence to confirm it.

But, if the Papias story is fiction, where where did it come from?

How did it arise? It is Austin Farrer who in *A Study in St Mark* (pp. 10-21) most comprehensively demolishes the Papias tradition, and we outline the essentials of his argument.

In the case of R.H. Lightfoot and D.E. Nineham the Papias tradition is gone, because they do not believe that Mark was written in that way. They begin without Papias; they examine the gospel; they come to the conclusion that it is a community product, produced over some length of time. The whole process leaves no room for Papias. He is not so much evicted as simply forgotten. Austin Farrer is much more deliberate; he does not so much forget Papias as attack him.

Eusebius in his *History* (3.39.13) passed the famous verdict on Papias, that he was a man of very limited intelligence. Farrer disagrees strongly with this judgment; he believes that Papias was an extremely shrewd and ingenious person indeed. By the time of Papias the four gospels were established as the only ones. Papias deals with only two of them. Why? About the two with which Papias did not deal nothing required to be said. Luke had written his own preface. He was admittedly not an eyewitness, and depended on documents produced by eyewitnesses. John's was a 'spiritual gospel', obviously different from the other three. So then in John we have a *spiritual and apostolic* gospel; in Luke we have a *literal and non-apostolic* gospel. What about the gospels which are *apostolic and literal*? The first and obvious question is – why are there two of them and whence the discrepancies? If we compare Matthew and Mark, we find that Matthew has practically everything that is in Mark, but that Mark omits much that is in Matthew, and that there is a certain amount of difference in arrangement. This is the situation which Papias sets out to explain, and – according to Farrer – he explains it very cleverly. Let us remind ourselves what he in fact says about the matter. He says that Mark is the interpreter of Peter, and he says that Matthew wrote in Hebrew, and everyone interpreted the Hebrew as he could. So then the answer to the question, 'Why are there two gospels?' is, 'There are two gospels *because there are two languages*.' Matthew begins by being in Aramaic – which all the original apostles spoke. Peter is transplanted into Greek. Mark is therefore read to the Greek-speakers; and so also is Matthew, each man making his own 'targum' of Matthew, each man interpreting, translating him as he could.

This is the situation when Luke comes to write. He cannot expect Theophilus to read Aramaic; he will not put the inadequate Mark into his hands. He might have translated Matthew, but he prefers to write a new book, using all the available sources. And shortly afterwards the Greek 'targum', oral interpretation of Matthew, is put into writing and quite displaces the original Aramaic version.

This explains the facts – there are two gospels because there are two languages; and it explains their relation to Luke. It also explains the discrepancies and shrewdly turns them to good effect. Peter did not mean to write a gospel at all; his teaching was in speech, and Mark set down the oral material piecemeal – and the very fact that he did not try to round it off neatly is the guarantee of his fidelity. The probability is that all the elder told Papias was that Mark was Peter's disciple – I Peter 5.13 was evidence enough for that – and that Matthew wrote in Aramaic – and Papias did the rest. And the whole clever theory collapses, given away by the statement that Matthew was originally written in Aramaic; for Matthew is obviously not a translation, but was written originally in Greek.

The whole ingenious theory is a production of Papias to ensure that Mark is given an apostolic origin and then to explain that there were two gospels on the grounds that there were two languages. It further met the difficulty that it is odd that the non-apostolic Mark precedes the apostolic Matthew with the theory that Mark is really the work of Peter and that Matthew is old, but was long in being translated. Farrer concludes that 'the Papian tradition must be simply given up as someone's ingenious but false construction'.

Are we then to assume that we can, and even must, in regard to the gospels, depart from the idea of history altogether? Are we to think entirely in terms of the *theology* of the gospels? Are we to say that what we are reading in the gospels is not at all what happened, but material which is illustrative of what certain people believed and thought about Jesus? We may put this even more acutely. If the gospels are preaching and not history must we think of them as being more than anything else essays in propaganda?

It is easy to see that there can be a situation in which, when history becomes propaganda, it ceases to be history. Peter Ustinov has written a short story called 'Add a Dash of Pity'.[14] In it two historians are talking. There is Zotin, the doctrinaire and dedicated Communist; and there is Zaryadko, a famous academic historian, much respected for his history of the Samaritans. Zotin has writen a book *Comrade Joan* in which the voices that the Maid of Orleans heard were the voices of the as yet unborn Marx and Engels. Zaryadko is disgusted with such a performance. 'You believe,' says Zotin, 'that history is static, whereas I believe that it is kissed to life by a variety of Prince Charmings'. 'No,' says Zaryadko, 'history has a proper beginning, middle and end.' Engels and Marx speaking to Joan is a gross piece of nonsense. 'You are wrong,' says Zotin. He continues:

> History is inherited like a furnished house, and we do with it what we wish. It is material which has only been left behind for us to use in influencing the present. If it will serve a political purpose for me to present Joan of Arc as a Marxist, or Martin Luther as a free-thinker, I will not

hesitate to do so. I am convinced that, if Joan of Arc had lived now, she would have been one of us.

Zaryadko retorts that this is simply making the past subservient to the whims of the present. 'Should there be a Christian revival,' he says, 'you would have Lenin listening to the voice of Moses.' There the use of history as propaganda is taken to its limits, to a *reductio ad absurdum*. Are we to think that the gospel writers presented Jesus exercising a power he never possessed, speaking with a wisdom with which he never spoke, living with a purity and beauty and courage which never did clothe his life, and all in an attempt to 'sell' Christianity?

There are two answers to that. The first is quite simply that the best propaganda is the truth. And the second is that, if you write about Joan of Arc in the twentieth century, you are some hundreds of years away from her. The Christian story was being told at a time when there were still many people alive who had seen and heard Jesus, and to whom it would have been difficult to put across something between a fiction, a legend and a tissue of inventions. No one is going to dispute the fact that the gospel writers were writing to commend Jesus; and the best way to commend him was to tell the truth about him.

Are we really to abandon Papias? The basic story which Papias transmits is that the gospel of Mark has an intimate connection with Peter. We have already seen that the early church consistently and universally accepted this story; Justin Martyr, Irenaeus, Clement of Alexandria, Origen, Tertullian, Jerome (quoted on pp. 120f. above) all repeat it. There is an inevitable subjectivism in any judgment. You may either ignore Papias as if he had never been, and then, from the study of Mark, say that you have reached the conclusion that Mark was not written that way, that it is no one's reminiscences, that it is a community production over a period. Or you can start from Papias, and you can be astonished at the amount of evidence there is in Mark to support the Papias story. To take but one instance, surely the trial of Jesus is one of the great moments of his life. In Mark the Jewish trial scene occupies 20 verses, 8 of which are taken up with the story of Peter's denial. In the other three gospels the proportion is even greater: the story of the denial takes up 8 out of 18 verses in Matthew, 9 out of 17 in Luke, and 7 out of 16 in John.[15] In the story of the trial and condemnation by men of the Saviour of the world and the Son of God – for that is what the gospel writers held Jesus to be – very nearly fifty per cent of the space is occupied with the story of Peter's private tragedy.

There is no possible way of proving or disproving the Papias story of the origin of Mark; in the end any judgment will be a subjective judgment; and in my own opinion there is no good reason to abandon Papias.

If we have to abandon the historicity of the gospel narratives, certain serious consequences follow. We may pick out four of these consequences.

(i)   It would have grave repercussions on the idea of Jesus as an example. As Peter said (I Peter 2.21), he left 'you an example that you should follow in his steps'. But if in the gospels what we have is not the historical story of what Jesus actually was but the theological account of what he theoretically should have been, then what happens to the example? There is then no divine example, only a human idea of what the example should be.

(ii)   Closely related with that would be the repercussion on the belief that Jesus is the revelation, the demonstration of God. It is the belief of the Christian that, when we see Jesus in action, we can say that this is the way in which God speaks and thinks and acts. But once again, unless we can be sure that Jesus did so act and speak, what we have is not the demonstration of what God is like but man's conception of what God is like. If John's great claim (1.14), 'The Word became flesh', that is, 'the mind of God became a human person' is to have any meaning or any value, it must mean that we do know what Jesus in fact did.

(iii)   This would also have repercussions on the claim of Jesus. It is the claim of Jesus to be Saviour, Master and Lord. That is to say, he asks for my complete submission to himself. And how can I submit to one about whose character and action and attitude I have no reliable information? It is often claimed that faith is not faith, if it depends on evidence. This is just not true. The biggest human act of faith that a man can make is to submit himself to a surgeon, who will take steps to render him unconscious, and who will then open up and reconstruct his body. But before I consent to this, I know that the surgeon is properly qualified; I know that he has passed all the necessary examinations, and that he has acquired all the necessary skills. Still further I may well know personally people on whom he has operated and whom his skill has healed; and if I do not know them personally, there will be others to tell me about them, and to point them out to me. My act of trust is based on my knowledge of the man and of what he has done for others. Just so, I cannot put my trust in Jesus, if all that he is to me is an unknown quantity X. I must know what he is like; what his attitude to men is; what he has done for others; if he is such that he has a right to demand my total submission. And where am I to get that information if not from the gospels? And suppose it is said to me: All right. The gospels, although not historical documents, show you *the kind* of person Jesus was, and *the kind* of things he did. Is it then so very great a step from saying that I can know the kind of things he did to saying that I can know the actual things he did? No one will submit to some one he knows nothing about. Even faith needs its evidences.

(iv) Lastly, we remake the point we made much earlier (pp. 22f. above). The conception of incarnation involves history. The conception of incarnation means that God became incarnate in a person, enmanned in a man, made human in a human being. And there can be no reality in any such statement, unless I have firm and reliable information about the person in whom that incarnation is claimed to have taken place.

I need not for one moment deny that the gospels are theology, but I abandon their history only at my peril.

11

REDACTION CRITICISM

Redaction criticism is the newest and in many quarters the most influential tool for the study of the New Testament. Literary criticism, form criticism, redaction criticism – thus runs the line of development in New Testament studies. What then is redaction criticism?

To put it very simply and very baldly – redaction criticism is the study of what an author does to the sources on which his work is founded. A reporter or an annalist may do nothing to his sources but simply transmit them; but an author in using his sources may make alterations in them. By studying these alterations it is possible to deduce something of the way in which his mind works and something of the theology which he holds.

At its simplest and its most basic this has long been done. We have already seen how the later gospel writers make significant and revealing alterations to Mark. To take only two already cited examples, Mark writes (6.5):

> And he (Jesus) could do no mighty work there (Nazareth), except that he laid his hands upon a few sick people and healed them.

Matthew (13.58), describing the same incident, says:

> And he did not do many mighty works there, because of their unbelief.

Matthew, with the increasingly reverential attitude to the earthly Jesus which came as the church grew more theologically conscious of who Jesus was, will not say that Jesus *could* not do many mighty works; he will not even in these circumstances ascribe inability to Jesus; he simply says that Jesus *did* not do many mighty works, thus implying that Jesus deliberately withheld his power. Again in the passage which tells of their ambitious request for the chief places in the kingdom, Mark (10.35) does not hesitate to show James and John themselves making the request, while Matthew (20.20), unwilling to show two leading apostles acting from less than worthy motives, ascribes the request to their mother.

That is redaction criticism at its simplest, but as it is more fully developed, redaction criticism goes far more deeply than that. In his Foreword to Perrin's book, *What is Redaction Criticism?*, Dan O. Via Jr. writes (p. viii):

The redaction critic investigates how smaller units – both simple and composite – from the oral tradition or from written sources were put together to form larger complexes, and he is specially interested in the formation of the Gospels as finished products. Redaction criticism is concerned with the interaction between an inherited tradition and a later interpretive point of view. Its goals are to understand why the items from the tradition were modified and connected as they were, to identify the theological motifs that were at work in composing a finished Gospel, and to elucidate the theological point of view which is expressed in and through the composition.

And Perrin himself begins his work by giving his own definition of the function of redaction criticism:

It is concerned with studying the theological motivation of an author as this is revealed in the collection, arrangement, editing, and modification of traditional material, and in the composition of new material or the creation of new forms within the traditions of early Christianity.

The name redaction criticism, *Redaktionsgeschichte*, was coined by Willi Marxsen in his book *Mark the Evangelist* (p. 21). But it may well be that a more correctly descriptive name would be composition criticism, *Kompositionsgeschichte*,[1] for redaction criticism is more concerned with the information which can be gained from the new pattern than with the examination of individual details.

From all this three things emerge. First, there will always be a subjective element in redaction criticism. The critic will have to make up his mind whether the changes the author makes in his source are deliberate, calculated, of set purpose and designed to present some definite point of view, or whether they are to be ascribed to what Schniewind called 'the carelessness of popular journalism'.[2] The answer to this question must depend on one which is even more basic: Is the material which the author is assumed to have redacted still extant? Can we see in black and white the changes that the redacting author has actually made? In other words, if we can assume the priority of Mark and the reconstruction of Q, then the study of redaction in Matthew and Luke can be carried out on some factual basis; the actual changes can be studied. But to talk of redaction in connection with Mark – and it is talked about – is sheer speculation, for the material which Mark redacted – if he redacted any – does not exist, and must be reconstructed by deduction, or, to give it a less dignified title, by guesswork.

Secondly, it is a basic assumption of redaction criticism that the findings of form criticism are to be accepted. From the point of view of redaction criticism the important findings of form criticism are two: that the gospel material began its existence in small units, and that there was no over-all order, no chronology, no development, no 'story'. Perrin (p. 15) quotes K.L. Schmidt, one of the 'founding fathers' of form criticism:

> On the whole there is [in the Gospels] no life of Jesus in the sense of a developing story, as a chronological outline of the history of Jesus, but only isolated stories, pericopes, which have been provided with a framework.[3]

This means that the gospel units are not like the pieces of a jigsaw puzzle, which can only be assembled in a certain fixed way; they can, so it is argued, be changed around as the author pleases and as suits his purposes, like beads on a string, which have no connection with one another and can be rearranged in any order. On this theory the gospel writers were not committed to any rigid historical outline of the life of Jesus, and so could rearrange the material as suited their purpose.

But there is a third assumption of redaction criticism which goes far beyond assuming that the gospel writers rearranged their material at will; it also assumes that in the authors there is a creative element, and that they produced new material as well as rearranging old. We can find this idea as far back as the eighteenth century, though used in a very different way. The first person to hold it was H.S. Reimarus (1694–1768). (See the account given by Schweitzer in *The Quest of the Historical Jesus*, pp. 13-26, and summarized by Perrin, *What is Redaction Criticism?*, pp. 3f.) Reimarus was a professor of oriental languages at Hamburg, and was a rationalist of the Enlightenment. In addition to his published works, he left unpublished at his death a manuscript of 4000 pages, parts of which Lessing later published under the title *Wolfenbüttel Fragments by an Unnamed Author* (Wolfenbüttel was the name of the town where Lessing was working at the time). Reimarus claimed that, if history is 'what actually happened', the gospels are not history. He held Jesus to be a politically motivated messianic pretender; he held that Jesus had never risen from the dead, but that the disciples had invented the story of the resurrection to avoid the necessity of going back to working for a living! The miracles, the stories which speak about the fulfilment of messianic prophecy, the universalistic traits, the predictions of the passion and the resurrection, are all later creations and not narratives of things that had happened. Reimarus had no doubt of the creative element in the tradition!

The creative element is again to the fore in D.F. Strauss's conception of the gospels. For Strauss the gospels were myths; that is to say, they were not attempting to write history; they were expressing in pictorial form religious convictions derived from the Old Testament, from Hellenistic thought or from Christian experience. Perrin (p. 5) summarizes his view in these words: 'The Gospel narratives are essentially concerned with purveying a Christ myth and this fact has to be recognized about them.'

But now we move on to another aspect of the history of the study of the synoptic gospels. Ever since the time of C. Lachmann in 1835 it had been a fixed point of synoptic study that Mark was the earliest gospel, and was in fact the basis of the other two synoptic gospels. The priority of Mark became one of the foundations of synoptic criticism, and it led to another conviction: that Mark, because it was the earliest of the gospels, was a simple and uncomplicated document, the historicity of which could be taken for granted. Perrin (p. 6) quotes some characteristic words from Westcott:

> The Gospel of Mark, conspicuous for its vivid simplicity, seems to be the most direct representative of the first Evangelic tradition, the common foundation on which the others were reared. . . . In substance and style and treatment the Gospel of St Mark is essentially a transcript from life. The course and the issue of facts are imaged in it in the clearest outline. If all the other arguments against the mythic origin of the Evangelic narratives were wanting, this vivid and simple record, stamped with the most distinct impress of independence and originality, . . . would be sufficient to refute a theory subversive of all faith in history.[4]

In short, it was held that Mark was the earliest of the gospels and that its historicity was self-evident.

Into this situation came Wrede with his book *The Messianic Secrete* (already discussed on pp. 137ff. above). As Perrin says (pp. 7f.):

> Wrede . . . sounded the death-knell for this kind of view . . . His book . . . is not so much a contribution to a discussion as a bomb-shell! . . . Nothing would ever be the same again.

Wrede notes certain very obvious features of Mark. There is the continuous misunderstanding of the disciples, a theme which runs right through the gospel (4.13, 40f.; 6.50-52; 7.18; 8.16-21; 9.5f.; 10.24-26; 14.37-41). In particular there is the misunderstanding of Jesus' prediction both of his passion and of his glory (8.31f.; 9.30-32; 10.32-4, 35-40). There is no suggestion of a developing comprehension on the part of the disciples; they are just as obtuse at the end as at the beginning. There are also the repeated injunctions to secrecy (1.25, 34, 43-5; 3.12; 5.37, 40, 43; 7.24, 33, 36; 8.23, 26, 30; 9.9, 30f.). One saying gives us a kind of clue, the saying of Jesus to the three disciples on the descent from the mount of transfiguration: 'And as they were coming down the mountain, he charged them to tell no one what they had seen, until the Son of man should have risen from the dead' (Mark 9.9). To Wrede the whole matter is obviously artificial. We have already set down his position in six propositions (pp.

137f. above). (i) Jesus never claimed to be Messiah. (ii) During his lifetime no one ever thought of him as Messiah. (iii) The resurrection gave men the idea that he was Messiah. (iv) The problem then arises why he was not recognized as such during his lifetime. (v) A whole series of passages are then constructed, together with appropriate sayings, to make it appear that during Jesus' lifetime on earth the fact of his messiahship was kept deliberately secret, except from the disciples, who however were supernaturally blinded, and who saw and realized the truth only in the light of the resurrection. (vi) Therefore none of the secrecy passages comes from the lips and life of Jesus at all. They are the construction of the church, and represent the faith of the church. And therefore Mark is not an historical work at all, but a dogmatic and theological production.

The view we have been outlining is that the gospel writers did far more than transmit material; they even went beyond arranging and adapting it; they created it. To put it crudely, the gospel writers did not only tell a story, they invented one. They did this in support of the theology which they desired to propagate. This is closely linked with another basic presupposition: from the beginning, the gospel material was preaching material. This is summed up in the famous remark attributed to Dibelius (quoted by Perrin, p. 15): 'In the beginning was the sermon.' The gospel material was from the beginning not history but propaganda, not the narrative of events but the presentation of theology, written not with the desire to inform but with the intention to convert.

On this view, the idea of Mark as a simple uncomplicated document of loving reminiscence is completely gone, and it becomes a highly complicated theological document. And, if Mark, how much more Matthew and Luke? What the science of redaction criticism attempts is to penetrate to the theological motivation behind the gospels by a painstaking examination of the way in which the gospel writers use their sources.

So then let us see redaction criticism in action, and let us begin by turning to *Tradition and Interpretation in Matthew* and examine Bornkamm's treatment (pp. 52-7) of Matthew's narrative (8.23-27) of the stilling of the storm.

(i) In the first place, Matthew includes this miracle in a complex of healing miracles, the leper (8.1-4), the centurion's servant (8.5-13), the healing of Peter's mother-in-law (8.14-17), and the healing of the Gadarene demoniac (8.28-34). By its very siting in the gospel pattern, Matthew has made it more than a nature miracle, more than the stilling of a storm.

(ii) Mark's narrative (4.35-41) is vivid and realistic and straightforward. There is the storm, there is the peril, there is the sleep of Jesus. There is the appeal of the disciples, and the appeal is in no way pious-sounding; it is 'secular': 'Master, don't you care that we are perishing?' The word of Jesus commands the wind to be silent, and the effect is immediate. Then comes the question of Jesus: 'Why are you afraid? Have you no faith?' Finally, there is the awe and the amazement of the disciples: 'Who is this that even wind and sea obey him?' It is not pious; it is pictorial and realistic. The centre of the story is in v. 39: 'He (Jesus) awoke and rebuked the wind and said to the sea, "Peace! Be still!"' The contrast between the great storm of wind (v. 37) and the great calm (v. 39) is vivid and dramatic. Herein is stressed the physical reality of the miracle, a reality underlined by the affirmation of the disciples that even the wind and the sea obey Jesus (v. 41).

(iii)   Matthew by no means abandons this. He too has the contrast between the great storm (8.24) and the great calm (8.26). But there is considerable and subtle modification to give the story a new slant.

(iv)   In Matthew the story is given a new context. Only in Matthew does it follow the stories of the scribe and the disciple who professed to wish to follow Jesus, and who were warned of what the cost of following is (8.18-22). In Luke (9.57-60), these two stories occur in a quite different context. Now in both these stories there occurs the characteristic word of discipleship, the word 'follow'. The scribe says (v. 19): 'Teacher, I will follow you wherever you go.' Jesus says (v. 22) to the would-be disciple who wishes to delay: 'Follow me, and leave the dead to bury their own dead.' It is a significant fact, therefore, that Matthew *and Matthew alone* begins the story of the storm at sea with a reference to *following*:

And when he (Jesus) had got into the boat, his disciples *followed* him.

Mark (4.36) has:

And leaving the crowd, they took him with them, just as was, in the boat.

Luke (8.22) has:

One day he got into a boat with his disciples, and he said to them, Let us go across to the other side of the lake.

Even if in Matthew the word 'follow' has its literal sense, it cannot wholly escape the specialized connection with discipleship which it has in the immediately preceding verses. So then, argues Bornkamm, Matthew is not simply handing on a narrative. He is the first exegete. He is the first to interpret the journey of Jesus with the disciples in the storm *with reference to discipleship, and that means with reference to the little ship of the church.* Tertullian (*On Baptism*, 12) was later to cite a suggestion that this miracle is a kind of baptism and that 'the apostles then served the turn of baptism when, in their little ship, they were sprinkled and covered with the waves'. But, be that as it may, Bornkamm presents Matthew here as writing not simply about a storm at sea – as Mark did – but in terms of discipleship and the church.

(v)   There are certain things which support this view. Only in Matthew are the words of the disciples 'an ejaculatory prayer: "Save, Lord; we are perishing"'. Only in Matthew (8.25) is the divine title *kyrie*, Lord, used. In Mark (4.38) it is *didaskale*, teacher, rabbi; in Luke (8.24) it is *epistata*, Master – both human titles. Further, from the beginning of ch. 8 this word *kyrie* occurs in every section, on the lips of those who were aware of Jesus' power. The leper says (v. 2): '*Lord*, if you will, you can make me clean.' The centurion says (vv. 6,8): '*Lord*, my servant is lying paralysed at home'; '*Lord*, I am not worthy to have you come under my roof.' It is the word which occurs on the lips of those who know and wish to experience the power of Jesus, on the lips of the blind men (9.28), of the woman with the daughter possessed by a demon (15. 25, 27), of the father of the epileptic boy (17.15), of the two blind men in Jericho (20.30f., 33). It is the word which the disciples themselves use to Jesus, as does Peter at Caesarea Philippi (16.22), at the transfiguration (17.4), at his question about the extent of forgiveness (18.21), as do the twelve at the last supper (26.22). It is the word used in the address to the coming Judge of the world (25.37, 44). The conclusion is that the use of 'Lord' in Matthew 8.25 is the word of prayer, and it contains a confession of discipleship. Again the discipleship motif is to the fore.

(vi)   The order of events in Mark and Luke is reversed in Matthew. In Mark (4.39) and Luke (8.24f.) the miracle comes first and then the rebuke. In Matthew (8.26) the rebuke comes first and then the miracle. 'In the midst of a mortal threat, the word of Jesus goes forth to his disciples, and puts them to shame.' Matthew regularly uses *oligopistos* 'of little faith', (and its noun *oligopistia*, 'little faith') with reference to that kind of faith which is too weak to meet the demands of the situation with which it is faced, of the anxiety which finds it impossible to trust even the God who clothes the wayside grass with splendour (6.30), here of the faith which collapses at the threat of danger (8.26), of the panic which made Peter sink in the water (14.31), of the disciples' worry that they had no bread (16.8), of the lack of faith which made them powerless to heal the epileptic boy (17.20).

Mark's way of telling the story makes it the story of one particular incident; in Matthew the story becomes, not the story of a special incident, but the story of a typical situation of discipleship as a whole.

(vii)   The weather term which Matthew uses is different from the term used by Mark and Luke, and is significant. Mark (4.37) and Luke (8.23) both speak of a storm of wind; and the word is *lailaps*, the normal word for such a storm; Matthew also speaks of a great storm, but the word he uses is *seismos*, which in the New Testament is regularly used of the crashing upheavals of the last times; it is an eschatological word. Matthew used it of the earthquake which shook Jerusalem and opened the tombs at the crucifixion of Jesus (27.54), and of the earthquake when the angel came and rolled away the stone in the garden (28.2). It is the word used for earthquakes in the apocalyptic picture of the last day (Matt. 24.7; Mark 13.8; Luke 21.11). It is a word characteristic of the apocalyptic scenes in the Revelation (6.12; 8.5; 11.13,19; 16.18). So the distress on the sea becomes not simply the story of a storm, but the symbol of the distresses inseparable from discipleship of Jesus.

(viii)   Lastly, Matthew has his own ending. Mark ends (4.41):

> And they were filled with awe, and said to one another, 'Who then is this, that even wind and sea obey him?'

Luke ends (8.25):

> And they were afraid, and they marvelled, saying to one another, 'Who then is this, that he commands even wind and water, and they obey him?'

And there is no doubt that the 'they' in these passages are the disciples. But Matthew's ending (8.27) is:

> And the men marvelled saying, 'What sort of man is this, that even winds and sea obey him?'

With Matthew it is the *men*, not the disciples. Bornkamm asks: What men? And then he answers his own question: 'Obviously . . . the men who are encountered by the story through preaching', and he cites as an illustration the saying of Paul (I Cor. 14.25) that when through prophecy a man is confronted with the secrets of his own heart, be he a member of the church or be he a stranger, 'he will worship God and declare that God is really among you'.

So Bornkamm says (pp. 56f.):

> The setting of the pericope is thus extended, its horizon is widened and from being a description of discipleship in which the disciples of Jesus experience trial and rescue, storm and security, it becomes a call to imitation and discipleship. . . . [In its new context and with its new interpretation,] the story of the stilling of the storm [is] a description of the dangers against which Jesus warns anyone who over-thoughtlessly presses to become a disciple; here is, in fact, the Son of Man who has not where to lay his head. At the same time, however, the story shows him as the one who subdues the demonic powers and brings the kingdom of God.

There are two further points which Bornkamm implies rather than states. First, the word that is used for Jesus *rebuking* the storm (*epitiman*) is regularly used when he rebukes demons (Matt. 17.18; Mark 1.25; 9.25; Luke 4.35; 9.42). And secondly, in the Old Testament the stilling of the storm is the function of the Almighty.

> The voice of the Lord is upon the waters;
>> the God of glory thunders,
>> the Lord, upon many waters (Ps. 29.3).

God is the one

> who dost still the roaring of the seas,
>> the roaring of their waves (Ps. 65.7).

The Psalmist says:

> Thou dost rule the raging of the sea;
>> when its waves rise, thou stillest them (Ps. 89.9).

(Cf. also Pss. 93.3; 107.25-30; 124.4f.) Jesus is depicted in divine terms as the conqueror of the demons and the master of the storm.

So then, as Bornkamm works it out, when we examine Matthew's redactional treatment of Mark's account of the stilling of the storm, we see how Matthew has taken an account of a marvellous nature miracle, and has made it a vehicle to show how Jesus is such that he can demand, and is able also to reward, the sacrifice which involves the abandoning of the closest earthly ties, as in the case of the second would-be follower. 'In this sense the story becomes a kerygmatic paradigm of the danger and glory of discipleship.'

We now turn to another investigation of Matthew's redactional activity. Also in *Tradition and Interpretation in Matthew* (pp. 165-300), H.J. Held has written of 'Matthew as Interpreter of the Miracle Stories'. It is Matthew's custom to compress and to abbreviate. But he does this in order to concentrate on what he regards as essential. The abbreviation is intended 'to direct attention to the main point'. Therefore Matthew's abbreviation is a method of interpretation. As Held sees it, Matthew's abbreviation is interpretation to bring out a christological scheme. Let us look at Held's examination of the story of the healing of Peter's mother-in-law (pp. 169-71). First let us set down the story as it is in each of the three gospels:

Matthew 8. 14f.	*Mark* 1. 29-31
And when Jesus entered Peter's house	And immediately he [some mss. read they] left the synagogue, and entered the house of Simon and Andrew with James and John. Now Simon's mother-in-law lay sick with a fever, and immediately they told him of her. And he came and took her by the hand and lifted her up, and the fever left her; and she served them.
he saw his mother-in-law lying sick with a fever;	
he touched her hand and the fever left her, and she rose and served him.	

Now let us see what Matthew does with this story.

(i)   In Matthew, although it is Peter's house, Jesus seems to enter the house alone.

(ii)   In Matthew Mark 1.30b is omitted; no one tells Jesus about the sick woman, and no one makes any request.

(iii)   In Matthew Jesus' 'treatment' of the woman is much abbreviated; it is not said that he took her by the hand and lifted her up, only that he touched her.

(iv)   In Mark the subject of the verbs changes. In v. 29 it is Jesus; in v. 30a it is Simon's mother-in-law; in v. 30b it is 'they'. In v. 31 it is Jesus again. In Matthew the subject never changes; it is Jesus all the way through. In the Matthew version there is no one there in the story but Jesus and the woman.

(v)   Mark finishes the story: 'She served *them*.' Matthew finishes the story: 'She served *him*.'

What Matthew has done is so to abbreviate the story that the attention is rivetted on Jesus; in Matthew's story no one acts but Jesus; no one indeed appears but Jesus; Jesus has the stage to himself.

Let us look at another of Matthew's abbreviations, the story of the Gerasene demoniac, also discussed by Held (pp. 172-5). Here Matthew's abbreviation is specially severe; Mark's 20 verses (5.1-20) are in Matthew cut to 7 (8.28-34). He omits the demoniac's request to be allowed to accompany Jesus (Mark 5.18-20), as well as the detailed description of the terrible nature of the man's illness (Mark 5.3-5), and much abbreviates the description of the miraculously healed demoniac (Mark 5.15). But Matthew retains the basic structure: the seriousness of the illness (v. 28); the technique used for the exorcism, and the departure of the demons into the swine as a proof of the healing (v. 32); the effect on the people (vv. 33f.); but what Matthew has done is to prune Mark's narrative almost savagely, in order to concentrate

---

Luke 4.38f.

And he arose and left the synagogue, and entered Simon's house.
Now Simon's mother-in-law was ill with a high fever, and they besought him for her.
And he stood over her and rebuked the fever, and it left her; and immediately she rose and served them.

everything on Jesus – and to concentrate on Jesus in a special capacity, a capacity which can be seen in the words of the demoniac to Jesus. In Matthew (v. 29) these words are:

> What have you to do with us, O Son of God? Have you come here to torment us before the time?

Mark (5.7) has:

> What have you to do with me, Jesus, Son of the Most High God? I adjure you by God, do not torment me.

Luke (8.28) has:

> What have you to do with me, Jesus, Son of the Most High God? I beseech you, do not torment me.

In Matthew there is no request at all; and in Mark and Luke there is an attempt at counter-magic – the adjuration, and the use of the name. Matthew has nothing about any counter-magic or any request. What Matthew is doing is making a christological statement, before the 'time', the final and complete inbreak of the reign of God; and the whole story is retold to concentrate on Jesus and on the christological claim that already the demons are delivered to the judgment of torment. There is no interest in the healing nor in the person healed; the whole point is the messianic destruction of the demons. The abbreviation is deliberately designed and carried out to make a christological statement.

A little later (pp. 178-80) Held shows how Matthew in certain of the miracle stories uses interpretive abbreviation to focus attention on the necessity for faith. He uses the passage which tells of the raising of Jairus' daughter and the woman with the issue of blood (Matt. 9.18-26; Mark 5.21-43; Luke 8.40-56). We begin by noting the simple fact that Mark takes 23 verses to tell the two stories, while Matthew takes only 9. The abbreviation is surgical, whatever the reason for it. Let us take first the story of the woman with the issue of blood. It is so good an example of Matthew's abbreviating method that it is worth setting down in full:

Mark 5.25-34

And there was a woman who had a flow of blood for twelve years, and who had suffered much under many physicians, and had spent all that she had, and was no better but rather grew worse. She had heard the reports about Jesus, and came up behind him in the crowd and touched his garment. For she said, 'If I touch even his garments, I shall be made well.' And immediately the hemorrhage ceased; and she felt in her body that she was healed of her disease. And Jesus, perceiving in himself that power had gone forth from him, immediately turned about in the crowd and said, Who touched my garments? And his disciples said to him, 'You see the crowd pressing around you, and yet you say, "Who touched me?"' And he looked round to see who had done it. But the woman, knowing what had been done to her, came in fear and trembling and fell down before him, and told him the whole truth. And he said to her, 'Daughter, your faith has made you well; go in peace, and be healed of your disease.'

Matthew 9.20-22

And behold, a woman who had suffered from a hemorrhage for twelve years

came up behind him and touched the fringe of his garment; for she said to herself, 'If I only touch his garment, I shall be made well.'

Jesus turned, and seeing her he said, 'Take heart, daughter; your faith has made you well.' And instantly the woman was made well.

In the original Greek Matthew has reduced Mark's 184 words to 63. Mark 5.25f., the vivid description of the course of the woman's trouble and her efforts to find a cure, is gone, as is the dramatic crowd scene (Mark 5.29-33). Matthew omits the crowd and omits the disciples; the meeting takes place, as it were, between the woman and Jesus alone. It is simply the meeting of a sick person with Jesus, with no real information about the place or the circumstances. For Matthew's purpose these things do not matter.

The essential point for Matthew is 9.22: 'Your faith has made you well.' The two things he has preserved are the behaviour of the woman, her thoughts and her actions, the things by which her faith became known, and, secondly, Jesus' attitude towards the woman's faith; to that faith he replies by his word and deed. The story is not for Matthew a narrative of healing; it is an instruction on the saying about faith.

We now turn to the story of the healing of Jairus' daughter, and again it is worth while to set the story down:

Mark 5.21-24, 35-43 | *Matthew* 9.18f., 23-26

And when Jesus had crossed again in the boat to the other side, a great crowd gathered about him; and he was beside the sea. Then came one of the rulers of the synagogue, Jairus by name; and seeing him, he fell at his feet, and besought him, saying, 'My little daughter is at the point of death. Come and lay your hands on her, so that she may be made well and live.' And he went with him. And a great crowd followed him and thronged about him.

While he was still speaking, there came from the ruler's house some who said, 'Your daughter is dead. Why trouble the Teacher any further?' But ignoring what they said, Jesus said to the ruler of the synagogue, 'Do not fear, only believe.' And he allowed no one to follow him except Peter and James and John the brother of James. When they came to the house of the ruler of the synagogue, he saw a tumult, and people weeping and wailing loudly. And when he had entered, he said to them, 'Why do you make a tumult and weep? The child is not dead but sleeping.' And they laughed at him. But he put them all outside, and took the child's father and mother and those who were with him, and went in where the child was. Taking her by the hand he said to her, 'Talitha cumi'; which means, 'Little girl, I say to you, arise.' And immediatley the girl got up and walked; for she was twelve years old. And immediately they were overcome with amazement. And he strictly charged them that no one should know this, and told them to give her something to eat.

While he was thus speaking to them

behold, a ruler came in

and knelt before him saying, 'My daughter has just died, but come and lay your hand on her, and she will live.' And Jesus rose and followed him with his disciples.

And when Jesus came to the ruler's house, and saw the flute players, and the crowd making a tumult, he said,

'Depart; for the girl is not dead but sleeping.' And they laughed at him. But when the crowd had been put outside,

he went in and took her by the hand,

and the girl arose.

And the report of this went through all that district.

We note first that Matthew has reduced Mark's thirteen verses to six. Once again he has severely abbreviated – and to what purpose?

As before, a great deal of Mark's detail is gone. There is no heightening of the miraculous. The magic word, Talitha cumi (Mark 5.41), is gone. The demonstration of the reality of the cure, the walking about of the girl, the giving her food, is gone. The disciples do not play any part in the story; the parents of the girl have disappeared from v. 25. Everything is between Jesus and Jairus.

But the most significant change that Matthew makes is in connection with the state of the child. Mark (vv. 22f.) has:

> And seeing him (Jesus) he (Jairus) fell at his feet, and besought him saying, My little daughter is at the point of death. Come, and lay your hands on her, so that she may be made well, and live.

Matthew (v. 18) has:

> Behold, a ruler came in, and knelt before him, saying, My daughter has just died; but come and lay your hands on her, and she will live.

As Held sees it, this is not, as it is usually taken to be, a heightening of the difficulty of the task facing Jesus; it is a demonstration of the ruler's faith. Even in the face of death, not just of illness, however serious, the ruler has complete faith. He does not need the encouragement to faith he receives in Mark's story (v. 36): 'Do not fear, only believe.' His faith is calm, confident and complete, and therefore it receives the perfect answer. As Matthew tells the story everything is concentrated on the encounter of the power of Jesus and the faith of the ruler, complete power and complete faith. For Matthew, this is not a miracle story, but a teaching narrative about faith.

We now look at Hans Conzelmann's book *The Theology of St Luke* (discussed by Rohde, *Rediscovering the Teaching of the Evangelists*, pp. 154-78, and by Perrin, pp. 28-33). Perrin says of Conzelmann's book: 'Neither the discipline of New Testament theology as a whole nor the understanding of Luke in particular will ever be the same again.' Luke who has always been highly regarded as a historian, now, thanks to Conzelmann, 'becomes a self-conscious theologian, and the details of his composition can be shown convincingly to have been theologically motivated'. What then is Conzelmann's position?

Conzelmann begins with two presuppositions (p. 12). First, he accepts the basic assumption that Luke is founded on Mark and Q. Second, he assumes the findings of form criticism. But Conzelmann is not as interested in the detail as he is in the whole pattern and framework of the tradition, and in what was happening to the tradition in the time of Luke. The first stage was the formation and stereotyping of the units of tradition. Next comes Mark's collecting of these units into a gospel. But with Luke we have a third stage

> in which the kerygma is not only transmitted and received, but itself becomes the subject of reflection. This is what happens in Luke. The new

stage is seen both in the critical attitude to tradition as well as in the positive formation of a new picture of history out of those already current, like stones used as part of a new mosaic.

What is the new view of history which dominates Luke, and what produced it? The central problem of Luke's days was the delay of the *parousia*, of Christ's coming again. The church had somehow to come to terms with the continued existence of the world as we know it. Early on, the return of Christ had been expected very soon, and the time of the duration of the world had been assumed to be very brief. A situation had now to be explained in which the time of the world's duration was to be indefinitely prolonged. So Luke formulated the conception of a three-stage salvation history.

The first period was the period of Israel, and to that stage John the Baptist belongs. 'The law and the prophets were until John; since then the good news of the kingdom of God is preached' (16.16). The second period is the ministry of Jesus, and that period comes to an end with the ascension. That period is 'the mid-point of time'. (The German title of Conzelmann's book on Luke was *Die Mitte der Zeit*, the centre of time.) Now comes Luke's positive, even epoch-making, contribution – the third period is that of the church in the world; in this period we can look backward to the time of salvation and the ministry of Jesus, and we can look forward to the *parousia*, the coming again of Jesus, which will bring this final period to an end, and which will be the climax of all things. But no longer did Luke think of this period as a short crisis period; it is a period of indefinite duration. Obviously, this change of outlook is going to give Luke a new slant on the gospel events.

In Jesus' ministry also, as Conzelmann sees it, there is a division into three parts (see Rohde, pp. 157f.). First, there is the time in Galilee (3.21-9.50), from Jesus' call at his baptism to be the Son of God, and the collection of witnesses to his call. Second, there is the travel account (9.51-19.27), with the disclosure of the decision to suffer, and the preparation of the disciples for the necessity of suffering. The journey is not to be taken as a geographical journey; Jesus' awareness that he must suffer expresses itself as a journey, but the journey is an invention. Third, there is the end of the story, from Jesus' entry into Jerusalem until his death (19.28-23.49). The framework of the gospel is neither chronological nor geographic; it is kerygmatic. The development of the gospel, says Conzelmann (p. 12), is 'the filling out of a given kerygmatic framework with the narrative material about Jesus and the traditional sayings of the Lord'. It is, as Conzelmann sees it, quite wrong to think of the gospel as the work of an historian. If we begin to ask questions about 'the reliability of Luke's reporting' we are asking the wrong kind of question altogether.

Luke's geography, according to Conzelmann, is theological geography. Galilee is the first place of the ministry of Jesus. Here there is no temptation, only a manifestation of the time of salvation. Judaea, and especially Jerusalem, is the second place of Jesus' ministry, but here there is temptation, for this is the place of the passion, and it is a necessary prelude to the resurrection and ascension. The ministry of John the Baptist does not belong to the ministry of salvation, and it is carefully and deliberately separated in its locale from Galilee and Judaea-Jerusalem which are the places of Jesus. It is located in the region of Jordan, which is the sphere of the old era, and it is significant that Luke (3.3) omits the statement (found in Mark 1.5 and Matt. 3.5) that people came from Jerusalem and Judaea to be baptized.

From Conzelmann's point of view the position of John in the scheme of things is altered. In Luke, he says (pp. 22f.), the Baptist,

> instead of being directly linked with the eschatological events . . . is given a definite place in a continuous story of salvation, the end of which is not yet in sight. John no longer marks the arrival of the new aeon, but the division between two epochs in the one continuous story, such as described in Luke 16.16. The eschatological events do not break out after John, but a new stage in the process of salvation is reached, John himself still belonging to the earlier of the two epochs which meet at this point.

For Luke John is no longer the preacher of repentance. So, according to Conzelmann, John is described in terms of the former epoch, as prophet, preacher of righteousness, but not in terms of the new epoch, in terms, for instance, of Elijah as forerunner. Acts (1.5; 11.16; 18.24-19.7) stresses that John's baptism is a baptism of repentance, rather than a baptism of the Spirit, and is therefore inferior. John is defined as the centre of salvation history (Luke 16.16), but as definitely subordinated to Jesus. John in Luke does not belong to the 'premonitory signs of the *parousia*', the coming again; to that only the resurrection of Jesus is the prelude, although long separated from it.

According to Conzelmann, Luke's topography has a theological significance.

> The mountain . . . is the place of prayer, the scene of secret revelations, of communication with the unseen world. No temptation can take place on it nor any public preaching (p. 29).

When Luke tells of the temptation in which the devil showed Jesus the kingdoms of the world, he says (4.5) that the devil took him up, but omits the words 'to a very high mountain' (as in Matt. 4.8). For Luke the mountain could not be the place of temptation. Rohde (p. 162) tells us that in Luke

> the people always remain behind when Jesus, alone or with his disciples, ascends a mountain (cf. Luke 9.37 with Mark 9.9 and Matt. 17.9). The

mount of transfiguration cannot be regarded as a geographical site either, but only as a site of an epiphany.

It is quite mistaken to try to identify it, or any other mountain which Jesus ascended, on a map. In Matthew (24.3) and Mark (13.3) the eschatological discourse takes place on the Mount of Olives; in Luke, (21.1-5) it takes place in the temple, for the mountain is the place of prayer, not of teaching.

On the lake, too, Conzelmann tells us, Jesus is always alone with his disciples. It is the setting for the manifestation of power, as in the stilling of the storm (8.22-25). Only at 5.1 does Jesus appear publicly on the shore, and this too is a 'scene of manifestation' (p. 42). Never again is he seen in public by the lake. In Mark (4.1) and Matthew (13.1) the parabolic discourse is delivered on the shore, but not in Luke (8.4). The place where Jesus meets people is the plain (6.17; 9.37).

As Conzelmann sees it, Luke is not primarily a historian but a theologian, and his geography and topography are not geography and topography but symbolism.

We next turn to Willi Marxsen and his book *Mark the Evangelist* (discussed by Perrin, pp. 33-39, and by Rohde, pp. 113-40), and to two of his dominant themes in particular. Marxsen (p. 30) quotes a famous remark by Martin Kähler: 'One could call the Gospels passion narratives with extended introductions.'[5] He emphasizes that there is nothing in the gospels which does not relate to Jesus. People and events are included, not for any interest in them as such, but because of their connection with Jesus. Any statement about anyone is in effect a statement about Jesus. This is particularly important in regard to John the Baptist. John the Baptist is introduced, not because of any interest in himself, not with any idea of 'showing things as they were', but with the intention of saying something about Jesus. There is no teaching either about John the Baptist or about his baptism. All that is said about him is in effect something said about Christ.

But, according to Marxsen, we can go further than that. As John the Baptist is there to interpret Jesus, so the Old Testament quotations in the text of the tradition are there to interpret John the Baptist. The words from Isaiah 40.3, quoted by Mark (1.3), have to do with the wilderness: 'The voice of one crying in the wilderness: Prepare the way of the Lord.' Immediately thereafter (Mark 1.4) John appears in the wilderness. Of this Marxsen goes on to say (pp. 37f.):

Now it is quite clear: the one who appears – in the wilderness – is the one who was already announced by the prophets. Thus in fact the 'in the wilderness' in v. 4 is an Old Testament quotation. The wilderness is not a locale. We ought not to speculate as to its location. The phrase does not intend to specify the Baptist's abode.... Rather, 'in the wilderness' qualifies the Baptist as the fulfiller of Old Testament predictive prophecy. Put in exaggerated form, the Baptist would still be the one who appears 'in the wilderness' even if he had never been there in his life.

Later, however (pp. 44-48) Marxsen argues that 'the reference to the wilderness (in Mark a theological statement) becomes in Matthew and Luke a geographical one' (Perrin, p. 37).

Marxsen goes on from a reference to place to a reference to time (pp. 38f.): Perrin (pp. 36f.) summarizes this:

> Although [Mark 1.]14 certainly refers to the arrest of John the Baptist by Herod, it does not necessarily indicate that the ministry of Jesus began only after John had been arrested. In its present place it simply means that, theologically speaking, John was the forerunner and Jesus the one who came after.

Therefore, from the theological pattern point of view – not from the historical and factual point of view – the story of John has to be brought to an end before the story of Jesus can properly begin; so John is delivered up in Mark 1.14, although the story of his arrest and death is not told until Mark 6.14-29. Mark's desire is not to write history, but to relate John and Jesus theologically.

The second characteristic contribution of Marxsen is the great stress that he lays on reference to Galilee. He holds that Mark was written about AD 66, at the beginning of the Jewish War against Rome, when the Christian community in Jerusalem had fled, or was about to flee, to Galilee, there to wait for the *parousia*, the coming again, which they believed to be imminent. In its theology, Marxsen holds, Mark's gospel reflects this situation. In view of this there are two Marcan sayings which are commonly held to be resurrection sayings, but which Marxsen takes to refer to the *parousia*: 'But after I am raised up, I will go before you to Galilee' (14.28); and secondly the announcement of the angel at the empty tomb: 'But go, tell his disciples and Peter that he is going before you to Galilee; there you will see him, as he told you' (16.7). These sayings, Marxsen holds, represent the point of view of a Christian community which had migrated from Jerusalem to Galilee at the outbreak of the war, there to await the almost immediate coming again of Jesus. In support of this he refers (p. 114) to a passage from the *Ecclesiastical History* of Eusebius (3.5.3);

> The people of the church in Jerusalem were commanded by an oracle given by revelation before the war to those in the city who were worthy of it to depart and dwell in one of the cities of Peraea which they called Pella.

(It is true that Pella was in Peraea, but Mark may have regarded it as a Galilean city.)

So Marxsen once again comes to the same conclusion which others reached about the other gospels, the conclusion that they are theological far more than historical documents, and that the gospel writers redacted their tradition in terms of their theology.

Finally, in regard to redaction criticism, let us look at the technique in operation. Perrin (pp. 40-63) gives us an actual sample of it, comparing Mark 8.27-9.1 with the parallel passages Matthew 16.13-28 and Luke 9.18-27. He begins with a description of the contents of the Mark passage. It is a passage with a clear structure. Jesus and his disciples are on the way to some villages in the district of Caesarea Philippi, when he asks them what the general public is saying about him (8.27). The answer is that some are saying that he is John the Baptist come back to life, or Elijah or one of the prophets (8.28). Then Jesus asks the disciples who they take him to be Peter responds with the fundamental confession of faith of early Christianity, 'You are the Christ'. Jesus accepts this confession, and enjoins secrecy (8.29f.).

Jesus then goes on to speak of the passion and death of the Son of man, against which Peter violently protests, whereat he is sternly reprimanded and identified with Satan (8.31-33).

This leads to a second block of teaching, addressed to the crowd (8.34) as well as to the disciples, in which Jesus proclaims that the disciple must be prepared to accept the possibility of martyrdom as the price of discipleship (8.34-37). The narrative then reaches its climax in two sayings, one that those who are disloyal to the Son of man in the present order will suffer for it at the final judgment (8.38), and the other that those who are loyal will be delivered, when the kingdom comes in power (9.1).

In his analysis (p. 41) Perrin points out 'the remarkable way in which the action moves backwards and forwards between the historical situation of the ministry of Jesus and the historical situation of the church for which Mark is writing'. The reply to Jesus' first question cites opinion about him which would be genuinely available in Palestine during his earthly life, whereas the reply to the second question is the basic confession of the early church. The block of teaching which follows is in pictures and language taken from the early church, the talk of taking up a cross, and taking it up for the sake of the gospel. The questions, the answers, the titles are on the lips of Jesus and Peter, but the titles involved are taken from the christological vocabulary of the early church. The names of the characters in the section come from the circumstances of Jesus' earthly ministry – Jesus, Peter, the multitude – but they represent just as much the circumstances of the early church.

'Jesus' is the Lord addressing his church, 'Peter' represents fallible believers, who confess correctly, yet go on to interpret their confession incorrectly, and 'the multitude' is the whole church membership for whom the general teaching which follows is designed.

The viewpoint of redaction criticism on the whole narrative is: 'It has the form of a story about the historical Jesus and his disciples, but the purpose is in terms of the risen Lord and his church.' It represents not what actually happened, but 'Mark's *understanding of what the risen Lord has to say to the church of his day*'. So Perrin sets out to examine the rest of the passage (8.31-9.1) to see what it tells us of Mark 'as one who *gathers, modifies* and *creates* tradition'. It has four constituent parts. As we examine Mark's material in the light of redaction criticism, we must remember that in this case we do not have the original source which Mark is redacting, and that therefore we are in the realm of deduction and even of speculation.

(i) There is the prediction of the passion (8.31). In Mark there are three such predictions (8.31; 9.31; 10.33f.). As Perrin reminds us (p. 43):

> The problem of a crucified Messiah was the major problem for the early church, both in terms of the development of her own theology and of the development of an apologetic to Judaism.

If the thought of a crucified Messiah was difficult for a Christian, it was next to impossible for a Jew. The problem was faced in the light of various approaches. There was the use of various Old Testament passages, such as Isaiah 53, in exegesis and in what Lindars calls 'passion apologetic'; there was speculative Son of man theology; there was the development of the idea of divine necessity; there was increasing emphasis on the cross as redemptive; and a similar emphasis on the resurrection as decisive victory.

Mark 8.27-10.52 is designed to serve as an introduction to the passion narrative itself; it is designed to make the passion narrative more intelligible; it is what Perrin calls 'a treatise on the cross in narrative form'. Perrin sees the whole section as a carefully constructed unit, held together by a series of three geographical references. In 8.37 there is the journey to the villages of Caesarea Philippi; in 9.30 it is said after the transfiguration and the healing of the epileptic boy: 'They went on from there and passed through Galilee.' In 10.1 after the Capernaum section we read: 'And he left there and went to the region of Judaea and beyond the Jordan.' Each section has its own passion prediction, and the tension continues to be heightened until in the last prediction Jerusalem is definitely named as the place of the passion (10.33). Clearly, the whole section is beautifully constructed, not so much as a journey to Jerusalem but as a journey to the cross.

(ii) Next comes teaching about discipleship (8.34-37). There are four sayings:

> If any man would come after me, let him deny himself and take up his cross and follow me (8.34).

> For whoever would save his life will lose it; and whoever loses his life for my sake and the gospel's will save it (8.35).

> For what does it profit a man to gain the whole world and forfeit his life? (8.36)

> For what can a man given in return for his life? (8.37)

All four passages occur together in Matthew 16.24-26; Luke has the first three together in 9.23-25; in addition Matthew has the first two joined at 10.38f.; Luke has the first two separately at 14.27 and 17.33. It is also to be noted that Mark 8.36 and 37 make two different points: that riches are of no avail at death (v.36) and that life is the highest good (v.37).

The collecting is standard editorial activity; but the placing of the collection here is theologically motivated; it lays down the principle that the path the Master trod is the path the disciple must tread.

There is a pattern within a pattern. Each passion prediction is followed first by misunderstanding, then by teaching.

(a)   8.31: the passion prediction.
    8.32f.: Peter's misunderstanding.
    8.34-37: the teaching about what discipleship really means.

(b)   9.31: the passion prediction.
    9.33f.: the dispute about who should be greatest, a complete misunderstanding about the meaning of discipleship.
    9.35-37: the teaching about the childlike spirit.

(c)   10.33f.: the passion prediction.
    10.35-41: the total misunderstanding of James and John about what constitutes true greatness.
    10.42-45: the teaching about the royalty of service, of which Jesus is the perfect example.

Clearly, there is deliberation here.

There is another sequence in regard to the essence of discipleship:

(a)   The disciple must be prepared to take up his cross, as his Master is (8.34).

(b)   The disciple must imitate the Master in 'servanthood' (9.35).

(c)   The cross and the servanthood are both taken up in a saying of Jesus, in which the theme of the cross is fully and finally presented: 'For the Son of man also came not to be served but to serve, and to give his life a ransom for many' (10.45).

Whatever one may think of certain aspects of redaction criticism, it is impossible to think that Mark is simply taking things as they come; out of his material he is deliberately shaping a pattern.

(iii)   Now we have what Perrin calls the climactic warning:

For whoever is ashamed of me and of my words in this adulterous and sinful generation, of him will the Son of man also be ashamed, when he comes in the glory of his Father with the holy angels (8.38).

Perrin thinks that this threat underwent a series of developments. He thinks that the earliest Aramaic form was:

Everyone who acknowledges me before man, he will be acknowledged before the angels of God.

When this was taken up into the tradition of the church it underwent alteration because the church was specially interested in the pronouncement of judgment by God upon offenders at the last time. So the parallels in Matthew 10.32f. and Luke 12.8f. provide a composite form with a basic pattern:

So everyone who acknowledges me before men, I (Luke: the Son of man) will also acknowledge before my Father who is in heaven (Luke: the angels of God); but whoever denies me before men, I also will deny before my Father who is in heaven (Luke: will be denied before the angels of God).

Two things have happened. First, the saying has become a 'double' saying using both verbs — 'acknowledge' and 'deny'. Second, the subject of the second clause can be either 'I' of 'the Son of man' or God (covered by the passive verb in Luke). Mark, says Perrin, originally knew the saying in some such form as has been thus reconstructed. He gives it in the form he does in order to remind his readers of the pronouncing of judgment which was so solemn a part of the church's eucharistic service (I Cor. 11.27-29). He makes two changes. First, the double emphasis of 'acknowledge-deny' becomes the more general 'be ashamed'. Second, he prefers 'Son of man' in the second clause to 'I' (or to the passive as an equivalent for 'God'). The first change is made, Perrin says, because 'the saying is now the warning part of a double climax of warning and promise (the promise being found in 9.1)'. To have had the promise twice would have unbalanced things. There are two reasons for Mark's use of 'Son of man'. First, its use in the warning balances 'kingdom of heaven' in the promise. Secondly, it picks up the 'Son of man' of 8.31. Thus, says Perrin in conclusion (p. 48), Mark is able, by the arrangement and redaction of his material, to make the point that 'the one whose cross is the example to be followed is also the one whose coming in judgment is to be anticipated'.

(iv) Lastly, there is what Perrin calls the climactic promise:

And he said to them, 'Truly, I say to you, there are some standing here who will not taste death before they see the kingdom of God come with power.'

Perrin regards this as a saying composed by Mark, and not as original. Let us look at his arguments (pp. 48-51) for this view. First, its language is Marcan. It is characteristic of Mark to speak about 'seeing' the *parousia* (9.1; 13.26; 14.62). Matthew and Luke speak about 'seeing' the *parousia* only when they are dependent on Mark. It is characteristic of Mark to associate 'power and glory' with the *parousia* (8.38; 9.1; 10.37; 13.26). Perrin therefore holds that the verse is characteristically Marcan in style. Where then did the verse come from? What is the model? Perrin holds it to be modelled on Mark 13.30:

> Truly, I say to you, this generation will not pass away before all these things take place.

What arguments does Perrin adduce for the connection of Mark 9.1 and Mark 13.30? They begin alike; both begin with the solemn words: 'Truly, I say to you'. They are alike in content; what they promise is very similar. They are alike in form; both introduce the words of Jesus with the *hoti* of direct speech, and both express the negative by means of a double negative with the subjunctive. They are alike in thought; both relate the promise to the coming of the last time. So Perrin concludes that Mark himself composed 9.1 with 13.30 as his model. His motivation was that the idea of the kingdom of God is most often used in a context of promise or blessing.

So, says Perrin, when we have examined this passage we have an excellent illustration of the characteristics of redaction. First we see the bringing together of previously existing independent sayings, or shorter combinations of sayings (8.36f.). Secondly, we see the modification of a saying which already existed in the tradition of the church. Thirdly, we see the creation of a new saying, using materials already present in the tradition of the church and of Jewish apocalyptic.

We must now look with Perrin (pp. 51-57) at the narrative as a whole, so that we may come to see Mark's overall aim and purpose behind it.

(i) In the first place, it would be hard to read the narrative without seeing the strong stress on persecution and suffering. The Son of man must suffer many things (8.31). The disciple must deny himself and take up his cross (8.34). There is the ever-present possibility of saving one's life only to lose it, and of losing it to save it (8.35). Perrin points out how the section keeps moving between the historical situation of the earthly ministry of Jesus and the circumstances of the early church. The whole section is clearly concerned on the one hand with the sufferings of the Christians 'for my sake and the gospel's'. The whole narrative presupposes a context of suffering; and the aim of the author is to prepare his readers for the persecution which is on the way, by connecting it backwards with the sufferings of Jesus and forwards with their own destiny, which will depend on whether or not they remain loyal and true. 'On the one hand, as went the Master, so must go the disciple; on the other hand, as goes the disciple now, so will go the Master with him at the End.' The whole section is 'a tract for the times', and the times are times of threatening persecution, for which the readers are being prepared.

(ii) As Perrin sees it, Caesarea Philippi remains 'the watershed of the Gospel' – but in a new sense. To an older generation of scholars Caesarea Philippi was the dividing line between 'the Galilaean spring-time' and the way of grief that led to the cross. That was, so to speak, an historical interpretation of the pattern of Mark's gospel, but on the new interpretation the approach should be theological, not historical.

Perrin believes that Mark is aiming to say something about Christology. This passage uses the title Christ. 'You are the Christ' (8.29). In the narrative Peter represents the early church, and he naturally uses the confessional title which the early church used. 'The light is focussed on this use of the title Christ.' 'Christ' occurs only seven times in Mark's gospel. In 1.1 it is part of the formal superscription to the whole gospel. In 9.41 'bear the name of Christ' really means 'are called Christians'. In 12.35; 13.21; 14.61; 15.32 it denotes the 'Anointed One' of Jewish messianic hope. Only here in Mark is Jesus 'formally acknowledged as the Messiah of Jewish expectation and the Christ of Christian worship'. Obviously, the narrative is of primary christological importance. As Perrin puts it, and on any grounds this is true, 8.29, Peter's confession marks a quite definite stage of development in the Marcan account of the understanding of Jesus in the minds of the disciples.

Perrin believes that in Mark's gospel there can be traced a development of the attitude of the disciples to Jesus.[6] In the first half of the gospel, from 1.16 to 8.21, the disciples are *imperceptive*. They are unable to perceive who Jesus is. His messiahship is constantly manifested in healings, in exorcisms, in nature miracles, but 'they remain amazingly obtuse in the face of their involvement in the messianic drama'. In the first half of the gospel they are granted very special privileges in their relationship to Jesus, but their perception of who he is seems much duller than that of people who only meet him once. Then comes the second stage, which emerges at Caesarea Philippi. At Caesarea Philippi Peter cannot grasp the idea of a suffering Messiah, even when the suffering is allied with resurrection. This is the change from imperceptivity to *misconception*. At the first stage they do not recognize Jesus as Messiah at all; at the second stage they recognize him as Messiah but misunderstand the nature of his messiahship. Finally there comes a third stage – *rejection*. Judas betrays him (14.10); Peter, James and John fail him in the Garden

(14.37-40); Peter even violently disowns him (14.66-72). Imperception, misunderstanding, rejection – so the development runs.

There would seem to be a clear pattern here, a deliberate sequence. What then was this misunderstanding, this mistaken conception, if you like, this heresy, which Mark regarded as so dangerous that he must write a gospel to correct it and to protect the church from it?

The Greek world knew all about the 'divine man', the 'Son of God', or of the gods, who descended into the world and demonstrated his divine power, and was able through his power to undergo ecstatic experiences and to perform miracles. To a Greek, Jesus might well seem an ideal example of the 'divine man'. And Perrin believes that one of Mark's main objects is 'to combat a "divine Man" understanding of Christology'. To achieve his purpose Mark adopts a definite plan. In the first half of the gospel he deliberately and of set purpose presents Jesus in terms of the 'divine man'.

> He saturates the first half of his gospel with wonder-working activities of Jesus, and intersperses summaries of this activity which can only be read in these terms (1.32-34; 3.7-12; 6.53-56), so that the reader . . . is left with only one possible conclusion: Peter confesses Jesus as a 'divine man'. In fact, if 1.1–8.29 were the only extant section of the Gospel, one would be forced to believe that from the Marcan perspective the only authentic understanding of Jesus was a 'divine man-Messiah' (p. 55).

This is the reason why the Caesarea Philippi incident remains central. Peter confesses Jesus as Messiah, and goes on to make it clear that by 'Messiah' he means 'divine man', and Jesus almost violently rejects this interpretation as the work of the devil: 'Get behind me, Satan!' (8.33). Perrin continues:

> The conclusion is inevitable: Mark presents a false understanding of Christology on the lips of Peter, a true understanding on the lips of Jesus. . . . The narrative is not concerned with the historical Peter's misunderstanding of the nature of Jesus' messiahship but with a false understanding of Christology prevalent in the church for which Mark is writing, i.e. with 'the heresy that necessitated Mark's gospel' (p. 56).

His aim is to produce in the church for which he is writing a 'suffering servant' Christology with which to replace the 'divine man' Christology. On this conclusion, Mark is not a historical but a thoroughly theological document.

Finally, Perrin concludes his exercise in redaction criticism by investigating what Matthew and Luke have done to this narrative. First (pp. 57-62) we look at Matthew's version (16.13-28). His layout is different; he has two distinct incidents, followed by a block of teaching.

(i) Matthew begins with what may be called the revelation to Peter. After Peter has made his confession of faith, Jesus says to him

(v. 17): 'Blessed are you, Simon Bar-Jona! For flesh and blood has not revealed this to you, but my Father who is in heaven.' For Matthew, Peter's discovery is the result of a divine revelation.

(ii)   The revelation to Peter is followed by his commissioning as the head of the Christian community (vv. 17-19). The implication is that it is the revelation which is the ground of the commission.

(iii)   Now there comes a break in Matthew's narrative. He proceeds (v. 21):

> From that time Jesus began to show his disciples that he must go to Jerusalem and suffer many things from the elders and chief priests and scribes, and be killed, and on the third day be raised.

In Matthew it is not at all necessary to suppose that the misunderstanding came immediately after the revelation, as it does in Mark. Matthew separates the revelation and the commission from the misunderstanding and the teaching.

This brings us to the problem of Matthew 16.17-19, a passage which has no parallel in any other gospel. Where does this appointment of Peter to headship in the church come from? Perrin (p. 58) accepts a suggestion of Bultmann's, elaborated by R.H. Fuller, that this encounter between Jesus and Peter was originally a story connected with Christ's *resurrection* appearance to Peter, and that Matthew has transferred to Caesarea Philippi a post-resurrection story.[7] It is by no means easy to see why the story should have been so transferred, but if this explanation is correct, we can then regard this as a story complete in itself, in which Peter receives a revelation, receives a commission, and acquires the power to determine the membership not only of the church but also of the kingdom of God. Perrin (p. 60) comments that, if this is a transferred resurrection appearance,

> Not only is Matthew following Mark in moving readily between the ministry of Jesus, which is past, and the ministry of the church, which is present, but he is also adding a third element in that he moves equally readily from the more distant past of the ministry of Jesus to the more immediate past of a resurrection appearance to Peter, to the present of the church. It is clear that in Gospel narratives past – both more distant and more immediate – and present flow into one another in a way that we must regard as remarkable.

Matthew changes the layout and introduces the new commission to Peter, and he also changes the wording. The first question now becomes: 'Who do men say that the Son of man is?' And Peter's answer becomes: 'You are the Christ, the Son of the living God' (16.13-16). Perrin points out that the introduction of 'Son of man' into the question makes it a 'nonsensical' question, since the answer is now given in the question. In fact this ceases to be a real, historical question, and becomes an affirmation of the church's faith. As for the addition to Peter's answer of the words 'the Son of the living God', this is part of the regular confession of the Christian church. Matthew used it, and it was particularly meaningful to him (8.29; 14.33; cf. also 2.15; 11.25-27). Perrin notes, however, that 'Son of God' was not a Jewish messianic title, and therefore, though perfectly natural on the lips of the church, it is impossible on the lips of Peter.

Finally there is Matthew's treatment of the climactic warning and the climactic promise:

Mark 8.38-9.1	*Matthew* 16.27f.
For whoever is ashamed of me and of my words in this adulterous and sinful generation, of him will the Son of man also be ashamed, when he comes in the glory of his Father with the holy angels.	For the Son of man is to come with his angels in the glory of his Father, and then he will repay every man for what he has done.
And he said to them, Truly, I say to you, there are some standing here who will not taste death before they see the kingdom of God come with power.	Truly, I say to you, there are some standing here who will not taste death before they see the Son of man coming in his kingdom.

Matthew redacted Mark's material in the interests of his very exalted doctrine of the place and power of the Son of man. Matthew is much more definite – 'The Son of man is to come.' Instead of being 'ashamed' of those who were ashamed of him, the Son of man has now become the Judge who will repay; the idea of the Son of man as Judge is characteristic of Matthew (13.41; 25.31). In Matthew the kingdom of God has become the kingdom of the Son of man. The Son of man for Matthew has done no less than assume the functions of God. So then Matthew has related the warning and the promise in terms of his doctrine of the Son of man.

Finally, we turn to Luke to see what he has done to the passage (9.18-27). Luke's initial sentence does not make sense as it stands:

Now it happened that as he was praying alone the disciples were with him.

Codex B, Vaticanus, no doubt in an attempt to make sense, has 'The disciples met him.' What has happened is that Luke is combining Mark 6.46, 'And after he had taken leave of them he went into the hills to pray', with Mark 8.27, 'And Jesus went on with his disciples to the villages of Caesarea Philippi.' Luke has no parallels to Mark 6.47-8.26; probably the pages were lost in the copy he was using, or perhaps, to put it more correctly, the papyrus roll was damaged there. So here he goes from Mark 6.46 to 8.27 and produces a sentence which is meaningless.

Luke omits altogether the dispute with Peter. Perrin makes two suggestions. He suggests that Luke was not concerned with christological questions, and he points out that in the dispute about greatness (Luke 22.24-27), Luke omits the great saying: 'For the Son of man also came not to be served, but to serve, and to give his life as a ransom for many' (Mark 10.45). His second suggestion is perhaps better – Luke may well have found the story of the likening of Peter to Satan offensive, and for that reason may have omitted it.

In 9.23 Luke adds one word: 'If any man would come after me, let him deny himself and take up his cross *daily* and follow me.' Mark (8.38) has: 'Whoever is ashamed of me and of my words in this adulterous and sinful generation . . .'; Luke (9.26) omits 'in this adulterous and sinful generation'. In 9.27 he has: 'There are some standing here who will not taste of death before they see the kingdom of God', omitting Mark's 'come with power'. This is simply Luke's revised eschatology. He is no longer thinking of any particular persecution; he is no longer looking forward to an imminent *parousia*, an immediate coming again; and so he removes the crisis urgency and gives instead a general command for permanent witness, pushing the coming of the kingdom into an indefinite future in the crisis sense of the term.

What then must be the assessment of redaction criticism? That there was such a practice as redaction is beyond doubt. The writers of the gospels did not just copy verbatim the sources which they possessed. Each began to write his gospel with his own purpose, and passed the material he possessed through his own mind, and stamped it with his own personality. It will clearly be possible to understand something of the author's mental processes by studying the changes he makes in his material, and, if the changes follow any kind of pattern or consistent line of thought, then it will be possible to deduce something of the writer's theology. But certain things have to be said.

First and foremost, as we have said more than once, redaction criticism can be a valid and scientific process if the material redacted is available, as with the use of Mark by Matthew and Luke; but if that original material is not available, then there is an element of speculation and even of guesswork about the whole process. This is why it seems to me that the work of Bornkamm, Barth and Held is much more attractive and much more illuminating than the work of Marxsen and Conzelmann in this sphere.

Second, it does seem that it would have been more accurately descriptive to have called this discipline Composition Criticism, for it is much less concerned with changes in detail, however revealing these changes may be, than it is with the rearranging of the material to form new patterns which will serve the author's theological interests and aims.

Third, another aspect of the question emerges when it is argued that the authors did not only adapt and rearrange, but that they also invented new material, even if that material was based on already existing tradition. That the authors would expand and explain and adapt the teaching of Jesus to meet the demands and the dangers of their own day is a proposition to which we can easily agree; that they produced their own material is more doubtful.

Fourth, most difficult of all is the acceptance of the claim that the geography and topography of the gospels are symbolic and theological rather than literal and phyiscal. It is difficult to agree with Marxsen that John the Baptist's 'wilderness' was a theological wilderness, or to accept Conzelmann's interpretation of Galilee and Jerusalem, of mountain and lake and plain, as phases of the ministry of Jesus rather than as geographical places. The difficulty in this is quite simple – it is the fact that no one would have thought that it was so, and indeed, to take but one instance, in the case of the Baptist's wilderness not even Matthew and Luke thought that it was so. It is perhaps a little difficult to believe that we had to wait until the twentieth century to find out what the gospel writers were really trying to say.

On the whole, it is true of redaction criticism, as it is true of so many things, that it is an exceedingly useful tool, and a very valuable means of gospel interpretation, but that it can also be used to support views and to reach conclusions which are so speculative that they must be viewed with extreme caution.

ABBREVIATIONS

AV   Authorized Version of the Bible

BNTC   Black's New Testament Commentaries, A. & C. Black and Harper

DSB   Daily Study Bible, Saint Andrew Press and Westminster Press

ET   English translation

ICC   International Critical Commentary, T. & T. Clark and Scribner

MNTC   Moffatt New Testament Commentary, Hodder & Stoughton and Harper

NEB   New English Bible

PNTC   Pelican New Testament Commentaries, Penguin Books

RSV   Revised Standard Version of the Bible

SBT   Studies in Biblical Theology, SCM Press and Allenson

Biblical quotations are normally from RSV.

NOTES

1 · THE NATURE OF THE GOSPELS

1. Karl Barth, *Church Dogmatics* I, *The Doctrine of the Word of God*, Part 1, ET T. and T. Clark 1936, p. 188.

2. Justin Martyr, *Exhortation to the Greeks*, 8.

3. Athenagoras, *Embassy*, 9.

4. Chrysostom, *Homilies on John*, 1.1.

5. Philo, *Who is the Heir of Divine Things?*, 249-66.

6. Tertullian, *Apology*, 18.

7. Methodius, *On the Resurrection*, 9 (1.48 in some editions).

8. Origen, *On Matthew*, 17.12

9. Origen, *Commentary on John*, 6.34 (18).

10. Novatian, *On the Trinity*, 30.

11. See V.H.H. Green, *Religion at Oxford and Cambridge*, SCM Press 1964, pp. 308-13.

12. Quoted by Paul Althaus, *The So-called Kerygma and the Historical Jesus*, pp. 27f.

13. Barth, *Church Dogmatics* I, *The Doctrine of the Word of God*, Part 2, ET T. and T. Clark 1956, pp. 137f. (summarized by Baillie, *God was in Christ*, p. 36).

14. A. Harnack, *What is Christianity?*, ET (1901), Harper Torchbooks 1968, p.144.

15. Quoted by Althaus, op. cit., pp. 19f.; cf. *The So-called Historical Jesus* ..., pp. 72f., 102f., 74 (in a different translation).

16. R.W. Hepburn, *Christianity and Paradox*, Watts 1958, p. 94.

2 · THE INITIAL STAGE

1. Quoted by Eusebius, *Ecclesiastical History*, 3.39.4.

2. Quintilian, *The Institutes of Oratory*, 2.2.8.

3. The text of Diocletian's Edict, with a translation, is given in an Appendix to Tenney Frank, *An Economic Survey of Ancient Rome* V: *Rome and Italy of the Empire*, Johns Hopkins Press 1940, pp. 305-421.

4. Quoted by Eusebius, op. cit., 6.12.3.

5. Quoted by Eusebius, ibid., 6.14.5.

6. Tertullian, *Against Marcion*, 4.5.

7. Jerome, *On Famous Men*, 8.

8. A. Dieterich, *Abraxas*, Leipzig 1891, p. 202 lines 15f.; the papyrus is P Leid. J385.

9. Dieterich, *Eine Mithrasliturgie*, Leipzig 1903, p.6 line 4; p.10 line 23.

10. Dibelius (p. 88) cites Clement of Alexandria, *Protrepticus*, 2.17.1, and also a scholion on Lucian's *Dialogues of the Courtesans*.

11. Quoted by E.B. Redlich, *Form Criticism: its Value and Limitations*, London 1939, p. 127, from Bultmann's essay in F.C. Grant, *Form Criticism*.

12. Aelius Aristides, *In Serapeum*, 29f.

13. Bultmann, 'New Testament and Mythology' in *Kerygma and Myth*, ed. H.W. Bartsch, ET SPCK 1957, p. 10.

3 · FORM CRITICISM ASSESSED

1. The Monarchian Prologue to Matthew, quoted by D.J. Theron, *Evidence of Tradition*, pp. 56f.

2. Jerome, preface to the *Commentary on Matthew* (quoted by Theron, op. cit., pp. 50f.): *'qui ... conati sunt magis ordinare narrationem quam historiae texere veritatem.'*

7 · THE GOSPEL OF MARK

1. These extracts from lost works by Clement and Origen are preserved by Eusebius in his *History*, 6.14.5 and 6.25.5.

2. J.B. Lightfoot, *Essays on the Work entitled Supernatural Religion*, London 1889, p. 176.

3. F.H. Colson, '*Taxei* in Papias', *Journal of Theological Studies* 14, 1912-13, pp. 62-9.

4. A.E.J. Rawlinson, *The Gospel according to Mark*, p. xv, quoting Maurice Goguel, *Introduction au Nouveau Testament*, Paris 1923, pp. 41f.

5. W. Sanday, *The Life of Christ in Recent Research*, Oxford 1907, pp. 69-72.

8 · THE GOSPEL OF MATTHEW

1. Quoted by Eusebius, *Ecclesiastical History*, 6.25.14.

2. J.B. Lightfoot, *Essays on the Work entitled Supernatural Religion*, pp. 172-77.

3. Cicero, *De Officiis*, 1.42; Lucian, *Menippus*, 11.

4. Clement of Alexandria, *Miscellanies*, 4.9; *Paedagogus*, 2.1.

5. Quoted by Goodspeed, *Introduction to the New Testament*, p. 170, and by Filson, *Commentary on Matthew*, p.1.

9 · THE GOSPEL OF LUKE

1. Frequently quoted, e.g. by F.C. Grant, *The Gospels*, p. 133.

2. T. Zahn, *Introduction to the New Testament* III, p. 1.

3. A. Souter, 'Luke', in Hastings' *Dictionary of Christ and the Gospels* II, Edinburgh and New York 1908, pp. 84f.

4. W.K. Hobart, *The Medical Language of St Luke*, Dublin 1882.

5. Franz Overbeck, *Christentum und Kultur*, Basel 1919, p. 79.

6. Lucian, *On how to Write History*, 23.

7. Dio Cassius, 67. 14; Suetonius, *Domitian*, 10, 15, 17; Eusebius, *Ecclesiastical History*, 3.18.4.

8. J.G. von Herder, quoted by J.M. Creed, *The Gospel according to St Luke*, pp. xlv-xlvi.

9. T. Zahn, op. cit., vol. III, pp. 61f.

10. T.R. Glover, 'The Study of Ancient History', *Greek Byways*, Cambridge 1932, pp. 275-92.

11. A.H. McNeile, *Introduction to the Study of the New Testament*, pp. 17, 15.

10 · THE DEVELOPMENT OF GOSPEL CRITICISM

1. Quoted by T.R. Glover in 'The Study of Ancient History', *Greek Byways*, Cambridge 1932, p. 276.

2. T.R. Glover, 'Polybius at Rome', *Springs of Hellas*, Cambridge University Press 1954, p. 114, quoting Polybius 12.25h.3.

3. P.W. Schmiedel, 'The Gospels', *Encyclopaedia Biblica* II, ed. T.K. Cheyne and J.S. Black, London and New York 1901, cols. 1761-1898.

4. AD 37: Josephus, *Antiquities*, 19.275 (also in *The Jewish War* 2.215); AD 53: *Antiquities* 20.138.

5. A. Deissmann, *The New Testament in the Light of Modern Research*, ET London 1929, p. 14.

6. Deissmann, op. cit., p. 155.

7. C. Guignebert, *Jesus*, ET London 1935, p. 93.

8. E. Stauffer, *Jesus and his Story*, ET SCM Press 1960, pp. 36-8.

9. B.F. Westcott, *Introduction to the Study of the Gospels*, 4th ed., London 1872, p. 367.

10. Nineham (p. 25) is quoting A. Menzies, *The Earliest Gospel*, p. 24; H.A. Guy, *The Origin of the Gospel of Mark*, Hodder & Stoughton 1954, pp. 109f.; Dibelius, *A Fresh Approach to the New Testament*, pp. 34f.

11. Vernon Bartlett, 'Papias', Hastings' *Dictionary of Christ and the Gospels* II, Edinburgh and New York 1908, p. 309.

12. J.B. Lightfoot, *Essays on . . . Supernatural Religion* (see ch. 7 n. 2), p. 165.

13. 'They' is the reading of NEB and of the United Bible Society text; RSV has 'he' in the text and 'they' in the margin.

14. Peter Ustinov, *Add a Dash of Pity. Short Stories*, Heinemann 1959, p.

15. The passages are as follows:

The trial of Jesus	Peter's denial
Mark 14.53-72	vv. 54, 66-72
Matt. 26.57-75	vv. 58, 69-75
Luke 22.44-71	vv. 54-62
John 18.12-27	vv. 15-18, 25-27

11 · REDACTION CRITICISM

1. This is the name suggested by E. Haenchen in his book *Der Weg Jesu*, Berlin 1966, p. 24 (quoted by Perrin, *What is Redaction Criticism?*, p. 1).

2. J. Schniewind, 'Zur Synoptikerexegese', *Theologische Rundschau*, NF 2, 1930, p. 139.

3. K.L. Schmidt, *Der Rahmen der Geschichte Jesu*, Berlin 1919, p. 317.

4. B.F. Westcott, *Introduction to the Study of the Gospels*, 4th ed., London 1872, pp. 204, 367.

5. M. Kähler, *The So-called Historical Jesus and the Historic, Biblical Christ*, p. 80 n. 11.

6. In this section Perrin (pp. 54-6) acknowledges his debt to T.J. Weeden's thesis, 'The Heresy that Necessitated Mark's Gospel', now published as *Mark – Traditions in Conflict*, Fortress Press 1971.

7. Bultmann, *History of the Synoptic Tradition*, pp. 258f.; R.H. Fuller, 'The *"Tu es Petrus"* Pericope', a paper read to the Society of Biblical Literature on 29 December 1966.

BIBLIOGRAPHY

GENERAL

Abbott, E.A., *The Fourfold Gospel*, 5 vols., London and New York 1913-17

Althaus, P., *The So-called Kerygma and the Historical Jesus*, ET Oliver & Boyd 1959 (= *Fact and Faith in the Kerygma of Today*, Muhlenberg 1960)

Bacon, B.W., *An Introduction to the New Testament*, New York 1900

Baillie, D.M., *God was in Christ*, 2nd ed., Faber & Faber and Scribner 1955

Barrett, C.K., *Luke the Historian in Recent Study*, Epworth Press and Allenson 1961, reissued Fortress Press 1970

Bea, Augustin, Cardinal, *The Study of the Synoptic Gospels*, ET Geoffrey Chapman and Harper 1965

Bornkamm, G., *Jesus of Nazareth*, ET Hodder & Stoughton 1960, Harper 1961

Bornkamm, G., Barth, G., and Held, H.J., *Tradition and Interpretation in Matthew*, ET SCM Press and Westminster Press 1963

Bultmann, R., *Jesus Christ and Mythology*, Scribner 1958, SCM Press 1960
– *Jesus and the Word*, ET 1934, quoted from Fontana ed., 1962
– *The History of the Synoptic Tradition*, ET Blackwell and Harper 1963

Burkitt, F.C., *The Earliest Sources for the Life of Jesus*, rev. ed., London and New York 1922
– *The Gospel History and its Transmission*, Edinburgh 1906, New York 1907

Butler, B.C. *The Originality of St Matthew*, Cambridge University Press 1951

Cadbury, H.J., *The Making of Luke-Acts*, 1927, reissued SPCK and Allenson 1964
– 'The Tradition' in *The Beginnings of Christianity* II, ed. F.J. Foakes Jackson and K. Lake, pp. 209-64

Cadoux, A.T., *The Sources of the Second Gospel*, London 1935

Cairns, D., *A Gospel without Myth?*, SCM Press 1960

Carpenter, J.E., *The First Three Gospels*, London 1890

Carrington, P., *The Primitive Christian Calendar: A Study in the Making of the Marcan Gospel*, Cambridge University Press 1952

Cerfaux, L., *An Historical Introduction to the Four Gospels*, ET Darton, Longman & Todd and Newman Press 1960

Chapman, J., *Matthew, Mark and Luke*, London and New York 1937

Clogg, F.B., *An Introduction to the New Testament*, 3rd ed., University of London Press 1948

Conzelmann, H., *The Theology of St Luke*, ET Faber & Faber 1960, Harper 1961

Dibelius, M., *A Fresh Approach to the New Testament and Early Christian Literature*, ET London and New York 1936

– *From Tradition to Gospel*, ET 1934, reissued James Clarke 1971

– *Jesus*, ET Westminster Press 1949; quoted from new ed., SCM Press 1963

Dodd, C.H., *According to the Scriptures*, 1952, quoted from Fontana ed., 1965

Easton, B.S., *The Gospel before the Gospels*, New York 1928

Farmer, W.R., *The Synoptic Problem*, Macmillan 1964

Farrer, A.M., *A Study in St Mark*, A. & C. Black 1951, Oxford University Press, New York, 1952

Fuchs, E., *Studies of the Historical Jesus*, ET (SBT 42), 1964

Fuller, R.H., *The New Testament in Current Study*, Scribner 1962, SCM Press 1963

Goodspeed, E.J., *An Introduction to the New Testament*, Chicago and Cambridge 1937

Grant, F.C., *The Gospels*, Harper 1957, Faber & Faber 1959

– *Form Criticism*, containing translations of 'The Study of the Synoptic Gospels' by R. Bultmann and 'Primitive Christianity in the Light of Gospel Research' by K. Kundsin, Chicago 1934

Grant, R.M., *A Historical Introduction to the New Testament*, Collins and Harper 1963

– *The Earliest Lives of Jesus*, SPCK and Harper 1961

Guy, H.A., *The Study of the Gospels*, Macmillan 1952

– *A Critical Introduction to the Gospels*, Macmillan 1955

Harnack, A., *Luke The Physician*, ET London and New York 1907

– *The Acts of the Apostles*, ET London and New York 1909

Hawkins, *Horae Synopticae*, Oxford and New York 1909

Henderson, I., *Myth in the New Testament* (SBT 7), 1952

Hoskyns, E., and Davey, N., *The Riddle of the New Testament*, 3rd ed., Faber & Faber 1947

Hunter, A.M., *Introducing the New Testament*, rev. ed., SCM Press and Westminster Press 1957

– *The Words and Works of Jesus*, rev. ed., SCM Press 1973

Jackson, F.J. Foakes, and Lake, K. (eds.), *The Beginnings of Christianity* II, 1922, reissued Eerdmans 1966

Jameson, H.G., *The Origin of the Synoptic Gospels*, Oxford 1922

Jones, M., *The New Testament in the Twentieth Century*, 3rd ed., London and New York 1934

Jülicher, A., *An Introduction to the New Testament*, ET London and New York 1904

Kähler, M., *The So-called Historical Jesus and the Historic, Biblical Christ*, ET (of German original of 1896), Fortress Press 1964

Käsemann, E., *Essays on New Testament Themes*, ET (SBT 41), 1964

Kleist, J.A., *Memoirs of St Peter or the Gospel according to St Mark*, Milwaukee 1932

Kümmel, W.G., *Introduction to the New Testament*, ET SCM Press and Westminster Press 1966

Lake, K. and S., *An Introduction to the New Testament*, New York 1937, London 1938

Lightfoot, R.H., *History and Interpretation in the Gospels*, Hodder & Stoughton 1935

McNeile, A.H., *Introduction to the Study of the New Testament*, 2nd ed. revised by C.S.C. Williams, Oxford University Press 1953

Malevez, L., *The Christian Message and Myth*, ET SCM Press 1958, Newman Press 1960

Manson, T.W., *Studies in the Gospels and Epistles*, ed. M. Black, Manchester University Press and Westminster Press 1962

Marxsen, W., *Mark the Evangelist*, Abingdon Press 1969

Moffatt, J., *Introduction to the Literature of the New Testament*, Edinburgh and New York 1911

Moule, C.F.D., *The Birth of the New Testament*, A. & C. Black and Harper 1962

Neill, S., *The Interpretation of the New Testament 1861-1961*, Oxford University Press 1964

Ogden, S.M., *Christ without Myth*, Harper 1961, Collins 1962

Peake, A.S., *A Critical Introduction to the New Testament*, London and New York 1909

Perrin, N., *What is Redaction Criticism?*, Fortress Press and SPCK 1970

Ramsay, W.M., *Luke the Physician*, 1908, reissued Baker Book House 1956

Redlich, E.B., *Students' Introduction to the Synoptic Gospels*, London and New York 1936

Richardson, A., *The Gospels in the Making*, London 1938

Robertson, A.T., *Luke the Historian in the Light of Research*, Edinburgh and New York 1920

Robinson, J.M., *A New Quest of the Historical Jesus* (SBT 25), 1959

– *The Problem of History in Mark* (SBT 21), 1957

Rohde, J., *Rediscovering the Teaching of the Evangelists*, ET SCM Press and Westminster Press 1967

Ropes, J.H., *The Synoptic Gospels*, 2nd impression with new preface, Oxford University Press 1960, Harvard University Press 1961

Sanday, W., *Studies in the Synoptic Problem*, Oxford and New York 1911

Schweitzer, A., *The Quest of the Historical Jesus*, 3rd ed., A. & C. Black 1954

Scott, E.F., *The Literature of the New Testament*, New York and London 1932

Stanton, V.H. *The Gospels as Historical Documents*, 3 vols, Cambridge 1903-30

Stonehouse, N.B., *Origin of the Synoptic Gospels*, Eerdmans 1963, Inter-Varsity Press 1964

Strauss, D.F., *The Life of Jesus Critically Examined* (George Eliot's translation of 1846), Fortress Press 1972, SCM Press 1973

Streeter, B.H., *The Four Gospels: a Study of Origins*, 5th imp. revised, London and New York 1936

Taylor, V., *The Gospels*, London 1930

– *The Formation of the Gospel Tradition*, 2nd ed., Macmillan 1933, reissued 1953

– *Behind the Third Gospel*, Oxford and New York 1926

Theron, D.J., *Evidence of Tradition*, Bowes & Bowes and British Book Service, Toronto, 1957

Turner, H.E.W., *Historicity and the Gospels*, Mowbray 1963

Unnik, W.C. van, *The New Testament*, Collins 1964, Harper 1965

Wikenhauser, A., *New Testament Introduction*, ET Nelson and Herder & Herder 1958

Wrede, W., *The Messianic Secret*, ET (of German original of 1901) James Clark 1971

Zahn, T., *Introduction to the New Testament*, 3 vols., ET Edinburgh and New York 1909

COMMENTARIES
(on English text unless otherwise stated)

Synoptic Gospels

Bruce, A.B., Expositor's Greek Testament, London 1897

Montefiore, C.G., 2nd ed., London and New York 1927

Matthew

Allen, W.C., ICC, 1907

Barclay, W., DSB., St Andrew Press 1956-7, Westminster Press 1959

Fenton, J.C., PNTC, 1963

Filson, BNTC, 1960

McNeile, A.H., Macmillan 1915 (Greek text)

Plummer, A., 1910, reissued Eerdmans 1953, James Clarke 1960

Robinson, T.H., MNTC, 1928

Tasker, R.V.G., Tyndale Commentaries, Inter-Varsity Press and Eerdmans 1961

Mark

Barclay, W., DSB, St Andrew Press 1954, Westminster 1957

Carrington, P., Cambridge University Press 1960

Cole, R.A., Tyndale Commentaries 1961, Eerdmans 1962

Cranfield, C.E.B., Cambridge Greek Testament, Cambridge University Press 1959

Grant, F.C., *The Earliest Gospel*, New York 1943

Hunter, A.M., Torch Commentary, SCM Press and Macmillan 1949

Lightfoot, R.H., *The Gospel Message of St Mark*, Oxford University Press 1950

Menzies, A. *The Earliest Gospel*, London 1901

Nineham, D.E., PNTC, London 1963, Baltimore 1964

Rawlinson, A.E.J., London 1925

Swete, H.B., London 1898, New York 1908 (Greek text)

Taylor, V., Macmillan 1952 (Greek text)

Turner, C.H., London and New York 1931 (reprinted from *A New Commentary on Holy Scripture*, ed. C. Gore, H.L. Goudge and A. Guillaume, London 1928)

Luke

Barclay, W., DSB, St Andrew Press 1953, Westminster Press 1959

Caird, G.B., PNTC, London 1963, Baltimore 1964

Creed, J.M., Macmillan 1930 (Greek text)
Easton, B.S., New York 1926
Leaney, A.R.C., BNTC 1958
Manson, W., MNTC 1930
Plummer, A., ICC 1896

TRANSLATIONS OF ANCIENT AUTHORS

Many of the more important works by the church fathers were translated in the *Ante-Nicene Christian Library*, ed. Alexander Robertson and James Donaldson (24 vols., Edinburgh 1867-72, reissued in 8 vols., New York 1884-6), and the *Select Library of the Nicene and Post-Nicene Fathers*, ed. Philip Schaff and Henry Wace, New York and London 1886ff., which may be found in libraries.

The Loeb Classical Library (Greek or Latin text with English translation on the facing page), published by Heinemann and Putnam, contains most classical authors and Hellenistic writers such as Josephus, and also includes some Christian authors and works such as the Apostolic Fathers and the *Ecclesiastical History* of Eusebius.

A *New Eusebius*, ed. J. Stevenson, SPCK 1957, gives short extracts from many authors illustrative of the history of the church to AD 337.

INDEX OF NAMES

INDEX OF BIBLICAL REFERENCES